Child Abuse and Neglect

Child Abuse and Neglect: Legislation, Reporting, and Prevention

Joseph J. Costa
Gordon K. Nelson
The Pennsylvania State University

Lexington Books
D.C. Heath and Company
Lexington, Massachusetts
Toronto

Library of Congress Cataloging in Publication Data

Costa, Joseph J
  Child abuse and neglect.

  Bibliography: p.
  1. Child abuse—United States. 2. Parents Anonymous. I. Nelson,
  Gordon Kenneth, 1947- joint author. II. Title.
HV741.C658   362.7'1   77-3836
ISBN 0-669-01670-5

Copyright © 1978 by D. C. Heath and Company

Published simultaneously in Canada.

Printed in the United States of America.

International Standard Book Number: 0-669-01670-5

Library of Congress Catalog Card Number: 77-3836

Contents

Foreword

Social concern over child abuse has been largely a child-oriented matter. Since the early work of Jane Addams and other social workers of her time, most of the concern has been devoted toward servicing the needs of the abused child. "Let's save these little babies from the sweat houses and from the depraved conditions" was a familiar cry of that time. The classic example is the case of Mary Ellen—a child whose case was brought before the court and the public's eye for being chained to a bed and beaten. Still there was no emphasis on the perpetrator, but "save that baby, Mary Ellen."

In time, concern over cases like Mary Ellen and other unfortunate victims took a different turn. It soon became evident that these poor babies presented a medical problem. Broken bones and various other kinds of injuries had to be given direct medical attention. A broken bone is a broken bone no matter how it was caused or who is responsible for it. The physician must set the bone just the same. But, eventually, social concern came around to the question of the person who broke this child's arm, in which case it became a legal concern. We then had to establish that *this* is the party who is the victim of a crime, and *that* is the party who is the perpetrator. From that point forward, the real shift of emphasis occurred in getting the perpetrator.

Although medical attention was readily found to be warranted in child abuse cases, it was not from the standpoint of willful injury. Morally it became unacceptable for children in our society to enter hospital wards with a medical problem as the result of inflicted trauma. Socially it is quite acceptable to come into a hospital with accidental trauma if, for example, one should receive slash wounds after having fallen through a plate glass window. On the other hand, it is not socially and morally acceptable to come into a hospital with slash wounds that had been deliberately inflicted with a knife. Injury is injury, with the possibility that one may live or die. The medical techniques involved are generally the same, sometimes requiring the use of suturing, plasma, and various other procedures. But what brought it on in that one instance of inflicted injury, as far as the causative factors are concerned, somehow rubs against the moral fiber of society. One is socially acceptable while the other is not.

Too often concern over child abuse and other social ills of our time becomes manifest in a meaningless search for acceptable explanations. We look to possible clues and variables that may provide acceptable answers. Why did I abuse my child? Well, let me tell you why. The people down the street use different kinds of light bulbs to illuminate their house. You mean this is not acceptable enough for a reason? Well, then, my neighbor's barking dog wakes me up each morning at six o'clock which leaves me tired the whole day. That is a little more reasonable; you are possibly a little more willing to accept that for an explanation. Or, better yet, the reason is my child is hyperactive. Aha! This is even more plausible to accept as a reason for my behavior.

After having explored all these possible clues, the fact remains that I have abused my child. All these "reasons" do not tell us much and are not really relevant to the main fact. We are all attempting to find "reasonable reasons." Yet all the "reasons" are unreasonable. By our very human nature, we have created a smoke screen in an effort to understand the nature of child abuse, and in the process we ourselves have been caught up in this smoke screen.

The smoke screen consists of leading people in a search for the tip of the iceberg. What do we even accept as child abuse? Some people by the nature of their profession look at child abuse from a legal definition. But this presents, at best, the very difficult task of trying to come up with a truly legitimate legal definition. For instance, *inflicted nonaccidental trauma* may mean many different things at different levels. If I snapped my finger against my child's mouth and he received a little cut on the lip from the teeth, this is inflicted trauma. In many states inflicted nonaccidental trauma is a felony, in which case I should be in superior court facing felony charges. But I probably will not even find myself in civil court.

We have cases of children presented in court with bruises covering their bodies, and they are returned home; and we have other cases of children who present no evidence of abuse and end up for years in a series of foster homes. So while we have a legal definition of child abuse which includes physical and sexual abuse, as well as neglect (which is one kind that is very difficult to determine), there is limited utility to be found in that definition from a legal standpoint. The smoke screen is created because of the restricted definition and the kinds of evidence marshaled in support of that definition. One problem is that it does not make any allowance for those children who should have an authoritative body making decisions for them.

The social definition of and criteria for child abuse may include considerations beyond the legal definition. For example, the social definition is more likely to embrace aspects of neglect; even the use of harmful drugs around children and sexual deviance in the home may be viewed as forms of child abuse. Sociologists, in particular, are inclined to examine child abuse in the context of the social environment and the impact of life situations. The abused child may be viewed as the victim of an unhealthy home environment, and the parent as the victim of poverty, lack of resources, and ignorance.

Here, again, we throw up the smoke screen in attempting to identify the origins of child abuse by exploiting social and cultural differences. Take as an example the people who live in regions of the Appalachian Mountains. They are sometimes regarded as the poorest people of our society. Nevertheless, among the impoverished conditions in which they live, you will find television sets, freezers, and automobiles which consume gasoline at the same prices or higher than in other parts of the country. Why a person in the Appalachians is less able to obtain a quart of milk for children with some of these advantages than someone else living near a store in downtown Los Angeles is difficult to explain. Is it more justifiable to abuse and neglect my children if I am impoverished and living in the Appalachian Mountains than if I am impoverished and living in Los Angeles? Is it more acceptable if I am black and abusing my children than if I am white and abusing my children? Is it more acceptable if I am uneducated and abusing my children than if I am educated and abusing my children? A smoke screen is created when we choose to accentuate these other differences. What makes it acceptable in one case but not the other? The point is that while we can or cannot understand the reasons for child abuse, the fact remains that it is happening.

Another frequently cited reason for abuse is parental ignorance. However, in view of much of the published research, which indicates that the highest percentage of abuse occurs among parents who abuse only one of their children, it is difficult to see why parental ignorance, lack of education, and lack of knowledge of child development skills might play a role. If they are suffering from parental ignorance, then why is that same ignorance not being applied to the other children in the home?

Similarly, psychologists may look to "mothering imprint" as a plausible explanation for child abuse. The reason parents abuse their children is that they did not receive a healthy mothering imprint. If the lack of a mothering imprint is a prerequisite to becoming a child abuser, what enables that same person who lacks a mothering imprint to mother the other children? Let us suppose that a parent abuses all the children. How do you explain why that parent does not abuse other people's children with whom they are around and toward whom they may even show nurturing? Parents Anonymous has worked with parents having as many as 10 children, and yet in each of these cases the parent has abused only *one* child. There is usually only one distinct target child or scapegoat who receives abusive treatment. Of all the research carried out on this subject, no predictability can be determined which child the scapegoat child will be in the birth order. There are no trends that can be clearly established with current data.

Furthermore, psychological interpretations dealing with the lack of modeling and identification provide inadequate causal explanations. With the high percentage of television sets available in American homes, and with the abundance of television programs emulating parenthood (e.g., "Eddie's Father," "Partridge

Family," "Happy Days," "All of My Children"), it is blind not to recognize the availability of models. While television parenting may not provide models par excellence, the availability of such models serves the purpose of comparing parenting in the home and parenting elsewhere. Parents are able to draw comparisons between their own practices and the practices they discover in other homes, or at least with the practices they are deluged with through television or magazines like *McCall's* and *Good Housekeeping.*

A recent review of national survey data (Nagi, 1976) indicates no clearly defined epidemiological patterns in the incidence of child maltreatment. Sizable proportions of reported abuse and neglect were found across all levels of measurement, including age, sex, and ethnic categories. These and similar findings would defy almost any attempt at labeling and classification, and at best would represent a complex interaction among many constellations of factors.

In order to begin to really understand the nature and origin of child abuse, one must begin always with the fact. After exploring all the many possible explanations of why parents have intended harm toward their children, very little actually has been revealed. For analogy, it is like looking at alcohol—what it is in alcohol—to determine what makes an alcoholic. Do not look at the child in order to find out why the parent is an abuser. Look at the individual and how that individual perceives the child. However, if you look at the child, do so for another reason: the abuse is going to cause that child some problems.

Family Life and Culture

The institutions of marriage and the family and the makeup of these institutions are sometimes linked to possible causes for child abuse (Barnes, Chabon, and Hertzberg, 1974; Calef, 1972; Forrest, 1974). There is some apparent widespread disenchantment to be found among Americans with these institutions, as evidenced by the rising number of divorces, broken homes, out-of-wedlock births, abortions; even the upsurge in day-care centers, advocacy of women's rights, and fastfood restaurants might be taken as symptoms of dissatisfaction. Again, in searching for factors contributing to the problem, we must examine these only within the context of the individual who is abusing his or her child. These factors may be relevant to certain individuals, but in and of themselves these factors cannot account for all the exceptions. At the same time it is necessary to look at healthy individuals and healthy homelife situations.

It is appalling to find how few adequate controls are being applied in child abuse research. Not all divorced persons abuse their children. There is little effort in present research to ascertain the extent to which these much-discussed characteristics prevail in healthy families. We do not ask families in which there is the absence of abuse to reveal their knowledge of child development. We do not sub-

ject healthy families to the same scrutiny of observation and questioning as we
do families with abuse.

In a highly funded research project being carried out in Denver, Colorado
attempts are being made to ascertain the effects of the birth process and immediate interaction of mother and newborn on subsequent patterns of child abuse
(Grey, Cutler, Dean, and Kempe, 1976). One implication is that failure to see the
infant during the first 24 hours after birth might be related to a higher incidence
of child abuse later. Yet, in most hospitals, a newborn is wisked off to the
nursery and is not seen by the mother for several hours in order to permit her
recovery. Is it sensible to identify this as a variable when there are many mothers
who experience these same conditions and yet do not abuse their children? It
may be desirable from the standpoint of some individuals to extend the amount
of time for contact with newborns; it may even be a good practice in general. But
we cannot expect that by focusing our attention on and devoting large resources
toward this variable the problem will be eliminated.

Similarly, the enactment of divorce proceedings or the establishment of day-
care facilities may be appropriate for certain individuals and families. But it is
foolish to believe that these measures alone will solve problems without regard
to the individuals. A day-care center may temporarily remove the child from a
troubled home situation, but do not expect the day-care center to solve the
problem. Day-care centers may be highly appropriate, and we may need more of
them, but for other reasons.

We have witnessed a gradual disintegration of American family life as we
have known it traditionally. Extended families were very fashionable at one time,
with many members living together as a unit on the same farm or on the same
flat, out of economic necessity. Today even the basic nuclear family has shown
signs of breaking down, with some relegation of parental responsibilities to television, babysitters, and paraprofessionals. This transition over the years has
worked out well with some families, although not with others. The extended-
family arrangement may still be a desirable structure for some individuals in
rearing children. For others, it may be undesirable and even devastating, especially in cases where abuse is perpetuated from generation to generation.

The reality is that the nuclear family still remains as the most prominent
form of family life in contemporary American society, and within this structure
we must work toward curbing child abuse. From the perspective of children, it
may make little difference in how the family is constituted—extended, nuclear,
broken, or otherwise—so long as they receive nurturing from somebody. Children
naturally gravitate toward pleasant nurturing experiences. They tend to move
toward persons who fulfill their needs at any given time, while pulling away from
persons who do not fulfill their needs. One child might incorporate a system of
parent surrogates in the neighborhood by visiting households that provide some
form of nurturing. A three-year-old who is despondent might look to a sympa-

thetic four-year-old who is able to fulfill the other's needs. In the future we may have to look at an entirely new concept of "extended family," one that includes either relatives or nonrelatives, professionals or nonprofessionals, institutions or noninstitutions. The task of parenting presents some awesome responsibilities that cannot always be assumed by one individual.

Parents can become very apprehensive at the idea of letting children receive nurturing from other people. For many of them it is difficult not to allow their personal needs to supersede or interfere with the needs of their children. Children have been accustomed to believing that if they are to get any nurturing, it is only to come from their parents. A child may fear nurturing from a stranger because of being told that strangers cannot give nurturing. As a result, the child may grow up believing that nurturing is obtainable only from a significant few.

This aspect of child rearing needs to be enlarged. Parents should be less fearful and mistrusting of the ability of others to attend to their children's needs. Certainly there is always the possibility that this loosened attitude could lead to some danger. But is it not better to be free of paranoia and open to the experiences of nurturing given by many people? In other cultures we find many kinds of community nurturing being practiced. Given a variety of situations, a child belongs to whomever is watching that child at the time. If the child is playing in the street, then the welfare of that child belongs to everyone nearby. The number of people showing this responsibility and providing the necessary nurturing makes little difference.

Mandatory Reporting Laws

Quite recently we have seen the enactment into law of federal legislation which now makes the reporting of alleged child abuse a mandatory procedure (Senate Bill 1191, 1973). All 50 states have now complied with federal legislation by enacting mandatory reporting laws of their own. These laws are designed to identify individuals with suspected family problems of child abuse, endangerment, abandonment, sexual abuse, or neglect. The laws stipulate that suspicions of these kinds are to be investigated by designated authorities. School teachers, physicians, caseworkers, and other persons are required to make their reports within a short time and to supply pertinent information.

The mandatory reporting laws are generally good laws. Some concern arises as to how these laws are to be carried out in actual practice. There is sometimes the fear that such reporting and investigating procedures may violate the rights of a suspected party. These concerns are unwarranted from the standpoint of attacking the new laws. Reporting in itself is not persecutory. How we carry out these laws is a different matter. The fact that it becomes necessary to file a report on a suspected family does not make reporting a vindictive measure.

How do I report? How do I investigate? Do we attack the law in that sometimes it is not carried out in the manner intended? Let us not attack mandatory reporting; let us go after what makes us feel like persecuted people. "I don't like getting reported" may be the cry of individuals who fear incrimination. If that is the case, then those same individuals should refrain from obtaining driver licenses, birth certificates, and social security numbers. They should not seek jobs or file for unemployment because in all of these situations they will be reported. The law should be regarded as a neutral and acceptable instrument. It may be as natural as a parent's urge to strike out. Is there something wrong with me for wanting to strike out, or is there something wrong in how I do it? Is there something wrong with me for reporting or investigating a family, or is there something wrong in the way I do it?

Parents Anonymous is finding an increased willingness on the part of parents to accept the reporting formalities. Parents are being persuaded that if the reporting agencies can remove the negative feelings of having to identify and report families with problems, then perhaps the reported familes can, in turn, reduce their own negative feelings about being reported. How can we begin to effectively carry out the law by feeling persecuted about it? Reported parents, in fact, are becoming more willing to remove these feelings and to do so faster than are the reporting agencies. It is recognized that in being reported, one can be identified as a potential recipient of services that may resolve the conflict at home. It is a myth to think that abusive parents do not want meaningful help.

The Schools

The school system is generally regarded as the transducer of the mores and values of our society, an agency to whom we entrust the care of our children. The school system is also a place where we find widespread abuse in the form of corporal punishment. This paradox raises some concern as to whether the school system is an appropriate place to begin teaching children the values of parenthood.

The schools are as good as any place for instilling character and morality in our children. It functions much like the law in that we do not attack the system because it does not produce the intended result. Here we need to look at the system in its operation to determine which features do not enhance the growth of our children.

In looking at this sysem, we are faced with the discrepancy that corporal punishment is appropriate in the school but not in the home. How do we shift our values and placate ourselves to think that it is acceptable in one place but not in another? It is like saying that premeditated murder is wrong in all instances except in the instance of capital punishment. By social standards it is wrong for a mother to place her child in numerous foster homes, but it is acceptable for the courts to sanction her decision and for the taxpayers to provide support. It would not be socially acceptable for a parent to lock up a child in a stripped down room without any external stimuli except food, but it is acceptable to do this in a juvenile detention facility at the expense of the state. If it is considered to be abuse in the home, what makes it acceptable in another institution? To be consistent with our social values, we are presented with this proposition: Either corporal punishment is appropriate both within the home and school or it is not appropriate in either place.

The school system performs an important function in imparting our values to the young, despite the fact that this role is sometimes carried out in negative ways. Schools can produce many exciting and varied learning experiences. Aside from the traditional emphasis on intellectual stimulation, schools can enhance emotional and psychological growth. We can use this system to teach the values of parenthood, child rearing, and child development. Classroom experiences may provide for excellent emotional self-growth. However, through this process we cannot expect to solve all our individual and social problems. Education is not a panacea for social ills. We can teach the principles of driving in a classroom to someone who is inexperienced, but the classroom lessons and the experiences of a teacher are not going to teach an individual how to drive. A similar approach can be taken toward emotional growth. We can turn that into a type of classroom experience for deriving intellectual know-how of what to expect later, but the classroom experiences will not teach us everything.

Working with Individuals

Child abuse must be regarded as a form of coping. It is one method of coping, as are excessive drinking, overeating, running away, homicide, catatonia, and various other psychoses. Parents who abuse their children have not invented any new psychiatric or emotional wheel. There is no new set of feelings that has been unfelt by other human beings. We all have the need to cope. Some of us cope in acceptable ways, while others do so in unacceptable or hurtful ways, either in terms of ourselves or others. We all have the capacity to harbor harmful thoughts, the urge to kill. The difference between those who carry out those thoughts and those who do not is related to the way one chooses to cope.

All the intellectual know-how in the world will not alter the situation in which an individual chooses to cope in undesirable ways. When your guts are churning, your intellectual capacity to use knowledge is overrun, and you see your child's behavior as the reason for these feelings. Knowledge will not stop you. So we come back to working with individuals who are so vulnerable to having their "buttons" pushed that this is a way of getting rid of presssure.

Parents Anonymous looks to other more appropriate and less hurtful ways of handling explosive situations. There is nothing wrong with exploding; it shows that you are a person who is capable of having feelings. There is nothing wrong with harboring dreadful thoughts or fantasizing. However, things do get mucked up when we explode in undesirable ways: "So you ticked me off. I've just demonstrated my capacity to get ticked off. And you are part of the circumstances which created this situation."

The emphasis of Parents Anonymous is not on doing something about the person who is a part of an explosive situation. The emphasis is on the fact that your "buttons" do get pushed in life, and you must do something about it. We already know what you have done in the past. You have abused your children or yourself. The goal is to break that one pattern of behavior and to help develop alternative ways of acting out and expressing yourself when your "buttons" are pushed. We do not want you to go catatonic; we do not want you to use denial, regression, child abuse, alcohol, overeating, or other unacceptable and hurtful means. Perhaps the next time an explosive situation occurs you decided to cry, throw a pillow, flop on the bed with a big sigh, or honk the horn while out driving. These are far more preferable ways of coping with stressful situations.

As people, we are a bundle of emotional attributes. Why should we deny that we have all kinds of feelings? We are predisposed to find a variety of ways of displaying our feelings, and in that predisposition we might pick violence as one way of showing feelings. We are also predisposed to think of many alternatives. Sometimes we get locked into thinking of one general set way, as in the case of violence. There are a lot of people who are angry but do productive things with their anger—public speaking, writing, taking stands on public issues, etc. The main thrust of Parents Anonymous is in finding appropriate ways of dealing with our feelings without saying that feelings are good or bad; they are just feelings.

References

Barnes, G.B., Chabon, R.S., & Hertzberg, L.J. Team treatment for abusive families. *Social Casework* 55 (1974):600–611.

Calef, V. The hostility of parents to children: Some notes on inferiority, child abuse, and abortion. *International Journal of Psychoanalytic Psychotherapy* 1 (1972):76–96.

Forrest, T. The family dynamics of maternal violence. *Journal of the American Academy of Psychoanalysis* 2 (1974):215–230

Grey, J., Cutler, C., Dean, J., and Kempe, C.H. Parental assessment of mother-baby action. In C.H. Kempe and R. Helfer, eds. *Child abuse and neglect: The family and the community.* Philadelphia: Ballanger, 1976.

Nagi, S.Z. Child maltreatment in the United States: A cry for help and organizational response. Children's Bureau, Office of Child Development, Department of Health, Education, and Welfare, 1976.

Jolly K., Founder
Parents Anonymous Incorporated
in collaboration with
Gordon K. Nelson

Acknowledgments

Any book is the product of the contributions of a number of people. The authors feel indebted to several individuals, more than can be acknowledged by naming them here. We are especially indebted to Henry I. Herring of the Pennsylvania State University for providing a broad level of support in getting this project "off the ground"; to Bruce Bonta, reference librarian, Pattee Library, Pennsylvania State University for invaluable assistance in developing our computer search; to former Pennsylvania State Senator Frederick H. Hobbs and Senator Michael O'Pake for their assistance in providing us with sources to expedite our research; to Ms. Perry Frank, Editor, *1976-77 Public Welfare Directory* for permission to use various segments of that Directory; to Donald C. Bross, Instructor in Pediatrics, University of Colorado for valuable advice and comments; to William S. Hildenbrand, Staff Assistant, Children's Division of the American Humane Association for advice and guidance; and very specially, to Phil Fox, Assistant Director, Child Abuse and Neglect Project of the Education Commission of the States for his personal advice, suggestions, direction, and permission to use the Commission's materials.

Gratitude is also due to those who have helped directly and indirectly with the preparation of this book. The authors have been ably assisted by Ruth Squyres and Edith Fenstemacher for typing of the manuscript, and by the efficient staff of the publisher.

Finally, this book would not have been possible without the close and complete collaboration of its authors.

Child Abuse and Neglect

Introduction

Not until recently has there been a significant change in the study of child abuse and neglect. The recent change, however, reflects a greater willingness to admit the complexity and multiformity of issues involved. Up to now, the vast bulk of literature on child abuse has been replete with case studies describing the physical beatings and injuries, even photographs, of young children. The response on the part of many readers, both among professionals and the general public alike, has been one of outrage and disgust. "Why can't something be done for those children? The courts should take the children away from their parents. The authorities should punish the parents." These are common reactions among readers whose emotions are stirred up over vividly dramatized accounts.

What readers sometimes fail to realize is the pervasive nature of the problem, that the very factors contributing to child abuse and neglect are latent in almost any neighborhood and home. Still a common misconception persists that child abusers suffer from some severe psychological disorder and that the families are basically pathological units. They are condemned as common criminals rather than viewed as victims of the conditions surrounding their lives, and their own childhood experiences. Although the outcomes are very similar—battered, neglected, isolated, and abandoned children—the parents are different in terms of their social, cultural, and eocnomic backgrounds. Even the general lifestyles and personalities can be different.

Mistreating children is something that characterizes people from all walks of life, not just the poor and the nonwhite. As Fontana (1973) pointed out, we hear a lot said about the high incidence of child abuse among the poor and less educated families. But closer scrutiny of this problem leads one to suspect that the more advantaged families can seek out private physicians for treatment and can avoid censure from public authorities. Problems leading to child abuse in lower social classes are, if anything, compounded by the problems of lack of income and lack of information. It is multiple factors like these that serve as the catalyst for child abuse and neglect, factors that are unique to almost every situation.

There are many types of problems and dynamics involved in child mistreatment. There are many types of persons that can fit into the role of perpetrator.

1

They may be individuals who have experienced adjustment difficulties of one kind or another in their personal lives, in marriage, in occupation, or in finances. Above all, they are human beings, too, whose difficulties cannot be overgeneralized. They are not the subject of aberrant personality disorders. In fact, only about 10 percent of abusive parents suffer from some serious psychological difficulties (Steele, 1975). Psychotic conditions are normally distributed in the abusive parent population as they are in the general population. So often we have concerned ourselves solely with the child who has become mistreated while ignoring the situational factors giving rise to the problem and simply condemning the parent.

A set attitude about child mistreatment phenomena is neither helpful for the troubled parent nor the child. Community agencies—social welfare and law enforcement officials—are seen as threatening influences to the parent who is in need of help. Agencies, in turn, often prove ineffective when they are not operating in the interest of the parent, or when they do not attempt to enlist parental cooperation. At best the legal intervenings and court hearings can only temporarily control volatile family situations. This is not to say that community authority should not be exercised, but rather that it often misfires; and when successfully applied, one problem (child abuse) is inevitably substituted for another problem (foster care).

If there is any one lesson to be learned from the early research on maternal deprivation (Bowlby, 1958, 1960, 1961, 1969; Spitz, 1945, 1946), it is the conviction that leaving the child in its own home is far more desirable than in a foster home. A foster home is no more than a temporary caretaking facility. It protects children by providing temporary relief, but does not provide for their psychological needs. Only when the family situation has become seriously disturbed might it be desirable to separate child from family, and even then no real solution to the problem is rendered. Moss (1966) has described the feelings of children in a child-care institution after having been separated from their parents. Under such conditions children become extremely dependent upon the institution; they experience the anxiety of being rejected and find it exceedingly difficult to trust any human relationship.

For this reason relatively greater emphasis is now being placed on self-help programs for troubled parents. Programs like Parents Anonymous (PA) help abusive parents help themselves and each other through self-understanding and self-control. Helping parents is certainly a more constructive way of changing child rearing patterns and protecting children.

The reader will note, thus far, that we do not separate aspects of the problem of child abuse from related breakdowns in parenting functions, like child neglect and abandonment. We do, however, recognize that there are some subtle differences in the psychodynamics of these problems. For instance, Steele and Pollock (1974) indicated that the neglectful parent generally fails in providing basic caretaking duties for the child, such as keeping the infant properly fed and cleaned. On the other hand, the abusive parent usually meets these physical needs but fails in providing a healthy psychological environment.

Still we feel that there are some overriding similarities to be found in both cases, and that child neglect is not altogether different as a problem from child abuse. The results are often the same. In one case, the parent fails in view of actions that are taken; in the other case, the parent fails in view of actions that are not taken. Moreover, can we be certain that a neglected child, one who is deprived of physical needs, is not being deprived of an adequate amount of love? On practical grounds, intervention and treatment requires careful and sensitive understanding of the factors leading to these related problems. Abused and neglected children and the parents of these children are all locked into a vicious cycle which is established from one generation to the next. The child is adversely affected in each case, whether out of neglect or abuse. The parent is caught up in social conflict and interpersonal difficulties.

Toward a Working Definition

Various inclusions and exclusions can be found for the terms *child abuse* and *child neglect*. Typically, state laws require ample proof that children have been deliberately inflicted with serious physical injury (e.g., broken bones, burns, internal injuries) by their parents or caretakers. Similarly, but somewhat more difficult to establish, there must be proof that neglected children have been left alone or unsupervised for a lengthy period of time, or abandoned (complete neglection). An inadequate supply of food (malnutrition and starvation), clothing, shelter, or medical needs is frequently taken as evidence of child neglect.

Helfer (1975) has identified three major criteria in the child abuse and neglect pattern: the potential to abuse, the existence of a special or different child, and crises. Parents who have the *potential to abuse* their children are said to include isolated persons with poor self-images, having passive spouses and unrealistic expectations of their children, and persons reared in certain deficient ways. A *special* or *different child* is one who is singled out for failing to meet parental expectations (e.g., stubborn, demanding, hyperactive, or retarded child). *Crises* can be either major or minor; in either case, they trigger acts of aggression.

The difficulty here is in providing clear operational definitions for these terms. As it stands, Helfer's (1975) criteria would implicate a very large segment of the parent population. Many parents who do not abuse or neglect their children still may have the potential to do so, and many may have crises in their lives and children who are not perceived exactly as being "normal." It would be highly desirable, if at all possible, to give greater precision to these terms.

In the case of child abuse, a problem exists in distinguishing physical abuse from the other less severe forms of physical discipline used by many parents. Presumably, physical force is applied by no mere accident, nor is it an isolated encounter; it is more likely to be construed as a repeated demonstration in the use of physical force by a parent. Other attributes would possibly include a dysfunctional family life, lack of sensitivity and communication between family members, and similar situations leading to the intentional use of force as applied to a child.

The critical line of departure from ordinary acts of physical discipline (e.g., spanking a child who insists on getting more cookies) seems to center on the word *some* and the circumstances that prompted the action. Clearly when the parents' response is made during a time of emotional stress, frustration, or out of rage, it is not likely to serve the purpose of disciplining a child. Parents who "discipline" their children under these circumstances undoubtedly have a distorted concept of discipline. Similarly, if the response pattern is not provoked by the actual behavior of the child, or if it is applied routinely without much thought or consideration as to the purpose, then we are likely to encounter a problem involving child abuse.

Child abuse need not result in the use of physical force alone. The Child Welfare League of America defines *child abuse* in terms of not only what has been done to the child, but also in terms of what has not been done, as in the case of children being deprived of affection and love. Severe emotional or psychological abuse can occur without any physical mistreatment. Prugh and Harlow (1962), for instance, have discussed a kind of "masked deprivation" which occurs when parents are unable to relate warmly to their children. Because of personal problems some parents may have distorted perceptions of their children and simply cannot give them any affection.

Many child welfare specialists regard emotional abuse as abuse of the worst kind. The effects go much deeper and can seriously threaten the child's mental health. In spite of the many inherent dangers of physical abuse, the broken bones, the burns, the various injuries usually do heal. However, when a mother, for example, is prone to verbally abuse her child, pointing out weaknesses and undesirability, these scars go much deeper and probably never heal completely. For this reason, statutes of the law are difficult to invoke because of a lack of clear evidence and because children are usually unwilling (or unable due to their age) to report the abuse they received from their parents. Most important, family intervention and treatment for both parent and child is extremely difficult to attempt in these circumstances without prior diagnosis.

Cultural Sanctions

Many parents believe it is their right to physically discipline children in the manner they see fit. The belief in physical disciplinary methods has become so accepted in our common thinking that few attempt to question its validity.

Child rearing practices that do not conform to this standard are often regarded with contempt, and the general thinking is that it is "permissive" to do otherwise. Parents who hold a high esteem for physical discipline in child rearing seldom recognize children as having rights of their own. Children's needs are seen as unimportant and subordinate to the needs of parents. The prevailing attitude can best be summed up in a common parental expression "Children should be seen and not heard."

Hardly anyone denies the importance of instilling a sense of discipline in one's children. However, the manner in which discipline is brought about is not so easily agreed upon. We find a range of parental practices displayed in our culture. At one end of the spectrum we find parents who make it a regular practice to beat their children; at the other end are those who refrain from all physical measures or employ different methods of disciplining. Perhaps somewhere in the middle can be found the bulk of the parenting population, those who sometimes physically discipline their children and sometimes employ other methods (e.g., restrictions and loss of privileges).

At the root of the whole issue of child abuse and neglect are competing philosophies and beliefs on how we ought to rear our children. Unlike the Soviet Union (Bronfenbrenner, 1970) and certain other countries, we do not have a national social policy regulating parenting functions. Any attempt at implementing one would meet with substantial opposition, nor would there be unequivocal agreement on a policy that best serves the national interest.

In the Soviet Union child rearing is a public affair, a matter that is clearly defined, and a practice to be followed by everyone. Obedience and self-discipline are discussed frequently in the media and in manuals that are specially developed on these subjects. People are encouraged to discipline their children, but without the use of physical force. In that particular system, a type of reinforcement schedule is set up with the child. Encouragement and praise are administered, for example, if a child is doing well in school. If the child is not doing so well, praise is withheld. Reprimands and the temporary denial of affection are some of the common techniques utilized in achieving discipline for every child.

Pearlin (1972) has found that parental disciplinary practices are also a result of the socialization process. In a cross-national investigation of parent-child relationships, Turinese (Italy) parents were noted to hold values and aspirations similar to American parents. From their own experiences, parents adopted disciplinary methods that coincided with their own social values and expectations. Parents who held high expectations of their children generally relied more frequently on physical punishment.

The basic problem in Western countries, like our own, is that parenting practices are entirely left to the whims of parents. We have no broadly accepted child rearing philosophy, and much of the child rearing literature, with the possible exception of Dr. Spock (1946), is confined to academic quarters and is not made easily accessible to the public through the media. Consequently, parenting functions become established out of habit, tradition, and particularly by the way parents themselves were raised as children.

Given this state of affairs, it is not difficult to see why child mistreatment still looms in our culture. For people to re-examine their attitudes and actions as parents will require intensive public discussion through mass media. Parents who continue to use harsh and cruel punishment can only assume that other parents are doing the same without concensus.

Childhood Experiences

Of considerable importance is the role of childhood experiences. Much of the recent literature indicates that abusive parents were themselves abused as children (Bakan, 1971; Blumberg, 1974; Elmer, 1956; Fontana, 1968; Galdston, 1965; Kempe & Helfer, 1972; Steele, 1975; Stolk, 1974; Young, 1964). Since child-rearing practices are not clearly articulated in western culture, it is only natural for parents, consciously or unconsciously, to follow the precedents set by their own parents. Oliver and Taylor (1971) have found physical and emotional mistreatment patterns across as many as five generations in a single family.

Green, Gaines, and Sandgrund (1974) have examined various patterns of family interaction in 60 reported cases of child abuse. One of the three potentiating factors they observed in their sample was mothers of abused children having reported difficulties with their own parents. Abusive mothers described the relationships with their parents in terms of rejection, criticism, and physical punishment. The resulting guilt and low self-esteem, or "bad" self-image, were interpreted as being displaced onto the child in the form of a defense mechanism. The mothers were said to be unconsciously identifying with their "bad" mothers, while attacking their children who symbolized the "bad child and self."

Nurse (1964) abstracted child abuse data from court records in order to ascertain familial patterns. Of the 20 long-term cases selected for study, half the group were found to experience extreme material and emotional deprivation. In 13 of the cases, parents spoke of having been rejected by their own parents, which took the form of desertion, sending the child away, or blaming the child for family troubles. Half this group were noted to be extremely dependent in relationships with their parents, a pattern that was later transformed to spouses. Most important, it was discovered that in none of the cases had parents experienced positive relationships as children.

Steele and Pollock (1974) also found life histories of child abuse in their clinical study group. Invariably they found abusive parents raised in living patterns similar to those which they had provided for their own children. The patterns of rearing were reported in the form of physical beatings and severe and excessive demands imposed by parents; the latter included strict obedience, submissive behavior, solacing parents, and never making mistakes. All the patients were found to have been deprived of "basic mothering," described in terms of a breakdown in the maternal affectional system of being cared for and cared about.

The concept of *transference psychosis*, as applied by Galdston (1965) and reviewed by Gelles (1973), has been used to describe the abusive parent's distorted perception of the child as a hostile adult. The abusive parent supposedly sees former guilt in the child, and as a result, projects negative feelings onto the child. The mere appearance of the child can evoke unpleasant emotions of the past. Consequently, the parent perceives the child as embodying attributes of an adult. In early childhood experiences a life pattern of violence is established which later becomes the adult's chief means of communication.

Whether or not there is any psychological validity to the concept of transference psychosis, the fact remains that abusive parents were themselves abused or neglected—physically or emotionally—as children.

Concept of Child

Another way of understanding some of the basic problems leading to child abuse is to examine parental attitudes toward children. Abusive parents characteristically see their children differently from nonabusive parents. From the time of early infancy the children are perceived as individuals who are quite capable of accomplishing adult tasks. They are not regarded as helplessly dependent creatures who are in constant need of parental support, but rather as individuals who are self-reliant and capable of satisfying parental emotional needs. Spinetta and Rigler (1972) make the point that abusive parents lack appropriate knowledge of child rearing, and as a result, demand and expect a great deal in terms of the child's performance.

Curiously enough, these parental attitudes in some sense reflect a highly developed concept of child. True, infants are not helpless and expressionless beings; anyone who has taken the time to carefully observe the actions of infants can see clearly that they are incredibly competent. Piaget, the internationally noted Swiss psychologist, has remarked often about the infant's competence in terms of successfully accomplishing a "miniature Copernician revolution" within the short space of two years. Psychoanalysts, too, are often infatuated with the social attachment that evolves between infant and mother during the first eight months, and speak of how this is such a critical period in the infant's ego development. For very early in life the child learns to seek out and interact with the mother because of reciprocal satisfaction.

But unfortunately, how much can one actually expect from a young child? A problem seems to occur when parents begin to depend heavily on their young children as providers of affection and emotional security. The mother who slaps her six-month-old infant for spilling his milk is making unreasonable demands on a child who has not yet developed hand coordination. The father who hits his

12-month-old child for constantly crying does not recognize that this is a basic means of communicating when the infant is unable to verbalize. In either case the punishment is unjustified. Parents respond in the manner they do because the children cannot fulfill their needs and expectations. The child's behavior might be interpreted as criticism of the parent's efforts, which undermines the parent's self-esteem (Steele and Pollock, 1972). The parent, of course, reacts with physical punishment.

Conceptual Models

Psychiatric Perspective

Varied interpretations of child abuse have been offered from the perspective of psychiatry. These views focus on underlying psychological processes that somehow have become disturbed, ranging from character disorders to psychoses. Kempe et al. (1962), in an attempt to delineate psychiatric factors of abusive parents, identified a general defect in character structure involving the control and release of aggressive impulses. Galdston (1965), having gone further in diagnosis, declared that the abuse syndrome can be understood as a "transference psychosis," in which the parent has a distorted perception of the child in developmental terms.

The "Medea complx" (Stern, 1948) has also been used to explain a mother's active hatred and homicidal wishes toward her child. Occasional death wishes against children are said to occur in most parents, usually as a revenge against the father figure. Although death wishes are harbored with common frequency, they are consciously resisted in view of what they represent. As a result, these thoughts generally remain at an unconscious level of covert hostility toward the child, evidencing themselves in difficulties of pregnancy and nursing. Still, on occasion, the situation may reach the level of overt hostility where a mother may show outright neglect and cruelty toward her child.

Most clinicians however prefer to deal with abusive parents in more flexible terms. Steele and Pollock (1974), for example, found a wide range of emotional disorders in their clinical observations of parents including hysteria, depression, anxiety, schizophrenia, obsessive-compulsive behavior, and related emotional problems. Some have suffered organic brain damage which produced deficits in intelligence and language; this, in turn, may have diminished the capacity of such individuals to make use of child rearing information. More commonly, abusive parents share characteristics of helplessness, dependency, low self-esteem, and isolation. They are emotionally deprived individuals with needs that have gone unsatisfied. Their interpersonal relationships usually suffer on account of this emotional impoverishment.

Zalba (1966) developed a typology of abusive parents based on an extensive review of case studies. The parents varied from violent and episodic schizophrenia to immature and impulsive character disorders. In attempts to deny their inner hostility and aggression, parents have projected these feelings onto their children and thus have made them targets of violence. Zalba also comments that an unfavorable family environment leads to a dependent, impulsive, unstable adult who can become a poor parent.

Wasserman (1967) acknowledged that while few abusive parents are psychotic, all have an inability to establish genuine interpersonal relationships. They are said to have suffered "severe damage" in their personalities. They are absorbed with their own feelings and cannot sympathize with those of others. This kind of person is believed to need a child for a "hostility sponge" for the purpose of preserving mental balance. Without a scapegoat an abusive parent would quite simply transfer aggression toward another child.

In an article entitled "Psychopathology of the Abusing Parent," Blumberg (1974) characterized the personality of abusive parents in terms of narcissism, poor self-image, uncontrollable aggression, rejection, denial, projection, and a strong need for mothering. Since abusive parents were themselves reared in an environment of abuse and neglect, they have not been able to develop the ability to love. Consequently, they cannot accept criticism and are prone to react impulsively with violence. Blumberg also warns therapists to be on guard in controlling their feelings, so as not to overidentify with the narcissistic patient.

Social Learning Perspective

As infants and young children, abusive parents were treated much like they treat their own children. They learned to accept physical punishment as a natural part of the growing-up process. They also learned to accept it as part of the discipline by which they should raise their own children, believing in the end that children are better off because of it.

The social learning perspective contrasts with psychiatric views of child abuse with respect to the relative emphasis placed on the source of aggressive behavior. The psychiatric view generally places greater emphasis on inner forces residing in an individual's personality—the emotional disturbances and aggressive impulses. These impulses are often unrecognized by the person responsible for them, and as such, they operate almost entirely at a subconscious level of thought. For example, the parent who repeatedly beats a child may have a distorted perception of that child to the extent of projecting inner hostility and anxiety-motivated forces from childhood.

Social learning theories, on the other hand, give greater emphasis to knowledge of the social contexts (e.g., home, school, society) where aggressive behavior is expressed. Adverse living situations increase the probability of child abuse and rejection. Parental modeling is seen as particularly important. When children suffer mistreatment at the hands of their parents, they themselves are likely to engage in abusive behavior in the future.

Gelles (1973) has presented a sociological analysis of child abuse to counter psychiatric claims concerning psychopathological disturbances, mental illnesses, and defects of character. Among the possible social causes cited in child abuse are unemployment, unwanted pregnancy, and general economic conditions. Children become the victims of parental aggression because they, as unwanted children, are sources of stress for the family. An unwanted child is seen as the source of family troubles, and therefore a burden. Furthermore, individuals who grew up in violent households and were raised with physical force have learned from role models that this is an acceptable means of dealing with family problems. Thus, abusive patterns of child rearing are recapitulated from one generation to the next.

Gill (1975) has presented a somewhat similar conceptual analysis of the causes of child abuse based on social variables. He found abuse to occur on each of three basic levels: in the home and in child care settings, in institutions (e.g., educational, welfare, correctional agencies), and in society. The causal dimensions of child abuse are seen largely in terms of the prevailing social philosophy and value system that determine the quality of human relations and inevitably influence the rights of children. Society's attitude toward the use of force as a means of attaining goals and dealing with conflicts ultimately serves as a cause of abuse on the family level. A society that legitimizes the use of force reinforces abuse of young children. Also, stress and frustration stemming from poverty and alienation are "triggering contexts" that may facilitate abusive attacks.

Child abuse, viewed here as a social learning process, perhaps can best be understood in terms of Bandura's (1973; Bandura and Walters, 1963) theoretical formulation of aggression. The aggressive modeling provided by disciplinary actions during early childhood is extremely influential. Parents who inflict severe physical punishment on their children are, in effect, providing aggressive (negative) models for them to follow. Their children will learn how to forcibly influence and control the behavior of others through these models. Conversely, parents who provide more positive models (e.g., temporary loss of affection) are encouraging self-control. Children draw upon parental practices in efforts to solve their interpersonal problems. This is true both in terms of family and peer-group relations. Sometimes the disciplinary actions of parents do not serve the intended outcome. For example, a parent who beats a child for striking a playmate inadvertently may be reinforcing the aggressive behavior which was intended to be eliminated.

Therapy based on principles of social learning may concentrate on providing nonaggressive alternate models to reduce the likelihood of aggressive responses among parents. What is essentially needed from this standpoint is to reverse the cycle of parental violence through better alternatives. These alternatives require a process of unlearning present parenting practices, or "reparenting" (Davoren, 1975). Aggression would therefore be reduced by developing more effective means of handling parent-child interaction.

Cognitive-Developmental Perspective

The authors take the position that child abuse and related mistreatment practices found in parenting are largely cognitive-developmental matters. As mentioned previously, an understanding of parental attitudes toward children in terms of an evolving concept of the child as such may help to elaborate some of the causes of the general mistreatment syndrome. We believe that child mistreatment is not attributable to cultural conditioning alone or to psychiatric beliefs about disturbances that occur in personality. If, for example, social and cultural training were the chief determinant of abuse and neglect, then how is it explained that not all badly abused children grow up to become child abusing parents? Certainly cultural expectations and childhood history are acknowledged as powerful influences. But it is difficult to account for some forms of parenting behavior that are highly resistant to social learning.

Our view is based on the tenets of Piaget's developmental psychology. Child abuse is seen in this context as the result of an active structuring experience, not as the passive product of social training. As a developmental process, it would appear that early childhood experiences provide a continued pattern of abuse and neglect. Young children may be denied the love, warmth, and affection they are rightly entitled to from their parents. However, the real problem arises when these children later come to believe, as adults, that this is natural, perfectly acceptable, and certainly the way children ought to be reared. In other words, it is only when the experiences of childhood become internalized through complex cognitive processes that the pattern begins to manifest itself in terms of a syndrome. A child who is called "bitch" and treated harshly for the first five years of her life, later comes to internalize this label and actually believes she is one.

We know that a young infant, up to 18 to 24 months of age, cannot evoke concepts of people and things beyond immediate perceptual experience. A mother who comes into the room during feedings may represent, for that particular moment, a pleasing and satisfying object. When she leaves the room, it is as if she disappeared. There is no concept or memory trace left with the child. As the child becomes older, he or she begins to establish some cognitive organization of parent or caretaker as a loving (or unloving) object, and a goal partnership begins to emerge.

The infant who was once unaware of the existence of people and unable to differentiate self from world later becomes a child who must work with these people and allow for their needs as well as his or her own. Through the developmental process the child learns to make inferences about the internal psychological states of others. The mistreatment children receive in varied circumstances may be interpreted as a positive sign and believed justified. In this process children learn certain values and standards belonging to their parents, and through active exchanges with them they will develop and apply many of these concepts and ideas.

Intervention and Treatment

Treating abusive parents can take many forms. The recent relative shift of emphasis from child to parent also reflects changes in treatment. Psychotherapy, usually in the form of psychoanalysis, has been a predominant mode of treating abusive parents. The goal of most treatment programs is to change the pattern of parent-child interaction in order to minimize the risks of injury to children. From a traditional standpoint this has taken the form of resolving deep intrapsychic conflicts of patients. A therapist might probe into a patient's relationship with parent and attempt to resolve that conflict.

Aside from traditional psychoanalysis, more recent use is also being made of transactional analysis (TA) techniques to therapy involving several couples in a group. The therapy focuses on destructive patterns in human relationships and stresses misinformation about parenting matters. Occupational therapy is another approach now being instituted to treat abusive parents and their children. This particular program emphasizes development of socialization skills, perception of abilities and limitations of self, and bringing about order and structure into one's life.

Principles of behavior modification and social learning theory are also being applied presently to identify families with an abused child. The basic strategy of such efforts is to increase effective parental behavior while at the same time decreasing abusive behavior through goal setting and attainment, contingent reinforcement scheduling, and discrimination training.

In the public sector, there are various services available to families with personal and social problems related to child abuse and neglect. These services are usually rendered by social caseworkers from welfare agencies, and are primarily rehabilitative in nature. It is also the task of caseworkers to investigate reports of alleged abuse and to initiate proceedings, if warranted, for the removal of children from their homes and placement in foster care. For this reason, intervention into the affairs of families by caseworkers frequently meets with opposition. Caseworkers can be perceived as threatening influences whose only interests are removing children and punishing parents. Opposition can occur even when the motives are to provide guidance and counseling while leaving the children with their families. Emergency treatment care also is provided in the form of medical, psychiatric, and financial assistance to strengthen the families in whatever ways might be necessary. Most community efforts of this kind operate through a coordinated system of interagency and hospital communication.

More recent efforts to curb the influences of child abuse are being made by self-help programs. Parents Anonymous has been gaining increasing prominence in recent years due to encouraging results with rehabilitation. Adults, like the founder of PA, realize that they are caught up in an abusive pattern and seek help. Groups have been set up across the country for adults who wish to remain anonymous and not be subjected to vindictive measures. Thereapy for the group emphasizes developing the ability to handle tension and anger, and parenting education.

Purpose of Guide

The material presented herein is designed to serve several purposes. In recognizing the shifting emphasis now being given to the child abuse problem and the apparent shortcomings of much of the current literature and research, we still find a considerable value in assembling material for researchers and practitioners working in this field of inquiry.

In compiling a comprehensive bibliography on the subject, we have attempted to identify a knowledge base that in the past has been uncertain. Most program implementers and evaluators recognize the need to proceed systematically while investigating areas of concern, and to avoid previous errors of judgment. One way of achieving this end is to begin recognizing that some kind of knowledge base does exist—no matter how imperfect or invalid it might be—and that this can serve as a basis for launching newly and carefully conceived programs.

It is also recognized that an extensive bibliography of this kind is helpful in relating diversified concerns over the problem of child abuse and neglect. Professionals in the disciplines of medicine, law, social work, education, psychology, and psychiatry each have some stake in the problem. Many of these professionals frequently feel the frustrations of not being very effective because the problem has passed beyond their purview. Social workers and hospital medical personnel, for example, sometimes feel exasperation when the courts appear to take no decisive action in particular cases. For this reason, we have painstakingly categorized specific problem areas under the general heading of child abuse and neglect. This should facilitate the library research work of investigators who are interested only in a particular area, whether it be the legal process, parenthood and family relations, treatment and health care, social and cultural practices, the educational institution, or prevention and education. For readers who otherwise may have a general interest in the subject matter, we also have assembled literature dealing with definitions and characteristics of the problem.

A survey of the literature over the last 10 years will reveal, as we have stated, a striking change in the emphasis placed on treatment and the target of intervention efforts. No longer is just the child of concern in the problem of child abuse and neglect. Now it is parents and people experiencing varying difficulties in their lives that are the focus of concern. Perhaps only now are we beginning to tackle the real problems associated with child abuse, not just the innocent and unwitting victims, but also the multifaceted aspects of family life today.

Last, we have included in this guide extensive listings of local and nation-wide groups that are presently involved at some level with the problem of child abuse and neglect. Readers may find these listings advantageous for consulting with local organizations and participating in an exchange of ideas and information. A complete run-down of reporting requirements and current legislation covering child abuse and neglect is also made available on a state-by-state basis to facilitate the efforts of both individuals and organizations.

References

Bakan, D. *Slaughter of the innocents.* San Francisco: Jassey–Bass, 1971.

Bandura, A. *Aggression: A social learning analysis.* Englewood Cliffs, New Jersey: Prentice-Hall, 1973.

Bandura, A., and Walters, R.H. *Social learning and personality development.* New York: Holt, Rinehart & Winston, 1963.

Blumberg, M.L. Psycopathology of the abusing parent. *American Journal of Psychotherapy* 28 (1974):21–29.

Bowlby, J. The nature of a child's tie to his mother. *International Journal of Psychoanalysis* 39 (1958):350–374.

——. Separation anxiety. *International Journal of Psychoanalysis* 41 (1960): 89–113.

——. Separation anxiety: A critical review of the literature. *International Journal of Psychoanalysis* 1 (1961):251–269.

——. *Attachment and loss: Attachment.* Vol. 1. New York: Basic Books, 1969.

Bronfenbrenner, U. *Two worlds of childhood: U.S. and U.S.S.R.* New York: Basic Books, 1970.

Davoren, E. Working with abusive parents: A social workers view. *Children Today* 4 (1975).

Elmer, E. *Children in jeopardy: A study of abused minors and their families.* Pittsburgh: University of Pittsburgh Press, 1967.

Fontana, V.J. *The maltreated child: The maltreatment syndrome in children.* 2d ed. Springfield, Illinois: Charles C. Thomas, 1973.

Galdston, R. Observations on children who have been physically abused and their parents. *American Journal of Psychiatry* 122 (1965):440–443.

Gelles, R.J. Child abuse as psychopathology: A sociological critique and reformulation. *American Journal of Orthopsychiatry* 43 (1973):611–621.

Gill, D.G. Unraveling child abuse. *American Journal of Orthopsychiatry* 45 (1975):346–356.

Green, A.H., Gaines, R.W., and Sandgrund, A. Child abuse: Pathological syndrome of family interaction. *American Journal of Psychiatry* 131 (1974): 882–886.

Helfer, R.E. Why most physicians don't get involved in child abuse cases and what to do about it. *Children Today* 4 (1975).

Kemper, C.H., Silverman, F.N., Steele, B.F., Droegemueller, W., and Silver, H.K. The battered-child syndrome. *Journal of the American Medical Association* 181 (1962):17–24.

Kempe, C.H., and Helfer, R.E. *Helping the battered child and his family.* Philadelphia: J.B. Lippincott Company, 1972.

Moss, S.Z. How children feel about being placed away from home. *Children* 13 (1966):153–157.

Nurse, S.M. Familial patterns of parents who abuse their children. *Smith College Studies in Social Work* 35 (1964):11–25.

Oliver, J.E., and Taylor, A. Five generations of ill-treated children in one family pedigree. *British Journal of Psychiatry* 119 (1971):473–480.

Pearlin, L. *Class context and family relations: A cross-national study.* Boston: Little, Brown, 1972.

Prugh, D.G., and Harlow, H. Masked deprivation. In *Deprivation of maternal care.* Public Affairs Papers, no. 14. Geneva: World Health Organization, 1962.

Spinetta, J.J., and Rigler, D. The child-abusing parent: A psychological review. *Psychological Bulletin* 77 (1972):296–304.

Spitz, R.A. Hospitalism. In O. Fenichel et al. *The psychoanalytic study of the child.* Vol. 1. New York: International Universities Press, 1945.

Spitz, R.A. Hospitalism. In O. Fenichel et al. *The psychoanalytic study of the child.* Vol. 2. New York: International Universities Press, 1946.

Spock, B. *The pocket book of baby and child care.* New York: Pocket Books, 1946.

Steele, B.F. *Working with abusive parents from a psychiatric point of view.* National Center for Child Abuse and Neglect (DHEW/OHD), Washington, D.C., 1975.

Steele, B.F., and Pollock, C.B. A psychiatric study of parents who abuse infants and small children. In R.E. Helfer and C.H. Kempe, eds. *The battered child.* 2d ed, pp. 89–133. Chicago: University of Chicago Press, 1974.

Stern, E.S., The Medea complex: The mother's homicidal wishes to her child. *British Journal of Psychiatry* 94 (1948):321–331.

Stolk, M.V. Who owns the child? *Childhood Education* 50 (1974):258–265.

Wasserman, S. The abused parent of the abused child. *Children* 14 (1967):175–
    179.
Young, L. *Wednesday's children: A study of child abuse and neglect.* New York:
    McGraw-Hill, 1964.
Zalba, S.R. The abused child: I. A survey of the problem. *Social Work* 11 (1966):
    3–16.

Model Legislation for the States

Introduction

In December 1973, The Early Childhood Task Force of the Education Commission of the States (ECS) published its first model legislation for child abuse and neglect. Since then, a number of states have adopted in part or in whole its suggested language.

In January 1974, the federal government enacted Public Law 93-247, which outlined certain requirements each state must meet to be eligible for federal funding. Accordingly, ECS has asked Brian Fraser[a] to revise his first model legislation to meet the requirements of the new federal guidelines, and it is now in its second printing under the auspices of the ECS Child Abuse and Neglect Project. This model act, the work of Mr. Fraser in conjunction with Douglas Besharov,[b] meets the requirements of Public Law 93-247. It has been constructed from the original language of the commission's first model to meet the contingencies and problems that states will encounter in this area over the next decade.

Today, all 50 states as well as Washington, D.C., Puerto Rico, and the Virgin Islands have statutes requiring that physical abuse of children be reported to some state agency. Many of these laws, however, are limited in scope and consequently impact. Child abuse continues to be a major unresolved national problem. The general purpose of this suggested legislation is to encourage state legislators to review their existing laws and revise them where appropriate in order to deal more effectively with child abuse and neglect.

It is conservatively estimated that at least 60,000 children—for the most

This is adapted from Report Number 71 of the Child Abuse and Neglect Project.

---

[a]Brian Fraser, B.A., J.D., Faculty, University of Colorado School of Medicine, Department of Pediatrics; Staff Attorney, The National Center for the Prevention and Treatment of Child Abuse and Neglect, University of Colorado Medical Center.

[b]Douglas Besharov, B.A., J.D., LL.M., Adjunct Professor of Law, New York University School of Law; Director, Select Committee on Child Abuse and Neglect, New York State Assembly.

part under the age of three—are seriously physically abused each year; 700 die at the hands of their parents. If the definition of child abuse is expanded to include sexual molestation, neglect, and emotional abuse, the estimates increase astronomically.

Moreover, child abuse is not a single assault, but repeated assaults on the same child, growing more severe the longer the abuse continues. The damage, both physically and psychologically, is cumulative. The longer the abusive behavior continues unchecked, the greater the chance of serious and permanent disability to the child. Further, child abuse is conditioned behavior learned from parents and passed along from one generation to the next.

Obviously, all the complex factors driving a parent to abuse or neglect a child cannot be dealt with adequately in a single piece of legislation. There is a growing awareness that laws identifying the abused child and the abusing parent must be coupled with treatment programs. Further, it must be recognized that there is no single agency, either public or private, that can offer all the services necessary for the identification, treatment, and prevention of child abuse and neglect.

Child abuse and neglect are multidisciplinary problems that must be attacked from a multidisciplinary point of view. All community services and all community treatment programs must be fully utilized. Most critically, we must foster communication, coordination, and cooperation among all community resources.

The specific purposes of this suggested legislation are:

1. To encourage complete reporting of suspected child abuse and neglect cases by all persons who have contact with young children
2. To encourage a therapeutic and treatment-oriented approach to child abuse and neglect, rather than a punitive approach
3. To encourage uniformity in terms and concepts and to encourage communication and cooperation among states
4. To enable each state to meet the requirements of Public Law 93-247

Even if this suggested legislation were enacted in the form outlined here, there are two complementary efforts that each state must undertake to maximize the impact of the law. First, education and training must be made available for all persons dealing with child abuse and neglect. Second, there must be an effective utilization of all forms of media to identify the problems and needs in the area of child abuse and neglect. However, a word of caution is in order here. There is little value, and perhaps much danger, in saturating the public with tales of the evils of child abuse and neglect. Public awareness to increased reporting. solely for the sake of reporting, is counterproductive. If the media is to increase the number of reports, each state must be prepared to offer services and treatment to those so identified.

Federal Impact

On January 31, 1974, Public Law 93-247 was enacted into law. The primary purpose of this law was to provide federal financial assistance for the prevention, identification, and treatment of child abuse and neglect. For a state or its political subdivisions to qualify for funding under PL 93-247, 10 requirements must be met:

1. A state must provide for the reporting of known or suspected instances of child abuse and neglect.
2. A state must provide, upon the receipt of a report of known or suspected child abuse or neglect, an investigation of that report by a properly constituted state authority. Each investigation must be initiated promptly; however, the properly constituted state authority must be an agency *other than* the agency, institution, or facility involved in the acts or omissions, if the report of child abuse and neglect involves the acts or omissions of a public or private agency or other institution or facility. In addition, a state must provide, upon a finding of abuse or neglect, for immediate action to protect the health and welfare of the abused or neglected child and any other children who may be in danger in the same home.
3. In connection with the enforcement of child abuse and neglect laws and the reporting of suspected instances of child abuse and neglect, a state must demonstrate that there are, in effect, administrative procedures, trained personnel, training procedures, institutional and other facilities, and multidisciplinary programs and services sufficient to assure that the state can deal effectively and efficiently with child abuse and neglect. At a minimum, this must include a provision for the receipt, investigation, and verification of reports; a provision for the determination of treatment or ameliorative social service and medical needs; provision of such services; and, where necessary, recourse to the criminal or juvenile court.
4. A state must have, in effect, a child abuse and neglect law that provides immunity for all persons who in good faith report instances of child abuse or neglect (immunity to apply to both civil and criminal prosecution that might arise from such reporting).
5. A state must preserve the confidentiality of all records concerning reports of child abuse and neglect by having, in effect, a law that (a) makes such records confidential and (b) makes any person who permits or encourages the unauthorized dissemination of such records or their contents guilty of a crime.
6. A state must establish cooperation among law enforcement officials, courts of competent jurisdiction, and all appropriate state agencies providing human services for the prevention, treatment, and identification of child abuse and neglect.

7. In every case involving an abused or neglected child that results in a judicial proceeding, a state must provide that a guardian *ad litem* be appointed to represent the child in such proceedings.
8. A state must provide that the aggregate of state support for programs or projects related to child abuse and neglect shall not be reduced below the level provided during the fiscal year 1973.
9. A state must provide for public dissemination of information on the problems of child abuse and neglect, as well as the facilities and the prevention and treatment methods available to combat child abuse and neglect.
10. A state, to the extent feasible, must ensure that parental organizations combating child abuse and neglect receive preferential treatment.

Clearly, a state's child abuse and neglect reporting statute cannot by itself meet all the requirements outlined in Public Law 93-247. To the extent possible, and to the extent that it is required, the following model act meets the requirements of Public Law 93-247.

For a thorough discussion of all the requirements and how they can be met, please refer to the *Federal Register,* vol. 39, no. 245 (Thursday, December 19, 1974).

Model Legislation

Section I Purpose

It is the purpose of this Act, through the complete reporting of child abuse, sexual abuse, and neglect, to protect the best interests of the child, to offer protective services in order to prevent any further harm to the child or any other children living in the home, to stabilize the home environment, to preserve family life whenever possible, and to encourage cooperation among the states in dealing with the problems of child abuse and neglect.

Alternative: The public policy of this state is to protect children whose health and welfare may be adversely affected through injury and neglect; to strengthen the family and to make the home safe for children by enhancing the parental capacity for good care; to provide a temporary or permanent nurturing and safe environment when necessary; and for these purposes to require the reporting of child abuse, investigation of such reports by a social agency, and provision of services where needed by the child and family (based on *Conn. Gen. Stats. Ann.* §17-38(a), 1975).

Comments: The purpose of the Act is preventive and curative, not punitive. It is intended to encourage reporting within a state and cooperation among the states in order to identify child abuse as quickly as possible. With the identification of a specific instance of child abuse, the state's resources can be brought to bear in an effort to protect the child's health, to prevent abuse from occurring again, and to keep the family unit intact whenever possible.

Keeping the family unit intact, however, is not the primary purpose of the legislation. Protection of the child takes first priority. In many cases, the protection of the child's interests and keeping the family together will be one and the same, and need not be mutually exclusive. Unfortunately, in some situations they are. In these cases, the two should be separated and primary emphasis should be placed on the welfare of the child.

Section II Definitions

When used in this Act, unless the specific content indicates otherwise:

1. "Child" means any person under 18 years of age.
2. "Abuse" means any physical or mental injury inflicted on a child other than by accidental means, or an injury at variance with the history given of it.
3. "Neglect" means a failure to provide, or a refusal to provide when financially able, by those legally responsible for the care and maintenance of the child; the proper or necessary support; education, as required by law; or medical, surgical, or any other care necessary for the child's well-being.
4. "Institutional child abuse and neglect" means situations of child abuse or neglect where the person responsible for the child's welfare is in a foster home, residential home, or other public or private institution or agency.
5. "State department" means the state department responsible for the supervision or administration of child protective services at the local level.
6. "Child protective agency" means the agency designated by state law with prime child protective responsibility, including the receipt, investigation, treatment, or referral of reports of known or suspected child abuse or neglect.
7. "Unfounded report" means any report made pursuant to this act that is not supported by some credible evidence.
8. "A person responsible for a child's welfare" includes the child's parent, guardian, or other person responsible for the child's welfare, whether the child is in his home, a relative's home, a foster care home, or a residential institution.
9. "Subject of the report" means any child reported under this Act, or his or her parent, guardian, or other person responsible for his welfare.

Alternative 1: "Abuse" means any case in which a child exhibits evidence of skin bruising, bleeding, malnutrition, sexual molestation, burns, fracture of any bone, subdural hematoma, soft-tissue swelling, a failure-to-thrive, or death, and such condition or death is not justifiably explained, or the history given concerning such condition or death is at variance with the degree or type of such condition or death, or the circumstances indicate that such condition or death may not be the product of an accidental occurrence (based on *Colo. Rev. Stats. Ann.,* §19-10-101(1), 1973).

Alternative 2: "Definition for identification of children for reporting purposes": A child under the age of 18 who is suffering from physical injury (inflicted upon him by other than accidental means), or sexual abuse, or malnutrition, or physical or emotional harm or substantial risk thereof by reason of neglect. Reporting of neglect shall take into account the accepted child-rearing practices of the culture of which he or she is part (*Clinical Proceedings,* Children's Hospital, National Medical Center, vol. 30, no. 2, February 1974; definition suggested at the Conference on the Battered Child, sponsored by the D.C. Chapter of the American Academy of Pediatrics and Group Health Association, Inc., Washington, D.C., Sheraton Park Hotel, June 7, 1973).

Comments: This definition of "child," taken from Maryland legislation, is relatively uniform across the country. Washington State, however, noting that the purpose of an act of this type is to protect those persons who cannot protect themselves, has defined a child as: "Any person under the age of 18 years and shall include mentally retarded persons, regardless of age" (*Rev. Wash. Code Ann.,* §26.44.020(6), 1974). A definition that specifically includes the mentally retarded is preferable, although it greatly expands the scope of the bill and a generally agreed-upon definition of "mentally retarded" may be difficult to achieve. For other definitions of "child," incorporating a mental or physical disability, the statutes of Delaware, Nebraska, and Ohio are especially helpful. As defined, "abuse" has a broad context. It refers to any physical injury not accidental in nature. The word "serious," which in many states precedes "physical injury," has been purposely deleted because legislation designed to provide an effective child abuse program should be concerned with *all* injuries, not just serious ones. In many cases, simple physical injuries later become the serious physical injuries, and by that time it is too late to intervene and offer adequate assistance.

The definition also refers to "mental injury." This connotes emotional abuse or emotional neglect. A number of state statutes define abuse to include emotional abuse. Statutes in this category include those in Delaware, Louisiana, Kansas, Tennessee, and Texas. Although many state statutes refer to serious physical injury resulting in emotional harm or serious mental abuse resulting in physical injury, here "mental injury" is not defined to include physical injury. The definition as used here is intended to mean pure emotional abuse. An "injury at variance with the history given of it" is included because parents who have seriously injured their children often propose explanations that do not adequately explain the injury.

"Neglect" includes the willful commission or negligent omission of some act by the parent. This is intended to cover situations in which the child is not physically or mentally abused, but which, if unchecked, present as great a danger to the child. This is not intended to cover those situations in which there is a need, but the need springs from the family's financial inabilities. The context of neglect is broad enough to cover the failure-to-thrive, abandonment, and starvation clauses noted specifically in some state statutes for neglect.

This Act recognizes that children are often abused or neglected by the public and private agencies and institutions meant to serve them. The term "institutional child abuse and neglect" is intended to cover those situations in which a child is abused or neglected in some institutional setting.

The definition of an "unfounded report" is intended to solve the problem of the malicious, bad-faith report. In too many cases, reports of suspected abuse with no credible evidence to justify them are listed in a central registry. It is hoped that by labeling reports as founded or unfounded, reports with no credible evidence to support them will be expunged from the central registry records.

Section III Persons Mandated to Report Suspected Abuse, Sexual Abuse, and Neglect

When any physician, resident, intern, hospital personnel engaged in the admission, examination, care, or treatment of persons, nurse, osteopath, chiropractor, podiatrist, medical examiner or coroner, dentist, optometrist, or any other medical or mental health professional, Christian Science practitioner, religious healer, school teacher or other school official or pupil personnel, social service worker, day-care worker or other child care or foster care worker, or any peace officer or law enforcement official has reasonable cause to suspect that a child has been subjected to abuse, sexual abuse, or neglect, or observes the child being subjected to conditions or circumstances that would reasonably result in abuse or neglect, he shall immediately report it or cause a report to be made.

Whenever such person is required to report under this Act in his capacity as a member of the staff of a medical or other public or private institution, school, facility, or agency, he shall immediately notify the person in charge of such institution, school, facility, or agency, or his designated agent, who shall then also become responsible to report or cause reports to be made. However, nothing in this section or Act is intended to require more than one report from any such institution, school, or agency; but neither is it intended to prevent individuals from reporting on their own behalf.

In addition to those persons and officials specifically required to report suspected child abuse, sexual abuse, and neglect, any other person may make a report if such person has reasonable cause to suspect that a child has been abused or neglected, or observes the child being subjected to conditions or circumstances that would reasonably result in abuse or neglect.

Comments: The basic format for Section III is drawn from the New York statute, and the provision for the report of conditions or circumstances that would reasonably result in abuse is drawn from the Colorado law.

The number of individuals required to report under this section is extensive. Section III identifies all those persons who have contact with young children and who are able to identify suspected injuries to children at the earliest possible point in time. The key to any good piece of legislation pertaining to child abuse and neglect is to provide a means for identifying the child abuse and neglect case as quickly as possible.

Sexual abuse has not been specifically defined in Section III. It is expected that state courts would interpret sexual abuse or sexual molestation to include sexual physical assaults, consensual sexual activity with a minor, and nonphysical sexual assaults, such as exhibitionism. Connecticut's children's code has been amended to allow hospitals, physicians, and clinics to examine and treat a minor for venereal disease without his parents' consent; examination and treatment are confidential unless the minor is under 12 years of age, and then a report is required under the statute mandating reports of suspected child abuse. The assumption is that sexual contact with a child under 12, with or without the consent of the child, constitutes abuse and should be reported as such.

Finally, this section provides for voluntary reports by any person who has reasonable cause to suspect abuse or neglect. This is to encourage all persons to report suspected abuse and neglect and to make certain that such reports will be identified and processed. At the same time, it ensures that individuals making voluntary reports will not be subjected to criminal liability for a failure to report. Only those individuals specifically required to report are criminally and civilly liable for a failure to do so.

Section IV Mandatory Reporting to a Medical Examiner or a Coroner and a Postmortem Investigation

Any person or official required under Section III of this Act to report cases of suspected child abuse, sexual abuse, or neglect, including workers of the local child protective services, who has reasonable cause to suspect that a child has died as a result of child abuse, sexual abuse, or neglect shall report that fact to the appropriate medical examiner or coroner. The medical examiner or coroner shall accept the report for investigation and shall report his findings to the

police, the appropriate district attorney, the local child protective service
agency, and, if the institution making a report is a hospital, to the hospital.

Comments: Until a few years ago, coroners and medical examiners were not
routinely required to report suspected incidences of child abuse, sexual abuse, or
neglect that resulted in a death. As a result, a number of child abuse deaths were
never noted or reported. While it is axiomatic that a child who is dead is no
longer in danger, one of the primary purposes of child abuse legislation is to protect *all* children within the same home. To accomplish this, deaths resulting from
suspected child abuse should be reported by the coroner or medical examiner
and the same procedure should be followed as if the child were still alive. It
should be noted, however, that Section IV requires reports to a medical examiner or a coroner when someone other than a medical examiner or coroner suspects that a child has died as a result of child abuse, sexual abuse, or neglect.
The medical examiner or coroner is required to accept the report, make an investigation, and report his findings to the police, district attorney, and the welfare
department.

Section V Color Photography and X-rays

Any person required to report cases of child abuse, sexual abuse, and neglect
may take or cause to be taken, at public expense, color photographs of the areas
of trauma visible on a child and, if medically indicated, cause to be performed
radiological examinations of the child. Any photographs or x-rays taken shall be
sent to the mandated receiving agency as soon as possible. Whenever such person is required to report under this Act, in his capacity as a member of the staff
of a medical or other private or public institution, school, facility, or agency, he
shall immediately notify the person in charge of such institution, school, facility,
or agency, or his designated delegate, who shall then take or cause to be taken,
at public expense, color photographs of physical trauma and shall, if medically
indicated, cause to be performed a radiological examination of the child.

Comments: This section is intended to provide data to augment the department's file pertaining to child abuse. It is assumed that such photographs would
become a portion of the medical file and thus could be used in court proceedings. This section specifically states that color photography *may* be taken of the
physical trauma visible on a child. Legally, this means that individuals mandated
to report abuse do not need parental permission or release to take the necessary
photographs. The language of this section specifically states that any person required to report may take color photographs, but when such person is a member

of a staff of a hospital or any other private or public institution, school, facility, or agency, he *shall* notify the person who *shall* take such color photographs.

Section VI Protective Custody

A police officer or law enforcement official may take a child into protective custody, and any person in charge of a hospital or similar institution or any physician treating a child may keep that child in his custody without the consent of the parent or the guardian, whether or not additional medical treatment is required, if the circumstances or conditions of the child are such that continuing in his place of residence or in the care or custody of the parent, guardian, custodian, or other person responsible for the child's care presents an imminent danger to that child's life or health.

Any person taking a child into protective custody shall immediately notify the child protective services and the juvenile court and shall make every reasonable effort to inform the parent or the person responsible for the child's welfare of the place or facility to which the child has been brought. The place the child shall be taken to shall be designated for that purpose by the juvenile court or the local child protective service. It may include a hospital if the child is or will be presently admitted to the hospital. The local child protective service shall be responsible for attempting to avoid placement of a child in a foster home or an institution, whenever possible and appropriate. The local child protective service shall commence child protective proceedings in the juvenile court at the next regular weekday session of the court or, at that time, recommend to the court that a petition not be filed and that the child be returned to his parents or other person responsible for his welfare pending further action.

Comments: The right of a physician or the head of a hospital, clinic, or other similar institution to retain custody of a child in his care is beginning to gain wide acceptance. The right to retain custody under this section is permitted even if there is no immediate need for additional medical treatment and even if the parents object to the retention of custody. The requirement is that there exists some immediate danger to the child's life or health. With the addition of the word "health," the minimum requirement is simply that if the child were released, there would be a possibility that the child might suffer further injury. There is no requirement that the injury be "serious."

This section is intended to give doctors, hospitals, clinics, and other similar institutions more flexibility in dealing with what they believe may be a potentially explosive and dangerous home environment for a child. This section is particularly pertinent in those situations in which it proves difficult to obtain an immediate police hold or court order. In order to make this section as palatable as possible, it requires that the parents be notified as quickly as possible under the circumstances, and that the juvenile court be notified at the next regular weekday session.

Section VII Reporting Procedures

1. Reports of child abuse, sexual abuse, or neglect made pursuant to this Act shall be made immediately by telephone and shall be followed by a written report within 48 hours if so requested by the receiving agency. The receiving agency shall forward immediately a copy of this report to the statewide central registry on forms supplied by such registry.

2. All initial oral reports shall be made by telephone to a state center established by this Act. The state department shall establish and shall maintain in the state center a 24-hour, 7-day-a-week, toll-free telephone number to receive such calls. If the initial report is made to some local service, the local service shall forward such information immediately to the state center. When reports are made directly to the state center, they shall be immediately transferred to the appropriate local service.

3. To the extent possible, such reports shall include the following information: the names and addresses of the child and his parents or other persons responsible for his care; the child's age, sex, and race; the nature and the extent of the injuries, sexual abuse, or neglect to the child or any other child in the same home; the name and address of the person responsible for the injuries, sexual abuse, or neglect; the family composition; the source of the report, including the name of the person making the report, his occupation, and his address; any actions taken by the reporting source, including the taking of x-rays or color photographs, temporary custody, or notification of the coroner or medical examiner; and any other information that the person making the report believes may further the purposes of this Act.

4. A copy of this report shall immediately be made available to the appropriate law enforcement agency, the district attorney, or the coroner or medical examiner's office for consideration.

5. A written report from persons or officials required by this Act to report shall be admissible in evidence in any proceeding relating to child abuse, sexual abuse, or neglect.

6. Reports involving known or suspected institutional child abuse, sexual abuse, or neglect shall be made and received as all other reports made pursuant to this Act. However, the investigation of such reports shall be the responsibility of the agency designated to fulfill this purpose by an approved local plan for child protective services or by an agency designated by the state department.

Comments: The intent of this section is to require immediate reports so that appropriate and ameliorative action can be offered. Furthermore, this section established one statewide, 24-hour-a-day hotline for child abuse, sexual abuse, and neglect reporting. The state department is responsible for the creation and maintenance of a toll-free child abuse hotline and must establish and maintain a state center to coordinate all state activities. While local communities will be encouraged to develop their own child abuse plan, there must be some agency ultimately responsible for the coordination of all child abuse and neglect programs. This is the function of the state center under the auspices of the state department.

This suggested legislation provides for a written report at the discretion of the receiving agency. Some states require an immediate oral report to the receiving agency, followed by a written report within some specified time period. Other states simply require an oral report. It is suggested that requirements of a written report in *all* cases of suspected abuse, sexual abuse, and neglect may have a chilling effect on reporting. The primary purpose of the reporting statute is to identify the child in peril as quickly as possible. Anything that might compromise this identification process should be thoroughly analyzed.

The content of the initial report is extensive, as it is in a number of states, such as Connecticut, Oregon, West Virginia, and New York. The purpose is to identify the child in danger, any other children in the same home who might also be in danger, the probable abuser, and the name of the reporter. The information is then utilized to initiate the investigation, to cross-index in the central registry, and to begin appropriate legal proceedings where necessary.

Subsection 4 of this section provides that copies of the initial report will be "made available" to the appropriate law enforcement agency, local district attorney, or coroner. It does not require that a report be transferred immediately to the police department, district attorney, or coroner. Reports of physical abuse may be of concern to the district attorney; reports of neglect will not. Reports of suspected abuse leading to death will be of interest to the coroner, but simple reports of abuse will not. In any event, reports are made available as appropriate. Each community will probably set up its own procedures for transferring information concerning child abuse, sexual abuse, and neglect. The actual procedures utilized for the transfer, and the circumstances under which a transfer takes place, are left to the agencies themselves.

Subsection 6 of this section ensures that the agency investigating the report is not the same agency that has been reported as abusing the child.

Section VIII Immunity from Liability

Any person, official, or institution participating in good faith in any act permitted or required by this Act shall be immune from any civil or criminal liability that otherwise might result by reasons of such actions.

Comments: To encourage reporting, this section protects from civil and criminal liability *any* person who makes a report. At the present time, every state offers some form of immunity from liability under mandatory reporting statutes. This section provides immunity for individuals required or permitted to report, required or permitted to take color photography or x-rays, or permitted to assume temporary custody. The immunity extends to *any* action permitted or required under this Act.

Immunity is granted only to those persons acting in good faith (i.e., without a malicious purpose). Some states presume the good faith of actors making a report or performing an activity under the mandatory reporting statute. For all practical purposes, however, anyone bringing suit against a reporter must show that the reporter acted in bad faith. If the person bringing suit must demonstrate bad faith on the part of the reporter, there is already a presumption of good faith. It was felt that inclusion of a phrase "presuming good faith" would simply be redundant and was omitted.

Section IX Abrogation of Privileged Communications

The privileged quality of communications between husband and wife and between any professional person and his patient or his client, except that between attorney and client, is hereby abrogated in situations involving known or suspected child abuse, sexual abuse, or neglect. Such privileged communications, excluding those of attorney and client, shall not constitute grounds for failure to report as required or permitted by this Act, to cooperate with the child protective service in its activities pursuant to this Act, or to give or accept evidence in any judicial proceeding relating to child abuse, sexual abuse, or neglect.

Comments: This section abrogates the privileged status of confidential communications for purposes of reporting or participating in any proceeding relating to child abuse, sexual abuse, or neglect. In most cases of child abuse, the only eyewitnesses are the parents and the child, and the child is either too young or too intimidated to testify. The parent who actually abused the child cannot, of course, be forced to testify against his own interests. Rather than force the county attorney to rely on purely circumstantial evidence to prove child abuse, this section would allow the spouse who actually witnessed the attack to testify.

Section X Failure to Report

1. Any person, official, or institution required by this Act to report a case of known or suspected child abuse, sexual abuse, or neglect, or to perform any other act, who knowingly fails to do so or knowingly prevents another person acting reasonably from doing so, shall be guilty of a misdemeanor.

2. Any person, official, or institution required by this Act to report a case of known or suspected child abuse, sexual abuse, or neglect, or to perform any other act, who knowingly fails to do so or knowingly prevents another person acting reasonably from doing so, shall be civilly liable for the damages proximately caused by such failure.

Comments: Under Section X, individuals who are required to report and who knowingly fail to do so become civilly and criminally liable. Subsection 1 is little more than a slap on the wrist, a criminal sanction levied by the state for a failure to report. Subsection 2, however, clears the way for a civil suit on behalf of the child for damages caused by the knowing failure to report. Previously, a suit for damages on behalf of the injured child was via the writ of "negligence per se," which often proved complicated and lengthy. Today, 33 states provide criminal sanctions for failure to report a case of suspected child abuse, sexual molestation, or neglect.

In task force discussions, several members expressed reservations about recommending penalties for a failure to report, arguing that the establishment of liability for failure to report might tend to result in excess reporting by those fearing possible legal action. They felt that many reports might be motivated more by a fear of legal incrimination and penalty than by a real concern for the welfare of the child. It was also felt that the establishment of penalties for failure to report might instill a fear of becoming involved at all, and that a legal penalty for failure to report might foster the inclination toward minding one's own business, thus defeating the intent of the legislation. Instead of establishing penalties, it was felt that efforts should be directed at breaking down the resistance to reporting. This could best be achieved by persistent educational efforts to sensitize the public as to the seriousness of the problem and the importance of reporting.

On the other hand, the task force expressed equally strong feelings that penalties for a failure to report would not result in excess reporting and that there was no substantial evidence to support the arguments against penalties. It was felt that inclusion of a penalty for failure to report would not increase the resistance to reporting, but would have the opposite effect. One doubt expressed from a pragmatic point of view was whether anyone would be *criminally* prosecuted for a failure to report in a one-time situation, because the diagnosis is simply too subjective. There have been cases where pediatricians have been sued *civilly* for a failure to report; in these cases, children were seen more than once, and abuse was readily apparent.

After weighing the arguments for and against, the task force decided to include in the suggested legislation the section that provides for penalties for failure to report, but also to emphasize in the accompanying comments the significant differences of opinion on this question.

There was no disagreement, however, on the need to educate the public about the extent of the problem and what should be done in the event that individuals do become involved in reporting cases of child abuse, sexual abuse, and neglect.

Section XI Child Protective Services

1. The state department shall establish or designate in every county (or comparable political subdivision) a local child protective service to perform the duties and functions set forth in this Act.

2. Except in cases involving institutional abuse or in cases in which police investigation also appears appropriate, the child protective service shall be the sole public agency responsible for receiving, investigating or arranging for investigation, and coordinating the investigation of all reports of known or suspected child abuse, sexual abuse, or neglect. In accordance with the local plan for child protective services, it shall provide protective services to prevent further abuse, sexual abuse, or neglect of children and provide for, or arrange for, coordinate, and monitor the provision of those services necessary to ensure the safety of children. The local child protective service shall have a qualified staff sufficient to fulfill the purposes of this Act and shall be organized to maximize the continuity of responsibility, care, and service of individual workers for individual children and families.

3. Each local child protective service shall:
   a. receive or arrange for the receipt of all reports of known or suspected child abuse, sexual abuse, or neglect on a 24-hour, 7-day-a-week basis
   b. provide or arrange for emergency children's services to be available at all times
   c. within 24 hours of notification of a suspected case of child abuse, sexual abuse, or neglect, commence or cause to be commenced a thorough investigation of the report

4. a. The investigation shall include an evaluation of the environment of the child named in the report and of any other children that may be in the same home; a determination of the risk to those children if they continue to remain in the home; a determination of the nature, extent, and cause of any condition enumerated in the initial report of child abuse, sexual abuse, or neglect; and the name, age, and condition of any other children living in the same home.
   b. Upon completion of the investigation, where appropriate, the local child protective service shall offer services to the child or to the family.
   c. If, at any time before the investigation has been completed, the opinion of the investigators is that immediate removal is necessary to protect the child from further abuse, sexual abuse, or neglect, the juvenile

court or the district court with juvenile jurisdiction shall be so notified.

d. In those cases in which the local child protective service determines that the best interests of the child require juvenile court action, the local child protective service shall initiate the appropriate legal proceeding, and shall assist the juvenile court during all stages of that proceeding in accordance with the provisions of this Act.

e. The local child protective service shall be responsible for providing, directing, or coordinating the appropriate and timely delivery of services to abused children and their families, including services to those responsible for the child's care.

5. The local child protective service shall complete and forward to the state central registry, on forms supplied by such state central registry,

a. within 7 days of the receipt of a report of known or suspected child abuse, sexual abuse, or neglect, a preliminary report of the investigation made by the local child protective service, including an evaluation of the situation, potential danger to the child or children, and actions taken or completed

b. within 90 days of receipt of the initial report of known or suspected child abuse, sexual abuse, or neglect, a progress report, including a determination by the local child protective service that the report is founded or unfounded, a plan for rehabilitative or ameliorative treatment, services offered and accepted or refused, and the present status of the case

c. within 7 days of termination of a case, a report indicating the final disposition

6. To carry out the purposes of this Act, the local child protective service may request and shall receive from departments, boards, bureaus, or other agencies of the state or any of its political subdivisions, or from any duly authorized agency or any other agency providing services under the local child protective service plan, such cooperation, assistance, and information as will enable it to fulfill its responsibilities.

Comments: This section provides for the establishment of a child protective service to fulfill child abuse and neglect functions. Although this Act requires that a child protective service be established in each county, it is recognized that in predominately rural states this may be impractical or impossible. It is therefore suggested that in rural states one child protective service be established for a number of contiguous counties. The purpose of the child protective service is to coordinate all aspects of the child abuse case, including the receipt of reports, the investigation of reports, court action, and treatment. Each county child protective service must receive reports, initiate an investigation within 24 hours, offer appropriate services to the child and family, and, where necessary, petition the juvenile court on behalf of the injured child.

In an attempt to coordinate and evaluate progress, each child protective service must complete three reports as the case unfolds. The first is a *preliminary report* indicating what action has been taken once a report of known or suspected child abuse, sexual abuse, or neglect has been received. The second is a *progress report* indicating whether or not the original report has proven to be founded or unfounded, what treatment plan has been completed for the child and his family, and what services have been offered and accepted to date. The third is a *termination report* indicating the eventual disposition of the case. All reports are forwarded to the state central registry on forms provided by the state central registry.

It should be noted that the child protective service is responsible for the receipt and investigation of reports and for treatment. If the local child protective service cannot investigate the report or offer treatment, it may arrange for another local agency to provide the service. The primary responsibility of the child protective service is not to offer services, but to ensure that all requirements of this Act are met and to coordinate all related activities.

Section XII Child Protection Team and Local Plan for Child Protection

1. The local child protective service shall convene a communitywide, multidisciplinary child protection team to be known as the *Child Protection Team.* The team shall be comprised of the director of the local child protective service or his representative, who shall serve as team coordinator; a representative of the local law enforcement agency; a representative of the juvenile court, appointed by the court; and, to the extent possible, a·physician, a lawyer, a representative of mental health or public health, and one or more representatives of the lay community, to be appointed by the team coordinator. The team shall be composed of no less than three and no more than nine members.

The team coordinator shall be responsible for supplying the team with copies of the initial report, the preliminary report, the progress report, and the termination report in every case of child abuse, sexual abuse, and neglect. The coordinator shall also supply the team with any other information he considers germane to its deliberations. The Child Protection Team shall meet once a week or within a week of the date a report is made of suspected abuse, known child abuse, sexual abuse, or neglect. The team shall serve as a diagnostic and prognostic service for the child protective service. However, the Child Protection Team may, after an evaluation of the reports, file a petition in the juvenile court on behalf of the subject child if it believes this would serve the interests of the child. If the Child Protection Team files a petition in the juvenile court on behalf of the child, it shall notify the guardian *ad litem* in writing of its reason for initiating a petition, its suggested prognosis, and its suggested treatment program for the abused child and his family.

2. After consultation with local law enforcement agencies, the juvenile court, parental organizations, and other appropriate public and private agencies and societies, including social service, medical, mental health, and legal agencies or societies, each Child Protection Team shall prepare annually a local plan for the provision of child protective services.

   a. The local plan shall describe local implementation of this Act, including the organization, staffing, method of operations, and financing of the child protective service, as well as provisions made for the purchase of services and interagency cooperation. The local plan shall also describe programs in effect and programs planned in connection with the implementation of this Act. The plan shall also describe administrative procedures in effect or planned; personnel trained in child abuse, sexual abuse, or neglect; training programs in existence or planned; and institutions and multidisciplinary programs in existence or planned. At a minimum, local services must include provision for the receipt, investigation, and verification of reports; provision for the determination of treatment or ameliorative social service needs; provision for such services; when necessary, resort to criminal or juvenile courts; and provision for monitoring and planning of the entire process.

   b. The local plan shall specify the terms and conditions under which the child protective service may purchase and utilize services of any public or private agency to carry out its responsibilities under this Act. When services are purchased by the local child protective service pursuant to this section, they shall be reimbursed by the state to the locality or the agency in the same manner and to the same extent as if the services were provided directly by the local child protective service.

   c. The local plan shall be made available to the public for review and comment at least 60 days before a public hearing on the plan. A public hearing shall be held at least 30 days before the plan is to be submitted to the state department. The date of submission to the state department shall be determined by the state department to stagger the department's receipt of such plans throughout the year.

   d. The local plan may not take effect until at least 60 days after its submission to the state department. Within 30 days of its submission, the state department shall certify whether the local plan fulfills the purposes and requirements of this Act. If it certifies that the local plan does not do so, it shall state the reasons therefore, and the team shall have 30 days to submit an amended plan. The state department shall

then have 30 days to certify whether this amended plan fulfills the
purposes and requirements of this Act. If it again certifies that the
plan does not do so, the local child protective service shall have an
additional 30 days to submit an amended plan, which the state department shall have 30 days to certify, whether or not the amended plan
fulfills the purposes and meets the requirements of this Act. Anytime
thereafter, the state department may withhold state reimbursement
for all or part of the county's social service activities. Decisions of the
state department under this section shall be reviewable in the form
and manner prescribed by state law.

Comments: This section recognizes that child abuse is a multidimensional problem. The identification, prevention, and treatment of child abuse, sexual abuse,
and neglect are part medical pathology, part psychiatry, part legal, and a bit
social work. The creation of a multidisciplinary Child Protection Team should
provide enough collective expertise from the relevant professions to provide an
adequate diagnosis and prognosis and provide and coordinate an adequate treatment plan for the abused child and his family. The Child Protection Team can be
utilized as a sounding board for the local child protective service, but it is also
more than a tool for the local agency; the team serves as a monitoring device and
a safety valve as well. If the local protective service, after investigation, decides
that a case is not one of child abuse, sexual abuse, or neglect, and decides not to
proceed to the court, the team can reevaluate the case and independently file a
petition on behalf of the child.

Furthermore, the treatment aspect of child abuse, sexual abuse, and neglect
is a multifaceted problem. Many service organizations that could be utilized in
cases of child abuse are currently not involved (public health, mental health,
school social workers, school nurses, public health nurses, school counselors,
Red Cross, and the Salvation Army, to name a few). The Child Protection Team
has the option, in drafting a local plan and in suggesting treatment programs for
a particular case, of calling upon these various service organizations.

The concept of multidisciplinary child protection teams or consultation
boards is not new. There are currently hundreds of hospital-based teams, community teams, and suspected child abuse and neglect (SCAN) organizations in
existence. Massachusetts provides for the establishment of "consultation and advisory boards" throughout the state (Ann. Laws of Mass., §119-51(D), 1974).
Colorado requires that all counties with reports of 50 or more cases of child
abuse, sexual abuse, and neglect create a child protection team for the diagnosis,
prognosis, and treatment of child abuse, sexual abuse, and neglect (Colo. House
Bill 1482, June 1975).

This section also recognizes that counties may vary in population, population makeup, services, and treatment programs. Child abuse is not only a multidisciplinary problem, it is a community problem. By requiring the local child

protection team to draft a local plan in consultation with other local agencies, community weaknesses will be minimized and community strengths optimized. If child abuse is ever to be identified, treated, and prevented effectively, it must be a total community effort. This section attempts to bring together all community service organizations to draft a cooperative community plan in order to meet the requirements of Public Law 93-247. The requirement of a comprehensive community planning effort is not unique. It will be a condition precedent to federal funding under Title XX of the Social Security Act, and it is currently in existence in New York (McKinney's Consolidated Laws of New York, Social Services Laws, §423, (1975)).

Section XIII The Statewide Child Protection Center and the Central Registry

1. The state department shall establish and maintain a single statewide facility, to be known as the Statewide Child Protection Center, which shall be a separate organizational unit administered within the state department, with qualified staff and resources sufficient to fulfill the purposes and functions assigned to it by this Act.

2. The purposes of the Statewide Child Protection Center shall be to assign and monitor initial child protection responsibility; to assist in the diagnosis of child abuse, sexual abuse, and neglect; to coordinate and monitor referrals of known or suspected child abuse, sexual abuse, and neglect; to measure the effectiveness of existing child protection programs and facilitate research, planning, and program development; and to establish and monitor a statewide central registry for child abuse, sexual abuse, and neglect.

3. The state department shall establish and maintain within the Statewide Child Protection Center a statewide toll-free number, 24 hours a day, 7 days a week, which all persons may use to report known or suspected cases of child abuse, sexual abuse, or neglect.

4. a. The state department shall establish and maintain within the Statewide Child Protection Center a central registry for child abuse, sexual abuse, and neglect.

   b. Through the recording of initial reports, preliminary reports, progress reports, and termination reports of child abuse, sexual abuse, and neglect, the central registry may be utilized to identify prior reports of known or suspected child abuse, sexual abuse, or neglect involving the same child or the same family; to continuously monitor the status of all child protective cases involving child abuse, sexual abuse, and neglect; and to develop statistical and other materials for research.

   c. All initial reports, either written or oral, of child abuse, sexual abuse, or neglect made to any agency shall be immediately relayed to the

Statewide Child Protection Center, which shall cause them to be
entered into the central registry. As preliminary reports, progress reports, and termination reports become available, they shall be transferred to the Statewide Child Protection Center, which shall cause
them to be entered into the central registry. The registry shall also include the names, addresses, and professional status of any persons
requesting and receiving information from the central registry.

d. Immediately upon receipt of a report of known or suspected child
abuse, sexual abuse, or neglect to the Statewide Child Protection
Center, the central registry shall be utilized to determine if there is
any prior record concerning the same child or the same family. The
Statewide Child Protection Center shall immediately notify the local
child protective service of the report of known or suspected child
abuse, sexual abuse, or neglect, and at the same time shall indicate to
the local child protective service whether there is a previous report of
child abuse, sexual abuse, or neglect concerning the same child or the
same family.

e. All reports of child abuse, sexual abuse, or neglect contained within
the central registry shall be classified in one of three categories: under
investigation, founded, or closed. All initial reports of suspected child
abuse, sexual abuse, and neglect shall be classified as "under investigation." Upon receipt of the preliminary report or the progress report
from the local child protective services, the "under investigation" report shall be classified as "founded" or "unfounded." All cases classified as "unfounded" shall be immediately expunged. After the child
who is the subject of the report reaches the age of 18 years, his record
shall be classified as closed and shall be sealed. Access to a closed
record shall only be permitted if a sibling or offspring of the child is
reported as a suspected victim of child abuse, sexual abuse, or neglect.
All closed records shall be automatically expunged seven years from
the date the record was closed.

f. At any time and in any case, the Statewide Child Protection Center
may amend or remove from the central registry any record upon good
cause shown and upon notice to the subjects of the report.

g. At any time a subject of a report may receive, upon written request, a
copy of all information contained in the central registry that pertains
to him, provided, however, that the registrar is authorized to prohibit
the release of any data that would identify the person who made the
initial report or any person who cooperated in a subsequent
investigation.

h. At any time after the completion of the investigation, but in no event
later than 60 days after receipt of the report, at which time this Act
contemplates that the investigation be completed, a subject of the re-

port may request the state department to amend or remove the record of the report from the registry. If the department refuses or fails to act within 30 days of such request, the subject shall have the right to a fair hearing within the department. Records shall not be maintained and shall be removed if they are inaccurate or are maintained in a manner inconsistent with this Act. In any hearing initiated by the subject of a report, the burden of proof shall be on the state department and the local child protective service. However, in any case in which the juvenile court or criminal court has found that there was child abuse, sexual abuse, or neglect, this shall be *prima facie* evidence that the report is founded. All hearings must be held within a reasonable time after the request for a hearing has been made.

i. The central registry within the Statewide Child Protection Center shall be the only registry within the state.

Comments: Section XIII creates one statewide facility to fulfill the requirements and the purposes of this Act. That "center" houses both the toll-free child abuse hotline and the central registry.

The child abuse hotline, which is operational 24 hours a day, 7 days a week throughout the year, serves two purposes: to report suspected cases of child abuse, sexual abuse, and neglect, and to determine, in conjunction with the central registry, whether a particular child and his family have been involved previously in a case of child abuse, sexual abuse, or neglect. Section XIII should be read in conjunction with the following section to determine who has access to information contained within the central registry.

If a report of suspected child abuse, sexual abuse, or neglect is reported on the hotline, the operator must take the caller's name, the child's name, and the parents' names and address. The operator may then cross-reference the child's name and the parents' names in the central registry to determine if there is any previous report concerning the same child or the same family. The initial report and any collateral information in the central registry are then relayed immediately to the appropriate child protective service. It is then the responsibility of the local child protective service to investigate the case and to take any steps necessary to protect the children under Section XI, §§2 of this Act.

All initial reports of child abuse, sexual abuse, or neglect are automatically entered into the central registry as reports "under investigation." When the preliminary report or progress report is received from the local child protective service, an unfounded report is immediately expunged. When the child who is the subject of the report reaches 18 years of age, his record is sealed and marked "closed." The closed record may only be opened when a sibling or the offspring of the same child is reported as having been abused or neglected. Allowing access to a sealed record on these cases acknowledges that child abuse in many instances is passed from one generation to the next. In many cases, the child abused today becomes the abusing parent of tomorrow. In any event, all records are automatically expunged seven years from the date they were marked "closed." The central registry also records the names and addresses of any person who requests and receives information from it. Obviously, information would not be released unless the person requesting the information felt that the child had been abused or neglected. This in itself may be important information to someone investigating the case at a later date.

In an effort to limit the central registry to relevant and correct data, any subject of the report may request a fair hearing to determine if the information in the central registry is accurate and being held in a manner consistent with this Act. In these hearings the burden of proof is on the state department and the local child protective service. It should be noted, however, that reports are not to be expunged simply because there is not sufficient evidence to support a case of child abuse, sexual abuse, or neglect in the juvenile or criminal court. Only unfounded or malicious reports are expunged automatically. Reports supplemented by credible evidence are left within the central registry. There would be little pragmatic value in limiting the central registry to reports of adjudicated cases.

There are currently 43 statewide child abuse registries. Thirty-three are the result of legislation, while the remaining 11 have been created by administrative fiat. Most of the provisions for this section have been drawn from the New York State statute, which provides for the most comprehensive of all central registries.

Section XIV Confidentiality of Records

1. In order to protect the rights of the child and his parents or guardian, all records concerning reports of child abuse, sexual abuse, or neglect, including reports made to the department, State Child Protection Center, state central registry, and local child protective services, and all records and reports generated as a result of such reports, shall be confidential except as specifically provided by this Act or other law. Any person who willfully permits, assists, or encourages the release of information contained in such reports or records, including those in the central registry, to persons or agencies not permitted by this section to have access shall be guilty of a misdemeanor.

2. No person, official, or agency shall have access to such records unless for the express purposes of this Act. Such persons include:
   a. a local protective agency
   b. a police or law enforcement agency investigating a report of known or suspected child abuse, sexual abuse, or neglect
   c. a physician who has before him a child he reasonably suspects may have been abused or neglected

   d. a person legally authorized to place a child in protective custody, but only when such person has before him a child he reasonably suspects may have been abused or neglected and such person requires the information in the report or record to determine whether or not to place the child in protective custody

   e. an agency with legal responsibility or authorization to care for, treat, or supervise a child who is the subject of a record or report, or other person responsible for the child's welfare

   f. any person who is the subject of a report, if such person is a child, the child's guardian *ad litem,* parent, guardian, or other person responsible for his welfare

   g. a court, upon finding that access to such records may be necessary for the determination of an issue before it; but such access shall be limited to *in camera* inspection, unless the court determines that public disclosure of the information contained therein is necessary for the resolution of an issue pending before it

   h. a grand jury, upon determination that access to such records is necessary in the conduct of its official business

   i. Any appropriate state or local official responsible for administration, supervision, or legislation in relation to child abuse, sexual abuse, or neglect, or prevention, or treatment when carrying out his official functions

   j. Any person engaged in bona fide research for a legitimate purpose, provided, however, that no information identifying the subjects of the report shall be made available to the researcher unless it is absolutely essential to the research purpose, that suitable provision is made to monitor the confidentiality of the data, and that the appropriate state official has given prior approval.

   3. A physician or person in charge of an institution, school, facility, or agency making the report shall receive, upon written request, a summary of the findings and action taken by the child protective service in response to the report. The amount of detail such summary shall contain will depend upon the source of the report, and shall be established by regulations adopted by the department.

   4. No information shall be released by the central registry unless the identity of the person, official, or agency requesting it is confirmed and the data to be released states whether the report is under investigation, founded, or sealed.

   5. A person given access to the names and other identifying information concerning the subjects of the report, except the subject of the report, shall not divulge or make public such identifying information unless he is a district attorney or other law enforcement official and his purpose is to initiate court action.

   6. Nothing in this section affects other state laws or procedures concerning the confidentiality of a criminal court and juvenile court system records.

Comments: Section XIV controls access to reports and records of child abuse, sexual abuse, and neglect. *All* records and *all* reports are confidential, not just the data in the central registry. Any person who willfully violates this confidentiality may be held criminally liable.

Those persons given access to records and reports under this section include a local child protective service agency; a law enforcement agency; a physician or person authorized to place a child in protective custody, but only in specified circumstances; any agency specifically authorized to care for or treat the abused or neglected child; any person who is the subject of a report; a court; a grand jury; and persons engaged in bona fide research. Persons specifically given access to records and reports under Section XIV must be currently working with the abused child or his family, and only for reasons that would further the purposes of this Act.

The subject of a report is entitled to access, but only in accordance with Section XIII of this Act. He is not entitled to data that would identify the person making the original report or persons who cooperated in any subsequent investigation. A guardian *ad litem,* appointed by the court to represent the child's interests in a child abuse, sexual abuse, or neglect proceeding, is entitled to relevant records and reports.

In an attempt to foster cooperation, communication, and coordination of resources, institutions, schools, facilities, and agencies that make reports of child abuse, sexual abuse, and neglect are entitled to progress reports on actions taken once the report has been initiated. Any information, reports, or records released to persons specified in this section must be identified as being under investigation, founded, or closed. Reports determined to have been unfounded are automatically expunged. Only in certain limited circumstances are "sealed records" released. Access to records under Section XIV meets the requirements of Public Law 93-247.

Section XV Education and Training

Within available funding, and as appropriate, the state department, the local child protective service, and the Child Protection Team shall conduct a public and professional training program with state and local department staff, persons, and officials required to report; the general public; and any other appropriate persons, in order to encourage maximum reporting of known and suspected child abuse, sexual abuse, and neglect, and to improve communication, cooperation, and coordination among all agencies involved in the identification, prevention, and treatment of child abuse, sexual abuse, and neglect. To the extent possible, such training and educational programs shall include information on the extent and nature of the problem; the duties and responsibilities of persons required to report; the duties and the functions of the state department, the

local departments of child services, the Statewide Child Protection Center, the
central registry, and local child protection teams; and the therapeutic treatment
programs available to abused and neglected children and their families.

Comment: Section XV requires training programs within a state for child abuse,
sexual abuse, and neglect. The actual guidelines and content for each program
will be incorporated in each community's annual plan for child abuse, drafted by
the local child protection team in conjunction with other agencies under Section XII, §§2 of this Act. The elements noted in Section XV constitute the minimum requirements for any plan adopted by a community. These requirements
satisfy the federal guidelines.

Section XVI The Guardian Ad Litem

In every case filed under this Act, the court shall appoint a guardian *ad litem* for
the child. The guardian *ad litem* shall be given access to all reports relevant to
the case and to any reports of examination of the child's parents or other cus-
todians pursuant to this Act. The guardian *ad litem* shall be charged with the
representation of the child's best interests, and to that end shall make such
further investigation as he deems necessary to ascertain the facts. He may interview witnesses, examine and cross-examine witnesses in both the adjudicatory
and dispositional hearings, introduce his own witnesses, make recommendations
to the court, and participate in the proceedings to the degree appropriate for
adequately representing the child.

Comments: This section provides a spokesperson for every abused, sexually
abused, and neglected child. The language requiring the appointment of a guardian *ad litem* does not require that the guardian *ad litem* so appointed be an
attorney. It is suggested, however, that an adequate protection of the child's
interests in these cases usually necessitates the appointment of a lawyer as guardian *ad litem.* When proceedings are initiated under this Act, the appointment of
the guardian *ad litem* is not discretionary with the court—it is mandatory.
    A guardian *ad litem,* by definition, is more than a lawyer; he is the guardian
of the child throughout the legal proceedings, as well as an advocate for the
child's long-range interests. To provide the guardian *ad litem* with the tools
necessary for accomplishing these ends, he is given access to all relevant records
and reports pertaining to the suspected abuse, sexual abuse, and neglect. In addition, he can make his own investigation, examine and cross-examine all witnesses, and call his own witnesses. The guardian *ad litem*'s recommendations are
not binding on the court. His role is akin to that of *amicus curiae.* The more pre-
cise his formulation of the problem and the more appropriate his recommendations, the more likely the court is to agree. The guardian *ad litem* is an excellent

assurance that all persons with knowledge will testify, that all facts will be ferreted out for the court's determination, and that all possible dispositions will be made available for consideration by the court.

Bibliography

Law Review Articles

Fraser. "Pediatric Bill of Rights." *South Texas Law Review* 16 (3):245, (1975).

Wald. "State Intervention of Behalf of Neglected Children." *Stanford Law Review* 27 (4):985, (1975).

Burke. "Evidentiary Problems of Proof in Child Abuse Cases." *Journal of Family Law* 13 (4):819, (1974).

Fraser. "Toward a More Practical Central Registry." *Denver Law Journal* 51 (4):509, (1974).

Fraser. "Legislative Approaches to Child Abuse." *American Criminal Law Review* 12:103, (1974).

"Appointment of Counsel for the Abused Child." 58 *Cornell Law Review* 177, (March 1972).

Belgrad. "Problem of the Battered Child." 11 *University of Maryland Law Forum* 37, (Winter 1972).

Gesmonde. "Emotional Neglect in Connecticut." 5 *Connecticut Law Review* 100, (1972).

Thomas. "Child Abuse and Neglect." 50 *North Carolina Law Review* 293, (Spring 1972).

"Appraisal of the New York State Statutory Response to the Problem of Child Abuse." 7 *Columbia Journal of Law and Social Problems* 51, (Winter 1971).

Ganley. "The Battered Child." 8 *San Diego Law Review* 364, (March 1971).

Donovan. "Legal Response to Child Abuse." 11 *William and Mary Law Review* 916, (Spring 1970).

Felder. "Lawyer's View of Child Abuse." 29 *Public Welfare* 188, (1970).

Fontana. "The Battered Child." 16 *Crime and Delinquency* 139, (April 1970).

Grumet. "Plaintiff." 4 *Family Law Quarterly* 296, (Fall 1970).

Raffile. "The Battered Child." 16 *Crime and Delinquency* 139, (April 1970).

"Child Neglect: The Environmental Aspects." 29 *Ohio State Law Journal* 1, (Winter 1968).

Paulsen, "Legal Protections Against Child Abuse." 13 *Children* 42, (1968).

Silver, Barton, and Dublin. "Child Abuse Laws—Are They Enough." 199 *Journal of the American Medical Association* 65, (1968).

Driscoll, "Child Abuse: Legal Aspects of the Physician's Duty." *Trail and Tort Trends* 395, (1967).

Paulsen. "Child Abuse Reporting Laws." 61 *Columbia Law Review* 1, (1967).

Paulsen. "Child Abuse Reporting Laws: Some Legislative History." 34 *George Washington Law Review* 3, (1966).

Paulsen. "Legal Framework for Child Protection." 66 *Columbia Law Review* 697, (1966).

Books

Helfer, Ray E., and C. Henry Kempe, eds. *The Battered Child,* 2d ed. Chicago: University of Chicago Press, 1974.

Kempe, C. Henry, and Ray E. Helfer, eds. *Helping the Battered Child and His Family.* Philadelphia: J. B. Lippincott Co., 1972.

Katz, Sanford N. *When Parents Fail: The Law's Response to Family Breakdown.* Boston: Beacon Press, 1971.

Young, Leontine. *Wednesday's Children: A Study of Child Neglect and Abuse.* New York: McGraw-Hill, 1971.

Flammang, C. J. *The Police and the Underprotected Child.* Springfield, Ill.: Charles C. Thomas, 1970.

James, Howard. *Children in Trouble.* New York: David McDay, 1970.

DeFrancis, Vincent. *Protecting the Child Victim of Sex Crimes.* Denver: American Humane Association, Children's Division, 1969.

Medical Articles

Smith, R. C. "New Ways to Help Battering Parents." *Toady's Health* (January 1973), p. 57.

Amiel, S. "Child Abuse in Schools." *Northwest Medicine* 71:808, (1972).

Caffey, J., F. Simverman, C. Kempt, H. Venters, and M. Leonard. "Child Battery: Seek and Save." *Medical World News* 13:21, (1972).

Caffey, J. "On the Theory and Practice of Shaking Infants: Its Potential Residual Effects of Permanent Brain Damage and Mental Retardation." *American Journal of Diseases of Children* (August 1972), p. 161.

Fleck, S. "Child Abuse." *Connecticut Medicine* 36:337, (1972).

Gil, D. G. "Violence Against Children." *Pediatrics* (April 1972), p. 641.

Havens, L. L. "Youth, Violence and the Nature of Family Life." *Psychiatric Annals* 2:18, (1972).

Holder, A. R. "Child Abuse and the Physician." *Journal of the American Medical Association* (October 23, 1972), p. 517.

Jackson G. "Child Abuse Syndrome: The Cases We Miss." *British Medical Journal* (June 24, 1972), p. 756.

James, J. "Child Neglect and Abuse.: *Maryland State Medical Journal* 21:64, (1972).

Jboisvert, Maurice. "The Battered Child Syndrome." *Social Casework* 21:64, (1972).

Robertson, I., and P. R. Hodge. "Hystopathology of Healing Abrasions." *Forensic Science* (April 1972), p. 17.

Spinetta, J. J. "The Child Abusing Parent; Psychological Review." *Psychological Bulletin* (April 1972), p. 296.

Tardieu, A., and F. Silverman. "Unrecognized Trauma in Infants and the Battered Child Syndrome." *Radiology* (August 1972), p. 337.

Gregg, G. S. "Infant Trauma." *American Family Physician* (May 1971), p. 101.

Lowry, T., and A. Lowry. "Abortion as a Preventative for Abused Children." *Psychiatric Opinion* 8:19, (1971).

Silber, D. L. "The Neurologist and the Physically Abused Child." *Neurology* (October 1971), p. 991.

Harris, M. J. "Discussion on the Battered Child Syndrome." *Australian Journal of Forensic Sciences* 3:277, (1970).

Public Documents

Canada, Manitoba. *Child Abuse.* Published by the Education Services, Manitoba Department of Health and Social Development.

U.S., Congress, Senate, Committee on Labor and Public Welfare. *Child Abuse Prevention Act, 1973: Hearings Before the Subcommittee on Children and Youth on S. 1191.* 93rd Cong., 1st sess., 1973.

Department of Health, Education, and Welfare

Administration of HEW

The Department of Health, Education, and Welfare was established in 1953 by the President's Reorganization Plan No. 1 of 1953. This legislation gave departmental status to the Federal Security Agency, which was established in 1939 to administer major programs in the areas of health, education, and welfare. Since that time, agencies and programs have been added to the Department in response to new legislation.

The Department is administered by a Secretary, assisted by an Under Secretary. Major Department components are administered by five assistant secretaries responsible for staff functions (Assistant Secretaries of Public Affairs, Planning and Evaluation, Comptroller, Administration and Management, and Congressional Liaison) and seven administrators in charge of program functions (Assistant Secretaries for Human Development, the Public Health Service, and the Division of Education; Commissioner for the Social Security Administration; Administrator for the Social and Rehabilitation Service; and Directors for the Office for Civil Rights and the Office of Consumer Affairs).

Departmental programs are carried out through 10 regional offices under the supervision of regional directors who are responsible for the general direction of HEW activities in their respective regions. Directors maintain close relationships with key state officials and HEW administrators in Washington in order to carry out their objectives. Regional offices are located in Boston, Massachusetts; New York, New York; Philadelphia, Pennsylvania; Atlanta, Georgia; Chicago, Illinois; Dallas, Texas; Kansas City, Missouri; Denver, Colorado; San Francisco, California; and Seattle, Washington.

Function and Programs

Staff and program functions at HEW are described as follows.

1. *Assistant Secretary for Legislation.* The Assistant Secretary for Legisla-

47

tion assists in development and implementation of the Department's Legislative program, and provides liaison with Congress.

2. *Assistant Secretary, Comptroller.* The Assistant Secretary, Comptroller develops the HEW budget and oversees the financial management of the Department.

3. *Assistant Secretary for Public Affairs.* The Assistant Secretary for Public Affairs serves as principal advisor to the Secretary and other staff offices on public affairs matters, and develops methods to keep the public informed about services and programs available to them from HEW.

4. *Assistant Secretary for Planning and Evaluation.* The Assistant Secretary for Planning and Evaluation coordinates economic, social, and program analyses with program evaluation, and provides the results of such studies for planning and development of Departmental policies.

5. *Assistant Secretary for Administration and Management.* The Assistant Secretary for Administration and Management carries out the administrative and management functions of the Department, including facilities construction and maintenance, personnel operations, training and employee development, management planning and technology, grants and procurement management, investigations and security, environmental affairs, equal employment opportunities, surplus property utilization, and general administration.

Office of Human Development

The Office of Human Development (OHD) was established in 1973 to supervise and coordinate previously scattered programs directed toward a wide variety of special status groups. The goal of OHD is to assist especially vulnerable Americans in developing to their greatest potential. Groups eligible for assistance include children and youth, the aged, the physically and mentally handicapped, native Americans, and persons living in rural areas.

OHD consists of 13 major agencies. Six of these agencies operate significant grant programs, in addition to acting as advocates and coordinators of departmental or governmentwide services. Seven other OHD offices, committees, or boards act as advocates and coordinators for special groups, although they do not operate grant programs. The one agency of concern for this particular publication is the Office of Child Development.

Office of Child Development (OCD)

OCD has five major functions: (1) to operate federally funded programs for children, such as Head Start and Parent and Child Centers; (2) to develop innovative programs for children and parents; (3) to serve as a coordination point for all federal programs for children and their families; (4) to administer the National Center on Child Abuse and Neglect; and (5) to act as an advocate for the children of the nation by bringing their needs to the attention of the government and the American public. OCD also awards grants for research, demonstration, and other social services involving children and their families.

Office of Human Development:

> 330 Independence Avenue, S.W.
> Washington, D.C. 20201
> Telephone: (202) 245-7246
> Stanley B. Thomas, Assistant Secretary

Office of Child Development

> 400 Sixth Street, S.W.
> Washington, D.C. 20201
> Telephone: (202) 755-7762
> John H. Meier, Director
> Saul R. Rosoff, Deputy Director
> Pauline Tait, Public Information Officer
>
> *Bureau of Head Start*
> (vacant) Associate Chief
> James Robinson, Deputy Chief
>
> *Day-Care Services Division*
> Preston Bruse, Director
>
> *Program Management Division*
> Dewitt C. Drohat, Chief
>
> *Indian and Migrant Programs Division*
> Dominic Mastrapasqua, Chief
>
> *Parent Involvement and Social Services*
> Richard Johnson, Director
>
> *Children's Bureau*
> Frank Ferro, Associate Chief
>
> *National Center on Child Abuse and Neglect*
> Douglas J. Besharov, Director

Department of Health, Education, and Welfare Regional Offices

Region 1: Boston (Connecticut, Maine, Massachusetts, Rhode Island, and Vermont)

John F. Kennedy Office Building
Boston, Massachusetts 02203
Telephone (617) 223-6831
Robert Fulton, Regional Director
Warren M. McFague, Regional Deputy Director

Region 2: New York (New Jersey, New York, Puerto Rico, and the Virgin
Islands)
26 Federal Plaza
New York, New York 10007
Telephone (212) 264-4600
Bernice L. Bernstein, Regional Director
Elwood Taub, Regional Deputy Director

Region 3: Philadelphia (District of Columbia, Delaware, Maryland, Pennsylvania,
and West Virginia)
3535 Market Street
P.O. Box 13716
Philadelphia, Pennsylvania 19109
Telephone (215) 596-6492
Gorham L. Black, Jr., Regional Director
Benjamin M. Guy, Regional Deputy Director

Region 4: Atlanta (Alabama, Florida, Georgia, Kentucky, Mississippi, North
Carolina, South Carolina, and Tennessee)
50 Seventh Street, N.E.
Atlanta, Georgia 30323
Telephone (404) 526-5817
Frank J. Groschelle, Regional Director
Charles F. Cain, Regional Deputy Director

Region 5: Chicago (Illinois, Indiana, Michigan, Minnesota, Ohio, and Wisconsin)
300 South Wacker Drive
Chicago, Illinois 60606
Telephone (312) 353-5164
Richard E. Friedman, Regional Director
George R. Holland, Regional Deputy Director

Region 6: Dallas (Arkansas, Louisiana, Oklahoma, New Mexico, and Texas)
1200 Main Tower Building
Dallas, Texas 75202
Telephone (214) 655-3301
Stuart H. Clarke, Regional Director
Scott Tuxhorn, Regional Deputy Director

Region 7: Kansas City (Iowa, Kansas, Missouri, and Nebraska)
    601 East Twelfth Street
    Kansas City, Missouri 64106
    Telephone (816) 374-3436
    Max M. Mills, Regional Director
    Richard E. Barnett, Regional Deputy Director

Region 8: Denver (Colorado, Montana, North Dakota, South Dakota, Utah, and
Wyoming)
    1961 Stout Street
    Federal Building, Room 11037
    Denver, Colorado 80202
    Telephone (303) 837-3373
    Rudlon R. Garfield, Regional Director
    Edwin R. LaPedis, Regional Deputy Director

Region 9: San Francisco (American Samoa, Arizona, Guam, Hawaii, Nevada, and
Wake Island)
    50 Fulton Street
    Federal Office Building
    San Francisco, California 94102
    Telephone (415) 556-6746
    Joe P. Maldonado, Regional Director
    Daniel M. Sprague, Regional Deputy Director

Region 10: Seattle (Alaska, Idaho, Oregon, and Washington)
    1321 Second Avenue
    Arcade Plaza Building
    Seattle, Washington 98101
    Telephone (206) 442-0420
    Bernard E. Kelly, Regional Director
    Thomas E. McLaughlin, Regional Deputy Director

**Reporting Requirements
Child Abuse Legislation
Programs and Agencies**

Alabama

Reporting Requirements

Persons mandated to report (compulsory) when reasonable cause to believe a child is or has been subjected to abuse or neglect: hospital, clinic, sanitarium, doctor, physician, surgeon, medical examiner, coroner, dentist, osteopath, optometrist, chiropractor, podiatrist, nurse, school teacher, official, peace officer, law enforcement officer, pharmacist, social worker, day-care worker or employee, mental health professional, or any other person called upon to render aid or medical attention to any child known or suspected to being abused or neglected

Permissive: any person who has reasonable cause to believe a child is abused or neglected

Form of report and when made: oral—immediately followed by a written report

To whom report is made: "a duly constituted authority" defined to include: chief of police or sheriff, if the report is made in an unincorporated territory of the state; department of pensions and security, or agency designated by it

Penalties: knowing failure to report is punishable as a misdemeanor by a sentence of up to six months or a fine of up to $500.

Immunities: anyone making a report shall be immune from any liability, either civil or criminal.

Adapted from child abuse and neglect project, Education Commission of the States. Denver, Colorado. Report Nos. 83 and 84. March, 1976; and reprinted with permission of the American Public Welfare Association, 1155 Sixteenth Street, N.W., Washington, D.C., 20036; from the 1976/77 Public Welfare Directory, Ms. Perry Frank, Editor.

55

Child Abuse Legislation

Citation: Act 1124; AC tit. 7, §177; tit. 13, §352(5,6)
Year enacted: 1975
Effective date: October 10, 1975
Purpose of legislation: mandatory reporting, yes
Reportable age: 0–18 years
Definitions: harm or threatened harm through nonaccidental physical or mental
    injury, sexual abuse or attempted sexual abuse. Negligent treatment/
    maltreatment: failure to provide adequate food, medical treatment, cloth-
    ing, or shelter
Education/school report: mandatory reporting, yes
Immunity: civil/criminal, yes
Mandatory investigation: yes, promptly
Confidentiality of records: yes; penalty: misdemeanor
Cooperation with law courts, state agencies: no specific provision
Guardian ad litem: yes
Administrative proceedings, trained personnel facilities: no specific provision
Dissemination of information: no specific provision

Programs and Agencies

Letters regarding general information about the service programs for children
and their families or individual cases involving the placement of minor children
in Alabama should be addressed to:

> Julia J. Oliver, Commissioner
> Department of Pensions and Security
> Administrative Building, 5th Floor
> 64 North Union Street
> Montgomery, Alabama 36130

Specific information:

> Bureau of Family and Children's Services
> Attention: Louise Pittman, Director (205)832-6150

County Sources:

Autauga County Mrs. Mary Brown, P.O. Box 250, Prattville 36067
    (205)365-6781
Baldwin County Mrs. Ann Fendley, P.O. Box 1029, Bay Minette 36507
    (205)937-2551

Barbour County James D. Trammell, P.O. Box 177, Clayton 36016
(205)775-3280

Bibb County Mrs. Kathleen Vandeford, Centreville 35042 (205)926-2461

Blount County Mrs. Frances Hill, P.O. Box 68, Oneonta 35121 (205)274-2351

Bullock County Mrs. Sara Jean Graham, P.O. Box 310, Union Springs 36089
(205)738-2740

Butler County Mrs. Myra W. Crenshaw, P.O. Box 26, Greenville 36037
(205)382-2631

Calhoun County Mrs. Margaret Copeland, 1200 Noble Street, P.O. Box 1869,
Anniston 36201 (205)236-5615

Chambers County Mrs. Ann Rucks, P.O. Box 409, LaFayette 36862
(205)864-2181

Cherokee County Mrs. Margaret Waldman, Courthouse Annex, Centre 35960
(205)927-5354

Chilton County Mrs. Mollye M. McKee, P.O. Box 446, Clanton 35045
(205)755-3250

Choctaw County Mrs. Delouise G. Dempsey, 117 South Mulberry Street, Butler
36904 (205)459-2404

Clarke County Mrs. Blanche Saunders, P.O. Box 95, Grove Hill 36451
(205)275-3235

Clay County Mrs. Margaret Patterson, P.O. Box 246, Ashland 36251
(205)354-2527

Cleburne County Robert Earl Hall, Jr., Courthouse, P.O. Box 25, Heflin 36264
(205)463-5633

Coffee County Mrs. Lucile McMinn, 321 Putnam Street, P.O. Box 448, Elba
36323 (205)897-2865

Colbert County Mrs. Louise F. Surratt, 120 West 5th Street, Tuscumbia 35674
(205)383-4855

Conecuh County Chester H. Ellis, 520 Belleville Street, Evergreen 36401
(205)578-1690

Coosa County Mrs. Mary Ann Thompson, Case Reviewer-in-Charge, P.O. Box 36,
Rockford 35136 (205)377-4381

Covington County Mrs. Virginia B. Mills, P.O. Box 786, Andalusia 36420
(205)222-3714

Crenshaw County Mrs. Betty W. King, P.O. Box 347, Luverne 36049
(205)335-3381

Cullman County Mrs. Dana J. Aycock, P.O. Drawer 987, Cullman 35055
(205)734-2731

Dale County Mrs. Jewell Hudson, P.O. Box 447, Ozark 36360 (205)774-5135

Dallas County Tarrilton E. Benton, 15 Riverview Avenue, P.O. Box 366, Selma
36701 (205)875-2770

DeKalb County Mrs. Bernice P. Parker, P.O. Box 49, Ft. Payne 35967
(205)845-0861

Elmore County Mrs. Eloise M. Wilson, P.O. Box 400, Wetumpka 36092
(205)567-5341

Escambia County Mrs. Audrey McLelland, Courthouse, P.O. Box 218, Brewton
36426 (205)867-5472

Etowah County Robert M. Galloway, Courthouse Annex, Gadsden 35901
(205)546-4651

Fayette County Miss Bess Savage, County Office Building, P.O. Box 7, Fayette
35555 (205)932-6775

Franklin County Mrs. Vermey K. Greene, P.O. Drawer M, Russellville 35653
(205)332-2032

Geneva County Mrs. Valinda Lolley, P.O. Box 385, Geneva 36340
(205)684-2608

Greene County Mrs. Margaret Fincher, County Activities Building, Eutaw
35462 (205)372-4331

Hale County Mrs. Virginia Glass, P.O. Box 441, Greensboro 36744
(205)624-8329

Henry County John A. Capps, County Office Building, P.O. Box 197, Abbeville
36310 (205)585-2616

Houston County James R. Enfinger, Sr., 1600 Ross Clarke Circle, S.E.,
P.O. Box 2027, Dothan 36301 (205)792-0981

Jackson County Miss Johnnie Bell, 110 East Appletree Street, P.O. Box 908,
Scottsboro 35768 (205)574-2791

Jefferson County Miss Joyce Clements, 1321 Fifth Avenue, South, P.O. Box
10725, Birmingham 35202 (205)322-5411 and Quality Control
(205)328-7002
Bessemer Branch: Mrs. Dean Leverett, Casework Reviewer-in-Charge, 1601
Carolina Avenue, Bessemer 35020 (205)428-2381

Lamar County Bill Weeks, P.O. Box 489, Vernon 35592 (205)695-7166

Lauderdale County Miss Virginia Clinton, Courthouse, P.O. Box 460, Florence
35630 (205)764-4041

Lawrence County Miss Frances Smith, Courthouse Annex, P.O. Box 398,
Moulton 25650 (205)974-0651

Lee County Mrs. Lucy K. Locklin, 1111 Auburn Street, P.O. Box 565, Opelika
36801 (205)749-8164

Limestone County Mrs. Betty G. Evans, P.O. Box 830, Athens 35611
(205)232-4120

Lowndes County Larry W. Owen, Hayneville 36040 (205)548-2216

Macon County Mrs. Darlene Collins, Worker-in-Charge, P.O. Box 210, Tuske-
gee, 36083 (205)727-1960

Madison County Mrs. Shirley J. Wolfe, P.O. Box T, Main Post Office, Huntsville 35804 (205)539-2211

Marengo County Mrs. Marguerite Wilkinson, P.O. Box 452, Linden 36748
(205)295-3531

Marion County Edwin D. Walker, P.O. Box 96, Hamilton 35570 (205)921-3141

Marshall County Ms. Cindy Sapp, Guntersville 35976 (205)582-3291

Mobile County Miss Doris Bender, Courthouse, P.O. Box 1906, Mobile 36601 (205)432-2751

Adult Services: Helen Thompson, Supervisor-in-Charge, 800 St. Anthony Street, Mobile 36603 (205)432-1681

Gordon Smith Center: (vacant), Assistant Director, 555 Stanton Road, Mobile 36617 (205)473-4462

Monroe County Mrs. Betty W. Shelley, P.O. Box 248, Monroeville 36460 (205)743-2282

Montgomery County Mrs. Ada Kate Morgan, 723 Forest Avenue, P.O. Box 6235, Montgomery 36106 (205)265-2331

Morgan County Miss Marilyn George, Courthouse Annex, P.O. Box 964, Decatur 35601 (205)353-8181

Perry County Mrs. Earle O. Anderson, P.O. Box 236, Marion 36756 (205)683-3651

Pickens County L. C. Keasler, P.O. Box 31, Carrollton 35447 (205)367-8186

Pike County Billy B. Carroll, County Activities Building, Church Street, Troy 36081 (205)566-1423

Randolph County Jeanette Dalrymple, P.O. Box 209, Wedowee 36278 (205)357-4311

Russell County Mrs. Shirley E. Hendrick, 1409 Fifth Avenue, P.O. Box 67, Phenix City 36867 (205)298-7882

Saint Clair County Mrs. Betty Jackson, Courthouse, Room 13, Pell City 35125 (205)338-3353

Shelby County Mrs. Nell J. Fulton, P.O. Box 1096, Columbiana 35051 (205)669-2111

Sumter County Mrs. Francis Rumley, P.O. Box 310, Livingston 35470 (205)652-5221

Talladega County Mrs. Jean O. Hobson, P.O. Drawer 539, Talladega 35160 (205)362-8711

Tallapoosa County Mrs. Susan B. Scott, 405 North Broadnax Street, Dadeville 36853 (205)825-4296

Tuscaloosa County Mrs. Mary D. Roberts, Courthouse, P.O. Box 2487, Tuscaloosa 35401 (205)758-8326

Walker County Mrs. Margaret Nuttall, P.O. Box 1772, Jaspar 35501 (205)387-1428

Washington County Mrs. Ruby M. Boykin, P.O. Box 383, Chatom 36518 (205)847-2216

Wilcox County Mrs. Camilla J. Selsor, Camden 36726 (205)682-4213

Winston County Dale Frank Hendrix, P.O. Box 116, Double Springs 35553 (205)489-5101

Alaska

Reporting Requirements

Persons mandated to report (compulsory) when reasonable cause to believe a child is or has been subjected to abuse or neglect: practitioners of the healing arts, school teachers, social workers, peace and corrections officers, or administrative officers of institutions

Permissive: same people in their nonprofessional capacities, anyone suspecting abuse or harm

Form of report and when made: not given

To whom report is made: nearest office of the department of health and social services, or a police officer if immediate action is necessary

Penalties: none

Immunities: criminal and civil immunity for persons making reports in good faith

Child Abuse Legislation

Citation: AS §47.17.010.070
Year enacted: 1971
Effective date: August 23, 1971
Purpose of legislation: mandatory reporting, yes
Reportable age: 0-16 years
Definitions: nonaccidental infliction of physical harm; failure to provide necessary food, care, clothing, shelter, and/or medical attention
Education/school report: mandatory reporting, yes
Immunity: civil/criminal, yes

Mandatory investigation: yes, no specific time frame
Confidentiality of records: yes; penalty: no specific provision
Cooperation with law courts, state agencies: no specific provision
Guardian ad litem: yes
Administrative proceedings, trained personnel facilities: no specific provision
Dissemination of information: no specific provision

Programs and Agencies

All correspondence pertaining to interstate placement of children, adoptions, and general information on child welfare should be directed to:

Director, Division of Social Services
Department of Health and Social Services
Pouch H-05
Juneau, Alaska 99811

Division of Social Services District Offices:

Anchorage Ann Lipson, 527 East Fourth Avenue, Anchorage 99501
Aniak Leo Morgan, P.O. Box 488, Aniak 99557
Barrow Lewis Frank, P.O. Box 587, Barrow 99723
Bethel Mike Price, P.O. Box 365, Bethel 99559
Dillingham Dorothy Emmons, P.O. Box 221, Dillingham 99576
Fort Yukon (vacant), P.O. Box 125, Fort Yukon 99740
Fairbanks Faye Guthrie, Lathrop Building, 2d Floor, Fairbanks 99740
Galena Dorothy Lee, P.O. Box 239, Galena 99741
Juneau Nola Capp, 315 Goldstein Building, Juneau 99801
Kenai Maurice Hamlin, P.O. Box 3613, Kenai 99611
Ketchikan Ernestine Zollman, P.O. Box 257, Ketchikan 99901
Kodiak Ronald Newcomb, P.O. Box 2515, Kodiak 99615
Kotzebue Carl Berger, P.O. Box 41, Kotzebue 99752
Kwigillingok Andrew Beaver, General Delivery, Kwigillingok 99622
Mountain Village Andrew Brown, P.O. Box 141, Mountain Village 99632
Nome Arthur Holmberg, P.O. Box 221, Nome 99762
Palmer Charmaine Mastriano, P.O. Box 901, Palmer 99645
Petersburg Marsha Schneider, P.O. Box 1089, Petersburg 99833
Seward Mary Savage, P.O. Box 755, Seward 99664
Sitka Brianne Surrey, P.O. Box 1069, Sitka 99835
Tok Nancy Fuller, P.O. Box 166, Tok 99780
Unalakleet Frances Degnan, P.O. Box 40, Unalakleet 99684
Valdez (vacant), P.O. Box 524, Valdez 99686

Arizona

Reporting Requirements

Persons mandated to report (compulsory) when reasonable cause to believe a child is or has been subjected to abuse or neglect: physician, hospital intern, or resident physician

Permissive: none

Form of report and when made: immediately—oral followed by a written report

To whom report is made: municipal or county peace officer

Penalties: for "violation of the provisions of this section" (presumably including failure to report): misdemeanor, with penalties up to $100 or 10 days or both

Immunities: civil and criminal immunity for those reporting under the statute, or those involved in a judicial proceeding resulting therefrom

Child Abuse Legislation

Citation: ARSA §8-535(D,E); §8-546.0-4
Year enacted: 1970
Effective date: May 18, 1970
Purpose of legislation: mandatory reporting, yes
Reportable age: 0-18 years
Definitions: nonaccidental physical or mental injury, causing of deterioration, failure to maintain reasonable care and treatment, failure to provide reasonable support
Education/school report: mandatory reporting, yes
Immunity: civil/criminal, yes
Mandatory investigation: yes, promptly

Confidentiality of records: yes; penalty: no specific provision
Cooperation with law courts, state agencies: State department of economic
    security may cooperate
Guardian ad litem: yes
Administrative proceedings, trained personnel, facilities: no specific provision
Dissemination of information: no specific provision

Programs and Agencies

Where to write: Communications regarding Department of Economic Security
programs and services should be sent to the appropriate District Office. When
the district is not known, correspondence will be forwarded by:

> Department of Economic Security
> P.O. Box 6123
> Phoenix, Arizona 85005
>
> Social Services Bureau
> Roger J. Hodges, Chief, (602)271-4450

Department of Economic Security District Offices:

Maricopa County (District I) 815 North 18th Street, Phoenix, Arizona 85006,
    John R. Foley, Manager, (602)271-3722
Pima County (District II) 151 West Congress Street, P.O. Box 3031, Tuscon,
    Arizona 85703, Milton F. Graf, Manager, (602)882-5435
Apache, Coconino, Navajo, and Yavapai Counties (District III) 2501 North
    Fourth Street, P.O. Box 3088, Flagstaff, Arizona 86001, Ronald D.
    Bachman, Manager, (602)779-0392
Mohave and Yuma Counties (District IV) 350 West Sixteenth Street, P.O. Box
    351, Yuma, Arizona 85364, Virginia Bryant, Acting Manager,
    (602)782-4343
Gila and Pinal Counties (District V) 900 East Florence Boulevard, P.O. Box
    1159, Casa Grande, Arizona 85222, W. J. Soltan, Manager, (602)836-2351
Cochise, Graham, Greenlee, and Santa Cruz Counties (District VI) 214 Bisbee
    Road, P.O. Drawer GG, Bisbee, Arizona 85603, Robert W. James, Manager,
    (602)432-5431

Department of Economic Security Area Offices:

District I

Area I. Manuel D. Martinez, 1209 West Madison, Phoenix, Arizona 85007
    (602)258-6361

Area II. Pat Cregar, 3003 North 35th Avenue, Phoenix, Arizona 85017 (602)269-1401

Area III. Frank A. Ivenz, 3406 North 51st Avenue, Phoenix, Arizona 85031 (602)247-5026

Area IV. James J. Malloy (Act.), 438 West Adams, Phoenix, Arizona 85003 (602)252-7771

Area V. James J. Malloy, 207 East McDowell, Phoenix, Arizona 85004 (602)254-5631

Area VI. Charles I. Sutton, 21 South Hibbert, Mesa, Arizona 85202 (602)834-7777

District II

Area I. James Anderson (Act.), 5151 East Broadway, Tucson, Arizona 85711 (602)882-5217

Area II. John Butler, 151 West Congress, Tucson, Arizona 85701 (602)882-5429

Area III. W. Lamar Ogden, 403 West Congress, Tucson, Arizona 85701 (602)882-5511

District III

Area I. Fred Lynde, 305 West Forest Avenue, Flagstaff, Arizona 86001 (602)779-3681

Area II. Harold Bahe, P.O. Box 307, Window Rock, Arizona 86515 (602)871-4729

Area III. Charles Tilson, 105 North Fifth Avenue, Box 399, Holbrook, Arizona 86025 (602)697-3542

Area IV. Barney Reardon, 143 South Cortez, Prescott, Arizona 86301 (602)445-1860

District IV

Area I. John Hunter, 3145 Stockton Hill Road, Box 989, Kingman, Arizona 86401 (602)753-6146

Area II. Ruth Bender, Tenth and Hopi Avenue, Bin 629, Parker, Arizona 85344 (602)669-9293

Area III. Virginia Bryant, 201 South Third Avenue, Box 1630, Yuma, Arizona 85364 (602)783-3551

District V

Area I. Hilda Wischman, 401 North Marshall Street, P.O. Box 579, Casa Grande, Arizona 85222 (602)836-7435

Area II. Josephine Walters, 177 East Oak Street, P.O. Box 643, Globe, Arizona 85501

District VI

Area I. Armando Elias, 1140 F. Avenue, Box 1099, Douglas, Arizona 85607 (602)364-4446

Area II. Jack P. Williams, 524 Third Avenue, P.O. Box 789, Safford, Arizona 85546 (602)428-2911

Area III. Henry R. Carrie, 44 Fry Boulevard, Box 938, Sierra Vista, Arizona 85635 (602)458-4000

Arkansas

Reporting Requirements

Persons mandated to report (compulsory) when reasonable cause to believe a child is or has been subjected to abuse or neglect: Physician, surgeon, coroner, dentist, osteopath, resident intern, registered nurse, hospital personnel (actually engaged in the care of patients), teacher, school official, social service worker, day-care center worker, or any other child or foster care worker, mental health professional, peace or law enforcement officer with reasonable cause to suspect abuse or conditions that would so result

Permissive: any other person with reasonable cause to suspect that a child has been abused or neglected

Form of report and when made: telephone immediately; written report within 48 hours if requested

To whom report is made: department of social and rehabilitative services; appropriate medical examiner or coroner if the child has died

Penalties: criminal: up to $100 and up to five days in jail for willful failure to report; civil: for willful failure, liability for all damages caused thereby

Immunities: civil and criminal immunity for reporting in good faith

Child Abuse Legislation

Citation: Act 397 of 1975
Year enacted: 1975
Effective date: March 14, 1975
Purpose of legislation: mandatory reporting, yes
Reportable age: 0–18 years

66

Definitions: physical or mental injury; sexual mistreatment other than accidental neglect; failure to provide necessary care and support, education, medical, surgical, etc.
Education/school report: mandatory reporting, yes
Immunity: civil/criminal, yes
Mandatory investigation: yes, promptly
Confidentiality of records: yes; penalty: misdemeanor
Cooperation with law courts, state agencies: yes
Guardian ad litem: yes
Administrative proceedings, trained personnel, facilities: yes
Dissemination of information: yes

Programs and Agencies

Where to write: Communications regarding public assistance, child welfare problems, visits to or from relatives, and emergency services should be sent in duplicate to the appropriate District Office. Communications regarding the Interstate Compact on Juveniles should be addressed to:

James B. Cartwright, Commissioner
Division of Social Services
Department of Social and Rehabilitative Services
P.O. Box 1437
Little Rock, Arkansas 72203

Arkansas Department of Social and Rehabilitative Services

National Old Line Building, Room 406
Little Rock, Arkansas 72201
Telephone: (501)371-1001
David B. Ray, Jr., Director

Field Operations Section
Telephone: (501)371-2486
Edward L. McMillan, Director, (501)371-2486
Ewing W. Kinkead, Administrative Assistant, (501)371-2540
Mrs. Jan Hayward, Field Representative, (501)371-2509
Mrs. Kathleen Underwood, Consultant, Child Welfare Services, (501)371-2181
Mrs. Lula Sager, Consultant, Child Development, (501)371-2433
Mrs. Jene Quick, Consultant, Adult Services, (501)371-2441
Ms. Mary Eddy Thomas, Consultant, Contract Services, (501)371-2433
Mrs. Polly McQuade, Consultant, Title XX Services, (501)371-2085
Miss Julia Westfall, Consultant, Staff Development, (501)371-2131

Social Services Division Regional Offices

I. Northwest Gordon C. Page, 612 North College Street, Fayetteville, Arkansas 72701 (501)521-7360

II. North Central Chester Clark, Highway 25-A N., P.O. Box 2676, Batesville, Arkansas 72501 (501)793-6893

III. Eastern Eugene V. Jones, Arkansas Services Center, 2920 McClellan Drive, Jonesboro, Arkansas 72401 (501)972-4056

IV. Southeast Kenny Whitlock, 3102 West 34th Street, P.O. Box 8967, Pine Bluff, Arkansas 71601 (501)534-5895

V. Central Richard L. Dietz, Hendrix Hall, P.O. Box 1766, Little Rock, Arkansas 72203 (501)371-2495

VI. West Central James R. Holden, 624 Malvern Avenue, Hot Springs, Arkansas 71901 (501)321-1271 or 1283

VII. Southwest William L. Card, Drawer J, Magnolia, Arkansas 71753 (501)234-7150

VIII. Western Calvin Mahan, 615 North 19th Street, Fort Smith, Arkansas 72901 (501)783-1183

Social Services Division District Offices

Region I: Northwest

Baxter (Baxter, Marion, and Searcy Counties) Courthouse Basement, Mountain Home, Arkansas 72653 Mabel Parks, Administrator, (501)425-3626

Benton (Benton County) P.O. Box 236, Bentonville, Arkansas 72712 Robert M. Arthur, Administrator

Boone (Boone and Newton Counties) 211 West Rush Street, Harrison, Arkansas 72601 Hersel Jefferson, Administrator, (501)365-8386

Carroll (Carroll and Madison Counties) Courthouse, Room 201, Berryville, Arkansas 72616 Madeline Jackson, Administrator, (501)423-2349

Washington (Washington County) 612 North College Street, Fayetteville, Arkansas 72701 Mary Helen Roper, Administrator, (501)521-7360

Region II: North Central

Independence (Independence County) 156 South Third Street, P.O. Box 3347, Batesville, Arkansas 72501 Jeryl Moore, Administrator, (501)793-3842

Fulton (Fulton, Izard, and Sharp Counties) Skyvue Shopping Center, P.O. Box 265, Salem, Arkansas 72576 Anthony Brown, Administrator, (501)895-3309

Jackson (Jackson County) P.O. Box 658, Newport, Arkansas 72112 Margaret Goss, Administrator, (501)523-6574

Van Buren (Stone and Van Buren Counties) P.O. Box 126, Clinton, Arkansas 72031 L. D. Parish, Administrator, (501)745-4192

White (Cleburne and White Counties) 302 West Center Street, Searcy, Arkansas
    72143   Rinda S. Miller, Administrator, (501)268-8696
Woodruff (Woodruff County) P.O. Box 493, Augusta, Arkansas 72006   Mary E.
    Wilson, Administrator, (501)347-2411, 5021, or 2351

Region III: Eastern

Clay (Clay and Greene Counties) P.O. Box 156, Piggott, Arkansas 72454   Josie
    Brandon, Administrator, (501)598-3324
Craighead (Craighead County) 2920 McClellan Drive, Jonesboro, Arkansas
    72401   Nellie Johnston, Administrator, (501)972-4059
Crittenden (Crittenden County) P.O. Box 70, Marion, Arkansas 72364   Melba
    Carpenter, Administrator, (501)739-3268
Cross (Cross County) P.O. Box 572, Wynne, Arkansas 72396   Lola Taylor,
    Administrator, (501)238-8553
Lawrence (Lawrence and Randolph Counties) P.O. Box 69, Walnut Ridge,
    Arkansas 72476   Winnie Cato, Administrator, (501)886-2408
Lee (Lee County) P.O. Box 248, Marianna, Arkansas 72360   Robert Evans,
    Administrator, (501)295-2597
Mississippi (Mississippi County) 218 North First Street, P.O. Box 1196, Blythe-
    ville, Arkansas 72315   Leroy Richardson, Administrator, (501)763-7093
Phillips (Phillips County) 615 Cherry Street, P.O. Box C, Helena, Arkansas
    72342   Juanita Milam, Administrator, (501)338-8391
Poinsett (Poinsett County) 212 East Street, P.O. Box 667, Harrisburg, Arkansas
    72432   Philip Smith, Administrator, (501)578-5491
St. Francis (St. Francis County) 517 Front Street, P.O. Box 899, Forrest City,
    Arkansas 72335   Harold Grobmyer, Administrator, (501)633-1242

Region IV: Southeast

Arkansas (Arkansas County) 101 Court Square, P.O. Drawer 512, DeWitt,
    Arkansas 72042   Shelby Moore, Administrator, (501)946-1860 or
    922-6736
Ashley (Ashley County) P.O. Box 390, Hamburg, Arkansas 71646   Lynetta
    Fowler, Administrator, (501)853-5208
Bradley (Bradley and Drew Counties) 404 East Central Street, P.O. Box 509,
    Warren, Arkansas 71671   Lizzie B. Williams, Administrator, (501)226-5879
Chicot (Chicot County) 400 Highways 82 and 65 S., P.O. Box 71, Lake Village,
    Arkansas 71653   Helen McAffrey, Administrator
Desha (Desha County) 126 Pine Street, P.O. Box 111, McGehee, Arkansas
    71654   Jack May, Administrator, (501)222-4144
Jefferson (Grant and Jefferson Counties) 1001 Linden Street, P.O. Box 5670,
    Pine Bluff, Arkansas 71601   Anne Guthrie, Administrator, (501)534-4200
Lincoln (Cleveland and Lincoln Counties) P.O. Box 187, Star City, Arkansas
    71667   Jimmie Nichols, Administrator, (501)628-4714

Region V: Central

Faulkner (Faulkner County) 724 Locust Street, Conway, Arkansas 72032
Edna Fay Gill, Administrator, (501)329-9831

Lonoke (Lonoke and Prairie Counties) P.O. Box 236, Lonoke, Arkansas 72086
Virginia White, Administrator, (501)676-3113, 6682, or 2736

Monroe (Monroe County) 148 South Second Street, Clarendon, Arkansas
72029 Marian K. Booker, Administrator, (501)747-3329

Pulaski North (Pulaski County) 313 East Fourth Street, P.O. Box 5791, North
Little Rock, Arkansas 72119 Bobby Joe Cook, Administrator,
(501)371-1495 or 2015

Pulaski South (Pulaski County) 1224 Louisiana Street, P.O. Box 2620, Little
Rock, Arkansas 72203 Ms. Shirley A. Rollans, Administrator,
(501)376-2041

Saline (Saline County) 315 North Main Street, P.O. Drawer 608, Benton,
Arkansas 72015 Paul Jeffus, Administrator, (501)778-0481

Region VI: West Central

Conway (Conway and Perry Counties) 305 East Broadway, P.O. Box 228,
Morrilton, Arkansas 72110 Anita Lou Dillard, (501)354-2415 or 2418

Garland (Garland County) 146 East Border Street, Hot Springs, Arkansas 71901
Allan Williams, Administrator, (501)321-2583

Johnson (Johnson and Pope Counties) 209 Cherry Street, P.O. Box 534, Clarksville, Arkansas 72830 Burley King, Administrator (501)754-2355

Pike (Clark, Hot Spring, and Pike Counties) 102 South Washington Street,
Murfresboro, Arkansas 71958 J. W. Walls, Administrator, (501)285-3111

Yell (Montgomery and Yell Counties) 401 Atlanta Street, P.O. Box 277, Danville, Arkansas 72833 John Kennedy, Administrator, (501)495-2723

Region VII: Southwest

Calhoun (Calhoun and Dallas Counties) Main Street, P.O. Box 718, Hampton,
Arkansas 71744 Harold Watson, Administrator, (501)798-4201

Columbia (Columbia and Lafayette Counties) 200 West Calhoun Street, Magnolia, Arkansas 71753 Don Miller, Administrator, (501)234-4190

Howard (Howard, Little River and Sevier Counties) County Courthouse, 421
North Main Street, Nashville, Arkansas 71852 Effie Jones, Administrator,
(501)845-4335

Miller (Miller County) County Courthouse Basement, Fourth and Laurel
Streets, Texarkana, Arkansas 75501 Kenneth E. Jones, Administrator,
(501)773-3441 or 5091

Nevada (Hempstead and Nevada Counties) 304 East Vine Street, Prescott,
Arkansas 71857 Twyla Arnett, Administrator, (501)887-3416

Ouachita (Ouachita County) 701 Viser Street, Camden, Arkansas 71701   Jessye
  L. Wood, Administrator, (501)836-8166 or 8178
Union (Union County) 728 Main Street, P.O. Box 609, El Dorado, Arkansas
  71730   Betty Thurmon, Administrator, (501)863-8123

Region VIII: Western

Franklin (Franklin and Logan Counties) Courthouse, P.O. Box 261, Ozark,
  Arkansas 72949   Thelma Harper, Administrator, (501)667-2379
Scott (Polk and Scott Counties) 310 Washington Street, P.O. Box 38, Waldron,
  Arkansas 72958   Bill Hogue, Administrator, (501)637-2330
Sebastian (Crawford and Sebastian Counties) 809 North Sixth Street, P.O. Box
  1724, Fort Smith, Arkansas 72901   J. Paul Ray, Administrator,
  (501)783-3149

California

Reporting Requirements

Persons mandated to report (compulsory) when reasonable cause to believe a child is or has been subjected to abuse or neglect: physician, surgeon, dentist, resident intern, chiropractor, religious practitioner, registered nurse, school superintendent, supervisor of child welfare and attendance, certified pupil personnel employee, school principal, teacher, licensed day-care worker or social worker, podiatrist, administrator of a private or public day camp, or teacher in a private or public school

Permissive: none

Form of report when made: telephone and written within 36 hours

To whom report is made: local police authority and the juvenile probation department, or the county welfare or health department

Penalties: misdemeanor; $500 and/or six months

Immunities: civil and criminal immunity

Child Abuse Legislation

Citation: CA 348, 309, 421-1974; Welfare & Instit. Code §681; Civil Code §237
Year enacted: 1974
Effective date: exact date not available
Purpose of legislation: mandatory reporting, yes
Reportable age: 0–18 years
Definitions: serious physical injury, harm, intentional neglect; malnutrition,

sexual abuse, willful mental injury, negligent treatment, or maltreatment; any condition which violates rights of physical, mental, or moral welfare; jeopardizes health, opportunity for normal development, or capacity for independence.

Education/school report: mandatory reporting, yes
Immunity: civil/criminal, yes
Mandatory investigation: yes, no specific time frame
Confidentiality of records: no specific provisions
Cooperation with law courts, state agencies: yes
Guardian ad litem: yes
Administrative proceedings, trained personnel, facilities: yes
Dissemination of information: yes

Programs and Agencies

Where to write: Communications regarding guardianships and civil suits should be sent directly to the county clerks. Communications regarding adoptions should be sent in triplicate to:

Adoption Services Section
Social Services Division
Department of Health
California Health and Welfare Agency
714 P Street
Sacramento, California 95814

Social Services Division

714 P Street, Room 364
Sacramento 95814
Gary Macomber, Department Director, (916)445-9222

Children's Services Section

Mary Sullivan, Chief, (916)322-5973
Roy Leber, Acting Chief, Adoptions Services Section

County Welfare Departments

Alameda County Librado Perez, 401 Broadway, Oakland 94607
(415)874-5009
Alpine County Ms. Janice Dean Lovett, P.O. Box 277, Markleeville 96120
(916)694-2235

Amador County Frank A. Earl, P.O. Box 877, Jackson 95642 (209)267-5237

Butte County Bob Crisan, 42 County Center Drive, Oroville 95965
(916)534-4572

Calaveras County John Crane, Government Center, San Andreas 95249
(209)754-4225

Colusa County Mrs. Lucy I. Lack, P.O. Box 370, Colusa 95932 (916)458-4985

Contra Costa County Robert E. Jornlin, 2401 Stanwell Drive, Concord 94520
(415)372-4640

Del Norte County Walter Hansen, 981 H Street, Crescent City 95531
(707)464-3191

El Dorado County Paul A. Berman, 2929 Grandview Street, Placerville 95667
(916)626-2455

Fresno County Reed Clegg, P.O. Box 1912, Fresno 93718 (209)255-9711

Glenn County Don K. Louderback, Willows 95988 (916)934-7714

Humboldt County Ms. Anne Luking, 211-5th Street, Eureka 95501
(707)445-7609

Imperial County Dardell McFarlin, Box 930, El Centro 92243 (714)353-1400

Inyo County Norman Paulson, P.O. Box 930, Independence 93526
(714)878-2411

Kern County O. C. Sills, P.O. Box 511, Annex, Bakersfield 93301
(805)861-3351

Kings County John T. Neyerlin, 330-11½ Avenue, Hanford 93230
(209)582-3211

Lake County D. L. Tryk, 1220 Martin Street, Lakeport 95453 (707)263-5461

Lassen County Martin J. Herzog, P.O. Box 1359, Susanville 96130
(916)257-5163

Los Angeles County Keith Comrie (Act.), P.O. Box 368, El Monte 91734
(213)572-5720

Madera County Mrs. Janice Edwards, P.O. Box 569, Madera 93637
(209)674-4641

Marin County Ron Usher, P.O. Box 4160, San Rafael 94903 (415)479-1100

Mariposa County Mrs. Lois Lewis, P.O. Box 7, Mariposa 95338 (209)966-3609

Mendocino County Dennis Denny, Courthouse, Ukiah 95482 (707)462-1461

Merced County Robert Whittaker, P.O. Box 112, Merced 95340
(209)726-7211

Modoc County J. Strother Boyd, P.O. Box 1707, Alturas 96101
(916)233-2561

Mono County Mrs. Ann Kurisky, P.O. Box 576, Bridgeport 93517
(714)932-8291

Monterey County Ben J. Kelley, P.O. Box 299, Salinas 93901 (408)757-2911

Napa County John Powell, P.O. Box 329, Napa 94558 (707)224-7843

Nevada County Eugene Newman, 205 Willow Valley Road, Nevada City 95959
(916)265-4571

Orange County William E. Erikson, P.O. Box 1957, Santa Ana 92702
(714)834-2270
Placer County David C. Echols, 11519 B. Avenue, E., Auburn 95603
(916)823-4481
Plumas County Mrs. Mona J. Green, P.O. Box 360, Quincy 95971
(916)283-2250
Riverside County Paul R. Wiley, 4080 Lemon Street, Riverside 92501
(714)787-2771
Sacramento County William Redmond, P.O. Box 487, Sacramento 95803
(916)440-7120
San Benito County Edward Anderson, 419-4th Street, Hollister 95023
(408)637-5336
San Bernardino County Fred F. Thies, 670 East Gilbert Street, San Bernardino
92404 (714)383-1024
San Diego County Homer E. Detrich, 7949 Mission Center Court Road, San
Diego 92108 (714)565-3601
San Francisco County Edwin Sarsfield, P.O. Box 7988, San Francisco 94120
(415)558-5913
San Joaquin County Harry Brodie, 133 Weber Avenue, Stockton 95201
(209)466-5231
San Luis Obispo County Thomas S. Ganoe, 1185 Islay Street, San Luis Obispo
93401 (805)543-5700
San Mateo County Robert Rippeto, 225-37th Avenue, San Mateo 94403
(415)573-2222
Santa Barbara County Arthur W. Nelson, 117 East Carrillo, Santa Barbara
93101 (805)965-0081
Santa Clara County Frederick B. Gillette, 55 West Younger Avenue, San Jose
95110 (408)299-2641
Santa Cruz County David B. Singleton, P.O. Box 1320, Santa Cruz 95060
(408)425-2291
Shasta County Mrs. Marian Babiarz, 1830 Yuba Street, Redding 96001
(916)246-5778
Sierra County Mrs. Connie Bennett, P.O. Box 38, Downieville 95936
(916)289-3532
Siskiyou County Wilbur M. van Over, Yreka 96097 (916)842-4471
Solano County Robert C. Granger, 321 Tuolumne Street, Vallejo 94590
(707)553-5311
Sonoma County Paul Allen, P.O. Box 1539, Santa Rosa 95403 (707)527-2715
Stanislaus County Wesley Jones, P.O. Box 1727, Modesto 95354
(209)526-6720
Sutter County Donald E. Currey, P.O. Box 1535, Yuba City 95991
(916)674-2160

Tehama County Mrs. Pauline Marinoff, P.O. Box W, Red Bluff 96080
    (916)527-1912
Trinity County Mrs. Allene A. Payton, P.O. Box 218, Weaverville 96092
    (916)623-2291
Tulare County Hilmi Fuad, P.O. Box 671, Visalia 93277   (209)732-7111
Tuolumne County Clifton T. White, 105 Hospital Road, Sonora 95370
    (209)532-3186
Ventura County James E. Isom, 3161 Loma Vista Road, Ventura 93003
    (805)648-6181
Yolo County Edward M. Curley, 20 Cottonwood Street, Woodland 95695
    (916)666-8203
Yuba County Dean P. Richmond, 935-14th Street, Marysville 95901
    (916)743-4681

Colorado

Reporting Requirements

Persons mandated to report (compulsory) when reasonable cause to believe a child is or has been subjected to abuse or neglect: physician or surgeon, including a physician in training; child health associate; medical examiner or coroner; dentist; osteopath; optometrist; chiropractor; chiropodist or podiatrist; registered nurse or licensed practical nurse; hospital personnel in admission, care, or treatment of patients; Christian Science practitioner; school official or employee; social worker; worker in a family care home or child care center; or mental health professional

Permissive: any other person

Form of report and when made: immediate oral; followed by a written report if requested

To whom report is made: county or district department of social services, or local law enforcement agency

Penalties: criminal: class two petty offense, fine up to $200; civil: liable for damages caused by failure to report

Immunities: making a report in good faith is presumed and results in full civil and criminal immunity

Child Abuse Legislation

Citation: HB 1482; CRS 19-10-101 *et seq.*
Year enacted: 1975
Effective date: June 30, 1975
Purpose of legislation: mandatory reporting, yes

Reportable age: 0–18 years

Definitions: act or omission which seriously threatens health or welfare of child; skin bruising, bleeding, malnutrition, burns, failure to thrive, bone fracture, death, sexual assault or molestation; failure to provide adequate food, clothing, shelter, and supervision.

Education/school report: mandatory reporting, yes

Immunity: civil/criminal, yes

Mandatory investigation: yes, immediately

Confidentiality of records: yes; penalty: misdemeanor

Cooperation with law courts, state agencies: yes

Guardian ad litem: yes

Administrative proceedings, trained personnel, facilities: yes

Dissemination of information: no specific provision

Programs and Agencies

Where to write: Inquiries regarding adoptions and general information concerning state policy on child welfare matters should be sent to:

> Director, Division of Title XX Services
> Department of Social Services
> 1575 Sherman Street
> Denver 80203

All letters pertaining to children should include full identifying information, including full names and addresses of parents and children and the birth dates of children. Especially in cases where placement is being requested, it is important to include information about the child's personality and behavior, school records, etc. Interstate inquiries concerning the ability of relatives to provide financial support should be sent to the relatives themselves and not to either the state or local agency.

Colorado Department of Social Services

> 1575 Sherman Street
> Denver 80203
> Telephone: (303)892-2561
> Henry A. Foley, Ph.D., Executive Director, (303)892-3515
> Frederick A. Langille, Executive Administrator, (303)892-3513

County Departments of Social Services

Adams County Paul L. Rayman, 4200 East 72nd Avenue, Commerce City 80022 (303)287-8831

Alamosa County Leland R. McDaniel, P.O. Box 1292, Alamosa 81101
(303)589-2581

Arapahoe County Braidwood Robinson, 5606 South Court Place, Littleton
80120 (303)798-8461

Archuleta County Fred Schmeir, Courthouse, Pagosa Springs 81147
(303)968-5530

Baca County Delbert Williams, Courthouse, Springfield 81073 (303)523-4131

Bent County Bert Hansen, P.O. Box 326, Las Animas 81054 (303)456-0515

Boulder County Lew Wallace, 3400 Broadway, Boulder 80301 (303)442-2828

Chaffee County David Sommerhauser, P.O. Box 1007, Salida 81201
(303)539-6627

Cheyenne County Carey C. Beek, Courthouse, Cheyenne Wells 80810
(303)767-5646

Clear Creek County Virginia Cattermole, Courthouse, Georgetown 80444
(303)569-2533

Conejos County Robert W. Beals, Courthouse, Conejos 81129 (303)376-5455

Costilla County Marbella V. Smith, P.O. Box 3, San Luis 81152 (303)672-3376

Crowley County Thomas O. Hobbs, Courthouse Annex, Ordway 81063
(303)267-3546

Custer County Arlie Riggs, Courthouse, Westcliffe 81252 (303)783-2371

Delta County Joseph T. Clark, P.O. Box 79, Delta 81416 (303)874-4489

Denver County Orlando Romero, 320 West 8th Avenue, Denver 80204
(303)292-4100

Dolores County Ogrita B. Vinger, Courthouse, Dove Creek 81324
(303)677-2250

Douglas County Eldon L. Bourquin, P.O. Box 357, Castle Rock 80104
(303)688-4825

Eagle County George B. Thatcher, Courthouse, Eagle 81631 (303)328-6328

Elbert County Charles B. Hawker, Simla 80835 (303)541-2369

El Paso County Alfred L. Gillen, P.O. Box 2692, Colorado Springs 80901
(303)471-0600

Fremont County Franklin S. Vecchio, P.O. Box 631, Canon City 81212
(303) 275-2319

Garfield County Ronald R. Johnson, P.O. Box 580, Glenwood Springs 81601
(303)945-5606

Gilpin County Virginia Cattermole, Courthouse, Central City 80427
(303)582-5444

Grand County Buster Turner, P.O. Box 648, Granby 80446 (303)887-3569

Gunnison County W. Anne Steinbeck, 200 East Virginia Street, Gunnison
81230 (303)641-1010

Hinsdale County W. Anne Steinbeck, 200 East Virginia Street, Gunnison
81230 (303)641-1010

Huerfano County Christine R. Schmidt, 121 West 6th Street, Walsenburg 81089
(303)738-2810

Jackson County Betty L. Sevison, Courthouse, Walden 80480 (303)723-4750
Jefferson County Nelson Nadeau, 8550 West 14th Avenue, Lakewood 80215
    (303)232-8632
Kiowa County Francis E. Frazee, P.O. Box 187, Eads 80136 (303)438-5541
Kit Carson County G. W. Asher, P.O. Box 878, Burlington 80807
    (303)346-8732
Lake County (vacant), P.O. Box 884, Leadville 80461 (303)486-0772
La Plata County Robert C. Agard, P.O. Box 1471, Durango 81301
    (303)247-3572
Larimer County Martin C. Coker, P.O. Box 2166, Fort Collins 80521
    (303)493-0750; and Loveland 80537 (303)667-6242
Las Animas County William Lancilia, 204 South Chestnut Street, Trinidad
    81082 (303)846-2276
Lincoln County Linda Fairbairn, Courthouse, Hego 80821 (303)743-2404
Logan County Robert B. Neimann, P.O. Box 1746, Sterling 80751
    (303)522-2194
Mesa County John C. Patterson, P.O. Box 1118, Grand Junction 81502
    (303)243-9200
Mineral County Robert W. Beals, Courthouse, Del Norte 81132
    (303)657-3381
Moffat County Emery E. Jones, Courthouse, Craig 81625 (303)824-6030
Montezuma County Maurine L. McNeill, P.O. Drawer GG, Cortez 81321
    (303)565-3769
Montrose County John A. Kramer, P.O. Box 216, Montrose 81401
    (303)249-3401
Morgan County Maynard Hesselbarth, Courthouse, Fort Morgan 80701
    (303)867-8291
Otero County William J. Ziegler, P.O. Box 494, La Junta 81050
    (303)384-8162
Ouray County Mary L. Tjossem, Courthouse, Ouray 81427 (303)325-4637
Park County Marshell McClung, Courthouse Annex, Fairplay 80440
    (303)836-2929
Phillips County (vacant), Courthouse, Holyoke 80734 (303)854-2280
Pitkin County Marion Stewart, P.O. Box 91, Aspen 81611 (303)925-7245
Prowers County Mark Tandberg, 900 Maple Street, Lamar 81052
    (303)336-7486
Pueblo County James H. Walch, 212 West 12th Street, Pueblo 81003
    (303)543-8000
Rio Blanco County Esme Conrado, P.O. Box 688, Meeker 81641
    (303)878-5856
Rio Grande County Robert W. Beals, Courthouse, Del Norte 81132
    (303)657-3381

Routt County Emery E. Jones, P.O. Box M, Steamboat Springs 80477
    (303)879-1540
Saguache County Margaret E. Raby, P.O. Box 215, Saguache 81149
    (303)655-2614
San Juan County Robert C. Agard, P.O. Box 396, Silverton 81433
    (303)387-5631
San Miguel County Kaythryn Critchell, Courthouse, Telluride 81435
    (303)728-3922
Sedgwick County Raymond Smikahl, Courthouse, Julesburg 80737
    (303)474-2626
Summit County Michael J. Rock, Courthouse, Breckenridge 80424
    (303)453-2561
Teller County Dolores Wzontek, Courthouse, Cripple Creek 80813
    (303)689-2525
Washington County Frederick Crawford, Courthouse, Akron 80720
    (303)345-2238
Weld County Eugene Mc Kenna, P.O. Box A, Greeley 80631   (303)352-1551
Yuma County Floyd Murphy, Courthouse, Wray 80758   (303)332-4877

Reporting Requirements

Persons mandated to report (compulsory) when reasonable cause to believe a child is or has been subjected to abuse or neglect: physician; surgeon, resident physician or intern; any hospital in the state; not registered, registered, or licensed practical nurse; medical examiner; dentist; psychologist; school teacher; principal or guidance counselor; social worker; police officer; clergyman; coroner; osteopath; optometrist; chiropractor; podiatrist; day-care center worker; mental health professional; or any other person not named above

Permissive: none

Form of report and when made: immediate, oral; written, within 78 hours

To whom report is made: state welfare commissioner or his representative, the local police department, the state police. If a person observing child is a member of any staff of any hospital, school, social welfare agency, or any other institution, he shall report to his superior who shall make the required report.

Penalties: fine of not more than $500

Immunities: full civil and criminal immunity for reports made in good faith

Child Abuse Legislation

Citation: CSA §17-38, as amended by PA 75-205, 270, 384, 492
Year enacted: 1975
Effective date: not available
Purpose of legislation: mandatory reporting, yes
Reportable age: 0–18 years
Definitions: nonaccidental physical injuries; maltreatment such as malnutri-

tion, sexual molestation, deprivation of necessities, emotional maltreatment, cruel punishment

Education/school report: mandatory reporting, yes
Immunity: civil/criminal, yes
Mandatory investigation: yes
Confidentiality of records: yes; penalty: misdemeanor
Cooperation with law courts, state agencies: yes
Guardian ad litem: yes
Administrative proceedings, trained personnel, facilities: yes
Dissemination of information: no specific provision

Programs and Agencies

Child welfare, including protective services, foster care, adoption, adoption resource exchange, placement of noncommitted children for specialized care, services to unmarried mothers, and correctional program services, are provided by the Department of Children and Youth Services. Communications regarding placement or return of children should be addressed to:

Department of Children and Youth Services
345 Main Street
Hartford 06115

Connecticut Department of Social Services

110 Bartholomew Avenue
Hartford 06115
Telephone: (203)566-2530
Edward W. Maher, Comm., (203)566-2008
Carolyn Perry, Department Comm., (203)566-2759

Department of Children and Youth Services

345 Main Street
Hartford 06115
Telephone: (203)566-3661
Francis H. Maloney, Comm., (203)566-3536
Mrs. Jeanette Dille, Department Comm., (203)566-3537
John Doermann, Department Administrator, Interstate Compact on
   Juveniles, Parolees, and Probationers, (203)566-5846
Dale Maynard, Director Social Services, (203)566-7303
Donna Pressma, Director Protective Services, (203)566-2387

Department of Children and Youth Regional Offices

Region A. Francis Daddona, 79 Linden Street, Waterbury 06702
    (203)573-1211

Region B. Abraham Chidekel, 110 Bartholemew Avenue, Hartford 06115
    (203)566-4416

Region C. Dorothy Shaw, 279 Main Street, Norwich 06360 (203)889-2351

Region D. Lucy Foster, 434 State Street, Bridgeport 06603 (203)384-1761

Region E. Donald Looney, 464 Congress Avenue, New Haven 06511
    (203)787-6181

Delaware

Reporting Requirements

Persons mandated to report (compulsory) when reasonable cause to believe a child is or has been subjected to abuse or neglect: physician; person in the healing arts, including any person licensed to offer services in medicine; osteopath; dentist; intern; resident nurse; school employee; social worker; psychologist; medical examiner; or any other person

Permissive: none

Form of report and when made: immediate oral; written if requested

To whom report is made: division of social services of the department of health and social services, and, if deemed necessary, to the local law enforcement agency

Penalties: knowing and willful violation of the statute: up to $100 and/or imprisonment for up to 15 days

Immunities: full civil and criminal immunity for reports made in good faith

Child Abuse Legislation

Citation: DC §1001-7
Year enacted: 1971
Effective date: June 25, 1971
Purpose of legislation: mandatory reporting, yes
Reportable age: mentally retarded or 0–18 years
Definitions: serious physical injury other than accidental; physical or emotional condition that gives indication of other serious abuse or maltreatment; mistreatment or nontreatment

Education/school report: mandatory reporting, yes
Immunity: yes
Mandatory investigation: yes, immediately
Confidentiality of records: yes; penalty: misdemeanor
Cooperation with law courts, state agencies: no specific provision
Guardian ad litem: no specific provision
Administrative proceedings, trained personnel, facilities: no specific provision
Dissemination of information: no specific provision

Programs and Agencies

Where to write: Communications regarding social information about recipients or relatives of recipients should be addressed in duplicate to the appropriate regional director. If the correct region is not known, address requests to:

Deputy Director, Division of Social Services
Department of Health and Social Services
P.O. Box 309
Wilmington 19899

Delaware Department of Health and Social Services

Delaware State Hospital
Administration Building
New Castle 19720
Telephone: (302)571-2011 for direct-dial number
John Sullivan, Acting Secretary, (302)421-6705
Dorothy B. Talbert, Assistant Director of Family and Children's Services
and Adult Services, (302)571-3172

Division of Social Services Regional Offices

Region I. Newcastle County: Wilmington 19899   Janice Lingan, Director,
(302)762-6860
Region II. Kent County: Dover 19901   Ruth Vehslage, Director,
(302)678-4800
Region III. Sussex County: Georgetown 19947   Irene K. Simpler, Director,
(302)856-5371

District of Columbia

Reporting Requirements

Persons mandated to report (compulsory) when reasonable cause to believe a child is or has been subjected to abuse or neglect: physicians, persons licensed under District of Columbia law to practice the healing arts (excludes dentists, podiatrists, optometrists, pharmacists, and nurses)

Permissive: none

Form of report and when made: oral immediately, followed as soon as possible with written

To whom report is made: District of Columbia metropolitan police department; if the person making the report is on the staff of a hospital, he makes the report to the director of the hospital, who makes it to the police department.

Penalties: none

Immunities: full civil and criminal immunity

Programs and Agencies

Inquiries in regard to children under the age of 18 living apart from their parents should be sent in duplicate to:

Bureau of Family Services
Social Rehabilitation Administration
Department of Human Resources
122 Center Street, N.W.
Washington 20001

District of Columbia Department of Human Resources

District Building
1350 East Street, N.W.
Washington 20004
Telephone: (202)629-3776
Joseph P. Yeldell Director, (202)629-5443
Albert P. Russo, Department Director, (202)629-3079
William J. Washington, M.D., Assistant to the Director for Health Services
    (202)629-3366

Bureau of Family Services

Betty Queen, Chief, (202)629-3766

Florida

Reporting Requirements

Persons mandated to report (compulsory) when reasonable cause to believe a child is or has been subjected to abuse or neglect: any person, including but not limited to any physician, nurse, teacher, social worker, or employee in a public or private facility serving children

Permissive: none

Form of report and when made: immediate oral, followed by written as soon as possible

To whom report is made: department of health and rehabilitative services; if person making report is on the staff of a hospital, he shall report to the director of the hospital, who in turn shall report to the department

Penalties: knowing or willful violation constitutes a second-degree misdemeanor

Immunities: any person making a report under the section is presumed to be acting in good faith and, as such, has full civil and criminal immunity

Child Abuse Legislation

Citation: FSA §827.07
Year enacted: 1975
Effective date: June 30, 1975
Purpose of legislation: mandatory reporting, yes
Reportable age: 0–18 years
Definitions: any willful or negligent act which results in neglect, malnutrition, sexual abuse, unreasonable physical injury, or material endangerment of mental sustenance, clothing, shelter, or medical attention.

Education/school report: mandatory reporting, yes
Immunity: yes
Mandatory investigation: yes, immediately
Confidentiality of records: yes; penalty: misdemeanor
Cooperation with law courts, state agencies: yes
Guardian ad litem: yes
Administrative proceedings, trained personnel, facilities: yes
Dissemination of information: yes

Programs and Agencies

Where to write: General inquiries regarding Department of Health and Rehabilitative Services programs, as well as communications regarding verification of legal residence and authorization to return; requests for social information and services; reports on continued eligibility for public assistance; interstate placement of children; and child welfare services should be sent in triplicate to:

Office of Social and Economic Services
Department of Health and Rehabilitative Services
P.O. Box 2050
Jacksonville 32203

Florida Department of Health and Rehabilitative Services

1323 Winewood Blvd.
Tallahassee 32301
Telephone: (904)488-7721
William J. Page, Jr., Secretary
David R. Beecher, Department Secretary
Emmett S. Roberts, Senior Advisor on Intergovernmental Operations
George Van-Staden, Acting Assistant Secretary for Operations
  (904)488-8901
George Van-Staden, Acting Assistant Secretary for Administrative Services
  (904)488-7851
James A. Alford, Ph.D., Assistant Secretary for Program Planning and
  Development

Bureau of Children's Services

(vacant), Chief

Department of Health and Rehabilitative Services District Offices

I. Escambia, Okaloosa, Santa Rosa, and Walton Counties: 3842 North Palafox
  Street, Pensacola 32522   Charles M. Daly, Director, (904)434-3581

II. *Bay, Calhoun, Franklin, Gadsden, Gulf, Holmes, Jackson, Jefferson, Leon, Liberty, Madison, Taylor, Wakulla, and Washington Counties:* Koger Executive Center, 2586 Seagate Drive, Turner Building, Suite 207, Tallahassee 32301   Charles H. Cox, Director, (904)488-9875

III. *Alachua, Bradford, Citrus, Columbia, Dixie, Gilchrist, Hamilton, Hernado, Lafayette, Lake, Levy, Marion, Putnam, Sumter, Suwanee, and Union Counties:* 2720 North West 6th Street, Suite B, Gainesville 32601   William H. McClure, Jr., Director, (904)377-7621

IV. *Baker, Clay, Duval, Flagler, Nassau, Saint Johns, and Volusia Counties:* Health Building, P.O. Box 210, Jacksonville 32211   James T. McGibony, M.D., Director, (904)354-3961

V. *Pasco and Pinellas Counties:* 9720 Executive Center Drive, St. Petersburg 33742   J. Thomas Herndon, Director, (813)893-2386

VI. *Hillsborough and Manatee Counties:* 915 North Ashley Street, Suite 4, Tampa 33602   Peter M. Kreis, Director, (813)272-3813

VII. *Brevard, Orange, Osceola, and Seminole Counties:* 1350 North Orange Avenue, Winter Park 32789   Mrs. Irene H. Burnett, Director, (305)628-4477

VIII. *Charlotte, Collier, De Soto, Glades, Hardee, Hendry, Highlands, Lee, Polk, and Sarasota Counties:* 1412 Jackson Street, P.O. Box 2258, Fort Myers 33901   Alvin J. Taylor, Director, (813)334-0093

IX. *Indian River, Martin, Okeechobee, Palm Beach and St. Lucie Counties:* Forum III, Suite 800, 1665 Palm Beach Lakes Boulevard, West Palm Beach 33401   Phyllis A. Roe, Director, (305)683-6603

X. *Broward County:* 2691 East Oakland Park Boulevard, Suite 305, Fort Lauderdale 33306   Robert P. Kelley, Director, (305)563-9661

XI. *Dade and Monroe Counties:* 2445 West Flagler Street, Miami 33135   Max B. Rothman, Director, (305)642-7900

Georgia

Reporting Requirements

Persons mandated to report (compulsory) when reasonable cause to believe a child is or has been subjected to abuse or neglect: physician, licensed osteopathic physician, intern, resident, dentist, podiatrist, public health nurse, social worker, teacher, school administrator, or child care or law enforcement personnel (provided that if person is on the staff of a facility, he shall report to the person in charge, who shall make the required report)

Permissive: none

Form of report and when made: immediate oral; written to follow if requested

To whom report is made: a child welfare agency providing protective services, or, in its absence, to an appropriate police authority

Penalties: none

Immunities: full civil and criminal immunity for report made in good faith

Child Abuse Legislation

Citation: GCA 24-A, §2001, 3301; 74-111
Year enacted: 1975
Effective date: April 24, 1975
Purpose of legislation: mandatory reporting, yes
Reportable age: 0–18 years
Definitions: physical or mental mistreatment, sexual abuse, physical maltreatment, unreasonable mental or emotional distress, failure to provide necessary care or support.
Education/school report: mandatory reporting, yes

Immunity: yes
Mandatory investigation: no specific time frame
Confidentiality of records: yes; penalty: no specific provision
Cooperation with law courts, state agencies: no specific provision
Guardian ad litem: yes
Administrative proceedings, trained personnel, facilities: no specific provision
Dissemination of information: no specific provision

Programs and Agencies

Inquiries concerning child welfare interagency correspondence (i.e., child welfare cases originating in Georgia county departments), correspondence relating to the interstate placement of children, and all other welfare cases should be routed in triplicate for forwarding to:

> Director, Division of Social Services
> Department of Human Resources
> 47 Trinity Avenue, S.W., Room 211-H
> Atlanta 30334

Georgia Department of Human Resources

> State Office Building
> 47 Trinity Avenue, S.W.
> Atlanta 30334
> Telephone: (404)656-4650 for direct-dial number
> T.M. Jim Parham, Commissioner, (404)656-5680
> David C. Evans, Department Commissioner, (404)656-4497
> Program Unit, Truman Moore, Chief, (404)656-4382

County Departments of Family and Children Services

Appling County A. Vance Faircloth, South Main Street, P.O. Box 387, Baxley 31513 (912)367-4691

Atkinson County Mrs. Margie W. Mansour, North Main Street, Pearson 31642 (912)422-3242

Bacon County Janice Greenway, P.O. Box 447, Alma 31510 (912)632-4682 or 4278

Baker County Mrs. Elma E. Andrews, Newton 31770 (912)734-5247

Baldwin County Mrs. Mary S. Hunter, 435 North Cobb Street, Milledgeville 31061 (912)453-4135

Banks County Johnny V. Lewallen, Highway 98, P.O. Box 116, Homer 30547 (404)677-2272

Barrow County Mrs. Elizabeth B. Petree, 103 Park Avenue, Winder 30680 (404)867-9696

Bartow County Miss S. Julia Weems, 212 Leake Street, P.O. Box 328, Cartersville 30120 (404)382-3855

Ben Hill County Mrs. Irene M. Barr, 400 East Swanee Street, P.O. Box 188, Fitzgerald 31750 (912)423-4358

Berrien County Mrs. Evie T. Connell, 206 North Jackson Street, Nashville 31639 (912)686-5568

Bibb County Mrs. Elaine Cochran, 601 Mulberry Street, P.O. Box 1078, Macon 31201 (912)321-6051

Bleckley County Mrs. Marjorie W. Wimberly, 104 Dikes Street, Cochran 31014 (912)934-2045

Brantley County Mrs. Leila H. Turner, Highway 84, Nahunta 31553 (912)462-5133

Brooks County Mrs. Carolyn T. Sheffield, 108 West Johnson Street, Quitman 31643 (912)263-7594 or 7283

Bryan County Mrs. Frances Williamson, P.O. Box 398, Pembroke 31321 (912)653-2805

Bulloch County Mrs. Marion L. Hitt, 7 North College Street, P.O. Box 1103, Statesboro 30458 (912)764-3233 or 4200

Burke County Mrs. Eunice M. Smith (Act.), Courthouse, Liberty Street, P.O. Box 390, Waynesboro 30830 (404)554-5112

Butts County John L. Hall, 375 McDonough Road, P.O. Box 3880, Jackson 30233 (404)774-7405

Calhoun County Mrs. Mary R. Clements, Highway 37, Morgan 31766 (912)849-2625

Camden County Mrs. Elizabeth L. Parr, P.O. Box 29, Woodbine 31569 (912)576-5405

Candler County Mrs. Mary Lou Hensley, 55-A North Lewis Street, Metter 30439 (912)685-2163

Carroll County James Huddleston, 627 Maple Street, P.O. Box 327, Carrollton 30117 (404)832-6351

Catoosa County Mrs. Catherine D. Fowler, Ringgold 30736 (404)935-2368

Charlton County James D. Crews, County Office Building, Folkston 31537 (912)496-2527

Chatham County Jimmy Sumner, 2 East Henry Street, P.O. Box 2566, Savannah 31402 (912)944-2151

Chattahoochee County Mrs. LaVerne N. Wright, Broad Street, P.O. Box 157, Cusseta 31805 (404)959-3643

Chattooga County Mrs. Janeese H. Pullen, 300 South Commerse Street, Summerville 30747 (404)857-4532

Cherokee County Mrs. Louvell L. Manous, 291 Main Street, P.O. Box 826, Canton 30114 (404)479-2692 or 3062

Clarke County Miss Mary H. Collier, 1125 Boulevard, Athens 30601 (404)546-6532

Clay County Mrs. Mary P. Morgan, 205 Washington Street, P.O. Box 189, Fort Gaines 31751 (912)768-2017

Clayton County Mrs. Anne T. Plant, 129 King Street, Jonesboro 30236 (404)478-0295

Clinch County Mrs. Ila S. Douglas, 100 Court Square, Homerville 31634 (912)487-5363

Cobb County Mrs. Ruth Williams, 325 Fairground Street, Marietta 30061 (404)424-7320

Coffee County Ms. Nora V. Riggle, 112 North Madison Avenue, P.O. Box 957, Douglas 31533 (912)384-3768

Colquitt County Mrs. Jean Garrison, 102-2nd Street, S.E., Moultrie 31768 (912)985-4430

Columbia County Mrs. Rubye P. Beasley, Courthouse Circle, Appling 30802 (404)541-1640 or 0139

Cook County Miss A. Virginia Bennett, North Parrish Avenue, Adel 31620 (912)896-3672

Coweta County James C. Hardy, 137 Jackson Street, Newnan 30263 (404)253-5080

Crawford County Mrs. Ellen B. McAfee, P.O. Box 97, Roberta 31078 (912)836-3565

Crisp County Ms. Mary G. Williams, 112-23rd Avenue, East, Cordele 31015 (912)273-2625

Dade County Mrs. Kathryn W. Hannah, P.O. Box 388, U.S. Route 11, Trenton 30752 (404)657-4110

Dawson County Mrs. Mary S. Smith, Courthouse Square, Dawsonville 30534 (404)265-2491

Decatur County Mrs. Mary W. Baell, 223 Donalson Street, Bainbridge 31717 (912)246-1208

De Kalb County Mrs. Louise D. Purdom, 430 North McDonough Street, Decatur 30030 (404)371-2491

Dodge County Ms. Diann Cheek, 6011½ Griffin Street, Eastman 31023 (912)374-4331

Dooly County Mrs. Doris D. Faulk, West Union Street, Vienna 31092 (912)268-4111

Dougherty County Mrs. Virginia H. Cadden, 406 Highland Avenue, Albany 31706 (912)439-4114

Douglas County Mrs. Elaine B. Riley, Church Street, Douglasville 30134 (404)942-4386

Early County Mrs. Marie S. Wilkerson, 319 South Church Street, Blakely 31723 (912)723-4331

Echols County Mrs. Allice S. Rampley, Statenville 31648 (912)559-5751

Effingham County Mrs. Ruth Lee, Laurel Street, P.O. Box 345, Springfield 31329 (912)754-6471

Elbert County Mrs. Dorothy M. Bailey, 10 West Church Street, P.O. Box 547, Elberton 30635 (404)283-3141

Emanuel County Mrs. Lillian K. Bird, West Moring Street, Swainsboro 30401 (912)237-6494

Evans County Mrs. Betty D. Smith, 107 West Liberty Street, Claxton 30417 (912)739-1222

Fannin County James E. Bennett, West 1st Street, Blueridge 30513 (404)632-2296

Fayette County Mrs. Annelle N. Burch, 200 Lanier Avenue, Fayetteville 30214 (404)461-8101

Floyd County Charles Ray Josey, Jr., P.O. Box 1188, Rome 30161 (404)295-7341

Forsyth County Ronald H. McClure, 117 Industrial Boulevard, Cumming 30130 (404)887-6158

Franklin County Mrs. Marie B. Loftis, Royston Road, Carnesville 30521 (404)384-4521

Fulton County Gilbert G. Dulaney, 800 Peachtree Street, N.E., Atlanta 30308 (404)894-5700

Gilmer County Mrs. Marie S. Reynolds, Broad Street, P.O. Box 331, Ellijay 30540 (404)635-2361

Glascock County Miss Kathy Chaulker, Main Street, Gibson 30810 (404)598-2955

Glynn County R. E. Keithcart, 1803 Gloucester Street, P.O. Box 1616, Brunswick 31520 (912)265-4207

Gordon County Stephen Hatcher, Oothcalooga Street, P.O. Box 217, Calhoun 30701 (404)629-9558

Grady County Mrs. Carolyn Childs, 80-2nd Avenue, S.E., Cairo 31728 (912)377-3154

Greene County Miss Jeannie Lewis, 201 North Main Street, Greensboro 30642 (404)453-7318 or 7611

Gwinnett County Frederick B. Webb, Chestnut Street, Lawrenceville 30245 (404)963-2481

Habersham County Irene Swain, Office Building 7, off Highway 98, Clarkesville 30523 (404)754-2148

Hall County Barbara E. Griffin, 472 East Enota Drive, Gainesville 30501 (404)532-5298

Hancock County Mrs. Mary G. Kennedy, P.O. Box 70, Sparta 31087 (404)444-6531

Haralson County Mrs. Irene K. Morgan, 2 Dallas Highway, Bushanan 30113 (404)646-5549

Harris County John D. Worton, P.O. Box 285, Hamilton 31811
(404)628-4226

Hart County Kenneth C. Black, Courthouse Annex, Courthouse Square, Hart-
well 30643   (404)376-5157

Heard County Jere B. Ridley, P.O. Box 385, Franklin 30217   (404)675-3361

Henry County Ms. Peggy Rice, P.O. Box 313, McDonough 30253
(404)957-2663

Houston County Ms. Kathryn Harris, Washington Street, P.O. Box 1298, Perry
31069   (912)987-2373

Irwin County Mrs. Blondean Cargile, Irwin Avenue and 4th Street, Ocilla 31744
(912)468-7406

Jackson County Mrs. Carolyn M. Balwin, Washington Street, Jefferson 30549
(404)367-5225

Jasper County Mrs. Larue Camp, 144 North Warren Street, Monticello 31064
(404)468-6461

Jeff Davis County Mrs. Saralyn Overstreet, Jeff Davis Street, Hazelhurst 31539
(912)375-2365

Jefferson County Mrs. Mervin F. Frost, 611 Walnut Street, Louisville 30434
(912)625-7259

Jenkins County Mrs. Cammilla M. Lane, Winthrope Avenue, Millen 30442
(912)982-1944

Johnson County William L. Colston (Caseworker-in-Charge), 110 West Elm
Street, Wrightsville 31069   (912)864-3475

Jones County Mrs. Maurine R. Bilderback, Courthouse Annex, Gray 31032
(912)986-3126

Lamar County Raymond R. Howard, 212 Gordon Road, Barnesville 30204
(404)358-2657

Lanier County Mrs. Mary S. Holland, Lanier County Courthouse, Lakeland
31635   (912)482-3686

Laurens County Miss Essie Mae Cobb, Courthouse, 3rd Floor, Dublin 31021
(912)272-1711

Lee County Mrs. Louise H. Forrester, U.S. Highway 19, Leesburg 31763
(912)759-6841

Liberty County Mrs. Helen E. Stanford, 135 South Main Street, P.O. Box 25,
Hinesville 31313   (912)876-5174

Lincoln County John G. Ludwig, School Street, Lincolnton 30817
(404)359-3135

Long County Mrs. Ada Hendrix, P.O. Box 373, Ludowici 31316
(912)545-2177

Lowndes County Mrs. Vivian S. Strom, 325 West Savannah Avenue, P.O. Box
1246, Valdosta 31601   (912)247-3477

Lumpkin County Mrs. Louise A. Riddle, Daholnega 30533   (404)864-2241

McDuffie County Mrs. Marcelle Morris, Whiteoak Road, P.O. Box 507, Thomson 30824 (404)595-2946

McIntosh County Mr. John E. Guthrie, Old American Legion Building, P.O. Box 483, Darien 31305 (912)437-4193

Macon County John Hammock, 100 Sumter Street, Oglethorpe 31068 (912)472-8128

Madison County Mrs. Elizabeth R. Holloway, Multi-purpose Building, Daniels-ville 30633 (404)795-2128

Marion County Mrs. Frances B. Rogers, Buena Vista 31803 (912)649-2311

Meriwether County Danny Fowler, P.O. Box D, Greenville 30222 (404)672-4244

Mitchell County Ms. Sarah Jorden, 20 Harvey Street, Camilla 31730 (912)336-8419 or 8709

Monroe County Mrs. Harriet T. Zellner, 13 North Lee Street, Forsyth 31029 (912)994-2561

Montgomery County Mrs. Willa S. Grist, 36 Railroad Avenue, Mt. Vernon 30445 (912)583-2562

Morgan County Mrs. Louise B. Bray, 384 Hancock Street, Madison 30650 (404)342-1371

Murray County Mrs. Barbara M. Weaver, P.O. Box P, Chatsworth 30705 (404)695-3322

Muscogee County Miss Virginia Heisler, 1718-8th Avenue, P.O. Box 2627, Columbus 31902 (404)324-7311

Newton County Steve Love, 6119 Adams Street, Covington 30209 (404)786-8161

Oconee County Mrs. Elizabeth M. Elder, P.O. Box 105, Watkinsville 30677 (404)769-5206

Oglethorpe County Mrs. Elizabeth T. Lanier, Boggs Street, Lexington 30648 (404)743-8152

Paulding County Mrs. Janet C. Tripcony, 248 Academy Dr., Dallas 30132 (404)445-2139

Peach County Miss Laura Nell Hardman, 305 West Church Street, Fort Valley 31030 (912)825-3372

Pickens County Von J. Hinton, 211 North Main Street, Jasper 30143 (404)692-2488 or 5312

Pierce County Mrs. Frances C. Talley, P.O. Box 620, Blackshear 31516 (912)449-6624

Pike County Alvin L. Milby, Sr., County Building Complex, Groyn Street, Zebulon 30295 (404)567-8427

Polk County Mrs. Margaret B. Woodruff, 302 Prior Street, P.O. Box 960, Cedartown 30125 (404)748-2942

Pulaski County Mrs. Judy S. Mullis, 610 Broad Street, Hawkinsville 31036 (912)892-9149

Putnam County Mrs. Helen L. Harrell, Marion Street, Eatonton 31024
(404)485-4921

Quitman County Mrs. Annie H. Redding, Georgetown 31754 (912)334-2427

Rabun County Robert Sexton, Courthouse, Hiawassee Street, Clayton 30525
(404)782-4283

Randolph County Mrs. Carol M. Simpson, Webster Street, P.O. Box 218, Cuthbert 31740 (912)732-3742

Richmond County Ms. Patsy P. Fitzgerald, 520 Fenwick Street, P.O. Box 2277,
Augusta 30903 (404)724-5711

Rockdale County Ms. Judith Giles, 1040 Oakland Avenue, Conyers 30207
(404)483-8606

Schley County Mrs. Jeannette H. Peede, 80 North Groad Street, Ellaville 31806
(912)937-2591

Screven County Mrs. Iva T. Clements, County Courthouse, Sylvania 30467
(912)564-2325

Seminole County Mrs. Patricia A. Miller, 2nd Street, Donalsonville 31745
(912)524-2365 or 2068

Spalding County Ms. Carole F. Johnson, 317 South 8th Street, Griffin 30223
(404)228-1386

Stephens County Gladelle M. Whitaker, West Tugalo Street, Toccoa 30577
(404)886-8478

Stewart County Robert R. Downer, P.O. Box 308, Lumpkin 31815
(912)838-4335

Sumter County Mrs. Marian M. Harris, 227 North Lee Street, Americus 31709
(912)928-1220

Talbot County Kenneth R. Duncan, P.O. Box 96, Talbotton 31827
(404)665-8524

Taliaferro County Wiley B. Jones, Courthouse, Crawfordville 30631
(404)456-2339

Tattnall County Mrs. Celina R. Sharpe, Courthouse Annex, Reidsville 30453
(912)557-4721

Taylor County Mrs. Patricia D. Brunson, P.O. Box 366, Butler 31006
(912)862-5221

Telfair County Mrs. Sylvia H. Smith, McRae 31055 (912)868-6481

Terrell County Mrs. Jean W. Lark, 210 East Lee Street, Dawson 31742
(912)995-4431

Thomas County Miss Josephine B. Craig, 401 East Jackson Street, Thomasville
31792 (912)226-1511

Tift County Mrs. Mary G. Veal, 1212 Chestnut Avenue, P.O. Box 745, Tifton
31794 (912)381-3388

Toombs County Mrs. Wynelle S. Odem, West Broad and Washington Streets,
P.O. Box 191, Lyons 30436 (912)526-8117

Towns County Mr. Jerry B. Kendall, Beroong Street, P.O. Box 156, Hiawassee
30546 (404)896-3524

Treutlen County Mrs. Frankie C. Ware, 108-1st Street, Soperton 30457

Troup County Mrs. Elizabeth H. Abercrombie, 504 East Depot Street, P.O. Box 1265, LaGrange 30240   (404)884-2331

Turner County Mrs. Brenda H. Lee, Rogers Plaza, Ashburn 31714 (912)567-4353

Twiggs County Ms. Vicki W. Rozier, P.O. Box 164, Jeffersonville 31044 (912)945-3258

Union County Mrs. Sandra B. Collins, Haralson Memorial Office Center, Blairsville 30512   (404)745-2931

Upson County Edward Moore, 209 East Thompson Street, Thomaston 30286 (404)647-7193

Walker County T. G. Brown III, North Cherokee Street, LaFayette 30728 (404)638-2270

Walton County Mrs. Lucy B. Bolton, Court Street, Monroe 30655 (404)267-5177 or 5815

Ware County William P. Denton, 201 State Street, Waycross 30501 (912)285-4410

Warren County John R. Howell, 105 Academy Street, Warrenton 30828 (404)465-3326

Washington County Mr. Leslie W. Davies, 155 East Church Street, Sandersville 31082   (912)552-3201

Wayne County Mrs. Carolyn D. Aspinwall, 135 South East Broad Street, Jesup 31545   (912)427-2093

Webster County Mrs. Ann J. Kirsey, Preston 31824   (912)828-3115

Wheeler County Mrs. Gwendolyn B. Cox, 411 McRae Street, Alamo 30411 (912)568-3211

White County Mrs. Charlotte P. Palmer, Courthouse, Cleveland 30528 (404)865-3128

Whitfield County Mr. Fred L. Jones, P.O. Box 1203, Dalton 30720 (404)278-4554

Wilcox County Mrs. Mary D. Cohen, 501 Gorden Street, Rochelle 31079 (912)365-2243

Wilkes County Mrs. Jeanne D. Beckum, Lexington Road, Washington 30673 (404)678-2814

Wilkinson County Miss Nancy P. Stewart, P.O. Box 195, Irwinton 31042 (912)946-2224

Worth County Mrs. Martha H. Rhodes, North Henderson Street, Sylvester 31791   (912)776-6921

Guam

Programs and Agencies

Where to write: Communications regarding requests for social information and services should be addressed to:

Division of Social Services
Department of Public Health and Social Services
P.O. Box 2816
Agana 96910

Guam Department of Public Health and Social Services

Government of Guam
P.O. Box 2816
Agana 96910
Telephone: (overseas operator) 734-9901
Pedro L. G. Santos, Director 734-9917
Joseph C. Cruz, Department Director 734-9914

Family and Children Services

Felicisima L. Quimpo, Supervisor
Trinidad R. Pangelinan, Child Protective Services
Rita Arlene Santos, Adoption Services
Isabel M. Sablan, Supervisor Licensing

Hawaii

Reporting Requirements

Persons mandated to report (compulsory) when reasonable cause to believe a child is or has been subjected to abuse or neglect: any doctor (person licensed to render services in medicine or the healing arts, including osteopathy and dentistry), any registered nurse, school teacher, social worker, coroner in his official capacity (provided that if person is on the staff of a hospital or similar facility, the person shall report to the person in charge, who shall make the required report)

Permissive: any other person who has reason to believe that a minor is abused or neglected

Form of report and when made: prompt oral report, followed as soon as possible by written report

To whom report is made: department of social services and housing

Penalties: none

Immunities: full civil and criminal immunity for report made in good faith

Child Abuse Legislation

Citation: HRS §350.5, 571-24
Year enacted: 1975
Effective date: February 13, 1975
Purpose of legislation: mandatory reporting, yes
Reportable age: 0–18 years
Definitions: physical or mental injury, sexual abuse, negligent treatment, or
  maltreatment

Education/school report: mandatory reporting, yes
Immunity: yes
Mandatory investigation: yes, immediately
Confidentiality of records: yes; penalty: no specific provision
Cooperation with law courts, state agencies: no specific provision
Guardian ad litem: yes
Administrative proceedings, trained personnel, facilities: no specific provision
Dissemination of information: no specific provision

Programs and Agencies

Inquiries regarding social welfare services and economic (public) assistance
should be sent to:

Edwin B. L. Tam, Public Welfare Administrator
Department of Social Services and Housing
P.O. Box 339
Honolulu 96809

Family and Children's Services

Marjorie Barrett, Administrator, (808)548-5846
Margaret Lee, Assistant Administrator, Family Services, (808)548-5801
Jane Okubo, Assistant Administrator, Foster Care Licensing, (808)548-5490
Beatrice Yuh, Assistant Administrator, Foster Care Adoption,
   (808)548-7502
Geraldine Senner, Assistant Administrator, Day Care, (808)548-6407

Related State Agencies

Executive Department of the Governor
Commission on Children and Youth
P.O. Box 3044
Honolulu 96802
Howard Yuh, Executive Secretary, (808)548-7582

Idaho

Reporting Requirements

Persons mandated to report (compulsory) when reasonable cause to believe a child is or has been subjected to abuse or neglect: physician, resident, intern, nurse, coroner, school teacher, day-care personnel, social worker, or other person having reasonable cause to believe that child is abused or in danger of being so (provided, that if the person making the report is on a staff, he shall inform the person in charge, who shall make the required report)

Permissive: none

Form of report and when made: no procedure given

To whom report is made: proper law enforcement agency

Penalties: none

Immunities: full immunity (criminal and civil) for good faith report; any person reporting in bad faith or with malice is not protected.

Child Abuse Legislation

Citation: IC §16-1624, 1641, 2000
Year enacted: 1973
Effective date: not available
Purpose of legislation: mandatory reporting, yes
Reportable age: 0–18 years
Definitions: abandonment, emotional maladjustment, neglect, abuse, skin bruising, bleeding, malnutrition, sexual molestation, burns, fractures of any bone, failure to thrive or death, or any such condition or death not justifiably explained

Education/school report: mandatory reporting, yes
Immunity: yes
Mandatory investigation: yes, immediately
Confidentiality of records: no specific provision; penalty: no specific provision
Cooperation with law courts, state agencies: no specific provision
Guardian ad litem: yes
Administrative proceedings, trained personnel, facilities: no specific provision
Dissemination of information: no specific provision

Programs and Agencies

Communications regarding transfer of juvenile delinquents should be addressed to:

> John Shuler, Administrator for Interstate Compact on Juveniles
> Division of Welfare
> Statehouse
> Boise 83720

Idaho Department of Health and Welfare

> Statehouse
> Boise 83720
> Telephone: (208)384-2336
> Milton G. Klein, Director

Family and Children's Services Section

> Telephone: (208)384-3340

Department of Health and Welfare Regional Offices

I. *Benewah, Bonner, Boundary, Kootenai, and Shoshone Counties:* P.O. Box 938, Coeur d'Alene 83814   David DeAngelis, Administrator, (208)667-8493

II. *Clearwater, Idaho, Latah, Lewis, and Nez Perce Counties:* P.O. Drawer B, Lewiston 83501   Ralph Colton, Ph.D., Administrator, (208)746-2651

III. *Adams, Canyon, Gem, Owyhee, Payette, and Washington Counties:* Highway 30, Route 3, Caldwell 83605   David Humphrey, Administrator, (208)459-7456

IV. *Ada, Boise, Elmore, and Valley Counties:* Statehouse, Boise 83720   Theo Murdock, Administrator, (208)384-2240

V. *Baine, Camas, Cassia, Gooding, Jerome, Lincoln, Minidoka, and Twin Falls*

Counties: 638 Addison Avenue West, Twin Falls 83301   Dennis
McDermott, Administrator, (208)734-4000

VI. *Bannock, Bear Lake, Bingham, Butte, Caribou, Franklin, Oneida, and Power
Counties:* P.O. Box 4166, Pocatello 83201   Jerry L. Harris, Administrator,
(208)233-6170

VII. *Bonneville, Clark, Custer, Fremont, Jefferson, Lemhi, Madison, and Teton
Counties:* 1655 South Woodruff Avenue, Suite A, Idaho Falls 83401
David Groberg, Ph.D., Administrator, (208)524-2060

Illinois

Reporting Requirements

Persons mandated to report (compulsory) when reasonable cause to believe a child is or has been subjected to abuse or neglect: physician, hospital, dentist, surgeon, osteopath, chiropractor, podiatrist, Christian Science practitioner, coroner, school teacher or administrator, registered or licensed nurse, truant officer, social worker, social services administrator, director or assistant of a nursery school or a child day-care center, law enforcement officer, or field personnel of the Illinois Department of Public Aid

Permissive: any other person with reasonable cause to believe the child has been abused or neglected

Form of report and when made: immediate oral; written, postpaid, U.S. mail, within 24 hours

To whom report is made: department of children and family services, local law enforcement agency

Penalties: none

Immunities: full civil and criminal immunity for good faith report; good faith presumed

Child Abuse Legislation

Citation: IRS Chap. 23, §1-12; Chap. 37, §704-5
Year enacted: 1975
Effective date: July 1, 1975
Purpose of legislation: mandatory reporting, yes
Reportable age: 0–18 years

Definitions: abuse: physical injury, sexual abuse, mental injury; neglect: failure
   to provide care and maintenance, proper and necessary support, education,
   medical, etc., abandonment, death
Education/school report: mandatory reporting, yes
Immunity: yes
Mandatory investigation: yes, 24 hours
Confidentiality of records: yes; penalty: misdemeanor
Cooperation with law courts, state agencies: no specific provision
Guardian ad litem: yes
Administrative proceedings, trained personnel, facilities: no specific provision
Dissemination of information: no specific provision

Programs and Agencies

Where to write: Case correspondence relating to the aid to families with dependent children program and the medical assistance program under Title XIX
should be sent, in duplicate, directly to the county departments of public aid.
Inquiries concerning general assistance and aid to the medically indigent should
be sent, in duplicate, to the county departments of public aid (except for Cook
County cases outside of Chicago) with the request that they be referred to the
proper supervisor of general assistance for action. For Cook County cases outside of Chicago, send inquiries to:

   County Representative
   Department of Public Aid
   624 South Michigan Avenue
   Chicago 60605

Illinois Department of Children and Family Services

   623 East Adams Street
   Springfield 62706
   Telephone: (217)782-7615

   1026 South Damen Avenue
   Chicago 60612
   Telephone: (312)793-4650

   Mary Lee Leahy, Director, (217)782-7615 and (312)793-4650
   Jess McDonald, Executive Department Director, (217)782-7615
   David Bankard, Department Director, Management Services, (217)782-0147
   Neil Matlins, Department Director, Planning, Research, and Evaluation,
      (217)782-2645

Dolores B. Reid, Department Director, Program Support Services,
(217)782-3627
William Ryan, Department Director, Program Operations, (217)782-6217
Jerry Stermer, Administrative Assistant, (312)793-4650
Cheryl Kahn, Administrative Assistant, (217)782-7615
Jan van Blommesteyn, Administrative Assistant, (217)782-7122
Marian Quinn Barnes, Chief Technical Advisor, Legal, (217)782-7122 and
(312)793-2410
Richard S. Laymon, Guardianship Administrator and Interstate Compact
Administrator, (217)782-6533

Office of Child Development

Thomas E. Villger, Administrator, (217)782-5134

Herrick House Children's Center

West Bartlett Road
Bartlett 60103
Telephone: (312)837-6010
Thomas Brennan, Administrator

Soldiers' and Sailors' Children's School

600 East Lincoln Street
Normal 61761
Telephone: (309)452-1136
Andrew J. Spelios, Superintendent

Department of Children and Family Services Area Offices

Aurora (DePage, Kane, and Kendall Counties): 48 West Galena Boulevard,
Aurora 60504   Karen Martin, Administrator, (312)896-0881
*Champaign (Champaign, Clark, Coles, Cumberland, Douglas, Edgar, Ford, Iro-
quois and Vermilion Counties):* 2125 South 1st Street, Champaign 61820
Willis D. Hartman, Administrator, (217)333-1037
Chicago East (Cook County): 1439 South Michigan Avenue, Chicago 60605
Elease D. Reed, Administrator, (312)341-7671
Chicago North (Cook County): 4320 West Montrose Avenue, Chicago 60641
Thomas A. Kmetko, Administrator, (312)282-9470
Chicago South (Cook County): 950 East 61st Street, Chicago 60637   Charles
Johnson, Administrator, (312)239-7070
Chicago West (Cook County): 1026 South Damen Avenue, Chicago 60612
Ronald L. Jennings, Administrator, (312)793-4697

Decatur (De Witt, Livingston, McLean, Macon, Moultrie, Piatt, and Shelby Counties): 125 North Franklin Street, Decatur 62523   Ralph Hanebutt, Administrator, (217)429-5731

East Saint Louis (Madison, Monroe, Randolph, and St. Clair Counties): Regional State Office Building, 10 Collinsville Avenue, East St. Louis 62201 Anthony Jenkins, Administrator, (618)875-9300, ext. 235

Joliet (Kankakee and Will Counties): 58 North Chicago Street, Joliet 60431 John Irwin, Administrator, (815)727-7675

Lake-McHenry (Lake and McHenry Counties): Waukegan Building, 6th Floor, 4 South Genesee Street, Waukegan 60085   R. Dennis Burns, Administrator, (312)244-4640

Marion (Alexander, Franklin, Gallatin, Hamilton, Hardin, Jackson, Johnson, Massac, Perry, Pope, Pulaski, Saline, Union, White, and Williamson Counties): 2209 West Main Street, Marion 62959   (vacant), Administrator, (618)997-4371

Moline (Henderson, Henry, Knox, Mercer, Rock Island, and Warren Counties): 2810-41st Street, Moline 61265   Jesse Viers, Administrator (309)762-9446

Ottawa (Bureau, De Kalb, Grundy, La Salle, Lee, Marshall, Putnam, Stark, and Whiteside Counties): 424 West Madison Street, Ottawa 61350   Dwight L. Lambert, Administrator, (815)433-4610

Peoria (Fulton, McDonough, Peoria, Tazewell, and Woodford Counties): 5415 North University Street, Peoria 61614   Jessie A. Hairston, Administrator, (309)691-2200, ext. 531

Quincy (Adams, Brown, Calhoun, Cass, Hancock, Jersey, Morgan, Pike, Schuyler, and Scott Counties): 410 North 9th Street, Quincy 62301   Don P. Robeson, Administrator, (217)223-7187

Rockford (Boone, Carroll, Jo Daviess, Ogle, Stephenson, and Winnebago Counties): 4302 North Main Street, P.O. Box 915, Rockford 61105   Margaret M. Kennedy, Administrator, (815)987-7640

Salem (Bond, Clay, Clinton, Crawford, Edwards, Jefferson, Lawrence, Marion, Richland, Wabash, Washington, and Wayne Counties): 205 East Locust Street, Salem 62881   George E. Ross, Administrator, (618)548-1692

Springfield (Christian, Logan, Macoupin, Mason, Menard, Montgomery, and Sangamon Counties): 4500 South Sixth Street Road, Springfield 62706 Barbara M. Ryan, Administrator, (217)786-6830

Indiana

Reporting Requirements

Persons mandated to report (compulsory) when reasonable cause to believe a child is or has been subjected to abuse or neglect: it shall be the duty of any person who has reason to believe that a child has had physical injury inflicted upon him other than by accidental means by a parent or the person responsible for his care

Permissive: none

Form of report and when made: immediate report upon actual discovery of injury; no time provision for reporting mere suspicion

To whom report is made: county department of public welfare or the proper law enforcement agency

Penalties: consciously failing to make the required report is a misdemeanor and upon conviction punishable by a fine of not more than $100 and/or imprisonment for a period not to exceed 30 days

Immunities: any person, except the person accused of infliction of physical injury on a child, who makes a report subject to this statute or who testifies at a judicial proceeding on the matter, has full civil and criminal immunity in the absence of a showing of bad faith or malice

Child Abuse Legislation

Citation: IC §12-3-3-2, 52-1426-1431
Year enacted: not available
Effective date: not available
Purpose of legislation: mandatory reporting, yes

Reportable age: not available

Definitions: a physical injury inflicted upon a child by other than accidental
    means by a parent or by other person who is responsible for his care

Education/school report: mandatory reporting, yes

Immunity: yes, civil/criminal

Mandatory investigation: yes, immediately

Confidentiality of records: no specific provision; penalty: no specific provision

Cooperation with law courts, state agencies: no specific provision

Guardian ad litem: yes

Administrative proceedings, trained personnel, facilities: no specific provision

Dissemination of information: no specific provision

Programs and Agencies

Where to write: All correspondence concerning child welfare services which involve interstate placement of children and/or children born out of wedlock and
requests for general information relative to child welfare-social services programs, including those regarding Title XX, should be sent in duplicate to:

Child Welfare
Social Services Division
Department of Public Welfare
141 South Meridian Street, 4th Floor
Indianapolis 46225

Division of Social Services

Lucille De Voe, Director, (317)633-4956

Division of Administrative Services

John B. Douglas, Director, (317)633-5247

County Public Welfare Departments

Adams County Meredith V. Rogers, P.O. Box 227, Decatur 46733
    (219)724-9169

Allen County John E. Heiny, 606 South Calhoun Street, Ft. Wayne 46802
    (219)423-7771

Bartholomew County J. Henry Blessing, 1971 State Street, P.O. Box 587,
    Columbus 47201   (812)376-9361

Benton County Mrs. Mary Forrest, Courthouse, Fowler 47944   (317)884-0120

Blackford County Mrs. Faye Daily (Act.), 203 East Washington Street, Hartford
    City 47348   (317)348-2902

Boone County Mr. Marion Robbins, Lawler Building, 124 East Washington
    Street, Lebanon 46052   (317)482-1630

Brown County Mrs. Elsie Wayman, Courthouse, P.O. Box 325, Nashville 47448
(812)988-2239
Carroll County Jack B. Good, Courthouse, Delphi 46923 (317)564-2409
Cass County Donald E. C. Leicht, Courthouse, Logansport 46947
(219)753-6386
Clark County Gordon Railey, City-County Building, Room 215, Jeffersonville
47130 (812)283-4451, ext. 18
Clay County Monica Tener (Act.), Courthouse, Brazil 47834 (812)448-8731
Clinton County Philip E. Brown, 54 West Street, Frankfort 46041
(317)654-8571
Crawford County Martin G. Wright, Courthouse, English 47118
(812)338-2701
Daviess County Virginia R. Arms, 300 East Walnut Street, Washington 47501
(812)254-0690
Dearborn County Mrs. Lyndall J. Breeden, Durbin Plaza, Lawrenceburg 47025
(812)537-0656
Decatur County David L. Baker, 119 East Main Street, Greensburg 47240
(812)663-6768
De Kalb County R. William Meier, Courthouse, Auburn 46706 (219)925-2810
Delaware County Glen Howard, 125 North Mulberry Street, Muncie 47305
(317)747-7750
Dubois County Robert L. Allen, 202 West 4th Street, Jasper 47546
(812)482-2585
Elkhart County Martha Spurgoen, Shoots Building, Room 36-38, 112-116
East Lincoln Avenue, Goshen 46526 (219)533-0402
Fayette County Mrs. Eileen C. Heineman, 119 West 4th Street, Connersville
47331 (317)825-5261
Floyd County C. Eugene McCoskey, New Albany 47150 (812)945-1126
Fountain County Mrs. Peggy W. McCoy, Courthouse, Covington 47932
(317)793-3331
Franklin County Chester E. Pickett, American Legion Building, 483 Main
Street, Brookville 47012 (317)647-4081
Fulton County Lawrence Seiwart, 112 East 8th Street, Rochester 46975
(219)223-3413
Gibson County Arthur L. Smith, Courthouse Annex, Princeton 47670
(812)385-4727
Grant County Mrs. Doris A. Miller, Courthouse Annex, 428 South Washington
Street, Marion 46952 (317)668-8871
Greene County Lysle E. Pittman, Courthouse, Bloomfield 47424
(812)384-8225
Hamilton County Harry Nicholson, 942 Maple Avenue, Noblesville 46060
(317)773-2183
Hancock County Mrs. Marie Walker, 9 East South Street, Greenfield 46140
(317)462-7748

Harrison County Allen F. Finkbiner, Courthouse, P.O. Box 366, Corydon 47112 (812)738-2296

Hendricks County Mrs. Patrician Skillman, Courthouse, P.O. Box 27, Danville 46122 (317)745-2586

Henry County Patricia B. Sales, 1219 Race Street, New Castle 47362 (317)529-3450

Howard County James R. McClean, Courthouse, Room 11, Kokomo 46901 (317)452-6083

Huntington County Verlin R. Jackson, Courthouse, Room 209, Huntington 46750 (219)356-4420

Jackson County Donald D. Cutts, Courthouse, Brownstown 47220 (812)358-2421

Jasper County Jack Musker, 119 Harrison Street, Rensselaer 47978 (219)866-4186

Jay County Gordon J. Hutson (Act.), Courthouse, Portland 47371 (317)726-7933

Jefferson County Mrs. Marjorie Hill, Courthouse Annex, 315½ East 2nd Street, Madison 47250 (812)265-2027

Jennings County David E. Grimes, Jackson Street, P.O. Box 367, Vernon 47282 (812)346-2254

Johnson County J. Fred Winslow, 2 East Jefferson Street, Franklin 46131 (317)736-5179

Knox County Mrs. Kathleen E. Powers, Courthouse Annex, Vincennes 47591 (812)882-3920

Kosciusko County Mrs. Peggy A. Shively (Act.), 110 North Buffalo Street, Warsaw 46580 (219)267-5185

Lagrange County Terry L. Graefnitz, 100 North Detroit Street, Lagrange 46761 (219)463-3451

Lake County John D. Kelley, 800 Massachusetts Street, Gary 46402 (219)883-4161
2010-167th Street, Hammond 46320 (219)845-1480

La Porte County Donald L. Snider, 1111 Washington Street, LaPorte 46350 (219)362-1510
106 Brinkman Street, Michigan City 46360 (219)879-8324

Lawrence County James H. Woodward, Courthouse Annex, 1410 North I Street, Bedford 47421 (812)279-9706

Madison County Clifford E. Bennett, 16 East 9th Street, Anderson 46016 (317)646-9351

Marion County Elizabeth Samkowski, 145 South Meridian Street, Indianapolis 46225 (317)633-3902

Marshall County Donald E. Patton, 109 North Walnut Street, Plymouth 46563 (219)936-3129

Martin County J. Wayne Mosier, U.S. Highway 50 and High Street, P.O. Box 88, Shoals 47581 (812)247-2871

Miami County Ronald W. Christiana, Courthouse, Peru 46970 (317)473-6611

Monroe County James R. Cummings, 125 West Kirkwood Avenue, Bloomington 47401 (812)336-6351

Montgomery County Roy R. Newman, 215 North Washington Street, Crawfordsville 47933 (317)362-5600

Morgan County Harry J. Lusk, P.O. Box 674, Martinsville 46151 (317)342-7151

Newton County Mrs. Gail K. Dawson, Courthouse, Kentland 47951 (219)474-5011

Noble County Lee Pearson (Act.), South Orange Street, Albion 46701 (219)636-2021

Ohio County Mrs. H. Marcella Kinnett (Act.), 502-2nd Street, Rising Sun 47040 (812)438-2530

Orange County C. Roscoe Boyd, Libery Building, Paoli 47454 (812)723-2278

Owen County Mrs. Anne H. Rein, Courthouse, Spencer 47460 (812)829-2726

Parke County Stanley L. Hartman, Courthouse, Rockville 47872 (317)569-3156

Perry County Larry K. Kleeman, Courthouse Annex, P.O. Box 337, Cannelton 47520 (812)547-7055

Pike County Mrs. Velma Fleming, Courthouse, Petersburg 47567 (812)354-9716

Porter County Thomas R. St.Myer, 157 Franklin St., Valparaiso 46383 (219)462-2112

Posey County Robert A. Webster, P.O. Box 534, Mt. Vernon 47620 (812)838-4429

Pulaski County Miss Cynthia L. Ines, Courthouse, Winamac 46996 (219)946-3312

Putnam County Gerald V. McCord, Courthouse, Greencastle 46135 (317)653-9780 or 3079

Randolph County John Carpenter, Courthouse, Winchester 47394 (317)584-2811

Ripley County Marvin B. Doyle, Courthouse, Versailles 47042 (812)689-6295

Rush County Mrs. Catherine Wilkinson, Courthouse, Rushville 46173 (317)932-2392

Scott County Mrs. Merredith Bridgewater, R.R. 2, Scottsburg 47170 (812)752-2503

Shelby County Mrs. June W. Himmel (Act.), Courthouse, Room 303, Shelbyville 46176 (317)398-9747

Spencer County Mrs. Betty Bauman, Courthouse, Rockport 47635 (812)649-9111

Starke County Dale N. Denny, R.R. 1, Box 17, Knox 46534 (219)772-3751

Steuben County Jan Lung, Courthouse Annex, Angola 46703 (219)665-3713 or 5162

St. Joseph County Wilmer H. Tolle, 306 North Michigan Street, South Bend 46601 (209)232-2021

Sullivan County Donald W. Bedwell, Courthouse, Sullivan 47882 (812)268-6326

Switzerland County Walter R. Reiman, 505 Vineyard Street, P.O. Box 98, Vevay 47043 (812)427-3232

Tippecanoe County David E. Ling, Courthouse Annex, 324 Main Street, Lafayette 47901 (317)423-2611

Tipton County Mrs. Carolyn Perry (Act.), Courthouse, Tipton 46072 (317)675-7441

Union County Gene Sanford, Courthouse, Liberty 47353 (317)458-5481

Vanderburgh County Robert Dale Work, City-County Complex, Room 108, P.O. Box 154, Evansville 47701 (812)426-5364

Vermillion County A. Malcom Sturm, Courthouse, P.O. Box 218, Newport 47966 (317)492-3396

Vigo County Ralph G. Baxter, 429 South 6th Street, Terre Haute 47808 (812)234-5526

Wabash County David H. Graham, Courthouse, Wabash 46992 (219)563-8471

Warren County Maurice A. Lenz, Courthouse, Williamsport 47993 (317)762-6125

Warrick County Mrs. Judith Harper, 319 South 3rd Street, P.O. Box 412, Boonville 47601 (812)3530 or 2270

Washington County Mrs. Carol L. Cox (Act.), Courthouse, Salem 47167 (812)883-4305

Wayne County Paul S. Hopwood, Courthouse, 3rd Street Entrance, Richmond 47374 (317)966-8381

Wells County Mrs. Elizabeth Diehl, Courthouse, Bluffton 46714 (219)824-3530

White County Mrs. Dorothy Custer, P.O. Box 365, Monticello 47960 (219)583-5742

Whitley County Carl F. Arntson, 115 South Line Street, Columbia City 46725 (219)244-6331

Iowa

Reporting Requirements

Persons mandated to report (compulsory) when reasonable cause to believe a child is or has been subjected to abuse or neglect: any health practitioner (if on a hospital or facility staff, the practitioner's superior in charge of the facility); social worker under the jurisdiction of the department of social services, public or private health care facility; psychologist; school employee; employee in a licensed day care facility; members of the staff of a mental health center; peace officer (if any are on a staff, the director of the facility shall report)

Permissive: any other person who believes that a child has had physical injury inflicted upon him as a result of abuse

Form of report and when made: immediate oral; written, within 48 hours; permissive reporter may make oral, written, or both

To whom report is made: department of social services, or local police agency if need is immediate

Penalties: criminal: knowingly and willfully failing to report, not more than $100 or not more than 10 days in the county jail; civil: knowing failure entails civil liability for damages caused by that failure

Immunities: full civil and criminal immunity for good faith report

Child Abuse Legislation

Citation: ICA §232.28, 1225, 235H, 1-H-24
Year enacted: 1974
Effective date: July 1, 1974
Purpose of legislation: mandatory reporting, yes

Reportable age: 0–18 years
Definitions: any nonaccidental physical injuries suffered by a child as a result
      of the acts or omissions of the child's parent, guardian, or other person
      legally responsible for the child
Education/school report: mandatory reporting, yes
Immunity: yes
Mandatory investigation: yes, promptly
Confidentiality of records: yes; penalty: misdemeanor
Cooperation with law courts, state agencies: yes
Guardian ad litem: yes
Administrative proceedings, trained personnel, facilities: yes
Dissemination of information: no specific provision

Programs and Agencies

All correspondence pertaining to interstate placement of children, adoptions,
and general information on child welfare should be directed in duplicate to:

> Jack Harvey, Chief
> Bureau of Family and Adult Services
> Division of Community Services
> Lucas State Office Building
> Des Moines 50319

Bureau of Family and Adult Services

> Jack Harvey, Chief, (515)281-3572

Department of Social Services District Offices

I. *Decorah* (Allamakee, Clayton, Fayette, Howard, and Winneshiek Counties):
      126 College Drive, Decorah 52101   Maurice (Ed) Hover, Administrator,
      (319)382-4231
II. *Mason City* (Cerro Gordo, Floyd, Franklin, Hancock, Kossuth, Mitchell,
      Winnebago, and Worth Counties): 1531 South Monroe Street, Mason City
      50401   Jack L. Baughman, Administrator, (515)424-1794 or 1637
III. *Spencer* (Buena Vista, Clay, Dickenson, Emmet, Lyon O'Brien, Osceola,
      Palo Alto, and Sioux Counties): 4 East 21st Street, P.O. Box 1068, Spen-
      cer 51301   John R. Stout, Administrator, (712)262-5251
IV. *Sioux City* (Cherokee, Ida, Monona, Plymouth, and Woodbury Counties):
      808-5th Street, P.O. Box 3063, Sioux City 51102   Charles H. Sweeney, Jr.,
      Administrator, (712)255-7923
V. *Ft. Dodge* (Calhoun, Hamilton, Humboldt, Pocahontas, Webster, and Wright

Counties): 1210 Central Avenue, P.O. Box 837, Ft. Dodge 50501   Jose T. Gownder, Administrator, (515)576-3193

VI. *Marshalltown* (Grundy, Hardin, Marshall, Poweshiek, and Tama Counties): K.F.J.B. Building, 2nd Floor, 133 East Main Street, Marshalltown 50158 Ross E. Orr, Administrator, (515)752-4668

VII. *Waterloo* (Black Hawk, Bremer, Buchanan, Butler, and Chickasaw Counties): First National Building, 5th Floor, 607 Sycamore Street, P.O. Box 2246, Waterloo 50705   Nancy Jane Law, Administrator (319)232-6595

VIII. *Dubuque* (Cedar, Clinton, Deleware, Dubuque, and Jackson Counties): Conlin Building, 2nd Floor, 1473 Central Avenue, Dubuque 52001   Jay D. Barfels, Administrator, (319)556-1945

IX. *Davenport* (Muscatine and Scott Counties): 1416 West 16th Street, Davenport 52804   Dennis R. Timmesmann, Administrator, (319)324-1021 or 383-0121

X. *Cedar Rapids* (Benton, Iowa, Johnson, Jones, Linn, and Washington Counties): Executive Plaza Building, 4403-1st Avenue, S.E., Cedar Rapids 52402 Roger L. Reid, Administrator, (319)393-8511

XI. *Des Moines* (Boone, Dallas, Jasper, Madison, Marion, Polk, Story, and Warren Counties): 1239-8th Street, P.O. Box 99, West Des Moines 50265 William C. Ketch, Administrator, (515)281-5281 or 3870

XII. *Carroll* (Audubon, Carroll, Crawford, Green, Guthrie, and Sac Counties): 611 North West Street, P.O. Box 367, Carroll 51401   Richard E. Philpot, Administrator, (712)792-1515

XIII. *Council Bluffs* (Cass, Fremont, Harrison, Mills, Montgomery, Page, Pottawattamie, and Shelby Counties): Executive Building, Room 204, 427 East Washington Avenue, Council Bluffs 51501   Arthur W. Anderson, Administrator, (712)322-7725

XIV. *Creston* (Adair, Adams, Clarke, Decatur, Ringgold, Taylor, and Union Counties): 625 West Taylor Street, Creston 50801   Marion E. Thorpe, Administrator, (515)782-8502

XV. *Ottumwa* (Appanoose, Davis, Jefferson, Keokuk, Lucas, Mahaska, Monroe, Van Buren, Wapello, and Wayne Counties): 2849 North Court Road, P.O. Box 899, Ottumwa 52501   John L. Zumwalt, Administrator, (515)684-4639

XVI. *Burlington* (Des Moines, Henry, Lee, and Louisa Counties): 403 Witte Building, Jefferson and Main Streets, Burlington 52601   Dorothy M. Bliesener, Administrator, (319)754-6561

Department of Social Services County Offices

Adair County Mrs. Velda I. Cole, 132 South East Court Drive, P.O. Drawer A, Greenfield 50849   (515)743-2119

Adams County Bev VerSteegh (Services) and Kathy Ortlund (Income Maintenance), P.O. Box 262, Corning 50841   (515)322-4031

Allamakee County Mary C. Ellinson, Courthouse, Waukon 52172
(319)568-4583

Appanoose County John F. Cassidy, 201½ North 13th Street, Centerville 52544
(515)856-2161

Audubon County Ted E. Simpson, Courthouse, Audubon 50025
(712)563-3644

Benton County Phil Dorothy (Services) and Nancy Boddicker (Income Maintenance), 114 East 4th Street, P.O. Box 454, Vinton 52349   (319)472-4759

Black Hawk County Karl Guetzlaff (Services) and Diane Olson (Income Maintenance), 1340 Logan Avenue, Waterloo 50703   (319)291-2441

Boone County Percy E. Berry, Courthouse, Boone 50036   (515)432-6387

Bremer County Verlyn Wieden, 107-3rd Street, S.E., Waverly 50677
(319)352-4233

Buchanan County Beth Kunkle (Services) and Sandra Kress (Income Maintenance), Courthouse, Independence 50644   (319)334-6091

Buena Vista County Mrs. Majorie E. Rhenstrom, Courthouse, P.O. Box 367,
Storm Lake 50588   (712)732-5409

Butler County Verlyn Wieden, 315 North Main Street, P.O. Box 306, Allison
50602   (319)267-2594

Calhoun County Ronald Walrod, 515 Court Street, Rockwell City 50579
(712)297-8524

Carroll County James R. Krambeer, 603 North Adams Street, Carroll 51401
(712)792-4391

Cass County Mrs. Dorothy Forristall, Courthouse, Atlantic 50022
(712)243-4401

Cedar County Mrs. Lynn Dunn, P.O. Box 391, Tipton 52772   (319)886-6036

Cerro Gordo County John Collins, Courthouse, Mason City 50401
(515)423-0013

Cherokee County Gerald Hemphill, 239 West Maple Street, P.O. Box 986,
Cherokee 51012   (712)225-2588

Chickasaw County Verlyn Weiden, Courthouse, New Hampton 50659
(515)394-4315

Clarke County Mrs. Wanda Craft, P.O. Box 377, Osceola 50213   (515)342-2161

Clay County Paul K. Williams, 218 West 6th Street, P.O. Box 790, Spencer
51301   (712)262-3586

Clayton County Goerge Scofield, Courthouse Annex, Elkader 52043
(319)245-1766

Clinton County Eizabeth Kruse (Services) and Ira DeHaven (Income Maintenance), 102 South 2nd Street, Clinton 52732   (319)242-7723 or 0573

Crawford County Ralph A. Bachmann, 1216 1st Avenue, South, Denison 51442
(712)263-5668

Dallas County Joan Mathews, 121 North 9th Street, Adel 50003
(515)993-4264
Davis County Robert E. Davis, 203 South Madison Street, Bloomfield 52537
(515)664-2239
Decatur County Carl Bernahl, Courthouse, Leon 50144 (515)446-4312
Delaware County (vacant), 214 South Franklin Street, Manchester 52057
(319)927-4512
Des Moines County Paul L. Radda, 512 North Main Street, Burlington 52601
(319)753-1605
Dickinson County Mrs. Hope McCown, Courthouse, P.O. Box 246, Spirit Lake
51360 (712)336-2555
Dubuque County (vacant, Services), and Harvey Burger (Income Maintenance),
1473 Central Avenue, Dubuque 52001 (319)583-9755 or 588-2041
Emmet County Mrs. Margaret A. Klinger, Courthouse, Estherville 51334
(712)362-4751
Fayette County Zaida E. McLaury, 113 North Vine Street, West Union 52175
(319)422-5634
Floyd County David R. Turner, Courthouse, Charles City 50616
(515)228-5713
Franklin County Mrs. Labena Jones, 17-1st Street, North West, P.O. Box 58,
Hampton 50441 (515)456-4763
Fremont County Mrs. Adelaide Wahling, Courthouse, Sidney 51652
(712)374-2512
Greene County Mrs. Mildred Stanley, Courthouse, Jefferson 50129
(515)386-2143
Grundy County Leland C. Reece, P.O. Box 126, Grundy Center 50638
(319)824-6941
Guthrie County Harold H. Beane, Courthouse, Guthrie Center 50115
(515)747-3618
Hamilton County Mark Dohmes (Services) and Margie Banks (Income Mainte-
nance), P.O. Box 54, Webster City 50595 (515)832-2231
Hancock County Mrs. Sandra Steiff, Courthouse Annex, Garner 50438
(515)923-2177
Hardin County Leland C. Reece, County Office Building, Eldora 50627
(515)858-3461
Harrison County John H. Stoner, Jr., Courthouse, Logan 51546
(712)644-2460
Henry County Sandra Shaull, P.O. Box 70, Mt. Pleasant 52641 (319)385-2350
Howard County LaVern R. Buttjer, P.O. Box 117, Cresco 52136
(319)547-2860

Humboldt County Allen Grooters, 16-6th Street, Humboldt 50548
   (515)332-3383
Ida County Dennis Tobin, 2nd and Main Streets, Ida Grove 51445
   (712)364-2631
Iowa County Lee Bergen (Services) and Mardelle Klein (Income Maintenance),
   Iowa Electric Building, P.O. Box 147, Marengo 52301   (319)642-3032
Jackson County Lucile Reynolds, 201 South Main Street, Maquoketa 52060
   (319)652-4954
Jasper County Ardell Welle, Courthouse, Newton 50208   (515)792-1955
Jefferson County Robert E. Drake, 51 East Hempstead Street, P.O. Box 987,
   Fairfield 52556   (515)472-5011
Johnson County Mrs. Cleo A. Marsolais, 911 North Governor Street, Iowa City
   52240   (319)351-0200
Jones County Tom Taylor (Services) and Elfrieda White (Income Maintenance),
   Courthouse, Anamosa 52205   (319)462-3557
Keokuk County Mrs. Marian McCreery, Courthouse, Sigourney 52591
   (515)622-2090
Kossuth County Mary Helen Cogley, Courthouse, Algona 50511
   (515)295-2123 or 3343
Lee County: North Mrs. Marjorie Roost, 613-6th Street, Fort Madison 52627
   (319)372-3651
Lee County: South Mrs. Marjorie Roost, 627 Main Street, Keokuk 52632
   (319)524-1052
Linn County Loren L. Jansa (Services), Executive Plaza Building, Suite I, Cedar
   Rapids 52402   (319)398-3950; Judy Bentley (Income Maintenance), 400-
   3rd Avenue, South East, Cedar Rapids 52401   (319)398-3525
Louisa County Mrs. E. Pauline Fuller, Highway 61, P.O. Box 136, Wapello
   52653   (319)523-6351 or 8126
Lucas County William E. Gottner, P.O. Box 735, Chariton 50049
   (515)774-5071
Lyon County William Berry, Courthouse, Rock Rapids 51246   (712)472-2669
Madison County Arling E. Smith, 110 West Green Street, Winterset 50273
   (515)462-2931
Mahaska County Mrs. Shirley Robertson, Courthouse, Oskaloosa 52577
   (515)673-3496
Marion County Carroll R. Anderson, 305 East Main Street, Knoxville 50138
   (515)842-5087
Marshall County William H. McCurdy, 704 May Street, P.O. Box 694, Marshall-
   town 50158   (515)752-6741
Mills County Mrs. Mary L. Barton, Courthouse, Glenwood 51534 (712)527-4803
Mitchell County David R. Turner, 509 State Street, Osage 50461
   (515)732-5524

Monona County Dennis Tobin, 1009 Pearl Street, Onawa 51040
    (712)423-1921
Monroe County Vera Newman, 112 South Main Street, P.O. Box 166, Albia
    52531 (515)932-5187
Montgomery County Mary Jane Gassner, Courthouse, Red Oak 51566
    (712)623-4838
Muscatine County Mrs. Elizabeth Masterson, 210 West 2nd Street, Muscatine
    52761 (319)263-9302 or 7644
O'Brien County Mrs. Jean Peterson, P.O. Box 400, Primgahr 51245
    (712)757-5135
Osceola County Mrs. Jean Peterson, Courthouse, Sibley 51249 (712)754-3622
Page County Allice Grafft, 307 East Washington Street, P.O. Box 215, Clarinda
    51632 (712)542-5111
Palo Alto County Mrs. E. Virginia Barringer, 2217 Main Street, P.O. Box 188,
    Emmetsburg 50536 (712)852-3523
Plymouth County Gerald G. Hemphill, 22-1st Street, North East, P.O. Box 630,
    LeMars 51031 (712)546-7076
Pocahontas County Allen Grooters, Courthouse, Pocahontas 50574
    (712)335-3565
Polk County Quenten L. Emery, 1249-8th Street, P.O. Box 756, Des Moines
    50303 (515)284-6495
Pottawattamie County Daniel Sparks (Services) and Marjorie Lidgett (Income
    Maintenance), 231 Pearl Street, Council Bluffs 51501 (712)328-5689 or
    5722
Poweshiek County Sue Longhurst (Services) and Ruby Simmerman (Income
    Maintenance), 819 Commercial Street, Grinnel 50112 (515)236-3149
Ringgold County Larry L. Brown, Courthouse, Mount Ayr 50854
    (515)464-2247
Sac County Glenn E. Major, 112 South 5th Street, P.O. Box 188, Sac City
    50583 (712)662-7776
Scott County Gary Redling (Services) and Mildred Whipple (Income Mainte-
    nance), 808 West River Drive, Davenport 52902 (319)326-8680
Shelby County Barry R. McKinley, 1012-6th Street, P.O. Box 126, Harlan
    51537 (712)755-3145
Sioux County William J. Berry, 215 Central Avenue, South East, Orange City
    51041 (712)737-2943
Story County Mrs. Florence Walter, Courthouse, 900-6th Street, Nevada 50201
    (515)382-6581
Tama County Monica Murray (Services) and Ruby Simmerman (Income Mainte-
    nance), 129 West High Street, Toledo 52342 (515)484-3406
Taylor County Fred Sheilds, Courthouse, Bedford 50833 (712)523-2129
Union County Harry Green, Courthouse, Creston 50801 (515)782-2173

Van Buren County Mrs. Marilyn G. Boley, Roberts Memorial Hall, R.R. 1, Box 22, Keosauqua 52565 (319)293-3791

Wapello County D. B. Arnold, Courthouse, Ottumwa 52501 (515)684-6586

Warren County Karen DeVore (Services) and Kathryn Wood (Income Maintenance), 215 Salem Street, Indianola 50125 (515)961-5353

Washington County Milan K. Thompson, 212 North Iowa Street, P.O. Box 519, Washington 52353 (319)653-5483

Wayne County Mrs. Mildreth M. Murphy, Courthouse, Corydon 50060 (515)872-1820

Webster County Mrs. Winifred Pray, 602-3rd Avenue, North, P.O. Box 1, Fort Dodge 50501 (515)573-8169

Winnebago County Dandra Steiff, 141 East K Street, P.O. Box 303, Forest City 50436 (515)582-3271

Winneshiek County Virginia L. Leidahl, P.O. Box 286, Decorah 52101 (319)382-2928

Woodbury County Ralph F. Klocke, 808-5th Street, Sioux City 51101 (712)279-6540

Worth County Grace Christiansen, 849 Central Avenue, Northwood 50459 (515)324-1013

Wright County Mrs. Roberta Bygness, Courthouse, Clarion 50525 (515)532-6645

Kansas

Reporting Requirements

Persons mandated to report (compulsory) when reasonable cause to believe a child is or has been subjected to abuse or neglect: persons licensed to practice the healing arts; dentists; persons in postgraduate training programs in the healing arts; certified psychologists; licensed social workers examining, attending, or treating a child under age 18; every licensed professional or practical nurse examining or caring for such child in the absence of the doctor; every school teacher, administrator, or employee; any law enforcement officer (director of hospital or facility shall report rather than staff)

Permissive: all other persons who have reason to believe that a child has been injured through abuse

Form of report and when made: prompt oral; written if requested

To whom report is made: juvenile court of the county, or the department of social rehabilitation services

Penalties: knowing and willful violation is a class B misdemeanor

Immunities: full civil and criminal immunity for reporting without malice

Child Abuse Legislation

Citation: KSA Chap. 231, §38-821; HB 2543
Year enacted: 1975
Effective date: April 23, 1975
Purpose of legislation: mandatory reporting, yes
Reportable age: 0–18 years

Definitions: physical or mental injury, causing of deterioration, sexual abuse, or
   maltreatment; endangerment of health, morals, emotional or well-being
Education/school report: mandatory reporting, yes
Immunity: yes
Mandatory investigation: yes, promptly
Confidentiality of records: yes; penalty: no specific provision
Cooperation with law courts, state agencies: no specific provision
Guardian ad litem: yes
Administrative proceedings, trained personnel, facilities: no specific provision
Dissemination of information: no specific provision

Programs and Agencies

Requests for general information on child welfare, evaluation of families living in
Kansas for the adoptive placement of a child residing in another state, supervision of children from other states or countries placed for adoption with families living in Kansas, and requests from private agencies pertaining to the
interstate placement of children should be directed to:

> Division of Children and Youth
> Department of Social and Rehabilitation Services
> State Office Building
> Topeka 66612

Kansas Department of Social and Rehabilitation Services

> State Office Building
> Topeka 66612
> Telephone: (913)296-3959
> Robert C. Harder, Secretary (913)296-3271
> Charles V. Hamm, General Consultant and Administrator, Interstate Com-
>   pact on Juveniles, (913)296-3967

Department of Social and Rehabilitation Services Area Offices

Chanute (Nesho, Montgomery, Wilson, and Woodson Counties): 2nd and Santa
   Fe Streets, P.O. Box 537, Chanute 66720 (316)431-3390; John Kirkwood,
   Director; Pauline Flynn, Chief of Social Services; Ervin Brune, Chief of
   Income Maintenance
Emporia (Chase, Dickinson, Lyon, Marion, and Morris Counties): 15 East 6th
   Avenue, Emporia 66801 (316)342-2505; Jol Myers, Director; Arlene
   Schroeder, Chief of Social Services; Phyllis Smith, Chief of Income
   Maintenance

Garden City (Clark, Finney, Ford, Gray, Greeley, Hamilton, Haskell, Hodgeman, Kearny, Lane, Meade, Ness, Scott, Seward, Stevens, and Wichita Counties): 1513½ East Fulton Street, Garden City 67846 (316)276-8228; James Claussen, Director; Ruth Walker, Chief of Social Services; Melvin Fager, Chief of Income Maintenance

Hays (Cheyenne, Decatur, Ellis, Grove, Graham, Logan, Norton, Osborne, Phillips, Rawlins, Rooks, Russell, Sheridan, Sherman, Smith, Thomas, Trego, and Wallace Counties): 1503 Vine Street, P.O. Box 688, Hays 67601 (913)628-1066; Gene Dawson, Director; David Schmidt, Chief of Social Services; Edward Grass, Chief of Income Maintenance

Hiawatha (Atchison, Brown, Doniphan, Jackson, and Jefferson Counties): 810 Oregon Street, Hiawatha 66434 (913)742-7186; Orveda Lewallen, Director; Don Madson, Chief of Social Services; Irvin Cantrell, Chief of Income Maintenance

Hutchinson (Harvey, McPherson, Reno, and Rice Counties): 129 West B. Street, Hutchinson 67501 (316)663-5731; William Paske, Director; Doris Gough, Chief of Social Services; James Johnson, Chief of Income Maintenance

Junction City (Clay, Geary, Marshall, Nemaha, Pottawatomie, Riley, Wabaunesee, and Washington Counties): 235 West 7th Street, P.O. Box 824, Junction City 66441 (913)762-5445; Faith Spencer, Director; Flordie Pettis, Chief of Social Services; Barbara Dunlap, Chief of Income Maintenance

Kansas City (Wyandotte County): I Gateway Center, P.O. Box 1248, Kansas City 66101 (913)371-6700; James Wann, Director; Hilde Farley, Chief of Social Services; Michael Van Landingham, Chief of Income Maintenance

Olathe (Johnson and Leavenworth Counties): Patrons Bank Building, Patrons Plaza, Olathe 66061 (913)782-6600; William Nesbit, Director; Sylvia Roberts, Chief of Social Services; Betty Friauf, Chief of Income Maintenance

Oswatomie (Anderson, Coffey, Franklin, Linn, Miami, and Osage Counties): P.O. Box 1000, Osowatomie 66064 (913)755-2162; Dorothy Martin, Director; William Pickering, Chief of Social Services; Georgia Wright, Chief of Income Maintenance

Parsons (Cherokee and Labette Counties): 122 South 22nd Street, P.O. Box 914, Parsons 67357 (316)421-4500; Martin Semonick, Director; Art Evans, Chief of Social Services; O. D. Sperry, Chief of Income Maintenance

Pittsburg (Allen, Bourbon, and Crawford Counties): 20th and Highway 69 Bypass, P.O. Box 420, Pittsburg 66762 (316)231-5300; Herbert Hickman, Director; Michael Harrison, Chief of Social Services; Kenneth Harton, Chief of Income Maintenance

Pratt (Barber, Barton, Commanche, Edwards, Harper, Kingman, Kiowa, Pawnee, Pratt, Rush, Stafford, and Sumner Counties): 420 South Jackson Street,

Pratt 67124   (316)672-5631; Warren Biel, Director; John Winderlin, Chief
of Social Services; Lester Lyden, Chief of Income Maintenance

Salina (Cloud, Ellsworth, Jewell, Lincoln, Mitchell, Ottwa, Republic, and Saline
Counties): 712 South Ohio Street, P.O. Box 86, Salina 67401
(913)827-9386; June Garrett, Director; Miriam Harper, Chief of Social
Services; Marlys Mattingly, Chief of Income Maintenance

Topeka (Douglas and Shawnee Counties): 2700 West 6th Street, P.O. Box 1424,
Topeka 66606   (913)235-9521; Cora Catt, Director; Theodore Mintun,
Chief of Social Services; Margaret Owens, Chief of Income Maintenance

Wichita (Sedgwick County): 535 North Main Street, P.O. Box 1620, Wichita
67203   (316)268-7440; John Alquest, Director; Velma Butler, Chief of
Social Services; Keith Massie, Chief of Income Maintenance

Winfield (Butler, Chautauqua, Cowley, Elk, and Greenwood Counties): Court-
house, P.O. Box 735, Winfield 67156   (316)221-6400; Billie Orr, Director;
Barbara Blue, Chief of Social Services; Marjorie Weaver, Chief of Income
Maintenance

Kentucky

Reporting Requirements

Persons mandated to report (compulsory) when reasonable cause to believe a child is or has been subjected to abuse or neglect: physician, osteopath, nurse, teacher, school administrator, social worker, coroner, medical examiner, or other persons having reasonable cause to suspect (administrator or director of hospital or other facility shall report rather than staff); death of the child does not relieve responsibility for reporting the circumstances surrounding the death

Permissive: none

Form of report and when made: immediate oral, followed as soon as possible with written

To whom report is made: representative of the department of human resources

Penalties: none

Immunities: full civil and criminal immunity for report upon probable cause

Child Abuse Legislation

Citation: KRS 199.335, 208.020, 208.990
Year enacted: 1964
Effective date: March 19, 1964
Purpose of legislation: mandatory reporting, yes
Reportable age: 0-18 years
Definitions: severe malnutrition; sexual abuse; severe neglect; serious physical
    injury; injuries other than by accidental means; gross neglect which would
    affect either the physical, mental, or emotional well-being; or death
Education/school report: mandatory reporting, yes

Immunity: yes
Mandatory investigation: search under warrant
Confidentiality of records: no specific provision; penalty: no specific provision
Cooperation with law courts, state agencies: no specific provision
Guardian ad litem: no specific provision
Administrative proceedings, trained personnel, facilities: no specific provision
Dissemination of information: no specific provision

Programs and Agencies

Where to write: The Department for Human Resources asks that inquiries concerning public assistance be addressed to:

    Bureau for Social Insurance
    Department for Human Resources
    Capitol Annex, Room 201
    Frankfort 40601

Inquiries concerning social services (except for Jefferson County) should be addressed to:

    Bureau for Social Services
    Department for Human Resources
    403 Wapping St.
    Frankfort 40601

Inquiries concerning social services in Jefferson County should be addressed to:

    Metropolitan Social Services Department
    Old First National Bank Building
    216 S. 5th Street
    Louisville 40202

Kentucky Department for Human Resources

    Capitol Annex
    Frankfort 40601
    (502)564-6785 for direct dial number
    C. Leslie Dawson, Secretary (502)564-7130
    Howard C. Lawson, Executive Assistant (502)564-7130

Office for Policy and Budget

    Joseph E. Smith, Administrator (502)564-7130

Office of the Ombudsman

316 Wilkinson Street
Frankfort 40601
Jack Reeves, Ombudsman (502)564-5497

Office of the Counsel

Executive Building, Room 100
209 St. Clair Street
Frankfort 40601
(502)564-7900
Kenneth A. Howe, Jr., General Consultant
John Godfrey, Assistant General Consultant

Bureau for Social Services

403 Wapping Street
Frankfort 40601
Jack Lewis, Commissioner (502)564-4650
Margaret Hockensmith, Executive Assistant (502)564-4650

Division for Field Services

Max Jackson, Director (502)564-3440

Bureau for Social Services Regional Offices

A. Western (District I—Purchase: Ballard, Calloway, Carlisle, Fulton, Graves,
Hickman, McCracken, and Marshall Counties; District II—Pennyrile: Caldwell,
Christian, Crittenden, Hopkins, Livingston, Lyon, Muhlenberg, Todd, and Trigg
Counties; District III—Green River: Daviess, Hancock, Henderson, McLean,
Ohio, Union, and Webster Counties; District IV—Barren River: Allen, Barren,
Butler, Edmonson, Hart, Logan, Metcalfe, Monroe, Simpson, and Warren
Counties: District V—Lincoln Trail: Breckinridge, Grayson, Hardin, Larue,
Marion, Meade, Nelson, and Washington Counties)

Western State Hospital, Hopkinsville 42240   Ben McClellan, Administrator,
(502)886-9427

District I—Purchase: Guthrie Building, 517 Broadway, P.O. Box 264,
Paducah 42001   Mary Lee King, Manager, (502)442-9191
District II—Pennyrile: Western State Hospital, Hopkinsville 42240   Joseph
Suitor, Manager, (502)885-6143

District III—Green River: DHR Building, 311 West 2nd Street, Owensboro
42301   William Horton, Manager, (502)685-4491
District IV—Barren River: 1010 College Street, P.O. Box 448, Bowling
Green 42101   Kenneth Royse, Manager, (502)781-2740
District V—Lincoln Trail: Carnes Building, 529 North Miles Street, Eliza-
bethtown 42701   Richard Appling, Manager, (502)769-2381

B. North Central (District VI—Kentuckiana: Bullitt, Henry, Jefferson, Oldham,
Shelby, Spencer, and Trimble Counties)

981 South 3rd Street, Louisville 40203   Nancy Fontenot, Administrator
(502)584-8351

District VI—Kentuckiana: Legal Arts Building, Room 400, 7th and Market
   Streets, Louisville 40202   Betty Triplett, Manager, Area A (502)585-5911,
   ext. 460; Nathaniel Green, Manager, Area D (502)585-5911, ext. 75
District VI—Kentuckiana (Areas B and C): 981 South 3rd Street, Louisville
   40203   Elizabeth Bealmear, Manager, Area B (502)588-4376; Mary J.
   Renner, Manager, Area C (502)588-4403

C. Southeastern (District XII—Kentucky River: Breathitt, Knott, Lee, Leslie,
Letcher, Owsley, Perry, and Wolfe Counties; District XIII—Cumberland Valley:
Bell, Clay, Harlan, Jackson, Knox, Laurel, Rockcastle, and Whitley Counties;
District XIV—Lake Cumberland: Adair, Casey, Clinton, Cumberland Green,
McCleary, Pulaski, Russell, Taylor, and Wayne Counties)

Route 2, Box 4, London 40741   Jim Roberts, Administrator (606)864-5121,
   ext. 45

District XII—Kentucky River: Greyhound Bus Station, P.O. Box 987, Hazard
   41701   Gene Rice, Manager, (606)439-2346
District XIII—Cumberland Valley: London TB Hospital, Route 2, Box 4,
   London 40741   Jim Wood Manager, (606)864-5121, ext. 45
District XIV—Lake Cumberland: 207 West Mt. Vernon Street, P.O. Box 619,
   Somerset 42501   Gerald Rossell, Manager (606)679-4436

D. Northeastern (District VII—Northern: Boone, Campbell, Carroll, Gallatin,
Grant, Kenton, Owen, and Pendleton Counties: District VIII—Buffalo Trace:
Bracken, Fleming, Lewis, Mason, and Robertson Counties; District IX—Gateway:
Bath, Menifee, Montgomery, Morgan, and Rowan Counties; District X—Fiveco:
Boyd, Carter, Elliott, Greenup, and Lawrence Counties; District XI—Big Sandy:
Floyd, Johnson, Magoffin, Martin, and Pike Counties; District XV—Bluegrass:
Anderson, Bourbon, Boyle, Clark, Estill, Fayette, Franklin, Garrard, Harrison,

Jessamine, Lincoln, Madison, Mercer, Nicholas, Powell, Scott, and Woodford Counties)

710 West High Street, Lexington 40502   Max Jackson, Administrator (606) 252-4037

District VII—Northern: 303 Court Street, Covington 41011   William Neuroth, Manager (606)291-1470

District VIII—Buffalo Trace: P.O. Box 446, Morehead 40351   Gladys McCartney, Manager (606)784-6687

District IX—Gateway: (same as District VII)

District X—Fiveco: P.O. Box 343, Ashland 41101   Ronald Moatz, Manager (606)324-4131

District XI—Big Sandy: 18 Front Street, Prestonburg 41563   George Quisenberry, Manager (606)886-6884

District XV—Bluegrass: 710 West High Street, Lexington 40508   Ted Marshall, Manager (606)252-3587 or 4037

Louisiana

Reporting Requirements

Persons mandated to report (compulsory) when reasonable cause to believe a child is or has been subjected to abuse or neglect: any person having cause to believe that a child's physical or mental health has been or may be further affected by abuse or neglect, such as licensed physicians, interns, or residents; nurses; hospital staff members; teachers; social workers; and other persons or agencies having responsibility for care

Permissive: any other person having cause to believe that the child's welfare has been or may be further affected by abuse or neglect

Form of report and when made: immediate oral; written, within five days

To whom report is made: parish child welfare unit, parish agency responsible for the protection of juveniles, or any local or state law enforcement agency

Penalties: implied that a knowing and willful failure to report is misdemeanor, up to $500 and/or six months

Immunities: civil and criminal immunity for good faith report

Child Abuse Legislation

Citation: LRS §14;403(6,7), 14:463
Year enacted: 1975
Effective date: September 12, 1975
Purpose of legislation: mandatory reporting, yes
Reportable age: 0–18 years
Definitions: physical or mental injury or causing deterioration; shall include

exploitation or overwork, to the extent that health, moral, or emotional
well-being is endangered
Education/school report: mandatory reporting, yes
Immunity: yes
Mandatory investigation: yes, promptly
Confidentiality of records: yes; penalty: misdemeanor
Cooperation with law courts, state agencies: no specific provision
Guardian ad litem: yes
Administrative proceedings, trained personnel, facilities: no specific provision
Dissemination of information: no specific provision

Programs and Agencies

Where to write: Public assistance correspondence with out-of-state agencies is
handled directly by the local offices of the Division of Family Services, and inquiries should be sent to the appropriate local office. If the office is not known,
the inquiry (in triplicate, or in cases involving more than one parish, a sufficient
number of additional copies) may be sent for forwarding to:

Division of Family Services
Health and Human Resources Administration
P.O. Box 44065
Baton Rouge 70804

Louisiana Health and Human Resources Administration

P.O. Box 44215
Baton Rouge 70804
William H. Stewert, M.D., Commissioner (504)389-5796
H. K. Sweeney, Department Commissioner (504)389-5366
Garland L. Bonin, Assistant Commissioner for Federal Programs
(504)389-6207

Division of Family Services
P.O. Box 44065
Baton Rouge 70804
Roy E. Westerfield, Director (504)389-6036
Alvis D. Roberts, Department Director (504)389-6036
George E. Clark, Special Assistant to the Director (504)389-6036
William M. Hightower, Special Assistant to the Director (504)389-6592
Miss Jane Ann Atkinson, Planning and Policy Formulation (504)389-6561
George W. Richards, Research and Statistics (504)389-6671

Operations

Mrs. Olive H. Randall, Department Assistant Director (504)389-6036
(vacant), Administrative Coordinator
Mrs. Jeanne G. Tregre, Management Analyst (504)389-2435 or 6423
Linden D. Claybrook, Emergency Welfare Services Coordinator
(504)289-2435
Don Fuller, Administrator, Social Services (504)389-5571

Division of Family Services Area Offices

Alexandria (Avoyelles, Grant, LaSalle, Natchitoches, Rappides, Sabine, Vernon,
and Winn Parishes): 900 Murray Street, P.O. Box 832, Alexandria 71301
Telephone: (318)487-4511; Miss Mathilde Bradford, Program Consultant,
Social Services; Mrs. Barbara Anderson, Program Consultant, Food Stamps;
(vacant), Program Consultant, Assistance Payments

Amite (East Feliciana, Livingston, St. Helena, St. Tammany, Tangipahoa, and
Washington Parishes): P.O. Box 206, Amite 70422   Telephone:
(504)748-2421; Maurice Badon, Jr., Program Consultant, Social Services;
Nick Lascaro, Program Consultant, Food Stamps; Gary M. Varnado, Program Consultant, Assistance Payments

Baton Rouge (Ascension, East Baton Rouge, Iberville, Pointe Coupee, West
Baton Rouge, and West Feliciana Parishes): Watkins Building, 2843 Vic-
toria Drive, Baton Rouge 70805   Telephone: (504)389-7161; Mrs. Laura
Strahorn, Program Consultant, Social Services; Louis Broussard, Program
Consultant, Food Stamps; Mrs. Carolyn Hopkins, Program Consultant,
Assistance Payments

Lafayette (Evangeline, Iberia, Lafayette, St. Landry, St. Martin, St. Mary, and
Vermilion Parishes): 302 Jefferson Street, Lafayette 70501   Telephone:
(318)233-4211; Miss Louise E. Bourne, Program Consultant, Social Services;
Ben A. Bearden, Program Consultant, Food Stamps; John S. Gardiner, Program Consultant, Assistance Payments

Lake Charles (Acadia, Allen, Beauregard, Calcasieu, Cameron, and Jefferson
Davis Parishes): 710 Ryan Street, P.O. Box 1807, Lake Charles 70601
Telephone: (318)433-0421; Mrs. Earline O. Coody, Program Consultant,
Social Services; Kenneth L. Reynolds, Program Consultant, Food Stamps;
Mrs. Pauline Rogers, Program Consultant, Assistance Payments

Monroe (Caldwell, Jackson, Lincoln, Morehouse, Ouachita, and Union Parishes):
State Office Building, 4th Floor, 122 St. John Street, Monroe 71201
Telephone: (318)322-6121; Terry McPhearson, Program Consultant, Social
Services; Don Wallace, Program Consultant, Food Stamps; (vacant), Program
Consultant, Assistance Payments

Orleans (Jefferson, Orleans, Plaquemines, and St. Bernard Parishes): 8000 For-
shey Street, P.O. Box 13276, Broadmoor Station, New Orleans 70185

Telephone: (504)486-3761; Miss Catherine Oberholtzer, Program Consultant, Social Services; Claude Carbo, Program Consultant, Food Stamps; (vacant), Program Consultant, Assistance Payments

Shreveport (Bienville, Bossier, Caddo, Claiborne, De Soto, Red River, and Webster Parishes): State Office Building, Room 306, 1237 Murphy Street, Shreveport 71101 Telephone: (318)424-6461; Miss Beatrice Enloe, Program Consultant, Social Services; James D. Simms, Program Consultant, Food Stamps; Marshall McKenzie, Program Consultant, Assistance Payments

Tallulah (Catahoula, Concordia, East Carroll, Franklin, Madison, Richland, Tensas, and West Carroll Parishes): State Office Building, 4th Floor, 122 St. John Street, Monroe 71201 Telephone: (318)322-6121; Miss Janice Robinson, Program Consultant, Social Services; Thomas H. Randell, Program Consultant, Food Stamps; James Milam, Program Consultant, Assistance Payments

Thibodaux (Assumption, Lafourche, St. Charles, St. James, St. John, and Terrebonne Parishes): 1000 Mabel Street, P.O. Box 797, Thibodaux 70301 Telephone: (504)447-7277; Mrs. Madeline A. Pineda, Program Consultant, Social Services; Joseph W. Harrer, Program Consultant, Food Stamps; Mrs. Dorothy P. Maness, Program Consultant, Assistance Payments

Division of Family Services Local Offices

Acadia Parish G. Rodney Young, 614 North Avenue G, P.O. Drawer 1060, Crowley 70526 (318)783-4540

Allen Parish Yvonne S. Smith, P.O. Drawer 280, Oberlin 70655 (318)639-4336 or 2596

Ascension Parish Celine M. Ganel, 204 Mississippi Street, P. O. Box 590, Donaldsonville 70346 (504)473-3825

Assumption Parish Philip A. Vitale, P.O. Box 39, Napoleonville 70390 (504)369-6406 and 6495

Avoyelles Parish Thomas E. Pegg, 303 South Main Street, Marksville 71351 (318)252-7557 and 6546

Beauregard Parish Edwina W. Courtney, 239 East 1st Street, P.O. Drawer 648, DeRidder 70634 (318)463-8601 and 3002

Bienville Parish Elbie M. Hall, P.O. Box 598, Arcadia 71001 (318)263-2815

Bossier Parish Ruth Longshore, P.O. Box 158, Benton 71006 (318)965-2311 and 2348

Caddo Parish Mr. Johnnie Bradley, 1237 Murphy Street, State Office Building, Room 104, Shreveport 71101 (318)424-6461

Calcasieu Parish Vincent J. Lamendola, 710 Ryan Street, P.O. Box 5245, Drew Station, Lake Charles 70601 (318)433-4622

Caldwell Parish Harrell C. Crockett, P.O. Box 738, Columbia 71418 (318)649-2673 and 2548

Cameron Parish Vincent J. Lamendola, P.O. Box 5245, Drew Station, Lake
   Charles 70601   (318)433-4622

Catahoula Parish Conrad Pierce, P.O. Box 306, Jonesville 71343
   (318)339-5011

Claiborne Parish Hardy A. Louviere, 500 North 3rd Street, P.O. Drawer 210,
   Homer 71040   (318)927-3518

Concordia Parish Mary M. Arnold, 301 Mississippi Avenue, Ferriday 71334
   (318)757-4547

DeSoto Parish Robert J. Brown, 405 Polk Street, P.O. Box 978, Mansfield
   71052   (318)872-0935

East Baton Rouge Parish Evelyn J. Yost, 1928 North Riverside Mall, P.O. Box
   3098, Baton Rouge 70821   (504)383-1500

East Carroll Parish Marie B. Parker, 301 1st Street, Lake Providence 71254
   (318)559-2039 and 2904

East Feliciana Parish William F. Town, P.O. Box 926, Clinton 70722
   (504)683-5142 and 5896

Evangeline Parish Willis Knighten, 410 West LaSalle Street, Ville Platte 70586
   (318)363-2155

Franklin Parish Arrie Lee Schooler, Loop Road, P.O. Box 551, Winnsboro
   71295   (318)435-5011

Grant Parish Edith Skinner, 513-8th Street, Colfax 71417   (318)627-3227

Iberia Parish Gilbert Ardoin, New Courthouse Annex Building, P.O. Box 219,
   Providence Street, New Iberia 70561   (318)365-8141

Iberville Parish Mrs. Mary G. Reinhardt, 721 Chinn Street, Plaquemine 70764
   (505)687-4315

Jackson Parish Jimmy F. Boyd, P.O. Drawer 610, Jonesboro 71251
   (318)259-2411 and 4401

Jefferson Parish Jean N. Abbott, 1111 Newton Street, P.O. Box 70, Gretna
   70053   (318)362-3000

Jefferson Davis Parish Margaret F. Ford, 742 East Plaquemine Street, P.O. Box
   801, Jennings 70546   (318)824-3694 or 6882

Lafayette Parish Harrison M. Kleimpeter, 302 Jefferson Street, Lafayette
   70501   (318)233-4211

Lafourche Parish Mary Lou Mire, 1000 Mable Street, P.O. Box 688, Thibodaux
   70301   (504)447-7380 and 446-6322

LaSalle Parish Norman O. Hicks, P.O. Drawer EE, Jena 71342   (318)992-4181

Lincoln Parish Ernest G. Harris, 802 East Georgia Street, P.O. Box 1366,
   Ruston 71270   (318)255-2143

Livingston Parish Dolores M. Clayton, P.O. Box 188, Livingston 70754
   (504)686-2261

Madison Parish Lloyd T. Erwin, P.O. Box 952, Tallulah 71282   (318)574-4524
   and 4530

Morehouse Parish Eddie J. Blackard, 641 East Hickory Street, P.O. Box 630, Bastrop 71220 (318)281-0621

Natchitoches Parish H. Shelton Johnson, 4th and Trudeau, P.O. Box 839, Natchitoches 71457 (318)352-6448

Orleans Parish Howard K. Sommers, 2601 Tulane Avenue, P.O. Box 51870, New Orleans 70151 (504)821-5200; 915 Lafayette Street, New Orleans 70113 (504)529-2771; 904 Summer Street, New Orleans 70114 (504)362-3030

Ouatchita Parish Rubye R. Taylor, 1505 North 19th Street, P.O. Box 1432, Monroe 71201 (318)325-6321

Plaquemines Parish Jessie C. Becnel, 2314 Belle Chasse Highway, South, P.O. Box 98, Belle Chasse 70037 (318)394-4370

Pointe Coupee Parish Marilyn B. Hess, 120 Almo Street, P.O. Box 130, New Roads 70760 (504)638-6324, 8056 and 3444

Rapides Parish James D. Peterson, State Office Building, 900 Murray Street, P.O. Box 4137, Alexandria 71301 (318)487-4511

Red River Parish Laura S. Duco, Red River Parish Administration Building, Carroll Street and Highway 71, P.O. Drawer I, Coushatta 71019 (318)932-4035

Richaland Parish Marjorie Holloway, Eugene Street, P.O. Box 837, Rayville 71269 (318)728-3253

Sabine Parish Marilyn M. Fullerton, P.O. Box 152, Many 71449 (318)256-2047

St. Bernard Parish Wendell S. Rundle, P.O. Box 235, Arabi 70032 (504)271-3452

St. Charles District Parish (all parts of St. Charles, St. John and St. James Parishes on southwest bank of Mississippi River) Sybil C. Pedeaux, P.O. Box 453, Hahnville 70057 (504)783-2242

St. Helena Parish N. Henry Bennett, P.O. Box 400, Grennsburg 70411 (504)222-6155

St. James Parish See St. John District and St. Charles District

St. John District (all parts of St. Charles, St. John, and St. James on northeast bank of Mississippi River) Emily C. Guidry, 102 West 4th Street, P.O. Drawer W, Reserve 70084 (504)536-1199 or 1190

St. Landry Parish Cecil C. Duplechin, 525 North Lombard Street, P.O. Box 1060, Opelousas 70570 (318)942-5611

St. Martin Parish Lite B. Bienvenu, P.O. Box 191, St. Martinville 70582 (318)394-3055

St. Mary Parish Evelyn C. Loustalot, 613-2nd Street, Franklin 70538 (318)828-0310

St. Tammany Parish Jerry R. Galloway, P.O. Box 788, Covington 70433 (504)892-4410

Tangipahoa Parish Isabelle K. Scarle, P.O. Box 188, Amite 70422
(504)748-8134

Tensas Parish Lucy M. Arnold, P.O. Box 6186, St. Joseph 71366
(318)766-3277

Terrebonne Parish Raynold J. Ponville, 511 Russell Street, P.O. Box 2118,
Houma 70361 (504)872-6871

Union Parish Edward Y. Burns, P.O. Box 156, Farmerville 71241
(318)368-3166

Vermilion Parish Annette N. Dauterive, 107 North Jefferson Street, P.O. Box
160, Abbeville 70510 (318)893-3742

Vernon Parish Mary A. Cleveland, P.O. Box 370, Leesville 71446
(318)239-3813

Washington Parish Porter B. Lee, 348 Jackson Street, P.O. Box 760, Bogalusa
70427 (504)732-7141

Webster Parish Viola Mansell, Courthouse Building, P.O. Drawer 820, Minden
71055 (318)377-4354 and 7470

West Baton Rouge Parish Ethel B. Marionneaux, 724 North Jefferson Avenue,
P.O. Box 560, Pt. Allen 70767 (504)344-6731

West Carroll Parish J. W. Alsbrooks, P.O. Box 370, Oak Grove 71263
(318)428-3211 and 2175

West Feliciana Parish Douglas Young, Public Welfare Building, P.O. Box 280,
St. Francisville 70775 (604)635-3374

Winn Parish Jerry G. Fullerton, 110 North Abel Street, P.O. Box 231, Winnfield
71483 (504)628-4751 and 4322

Maine

Reporting Requirements

Persons mandated to report (compulsory) when reasonable cause to believe a child is or has been subjected to abuse or neglect: physician, resident, intern, medical examiner, dentist, osteopath, chiropractor, podiatrist, registered or licensed practical nurse, Christian Science practitioner, teacher, school official, social worker, psychologist, child care personnel, mental health professional, or law enforcement official (director reports instead of staff at a facility)

Permissive: any person may report if reasonable belief or cause to suspect

Form of report and when made: immediate oral; written, within 48 hours if requested

To whom report is made: department of health and welfare, also to appropriate medical examiner in case of death

Penalties: knowing and willful failure to report, if that child has been subject to abuse or neglect which results in a conviction of a person, results in misdemeanor penalty for such failure, fine of not more than $500

Immunities: good faith in reporting is presumed; civil and criminal immunity for such reporting

Child Abuse Legislation

Citation: MRSA Tit. 22, §3851-60
Year enacted: 1975
Effective date: April 21, 1975
Purpose of legislation: mandatory reporting, yes
Reportable age: 0–18 years
Definitions: physical or mental injury, sexual abuse, negligent treatment, or maltreatment
Education/school report: mandatory reporting, yes
Immunity: yes, civil/criminal

Mandatory investigation: yes, no specific time frame
Confidentiality of records: yes; penalty: misdemeanor
Cooperation with law courts, state agencies: no specific provision
Guardian ad litem: yes
Administrative proceedings, trained personnel, facilities: no specific provision
Dissemination of information: no specific provision

Programs and Agencies

Where to write: The Department of Human Services will act as a forwarding center for inquiries. Letters should be addressed to:

David E. Smith, Commissioner
Department of Human Services
State House
Augusta 04333

Social Services Unit

Telephone: (207)289-3456
Edgar J. Merrill, Manager
Freda Plumley, Consultant, Substitute Care
Stephen Ludwig, Group Child Care and Licensing Consultant
Anne Kalwell, Manager, Day Care and Foster Care Licensing
George Odencrantz, Adult Protective Services Manager
Carolyn McTeague, Consultant, Child Protective Services
Mildred Hart, Early Childhood Program Consultant

Research Evaluation & Planning Unit

Clyde Nickerson, Manager (207)289-3356

Department of Human Services Regional Offices

I. Portland (Cumberland and York Counties): 509 Forest Avenue, Portland 04101   James Tierney, Director (207)774-4581
II. Lewiston (Androscoggin, Franklin, and Oxford Counties): 179 Lisbon Street, Lewiston 04240   Douglas Hall, Director (207)783-9151
III. Augusta (Kennebec, Knox, Lincoln, Sagadahoc, Somerset, and Waldo Counties): Vickery Hill Building, 11 Weston Street, Augusta 04333   Harry Bedigan, Director (207)289-2851
IV. Bangor (Hancock, Penobscot, Piscataquis, and Washington Counties): 117 Broadway, Bangor 04401   Ronald Schoppee, Director (207)947-0511
V. Houlton (Aroostook County): 5 Mechanic Street, Houlton 04730   Arthur Smith, Director (207)532-9531

Maryland

Reporting Requirements

Persons mandated to report (compulsory) when reasonable cause to believe a child is or has been subjected to abuse or neglect: every health practitioner (broadly defined), educator (teacher or administrator), social worker, or law enforcement official who contacts, examines, attends, or treats a child and has reason to believe that the child is abused; a person other than those in the above category who has similar reason to suspect abuse shall also report

Permissive: none

Form of report and when made: oral, followed by written within 48 hours

To whom report is made: local department of social services, or the appropriate law enforcement agency

Penalties: none

Immunities: full civil and criminal immunity for good faith report

Child Abuse Legislation

Citation: MCA Art. 27-35(a)-(i)
Year enacted: 1974
Effective date: July 1, 1974
Purpose of legislation: mandatory reporting, yes
Reportable age: 0–18 years
Definitions: physical injury or injuries sustained by a child as a result of cruel or inhumane treatment or as a result of malicious act or acts by any parent, adoptive parent, or other person who has permanent or temporary care, custody or responsibility of minor child; any sexual abuse of a child, whether physical injuries are sustained or not
Education/school reports: mandatory reporting, yes
Immunity: yes
Mandatory investigation: yes, no specific time frame

Confidentiality of records: no specific provision; penalty: no specific provision
Cooperation with law courts, state agencies: no specific provision
Guardian ad litem: no specific provision
Administrative proceedings, trained personnel, facilities: no specific provision
Dissemination of information: no specific provision

Programs and Agencies

Where to write: Inquiries should be addressed to the local departments of social services except in the following instances. Inquiries concerning the ability of relatives to provide financial support should be sent to the relatives themselves. Inquiries regarding the interstate placement of minor children in unrelated homes should be sent in duplicate to:

Social Services Administration
Department of Human Resources
1315 St. Paul Street
Baltimore 21202

Maryland Department of Human Resources

1100 North Eutaw Street, Baltimore 21201
Richard A. Batterton, Secretary (301)383-5528
William G. Sykes, Department Secretary (301)383-3472
Joel J. Rabin, Assistant Attorney General and Consultant (301)383-5648
Luther W. Starnes, Executive Assistant to the Secretary (301)383-5649
Linda L. S. Schulte, Director Public Information (301)383-5644
H. Branch Warfield, Assistant Director for Social Services Field Operations
   (301)383-3510

Local Departments of Social Services

Allegany County Ethel Wilderman, 218 Paca Street, Cumberland 21502
   (301)724-5500
Anne Arundel County John Isaac, The Arundel Center, Calvert Street, Annapolis 21404 (301)269-1350
Baltimore County Mrs. Katherine Cochran, 620 York Road, Towson 21204
   (301)494-2811
Calvert County Olin A. Dovel, Jr., Calvert Executive Building, Prince Frederick
   20678 (301)535-1642
Caroline County Steven Mood, Law Building, Denton 21629 (301)479-0890
Carroll County Lowell Haines, 95 Carroll Street, Westminster 21157
   (301)876-2190

Cecil County John Koch, County Office Building, 3rd Floor, Elkton 21921
(301)398-1414

Charles County B. L. Robinson, 8 Kent Avenue, White Plains 20695
(301)934-2700

Dorchester County Jeanne J. Cook, 407 Race Street, Cambridge 21613
(301)228-5100

Frederick County Mrs. Geneva Barthel, 400 East Church Street, Frederick
21701   (301)662-6151

Garrett County W. Perry Shaffer, 421 East Green Street, Oakland 21550
(301)334-9491

Harford County William Snyder, 119 South Hays Street, Bel Air 21014
(301)838-6121

Howard County Sam Marshall, Gorman Plaza, Suite 136, 8950 Route 108,
Columbia 21045   (301)730-9520

Kent County Mrs. Margaret W. Herring, 217 High Street, Chestertown 21620
(301)778-0820

Montgomery County Harriet Herrman, 5630 Fishers Lane, Rockville 20852
(301)279-1887

Prince George's County Williams Davidson, 6525 Belcrest Road, Hyattsville
20782   (301)779-1838

Queen Anne's County William Wise, 208 North Commerce Street, Centreville
21617   (301)758-0440

St. Mary's County Joseph Carter, P.O. Box 317, Leonardtown 20650
(301)475-2821

Somerset County Elizabeth Hall, 21, North Church Street, Princess Anne 21853
(301)651-0311

Talbot County Mrs. Elmire Heist, 10 South Hanson Street, Easton 21601
(301)822-1617

Washington County Francis J. Connolly, 112 West Baltimore Street, Hagers-
town 21740   (301)739-6370

Wicomico County George P. Karras, Elizabeth Street and Railroas Avenue,
Salisbury 21801   (301)742-9411

Worcester County Baine Yates, 424 West Market Street, Snow Hill 21863
(301)632-2705

City: Baltimore Mrs. Maud S. Harvey, 1500 Greenmount Avenue, Baltimore
21202   (301)234-2201

Reporting Requirements

Persons mandated to report (compulsory) when reasonable cause to believe a child is or has been subjected to abuse or neglect: physician, medical intern, medical examiner, dentist, nurse, public or private school teacher, educational administrator, guidance or family counselor, probation officer, social worker or policeman in his professional capacity (directors report rather than staff)

Permissive: any other person with reason to believe that child is suffering from or has died because of abuse or neglect

Form of report and when made: immediate oral; written, within 72 hours

To whom report is made: department of public welfare if the child has died; report also to the district attorney for the county and the appropriate medical examiners

Penalties: none

Immunities: absolute immunity for those required to report; immunity (civil and criminal) for others if report in good faith

Child Abuse Legislation

Citation: MGL Chap. 119, §29, 39F
Year enacted: 1973
Effective date: 1973
Purpose of legislation: mandatory reporting, yes
Reportable age: 0–16 years
Definitions: serious physical or emotional injury from abuse, including sexual,

146

or from neglect, including malnutrition; physically dependent on addictive
drug at birth

Education/school reports: mandatory reporting, yes
Immunity: yes
Mandatory investigation: yes, no specific time frame
Confidentiality of records: yes; penalty: fine and/or imprisonment
Cooperation with law courts: no specific provision
Guardian ad litem: yes
Administrative proceedings, trained personnel, facilities: no specific provision
Dissemination of information: no specific provision

Programs and Agencies

Inquiries concerning authorization to return unattached children or to offer any
other service to children should be addressed in duplicate to:

Office of Social Services
Department of Public Welfare
600 Washington Street
Boston 02111

Office of Social Services

Beth I. Warren, Assistant Commissioner (617)727-6100
John Hagenbuch, Coordinator, Protective Services (617)727-7020

Adoption Placement Service

Rosemary McAuliffe, Director (617)727-6180

Office of Research and Planning

Martin Abramowitz, Assistant Commissioner (617)727-6056

Office of Administration

Dot Levy, Assistant Commissioner (617)727-6153

Office of Finance

Andy Griffiths, Director (617)727-6176

Project Management Office

Val Asbedian, Director (617)727-6025

Department of Public Welfare Regional Offices

(Region)

Boston Austin A. O'Malley, 43 Hawkins Street, Boston 02114 (617)227-8320

Greater Boston John P. Riordan, 39 Boylston Street, Boston 02116
  (617)357-8250

Lawrence John J. Mahoney, 1 Mill Street, Lawrence 01840 (617)686-3971
  (617)997-3661

New Bedford James C. Caramello, 684 Purchase Street, New Bedford 02740

Springfield Edward Foley, 235 Chestnut Street, Springfield 01103
  (413)781-7510

Worcester Gerald F. Nugent, 75 Grove Street, Worcester 01605 (617)791-8571

Department of Public Welfare Community Service Area Offices

Boston Region

Area

Adams Street Alfred Washington, 1231 Adams Street, Dorchester 02124
  (617)296-6600

Morton Street Satellite Office William Murphy, 123 Morton Street, Jamaica
  Plain 02130 (617)524-1400

Roslindale Satellite Office Marjorie Maguire, 26 Cummins Highway, Roslindale
  02131 (617)325-4100

Church Street Bernice Rosenbaum, 20 Church Street, Boston 02116
  (617)542-4850

East Boston Robert Bailey, 154 Maverick Street, East Boston 02128
  (617)567-6140

Grove Hall Willie Sheriff, 515 Blue Hill Avenue, Roxbury 02121
  (617)442-1810

Washington Park Satellite Office Paul Berkowitz, 304 Martin Luther King
  Boulevard, Roxbury 02120 (617)445-7840

Academy Homes Satellite Office Kevin Brown, 2996 Washington Street,
  Roxbury 02119 (617)445-5710

Hancock Lawrence Durkin, 170 Hancock Street, Dorchester 02125
  (617)288-3340

Columbia Point Satellite Office Beulah Levangie (Supervisor), 320 Mt. Vernon
  Street, Dorchester 02125 (617)288-1612

D Street Satellite Office Emmanuel Feeney (Supervisor), 198 D Street, South
  Boston 02127 (617)268-8740

West Howell Street Satellite Office Nancy Dunphy (Supervisor), 20 West Howell
  Street, Dorchester 02125 (617)282-0010

Roxbury Crossing Paul Kussman, 1491 Tremont Street, Roxbury Crossing
  02120 (617)442-4800

South Huntington Teresa Taylor, 406 South Huntington Avenue, Jamaica Plain
    02130   (617)522-2010
Institutions, Nursing Homes and Medicaid Eugene J. Ryan, 1181 Washington
    Street, Dorchester 02124   (617)296-9600
Long Island Hospital Satellite Office Edwin B. Ryan (Supervisor), Boston
    Harbor, Quincy 02169   (617)328-1371

Greater Boston Region

Brookline (Brookline, Newton, Wellesley, and Weston): 320 Washington Street,
    Brookline 02146   Elizabeth Davis, Director (617)731-1500
Cambridge (Cambridge): 57 Inman Street, Cambridge 02139   Mrs. Ruth S.
    Malenka, Director (617)661-9390
Chelsea (Chelsea, Revere, and Winthrop): 300 Broadway, Chelsea 02150
    Cornelius J. Darcy, Director (617)884-7300
Revere Satellite Office: 85 Broadway, Revere 02151   William Keefe, Supervisor
    (617)289-4400
Winthrop Satellite Office: Town Hall, Winthrop 02152   David Foulkes, Super-
    visor (617)846-3060
Framingham (Ashland, Framingham, Holliston, Hopkinton, Millis, and Sudbury,
    Marlborough, Northborough, Southborough, Westborough, Dover, Natick,
    Sherborn, and Wayland): 354-A Waverly Street, Framingham 01701   Mrs.
    Eunice H. Smith, Director (617)879-4200
Hudson Satellite Office: Professional Building, 34-A Pope Street, Hudson 01749
    Nicholas J. Pagano, Supervisor (617)562-2842
Marlborough Satellite Office: City Hall, Room 1, Marlborough 01752   Yvette
    A. Kyle, Supervisor (617)481-4726
Lynn (Lynn, Lynnfield, Marblehead, Nahant, Saugus, and Swampscott):
    1 Washington Square, Lynn 01902   Thomas H. Spirito, Director
    (617)599-0700
Medford (Arlington, Everett, Malden, and Medford): 64 Salem Street, Medford
    02155   Ronald Newcomb, Director (617)391-5750
Arlington Satellite Office: Robbins House, 670 Massachusetts Avenue, Arling-
    ton 02174   Janice Marshall, Supervisor (617)646-7240
Everett Satellite Office: City Hall, Room 1, Everett 02149   Salvatore S. Abate,
    Jr., Supervisor (617)389-6931
Malden Satellite Office: 104-132 Exchange Street, Malden 02148   James M.
    Hall, Supervisor (617)321-3800
Norwood (Canton, Medfield, Needham, Norfolk, Norwood, Sharon, Walpole,
    Wrentham, Dedham, and Westwood): 10 Cottage Street, Norwood 02062
    Doris Carr, Director (617)762-6300
Dedham Satellite Office: Town Office Building, Bryant Street, Dedham 02026
    Charles Moloney, Supervisor (617)329-1030

Quincy (Braintree, Cohasset, Hull, Milton, Quincy, Randolph): 23-25 School
  Street, Quincy 02169   Leonard DeLory, Director (617)479-6868

Hingham Satellite Office: Town Office Building, 7 East Street, Hingham 02043
  Mrs. Richard Parker, Supervisor (617)749-2280

Randolph Satellite Office: Welfare-Veterans Building, 1 Turner Lane, Randolph
  02368   I. William Trostel, Supervisor (617)963-8210

Weymouth Satellite Office: 1431 Pleasant Street, East Weymouth 02189   John
  Morrisey, Supervisor (617)335-6000

Somerville (Somerville): 1 Davis Square, Somerville 02144   Ann M. Linnehan,
  Director (617)666-4910

Wakefield (Wakefield, Melrose, North Reading, Reading, and Stoneham): 7 Lincoln Street, Wakefield 01880   Andrew P. Ring, Director (617)245-2603

Melrose Satellite Office: 505 Main Street, Melrose 02176   Marcia Fischer,
  Supervisor (617)665-8950

Reading Satellite Office: 52 Sanborn Street, Reading 01867   William F.
  O'Keefe, Supervisor (617)944-7050

Waltham (Belmont, Waltham, and Watertown): 22 Church Street, Waltham
  02154   Mrs. Mary E. McDonald, Director (617)893-0146

Watertown Satellite Office: Administration Building, Watertown 02172   Joan
  Miller, Supervisor (617)926-9620

Lawrence Region

Beverly (Beverly, Hamilton, Manchester, Peabody, Wenham, Essex, Gloucester,
  Ipswich, Rockport, Danvers, Middleton, Peabody, Topsfield, and Salem):
  303 Cabot Street, Beverly 01915   Mrs. Carlotta Talbot, Director
  (617)927-6616

Gloucester Satellite Office: City Hall, Gloucester 01930   Neil Strong, Supervisor (617)283-2268

Peabody Satellite Office: City Hall Annex, Peabody 01960   Dorothy Baggan,
  Supervisor (617)531-3280

Salem Satellite Office: 209 Essex Street, 2nd Floor, Salem 01970   Thomas
  Walsh, Supervisor (617)745-8350

Haverhill (Haverhill, Amesbury, Merrimac, Newbury, Rowley, Salisbury, Box-
  ford, Georgetown, Groveland, West Newbury, and Newburyport): 42 Prim-
  ose Street, Haverhill 01830   Margaret N. Ring, Director (617)373-1935

Amesbury Satellite Office: 194 Main Street, Amesbury 01913   Dorothy Dube,
  Supervisor (617)388-2863

Georgetown Satellite Office: 48 Central Street, Georgetown 01830   Jarda
  Cragg, Supervisor (617)352-2832

Newburyport Satellite Office: City Hall, Newburyport 01950   George F.
  Cooper, Supervisor (617)462-6639

Lawrence (Andover, Lawrence, Methuen, and North Andover): 301 Essex
  Street, Lawrence 01840   William Healey, Director (617)686-9441

Methuen Satellite Office: 105 Haverhill Street, Methuen 01844   Robert Pent-
land, Supervisor (617)686-3883

North Andover Satellite Office: 168 Pleasant Street, North Andover 01845
Mary Alice Burke, Supervisor (617)682-8237

Lowell (Lowell, Billerica, Chelmsford, Dunstable, Dracut, Tyngsboro, Tewksbury, and Westford): 100 Merrimack Street, Lowell 01852   Arlene
Redmond, Director (617)454-8061

Billerica Satellite Office: 67 High Street, North Billerica 01862   Carl Abbati-
nozzi, Supervisor (617)663-2117

Chelmsford Satellite Office: Town Hall, Room 21, Chelmsford 01824   Doris
Mahoney, Supervisor (617)256-2731

Dracut Satellite Office: 482 Aiken Street, Dracut 01826   Barbara Madden,
Supervisor (617)458-8739

Tewksbury Satellite Office: Town Hall, Tewksbury 01876   John L. Kelley,
Supervisor (617)851-2382

Westford Satellite Office: Town Hall, Main Street, P.O. Box 21, Westford 01886
Edith M. Lowney, Supervisor (617)692-2937

Woburn (Burlington, Lexington, Winchester, Woburn, Acton, Bedford, Boxboro,
Carlisle, Concord, Harvard, Lincoln, Littleton, Maynard, Stow, Wilmington):
4 Federal Street, Woburn 01801   Francis O. Ryan, Director (617)935-5065

Concord Satellite Office: 747 Main Street, Concord 01742   Barbara P. Hayward, Supervisor (617)369-1290

Wilmington Satellite Office: 221 Lowell Street, Wilmington 01887   Walter F.
Coleman, Supervisor (617)658-2211

New Bedford Region

Attleboro (Attleboro, Foxboro, Mansfield, North Attleboro, Norton, and Plain-
ville): 15 Railroad Avenue, Attleboro 02703   Edward Silvia, Director
(617)266-0293

Brockton (Abington, Avon, Bridgewater, Brockton, East Bridgewater, Easton,
Holbrook, Stoughton, West Bridgewater, and Whitman): 75 Commercial
Street, Brockton 02401   Louis G. Silva, Director (617)588-3902

Fall River (Fall River, Freetown, Somerset, Swansea, and Westport): 66 Troy
Street, Fall River 02721   Lionel Garganta, Director (617)679-1981

Falmouth (Falmouth, Barnstable, Brewster, Dennis, Sandwich, Yarmouth,
Bourne, Nantucket, Chilmark, Edgartown, Gay Head, Oak Bluffs, Tisbury,
West Tisbury, Chatham, Eastham, Harwich, Orleans, Provincetown, Truro,
and Wellfleet): 344 Gifford Street, Falmouth 02540   Niles Peterson,
Director (617)548-8223

Barnstable Satellite Office: 269 Barnstable Road, P.O. Box 57, Hyannis 02601
Jon Tirrell, Supervisor (617)771-1201

Nantucket Satellite Office: Brush Road, Nantucket 02554   Marjorie E. Clute,
Supervisor (617)228-0470

Oak Bluffs Satellite Office: Douglas Way, Oak Bluffs 02557   Marjorie E.
     Murphy, Supervisor (617)693-0210
Orleans Satellite Office: Hilltop Plaza, Box 1045, Rte. 6-A, Orleans 02653
     Ann Slattery, Supervisor (617)255-4403
New Bedford (Acushnet, Dartmouth, Gosnold, New Bedford, Fairhaven, Marion,
     Mattapoisett, Rochester, and Wareham): 533 Mill Street, New Bedford
     02740   Francis Gilbert, Supervisor (617)997-1561
Fairhaven Satellite Office: 121 Sconticut Neck Road, Fairhaven 02719   Pauline
     Levaseur, Supervisor (617)997-7801
Wareham Satellite Office: 2510 Cranberry Highway, Wareham 02571
     Lawrence Weeden, Supervisor (617)295-0138
Plymouth (Carver, Plymouth, Duxbury, Kingston, Marshfield, Pembroke,
     Plympton, Halifax, Hanover, Hanson, Norwell, and Rockland): 88 Sand-
     wich Street, Plymouth 02363   Thomas Wood, Director (617)746-5180
Marshfield Satellite Office: 937 Webster Street Rear, Marshfield 02050   Helen
     Wyman, Supervisor (617)837-5161
Rockland Satellite Office: 346 Market Street Rear, Rockland 02370   Pearl M.
     Gilmore, Supervisor (617)878-1899
Taunton (Berkeley, Dighton, Lakeville, Middleboro, Raynham, Rehoboth, See-
     konk, and Taunton): 51 Broadway, Taunton 02780   Joseph F. Wade,
     Director (617)823-2571

Springfield Region

Pittsfield (Ashley Falls, Becket, Dalton, Hancock, Hinsdale, Housatonic, Lanes-
     borough, Lee, Lenox, New Ashford, Peru, Pittsfield, Richmond, Stock-
     bridge, Tyrington, Washington, West Stockbridge, Adams, Cheshire,
     Clarksburg, Florida, Monroe, North Adams, Savoy, Williamstown, Windsor,
     Great Barrington, Monterey, Mt. Washington, New Marlborough, Otis,
     Sandisfield, and Sheffield): 46 Summer Street, Pittsfield 01201   Donald J.
     Stack, Director (413)499-3250
Adams Satellite Office: 38 Hoosac Street, Adams 01220   Mrs. Anne M. Ciuk,
     Director (413)743-5300
Great Barrington Satellite Office: Castle Street, P.O. Box 478, Great Barrington
     01230   Anthony Pannozzo, Supervisor (413)528-2200
Northampton (Amherst, Chesterfield, Cummington, Easthampton, Florence,
     Goshen, Hadley, Hatfield, Haydenville, Middlefield, Northampton, Pelham,
     Plainfield, Whately, Williamsburg, Worthington, Ashfield, Bernardston, Buck-
     land, Charlemont, Conway, Colrain, Deerfield, Erving, Gill, Greenfield,
     Hawley, Heath, Leverett, Leyden, Montague, Northfield, Rowe, Shelburne,
     Shutesbury, Sunderland, Wendell, Blanford, Chester, Granville, Huntington,
     Montgomery, Russell, Southampton, Southwick, Tolland, Westfield, and

Westhampton): 355 Bridge Street, Northampton 01060   John R. Thompson, Director (413)586-3600

Greenfield Satellite Office: 31 Federal Street, Greenfield 01301   Robert Thompson, Director (413)774-2721

Westfield Satellite Office: 55 Broad Street, Westfield 01085   Sheila Harrington, Supervisor (413)568-8915

Holyoke (Belchertown, Granby, Holyoke, South Hadley, Chicopee, and Ludlow): 383 Dwight Street, Holyoke 01040   Gilbert F. Mueller, Director (413)536-2550

Chicopee Satellite Office: 5 Meadow Street, Chicopee 01014   Stanley H. Ciosek, Supervisor (413)536-7820

Springfield (Bonsville, East Meadow, East Longmeadow, Longmeadow, Springfield, Three Rivers, Wilbraham, Brimfield, Hampden, Holland, Monson, Palmer, Wales, Ware, Agawam, and West Springfield): 834 State Street, Springfield 01109   Earle A. Thompkins, Director (413)781-7670

Palmer Satellite Office: 512-518 North Main Street, Palmer 01069   Albert R. Dupsha, Supervisor (413)283-9757

West Springfield Satellite Office: 115 Elm Street, West Springfield 01089   Jane Nunn, Supervisor (413)788-4588

Worcester Region

Fitchburg (Ashby, Ayer, Fitchburg, Groton, Lunenburg, Pepperell, Shirley, Townsend, Bolton, Clinton, Lancaster, Sterling, and Leominster): 76 Summer Street, Fitchburg 01420   Margaret M. O'Connor, Director (617)345-2181

Clinton Satellite Office: 145 Church Street, Clinton 01510   (vacant), Supervisor (617)365-7316

Leominster Satellite Office: 29 Main Street, Leominster 01453   Kathleen Ward, Supervisor (617)537-4712

Gardner (Ashburnham, Gardner, Hardwick, Winchendon, Athol, New Salem, Orange, Warwick, Barre, New Braintree, Oakham, Princeton, Rutland, Hubbardston, Petersham, Phillipston, Royalston, Templeton, and Westminster): 82 Main Street, Gardner 01440   Michael J. Pandiscio, Director (617)632-0350

Athol Satellite Office: Memorial Building, Room 22, Athol 01331   Eleanor M. Clucus, Supervisor (617)249-3567

Rutland Satellite Office: 425 Main Street, Rutland 01543   William Duncan, Supervisor (617)886-4353

Templeton Satellite Office: P.O. Box 297, Templeton 01468   William Duncan, Supervisor (617)939-8975

Medway (Bellingham, Blackstone, Franklin, Hopedale, Medway, Mendon, Milford, Millville, Upton, Grafton, Douglas, Northbridge, Sutton, and Uxbridge): 89 Main Street, Medway 02053 Fredrick H. Hanny, Director (617)533-6647

Grafton Satellite Office: Central Square, P.O. Box 92, Grafton 01519 Fred Heaney, Supervisor (617)839-4761

Northbridge Satellite Office: 13 Douglas Street, Whitinsville 01588 B. Mae Wrona, Supervisor (617)234-8756

Southbridge (Charlton, Dudley, Oxford, Southbridge, Webster, East Brookfield, Hardwick, North Brookfield, Spencer, Brookfield, Warren, and West Brookfield): 399 Main Street, Southbridge 01550 Lillian G. Proulx, Director (617)764-4351

North Brookfield Satellite Office: Town Hall, 185 Main Street, North Brookfield 01535 (vacant), Supervisor (617)867-6727

Spencer Satellite Office: Main Street, P.O. Box 186, Spencer 01562 Lillian G. Proulx, Supervisor (617)867-6424

Worcester (Leicester, Millbury, Worcester, Boylston, West Boylston, Auburn, Holden, Leicester, Paxton, Berlin, and Shrewsbury): 9 Norwich Street, Worcester 01608 John P. Guilfoil, Director (617)791-3621

Boylston Satellite Office: Town Hall, Room 8, P.O. Box 105, Boylston 01505 Alice M. Brown, Supervisor (617)869-2841

Leicester Satellite Office: 3 Warren Avenue, Leicester 01524 John P. Guilfoil, Supervisor (617)895-5011

Shrewsbury Satellite Office: 100 Maple Avenue, Shrewsbury 01545 Annie Basilissa, Supervisor (617)845-5891

Michigan

Reporting Requirements

Persons mandated to report (compulsory) when reasonable cause to believe a child is or has been subjected to abuse or neglect: physician, coroner, dentist, medical examiner, nurse, audiologist, certified social worker, social work technician, school administrator, school counselor, teacher, law enforcement officer, or duly regulated child care provider (either staff or director of a hospital or other facility may make report)

Permissive: any person, including a child, who has reasonable cause to suspect child abuse or neglect

Form of report and when made: immediate oral; written, within 72 hours

To whom report is made: state department of social services; permissive reporters may report to the department or law enforcement agency; staff must inform directors in hospital or other facility

Penalties: civil liability for damages caused by failure to report

Immunities: identity of reporter is kept confidential, immunity (civil and criminal) for good faith reporting; extends only to acts taken with respect to this reporting act

Child Abuse Legislation

Citation: Act 238 of Pa., 1975 §1-16; MCL §25.240
Year enacted: 1975
Effective date: October 1, 1975
Purpose of legislation: mandatory reporting, yes
Reportable age: 0–18 years

Definitions: nonaccidental physical or mental injury, sexual abuse, maltreatment; harm caused by negligent treatment; failure to provide adequate care or support

Education/school reports: mandatory reporting, yes

Immunity: yes

Mandatory investigation: yes, 24 hours

Confidentiality of records: yes; penalty: misdemeanor

Cooperation with law courts, state agencies: yes

Guardian ad litem: yes

Administrative proceedings, trained personnel, facilities: yes

Dissemination of information: yes

Programs and Agencies

Where to write: The Department of Social Services prefers that interstate correspondence regarding requests for social information, child welfare services (including interstate placement of children), and persons receiving public assistance while residing in other states be routed directly to the local county with a copy to the state office, attention Assistance Payments or Social Services, depending on the subject matter.

Michigan Department of Social Services

> 300 South Capital Avenue
> Lansing 48926
> Telephone: (517)373-2035
> John T. Dempsey, Director (517)373-2000
> Mary J. Snyder, Administrative Assistant (517)373-2000
> Richard Miller, Executive Assistant (517)373-2000
> Milton Firestone, Legal Council (517)373-9100
> Paul M. Allen, Chief Department Director (517)373-9440
> Ernest E. Davis, Chief Administrative Officer (517)373-9440
> Eileen Courter, Public Information Specialist (517)373-2036

Office of Children and Youth Services

> Gerald G. Hicks, Director (517)373-0093
> Richard E. Higley, Placement Services (517)373-2083
> Richard Friz, Prevention Services (517)373-8225

County Departments of Social Services

Alcona County Bruce Vanden Bosch, 311 Lake St., Courthouse, Harrisville
48740 (517)724-6291

Alger County Philip Langloris, P.O. Box 354, Courthouse, Munising 49862 (906)387-4440

Allegan County Harold Leep, County Bldg. Annex, 2233-33rd St., Allegan 49010 (616)673-8411

Alpena County Gerald I. Kindt, 711 W. Chisholm, Alpena 49707 (517)356-9016

Antrim County Burrell Smith, Courthouse, Bellaire 49615 (616)533-8664

Arenac County William Thorp, County Bldg., P.O. Box 130, Standish 48658 (517)846-4551

Baraga County Kenneth J. La Berge, 2 N. Main St., L'Anse 49946 (906)524-6126

Barry County Richard Ritter, 110 W. Center St., Hastings 49058 (616)945-2437

Bay County Thomas E. Hanson, 912 Adams St., Bay City 48706 (517)894-4161

Benzie County Morley Bates, Courthouse, Beulah 49617 (616)882-4410

Berrien County Wesley Bowerman, 1134 S. Crystal St., Benton Harbor 49022 (616)926-7331

Branch County Gerald Schultz, Human Services Bldg., 809 Marshall Rd., Coldwater 49036 (517)279-8426

Calhoun County Ronald Rogers, 135 Hamblin Ave., P.O. Box 240, Battle Creek 49014 (616)963-1501

Cass County Mrs. Margaret Murray, 130 N. Broadway St., Cassopolis 49031 (616)445-3806

Charlevoix County Richard Tillen, County Bldg., Charlevoix 49720 (616)547-4471

Cheboygan County Preston H. Davis, County Bldg., Cheboygan 49721 (616)627-7194

Chippewa County Alvin Covell, 140 W. Spruce St., Sault Ste. Marie 49783 (906)632-3377

Clare County Patrick E. Redmond, P.O. Drawer 469, Harrison 48625 (517)539-7151

Clinton County George Eberhard, 911 E. State St., St. Johns 48879 (517)224-6751

Crawford County James W. Keighley, Jr., 303 James St., P.O. Box 702, Grayling 49738 (517)348-7691

Delta County Lawrence E. Curran, 2920-23rd Ave., S., Escanaba 49829 (906)786-5394

Dickinson County Nicholas Muraro, 800 Crystal Lake Blvd., P.O. Box 429, Iron Mountain 49801 (906)774-1484

Eaton County John L. Wittenberg, 528 W. Beech St., P.O. Drawer C, Charlotte 48813 (517)543-0860 or 645-7401 (local from Lansing)

Emmet County Jerry Joneson, 911 Spring St., Petoskey 49770 (616)347-2507

Genesee County Chester Bielaczyc, Walter Winchester Complex, P.O. Box 3010, Flint 48502 (313)767-6530

Gladwin County Victory R. Havens, Courthouse, P.O. Box 308, Gladwin 48624 (517)426-9258

Gogebic County Walter E. Bennetts, 210 N. Moore St., Bessemer 49911 (906)667-9711

Grand Traverse County Robert G. Wilson, 920 Hasting St., P.O. Box 466, Traverse City 49684 (616)946-0810

Gratiot County Avery Archer, 435 W. Filmore Rd., Rte. 4, Ithaca 48847 (517)875-4162

Hillsdale County Mrs. Caroline Harryman, 55 Hillsdale St., Hillsdale 49242 (517)437-7377

Houghton County Royce Koskinen, County Welfare Bldg., P.O. Box 630, Hancock 49930 (906)482-0500

Huron County James M. Sump, Huron County Bldg., Rm. 102, Bad Axe 48413 (517)269-9201

Ingham County Helen Reinhart, 930 W. Holmes Rd., Lansing 48910 (517)373-0013

Ionia County Melvin Haga, 227½ W. Main St., Ionia 48846 (616)527-4440 or 4700

Iosco County Benson B. Beck, 119 W. Harris Ave., Rte. 1, Tawas City 48763 (517)362-4421

Iron County Victor S. Shepich, 139 E. 1st Ave., P.O. Box 388, Caspian 49915 (906)265-9958

Isabella County Maynard Cole, 200 N. Main St., County Bldg., Mt. Pleasant 48858 (517)772-5961

Jackson County Robert D. Woodard, Lincoln-Hamp, Social Services Bldg., 950 W. Monroe St., Jackson 49202 (517)787-5600

Kalamazoo County Glen E. Momany, 666 Porter St., Kalamazoo 49007 (616)382-2870

Kalkaska County Wayne Williams, 215 S. Cedar St., P.O. Box 35, Kalkaska 49646 (616)258-8606

Kent County Evert W. Vermeer, 415 Franklin, S.E., Grand Rapids 49507 (616)247-6000

Keweenaw County Gerald Serbinski, Allouez Township Bldg., P.O. Box 348, Mohawk 49950 (906)337-3302

Lake County Jack Chase, 1090 Lake Ave., P.O. Box 278, Baldwin 49304 (616)745-4674

Lapeer County William M. Charles, 1575 Suncrest Dr., Lapeer 48446 (313)664-5961

Leelanau County Gregory Anspaugh, 108 Broadway, Suttons Bay 49682 (616)271-3442

Lenawee County Munroe Boersema, 150 Toledo St., Adrian 49221 (313)263-6761

Livingston County Ralph Patzer, 210 Highland Way, Howell 48843
(517)546-0310

Luce County Joseph Salbert, Luce County Government Bldg., Newberry 49868
(906)293-5144

Mackinac County Eugene Luoma, 10 N. State St., St. Ignace 49781
(906)643-9550

Macomb County Donald Vander Veen, 43533 Elizabeth Rd., Mt. Clemens
48043   (313)463-7011

Manistee County Floyd Adams, Courthouse, Manistee 49660   (616)723-2569

Marquette County Mrs. Mary Louise Fontaine, 300 S. 3rd St., Marquette 49855
(906)228-9692

Mason County Robert Ernst, County Services Bldg., 1110 S. Washington Ave.,
Ludington 49431   (616)845-7391

Mecosta County Charles Bryant, Courthouse, P.O. Box 1092, Big Rapids 49307
(616)796-3533

Menominee County Robert J. Malligren, Courthouse, Menominee 49858
(906)863-9965

Midland County H. M. Meredith, 1210 James Savage Rd., Midland 48640
(517)631-9430

Missaukee County Mark Hendges (Act.), 6180 W. Sanborn Rd., Box B, Lake
City 49651   (616)839-4356

Monroe County Dorman L. Harrington, 1414 E. 1st St., Monroe 48161
(313)242-6211

Montcalm County G. Thayer Hart, 617 N. State Rd., P.O. Box 278, Stanton
48888   (517)831-5211

Montmorency County Oral McMurphy, Courthouse, P.O. Box 427, Atlanta
49709   (517)785-4573

Muskegon County Robert Cordano, 376 Apple Ave., Muskegon 49442
(616)724-8221

Newaygo County Willard T. Ritter, 1038 W. Wilcox St., P.O. Box 217, White
Cloud 49349   (616)689-6617

Oakland County Howard E. Rosso, Walled Lake District Office, 1010 W. Maple,
Walled Lake 48088   (313)624-8800

Oceana County Clyde M. Lombard, 313 State St., P.O. Box 70, Hart 49420
(616)873-2101

Ogemaw County Mrs. Evlyne H. Sheltrown, 107 W. Main St., Rose City 48654
(517)685-2494

Ontonagon County Val K. White, Courthouse, 601 Trap St., Ontonagon 49953
(906)884-4951

Osceola County Walter Kwiatkowski, 115 N. Sears St., Reed City 49677
(616)832-2268

Oscoda County Ronald Keller, Courthouse Annex, P.O. Box 464, Mio 48647
(517)826-3228

Otsego County Karl David, 111 W. Mitchell St., Gaylord 49735
    (517)732-1702
Ottawa County Larry Hilldore, 329 N. River Ave., Holland 49423
    (616)396-1408
Presque Isle County Miss Beatrice Schornak, 216 S. 3rd St., Rogers City 49779
    (517)734-2108
Roscommon County Bradner Ameluxen, Courthouse, P.O. Box 147, Ros-
    common 48653   (517)275-5107
Saginaw County Ernst J. Smith, County Office Bldg., 615 Court St., Saginaw
    48602   (517)793-9150
St. Clair County Donald T. Wilson, 3415-28th St., Pt. Huron 48060
    (313)987-5500
St. Joseph County Donald Ve Casey, 612 E. Main St., P.O. Box 156, Centre-
    ville 49032   (616)467-6311
Sanilac County Mrs. Ruth I. Benedict, 61 W. Sanilac St., Sandusky 48471
    (313)648-2878
Schoolcraft County Douglas E. Kraatz, 131 River St., Manistique 49854
    (906)341-2114
Shiawassee County David Lorion, 701 S. Norton St., Corunna 48817
    (517)743-5661
Tuscola County Onalee Detwiler (Act.), 2266 W. Caro Rd., Caro 48723
    (517)673-4144
Van Buren County Charles Higgins, C.R. 681, P.O. Box 7, Hartford 49057
    (616)621-3151
Washtenew County Kenneth Oettle, 120 Catherine St., Ann Arbor 48108
    (313)994-1890
Wayne County R. B. Shelton, 640 Temple St., Detroit 48201   (313)256-1000
Wexford County Thomas Armstrong, 401 Lake St., Cadillac 49601
    (616)775-8566

Minnesota

Reporting Requirements

Persons mandated to report (compulsory) when reasonable cause to believe a child is or has been subjected to abuse or neglect: professional or assistant in the practice of the healing arts, social services, hospital administration; psychologist; psychiatrist; child care worker; educator; or law enforcement official (only one report needed from any institution, facility, school, or agency)

Permissive: any person with knowledge of, or reasonable cause to believe, a child is being neglected or abused

Form of report and when made: immediate oral; followed as soon as possible by written

To whom report is made: appropriate police department or local welfare agency

Penalties: failure to report as required: misdemeanor; falsifying reports: liable in a civil suit for damages, both proximate and punitive

Immunities: civil and criminal immunity when reporting in good faith and exercising due care

Child Abuse Legislation

Citation: MSA75-626, §260.155(4)
Year enacted: 1975
Effective date: June 2, 1975
Purpose of legislation: mandatory reporting, yes
Reportable age: minor child
Definitions: sexual abuse, physical injury, nonaccidental injury, which cannot be explained by history of injuries provided

Education/school reports: mandatory reporting, yes
Immunity: yes
Mandatory investigation: yes, immediately
Confidentiality of records: yes; penalty: misdemeanor
Cooperation with law courts, state agencies: no specific provision
Guardian ad litem: yes
Administrative proceedings, trained personnel, facilities: no specific provision
Dissemination of information: no specific provision

Programs and Agencies

Where to write: Correspondence regarding aid to families with dependent children, medical assistance, general assistance, Minnesota supplemental assistance, and requests for social information should be sent directly to the appropriate county department in duplicate. Correspondence regarding importation and exportation of children who are not in the custody of a parent and who are going to (1) the home of a parent who does not have custody, (2) the home of a relative, or (3) foster care (including adoption, temporary foster home care, or institutional care) should be sent in quadruplicate and addressed to:

> Division of Social Services
> Bureau of Community Services
> Department of Public Welfare
> Centennial Office Bldg.
> St. Paul 55155

Minnesota Department of Public Welfare

> Centennial Office Building
> St. Paul 55155
> Telephone: (612)296-6117
> Vera J. Likins, Commissioner (612)296-2701
> James J. Hiniker, Department Commissioner (612)296-6993
> Thomas L. Fabel, Department Attorney General (612)296-6671
> Ronald C. Young, M.D., Medical Director (612)296-3058
> Jon Darling, Accounting Director (612)296-5733
> Hearing Examiners (612)296-5764

Social Service Division

> Gary W. Haselhuhn, Director (612)296-2307

Service Development

> Dwaine R. Lindberg, Supervisor (612)296-6743

County Departments of Public Welfare

Aitkin County Dwight Miller, Courthouse, Aitkin 56431   (218)927-2141
(Aids) and (218)927-3744 (Social Services)
Anoka County John Elfelt, P.O. Box 290, Anoka 55303   (612)421-4760
Becker County Fred Kranstover, Courthouse, Detroit Lakes 56501
(218)847-5628 (Aids) and (218)847-5684 (Social Services)
Beltrami County Charles Melberg, P.O. Box 688, Bemidji 56601
(218)751-4310; Branch Office, Red Lake 56671   (218)679-3325
Benton County Donald Sykora, Courthouse, Foley 56329   (612)968-7263
Big Stone County Dale Szyszka, 340 N.W. 2nd St., Ortonville 56278
(612)839-2555
Blue Earth County Allen Sigafus, 420 Cherry St., Mankato 56001
(507)625-3031 (Aids) and 400 Washington Ct., Mankato 56001
(507)387-4111 (Social Services)
Brown County Thomas Henderson, 114 N. State St., New Ulm 56073
(507)354-8246
Carlton County P. Jerome Turnquist, Courthouse, Carlton 55718
(218)384-4281
Carver County Herbert Duncan, Courthouse, Chaska 55318   (612)448-3661
Cass County John Fjelstul, Welfare Bldg., Walker 56484   (218)547-1340
Chippewa County Norman G. Slagter, Courthouse, Montevideo 56265
(612)269-6581
Chisago County Robert Minor, Courthouse Annex, Center City 55012
(612)257-1300
Clay County Paul Sundberg, Courthouse, Moorhead 56560   (218)233-2781
Clearwater County Ordean A. Synstelien, Box X, Bagley 56221
(218)694-6512 (Aids) and (218)694-6164 (Social Services)
Cook County Raymond From, Courthouse, Grand Marais 55604
(218)387-2900 (Aids) and (218)387-1484 (Social Services)
Cottonwood County Albert C. Hoppert, P.O. Box 31, Windom 56101
(507)831-1891
Crow Wing County Wayne Larson, 1112 Willow St., Brainerd 56401
(218)829-0311 (Aids) and (218)829-3556 (Social Services)
Dakota County J. Paul Arneson, 820 Southview Blvd., South St. Paul 55075
(612)451-1741
Dodge County Ralph A. Winkle, Courthouse, Mantorville 55955
(507)635-2211
Douglas County Melvin Midboe, Courthouse, Alexandria 56308
(612)763-5183
Faribault County Stanley Lahti, County Office Bldg., P.O. Box 436, Blue Earth
56013   (507)526-3265
Fillmore County Rolf Huggenvi, Courthouse, Preston 55965   (507)765-3821
Freeborn County Fred Silbaugh, 410 S. Broadway, Albert Lea 56007
(507)373-6482

Goodhue County Philip M. McGonagle, Courthouse, Red Wing 55066
　　(612)388-2891 (Aids) and (612)388-7195 (Social Services)
Grant County Charles Hanson, Courthouse, Elbow Lake 56531　(218)685-4417
Hennepin County James Wiechers (Act.), A-1005 Government Center, 300 S.
　　6th St., Minneapolis 55487　(612)348-8125
Houston County W. J. Freeman, Courthouse, Caledonia 55921　(507)724-3344
Hubbard County Robert Sunderland, Courthouse, Park Rapids 56470
　　(218)732-3339
Isanti County Ronald Mooers, 221 S.W. 2nd St., Cambridge 55008
　　(612)689-4900 (Aids) and (612)689-1711 (Social Services)
Itasca County Edwin N. Yattaw, Courthouse, Grand Rapids 55744
　　(218)326-9441
Jackson County Norbert L. Bruegmann, Courthouse, Jackson 56143
　　(507)847-4000
Kanabec County Philip Peterson, 18 N. Vine St., Mora 55051　(612)679-3465
　　(Aids) and 209 E. Maple St., Mora 55051　(612)679-4740 (Social Services)
Kandiyohi County John Haines, Courthouse, Willmar 56201　(612)235-3014
　　(Aids) and (612)235-8317 (Social Services)
Kittson County John BeauLac, Courthouse, Hallock 56728　(218)843-6741
Koochiching County Elwyn Bow, Courthouse Annex, International Falls 56649
　　(218)283-8405
Lac Qui Parle County Dolores Bormann, Courthouse, Madison 56256
　　(612)598-7594
Lake County Wilbur J. Peterson, 616-3rd Ave., Two Harbors 55616
　　(218)834-2134 (Aids) and (218)834-2136 (Social Services)
Lake of the Woods County Robert Goudge, Courthouse, Baudette 56623
　　(218)634-2642
LeSueur County Lenz W. Rademacher, Courthouse, LeCenter 56057
　　(612)445-7543
Lincoln County Frank Moorse, Courthouse, Ivanhoe 56142　(507)694-1452
Lyon County Frank Moorse, Courthouse, Marshall 56258　(507)532-2201
McLeod County Leo H. Frank, Courthouse, Glencoe 55336　(612)864-5551
Mahnomen County Vernon L. Strandemo, County Office Bldg., Mahnomen
　　56557　(218)935-2568
Marshall County Arthur Kohlhase, Courthouse, Warren 56762　(218)748-5481
Martin County Michael Clancy, Courthouse, Fairmont 56031　(507)238-4447
Meeker County Robert L. Scott, Courthouse, Litchfield 55355　(612)693-2418
Mille Lacs County John McClure, Courthouse, Milaca 56353　(612)983-6161
Morrison County James A. Atkinson, Courthouse, Little Falls 56345
　　(612)632-9201
Mower County Robert Schultz, P.O. Box 189, Austin 55912　(507)433-3416
Murray County Frank Moorse, 2711 Broadway, Slayton 56172　(507)836-6144
Nicollet County Dayton R. Marinson, Courthouse, St. Peter 56082
　　(507)931-1170

Nobles County Dean R. Swanson, Courthouse, Worthington 56187
  (507)372-2157
Norman County Allen Zumach, County Office Bldg., Ada 56510
  (218)784-7136
Olmsted County Carl Maeder, 915-3rd Ave., S.E., Rochester 55901
  (507)288-2471
Otter Tail County Roland F. Winterfeldt, Courthouse, Fergus Falls 56537
  (218)739-2271
Pennington County Gary Erickson, P.O. Box 340, Thief River Falls 56701
  (218)681-2880
Pine County William McQuillan, Courthouse, Pine City 55063   (612)629-2544
  (Aids) and Village Hall, Sandstone 55072   (612)245-2313 (Social
  Services)
Pipestone County David Logan, Courthouse, Pipestone 56164   (507)825-3357
Polk County Emil J. Bagley, Courthouse, Crookston 56716   (218)281-3127
Pope County John V. DeMorett, Courthouse, Glenwood 56334
  (612)634-4591
Ramsey County James Edmunds, 160 E. Kellogg Blvd., St. Paul 55102
  (612)298-5351
Red Lake County Charles A. Stephens, Courthouse, Red Lake Falls 56750
  (218)253-4131
Redwood County Duane LeBrun, P.O. Box 27, Cliffwood Plaza, Redwood Falls
  56283   (507)637-2926
Renville County Richard M. Hoaglund, Courthouse, Olicia 56277
  (612)523-2202
Rice County Chester W. Pearson, 2855 N. Hwy. 3, P.O. Box 718, Faribault
  55021   (507)334-4357
Rock County Charles Olson, 107 E. Main St., Luverne 56156   (507)283-4481
Roseau County Victor Bettger, 307-3rd St., Roseau 56751   (218)463-2411
St. Louis County Miles J. Wangensteen, 422 W. 3rd St., Duluth 55806
  (218)727-8231; Courthouse, Hibbing 55746   (218)262-1008; Courthouse,
  Virginia 55792   (218)741-3500
Scott County Thomas Lindquist, 310 W. 4th Ave., Shakopee 55379
  (612)445-6676 (Human Services); 133 E. 1st Ave., Shakopee 55379
  (612)445-1723 (Aids); and 440 S. Atwood St., Shakopee 55379
  (612)445-5454 (Social Services)
Sherburne County Donald Strei, County Administration Bldg., Elk River 55330
  (612)441-1711
Sibley County Paul D. Hanson, Courthouse, Gaylord 55334   (612)237-2351
  (Aids); and 14-4th St., Gaylord 55334   (612)237-5266 (Social Services)
Stearns County Pasquale Serrano, 700 St. Germain St., St. Cloud 56301
  (612)251-3272
Steele County Harry K. Hoehne, 122 E. Rice St., Owatonna 55060
  (507)451-6740

Stevens County Mike Marxen, P.O. Box 111, Morris 56267 (612)589-1481

Swift County Ronald G. Laycock, 103-12th St., S., Benson 56215
(612)843-3161

Todd County Darryl Meyer, Courthouse Annex, Long Prairie 56347
(612)732-6181

Traverse County Mike Marxen, 15-10th St., S., Wheaton 56296 (612)563-8255

Wabasha County Wallace J. Walter, Courthouse, Wabasha 55981
(612)565-4544

Wadena County Dennis O. Johnson, Courthouse, Wadena 56482
(218)631-2832

Waseca County Donald F. Fisher, Security Bldg., Waseca 56093
(507)835-3240

Washington County Allen Main, 939 W. Anderson St., Stillwater 55082
(612)439-6901

Watonwan County Russell Lee, 715-3rd Ave., S., St. James 56081
(507)375-3329

Wilkin County Thomas Fawcett, Courthouse, Breckenridge 56520
(218)643-8561

Winona County Harold Thompson, Courthouse, Winona 55987 (507)452-8200

Wright County Robert A. Sullivan, Courthouse, Buffalo 55313 (612)295-5030

Yellow Medicine County Robert H. Lovell, Courthouse, Granite Falls 56241
(612)564-2211

Mississippi

Reporting Requirements

Persons mandated to report (compulsory) when reasonable cause to believe a child is or has been subjected to abuse or neglect: doctor (licensed), dentist, intern, resident, registered nurse, psychologist, teacher, social worker, school principal, child care giver, minister, law enforcement officer (director of agency, institution, or hospital shall make report instead of staff)

Permissive: none

Form of report and when made: immediate oral, followed as soon as possible by written report

To whom report is made: county welfare department

Penalties: none

Immunities: presumption of good faith in favor of the reporter results in civil and criminal immunity

Child Abuse Legislation

Citation: MCA §43-21-17, 93-15-5; HB 1065, Chap. 494
Year enacted: 1975
Effective date: April 7, 1975
Purpose of Legislation: mandatory reporting, yes
Reportable age: 0–18 years
Definitions: nonaccidental injury, sexual abuse, mental health adversely affected; failure to provide necessary care, support, education, other necessary care for well-being; lack of special care because of mental condition, i.e., mentally defective or mentally disordered

167

Education/school reports: mandatory reporting, yes
Immunity: yes
Mandatory investigation: yes, no specific time frame
Confidentiality of records: yes; penalty: no specific provision
Cooperation with law courts, state agencies: no specific provision
Guardian ad litem: yes
Administrative proceedings, trained personnel, facilities: no specific provision
Dissemination of information: no specific provision

Programs and Agencies

Where to write: Requests concerning general information regarding the department's programs should be sent to the proper state office division at this address:

> Department of Public Welfare
> P.O. Box 4321, Fondren Station
> Jackson 39216

Mississippi Department of Public Welfare

> P.O. Box 4321, Fondren Station
> Jackson 39216
> F. W. St. Clair, Comm. (601)982-6265

Division of Social Services

> Morris J. Priebatsch, Director (601)982-6621

Department of Public Welfare Regional Offices

Region I. (Alcorn, Benton, Coahoma, De Soto, Itawamba, Lafayette, Lee, Marshall, Monroe, Panola, Pontotoc, Prentiss, Quitman, Tate, Tippah, Tishomingo, Tunica, and Union Counties): P.O. Box 450, Pontotoc 38863 Lake W. Waldrop, Administrator (601)489-1232

Region II. (Calhoun, Carroll, Choctaw, Clay, East Bolivar, East Chickasaw, Grenada, Leflore, Lowndes, Montgomery, Oktibbeha, Sunflower, Tallahatchie, Webster, West Bolivar, West Chickasaw, and Yalobusha Counties): P.O. Drawer D, Grenada 38901   W. F. Watson, Administrator (601)226-1351

Region III. (Attala, Holmes, Humphreys, Issaquena, Kemper, Leake, Madison, Neshoba, Noxubee, Rawkin, Sharkey, Washington, Warren, Winston, and Yazoo Counties): P.O. Box 147, Brandon 39042   Claude Hartness, Act. Administrator (601)825-6716

Region IV. (Adams, Amite, Claiborne, Copiah, Covington, Franklin, Hinds, Jefferson, Jefferson Davis, Lawrence, Lincoln, Pike, Simpson, Smith, Walthall, and Wilkinson Counties): P.O. Box 4321, Fondren Station, Jackson 39216 (vacant), Administrator (601)982-6245

Region V. (Clarke, Forrest, George, Greene, Hancock, Harrison, Jackson, Jasper, Jones, Lamar, Lauderdale, Marion, Newton, Pearl River, Perry, Scott, Stone, and Wayne Counties): 1318 Hardy St., Hattiesburg 39401 Mrs. Vera Jaggers, Administrator (601)544-3860

Department of Public Welfare County Offices

Adams County Mrs. Margaret Ware, 150 E. Franklin St., Natchez 39120 (601)442-1482, 442-5461

Alcorn County William McCord, P.O. Box 1310, Corinth 38834 (601)286-3354, 286-5400

Amite County Julius A. Burris, P.O. Box 305, Liberty 39645 (601)657-3421

Attala County Mrs. Hope C. Ellis, E. Adams St., Kosciusko 39090 (601)289-4881, 289-3704

Benton County Mrs. Bonnie J. Ayres, P.O. Box 196, Ashland 38603 (601)224-6271

Bolivar County East, Mrs. Evelyn Wilkinson, 212 N. Pearman Ave., Cleveland 38732 (601)843-8311, 843-8611; West, Mrs. Clare C. Jackson, P.O. Box 368, Rosedale 38769 (601)759-3551, 759-6575

Calhoun County Mrs. Ada Ruth Hardy, P.O. Box 57, Pittsboro 38951 (601)983-2425, 983-4542

Carroll County George W. Turbeville, Jr., P.O. Box 208, Vaiden 39176 (601)464-5961; Carrollton Office (601)237-8171

Chichasaw County East, Mrs. Frances Sue Howell, Courthouse, Okolona 38860 (601)447-5511; West, Mrs. Martha B. Griffin, P.O. Box 151, Houston 38851 (601)456-3724, 456-2871

Choctaw County Mrs. Billye Gwyn Reid, P.O. Box 338, Ackerman 39735 (601)285-6269

Claiborne County Mrs. Gertrude Lum Dale, P.O. Drawer O, Port Gibson 39150 (601)437-5115, 437-4162

Clarke County Mrs. Annette S. Hutto, 209 N. Archusa Ave., Quitman 39355 (601)776-7021, 776-2911

Clay County Mrs. Martha Brand, P.O. Box 813, West Point 39773 (601)494-3483, 494-5736

Coahoma County Kenneth T. Dixon, Box 9, Clarksdale 38614 (601)624-2471, 624-8430, 627-4177

Copiah County F. D. Cliett, P.O. Drawer A, Whitworth St., Hazelhurst 39083 (601)894-2321, 894-4391

Covington County Mrs. Johnnie F. Miller, P.O. Box 507, Collins 39428 (601)765-7221, 765-8321

De Soto County Mrs. Jere Gale, 235 Hwy. 51 S., Hernando 38632
(601)368-4461, 368-8611

Forrest County Glenn Donald Grimsley, P.O. Drawer 1728, Hattiesburg 39401
(601)582-8311, 583-1576

Franklin County Mrs. Lola Barnett, P.O. Box 667, Meadville 39653
(601)384-2369, 384-5468

George County Mrs. Rachel D. Smith, P.O. Box 104, Lucedale 39452
(601)947-3116

Greene County Mrs. Clara Dearman, P.O. Box 497, Leakesville 39451
(601)394-5378

Grenada County Mrs. Barbara K. Whitworth, P.O. Box 945, Grenada 38901
(601)226-1971, 226-3521

Hancock County Mrs. Lucretia Fly, P.O. Box 151, Bay St. Louis 39520
(601)467-4565

Harrison County H. E. Walker, P.O. Box 262, Gulfport 39502 (601)864-1531

Hinds County Mrs. Sharon Whitt, P.O. Box 8777, 1775 Wilson Blvd., Jackson
39204 (601)373-1120

Holmes County Mrs. Jean McLellan, P.O. Box 480, Lexington 39095
(601)834-1221

Humphreys County Mrs. Carolyn Bridgers, P.O. Box 88, Belzoni 39038
(601)247-2323, 247-1876

Issaquena County Sydney Fernandez, P.O. Box 66, Mayersville 39113
(601)873-4728

Itawamba County Homer R. Tucker, P.O. Box 556, Fulton 38843
(601)862-4851

Jackson County W. Edward Goff, P.O. Box 489, Pascagoula 39567
(601)762-2782 or 1363

Jasper County Mrs. Bonnie S. Grantham, P.O. Drawer 350, Bay Springs 39422
(601)764-2151, 764-2605

Jefferson County Mrs. Elsie M. Dawkins, P.O. Box 97, Fayette 39069
(601)786-3571

Jefferson Davis County Mrs. Edna Bush Stephens, P.O. Box 336, Prentiss 39474
(601)792-4760, 792-4284

Jones County Mrs. Edna E. Coates, P.O. Box 869, Laurel 39441
(601)428-1568, 428-8797

Kemper County Mrs. Marvel S. Bates, P.O. Box 326, DeKalb 39328
(601)743-2683, 743-2850

Lafayette County Henry Grady Fuller, P.O. Box 286, Oxford 38655
(601)234-1861, 234-5316

Lamar County Willie Louis Grinsley, P.O. Box 788, Purvis 39475
(601)794-6315

Lauderdale County Walter Clyde Walker, Jr., P.O. Box 1891, Meridian 39302
(601)483-3337, 693-1956

Lawrence County Lloyd Huguley, P.O. Box 577, Monticello 39654
(601)587-5921
Leake County Billy Kendall McPhall, P.O. Box 47, Carthage 39051
(601)267-3242
Lee County Mrs. Jannie F. Owen, P.O. Box 1563, Tupelo 38802
(601)842-4321, 842-5836
Leflore County Mrs. Rosalie P. Witty, P.O. Box 292, Greenwood 38930
(601)453-3124, 453-1197
Lincoln County Carl Hunsucker, P.O. Box 538, Brookhaven 39601
(601)833-3311, 833-7391
Lowndes County Mrs. Mary Lee Sumrall, 223-22nd Street, North Columbus
39701 (601)328-5278, 328-3886
Madison County Mrs. Mary C. Lauderdale, P.O. Box 364, Canton 39046
(601)859-4813, 859-1276
Marion County Robert Earl Leggett, P.O. Box 129, Columbia 39429
(601)736-6383, 736-6431
Marshall County Jim B. Buchanan, P.O. Box 218, Holly Springs 38635
(601)252-4511, 252-4727
Monroe County Johnny J. Coleman, East Commerce Street, P.O. Box 788,
Aberdeen 39730 (601)369-2872, 369-8341; Amory Office
(601)256-5742
Montgomery County James E. Brister, P.O. Box 267, Highway 51, South,
Winona 38967 (601)283-2922, 283-1113
Neshoba County Mrs. June L. Posey, P.O. Box 177, 231 Beacon Street, Phila-
delphia 39350 (601)656-1451, 656-6511
Newton County Mrs. Mildred Pace, P.O. Box 158, Decatur 39327
(601)635-2346
Noxubee County J. P. Shelton Mullens, P.O. Box 404, Macon 39341
(601)726-5131
Oktibbeha County Edward F. Todd, P.O. Box 865, Starkville 39759
(601)323-1566, 323-7962
Panola County Mrs. Mary C. Carter, P.O. Box 128, Sardis 38666
(601)487-1751, 487-2891
Pearl River County Mrs. Dale T. Adams, 204 South Julia Street, Poplarville
39470 (601)795-4507, 795-4062; Picayune Office (601)798-7847
Perry County Mrs. Hilda R. Lee, P.O. Box 166, New Augusta 39462
(601)964-3658
Pike County Mrs. Maxene Williford, P.O. Box 967, McComb 39648
(601)684-3431, (601)684-1712; Magnolia Office (601)783-5242
Pontotoc County John A. Tutor, 227 Liberty Street, P.O. Box 419, Pontotoc
38863 (601)489-1852, 489-4182
Prentiss County Joseph B. Hill, P.O. Box 427, Booneville 38829
(601)728-5981

Quitman County Edgar Howard Shields, P.O. Drawer F, Marks 38646
  (601)326-8021, 326-7026
Rankin County Mrs. Inez B. Watson, P.O. Box 85, Brandon 39042
  (601)825-5081, 825-5213
Scott County Walter Dale McCann, P.O. Box 406, Forest 39074
  (601)469-2771, 469-4762
Sharkey County Mrs. Lucy J. Boykin, County Courthouse, Rolling Fork 39159
  (601)873-4338, 873-2645
Simpson County Mrs. Jewel Ates, P.O. Box 578, Mendenhall 39114
  (601)847-1233, 847-1771
Smith County Jacqueline Hard, P.O. Box 205, Raleigh 39153   (601)782-4505
Stone County Mrs. Alletha J. Kirker, P.O. Box 247, Wiggins 39577
  (601)928-4996
Sunflower County Mrs. Sonya Fox, P.O. Box 687, Indianola 38751
  (601)887-2051, 887-2732
Tallahatchie County Mrs. Virginia H. Taylor, P.O. Box 49, Charleston 38921
  (601)647-5571, 647-5868
Tate County Mrs. Virginia Lee Cox, 102 McKie Street, Senatobia 38668
  (601)562-6821, 562-8536
Tippah County Joe Terry White, Ripley 38663   (601)873-9307, 873-7665
Tishomingo County Mrs. Margaret June Woodley Riley, P.O. Drawer 280,
  Iuka 38852   (601)423-5203, 423-3411
Tunica County Mrs. Pattye Sue Tucker, P.O. Box 1026, Tunica 38676
  (601)363-1771, 363-1071
Union County Mrs. Beatrice Henry, P.O. Box 769, New Albany 38652
  (601)534-4758, 534-4651
Walthall County Mrs. Ava Pigott, P.O. Box 209, Tylertown 39667
  (601)876-2191, 876-2581
Warren County Charlotte Ann Helgason, 913 Jackson Street, Vicksburg 39180
  (601)636-1512, 638-2073
Washington County Raymond G. Messer, Sr., 903 Alexander Street, Greenville
  38701   (601)355-6051, 355-6021
Wayne County Charles Wayne Seeger, 810 Chickasaway Street, Waynesboro
  39367   (601)735-4752, 735-2847
Webster County Walter Kelly Land, P.O. Drawer B, Euphora 39744
  (601)258-4771
Wilkinson County Mrs. Bettye G. Plitt, P.O. 726, Woodville 39669
  (601)888-4311
Winston County Robert Franks Oakley, P.O. Box 270, Louisville 39339
  (601)773-2434, 773-9032
Yalobusha County Tomie R. Ashford, P.O. Box 191, Water Valley 38965
  (601)473-2951
Yazoo County (vacant), P.O. Box 570, Yazoo City 39194   (601)746-5821

Missouri

Reporting Requirements

Persons mandated to report (compulsory) when reasonable cause to believe a child is or has been subjected to abuse or neglect: physician, medical examiner, coroner, dentist, chiropractor, optometrist, podiatrist, resident, intern, nurse, hospital and clinic personnel (engaged in examination, care, or treatment), other health practitioner, psychologist, mental health professional, social worker, day-care center worker or other child care worker, juvenile officer, probation or parole officer, teacher, principal, other school official, minister, Christian Science practitioner, peace officer or other law enforcement official, or other person with responsibility for the care of children (director may make a report for staff)

Permissive: any other person with reasonable cause to believe that a child is or may be subjected to abuse or neglect

Form of report and when made: oral, followed within 48 hours by written

To whom report is made: Missouri division of family services; if child has died, report goes to appropriate medical examiner or coroner

Penalties: misdemeanor: $1,000 and/or one year in county jail

Immunities: civil and criminal immunity for good faith report

Child Abuse Legislation

Citation: AMS §211.471; HB574
Year enacted: 1975
Effective date: June 6, 1975
Purpose of legislation: mandatory reporting, yes
Reportable age: 0–18 years

Definitions: nonaccidental physical injury, sexual abuse, emotional abuse; failure to provide necessary support, education medical, surgical, or other care necessary for well-being of child

Education/school reports: mandatory reporting, yes

Immunity: yes

Mandatory investigation: yes, 24 hours

Confidentiality of records: yes; penalty: misdemeanor

Cooperation with law courts, state agencies: yes

Guardian ad litem: yes

Administrative proceedings, trained personnel, facilities: yes

Dissemination of information: yes

Programs and Agencies

General inquiries regarding public laws or policies, or inquiries where the local office cannot be determined, should be addressed to:

Division of Family Services
Department of Social Services
Broadway State Office Building
Jefferson City, Missouri 65101

Missouri Department of Social Services

Broadway State Office Building
Jefferson City, Missouri 65101
Telephone: (314)751-4815
Lawrence L. Graham, Director
Terry C. Bellora, Deputy Director, Administration
George Camp, Deputy Director

Social Services Section

Dwain Hovis, Deputy Director (314)751-2548

Division of Family Services County and City Offices

Adair Charles Silvey, P.O. Box 670, Kirksville 63501 (816)665-3785
Andrew Sherman S. Smolly, Savannah 64485 (816)324-3152
Atchison Mrs. Martha C. Austin, Rock Port 64482 (816)744-5318
Audrain Lewis DeHart, 400 E. Liberty, Mexico 65265 (314)581-3312
Barry William Moseley, Cassville 65624 (417)847-4761
Barton Mrs. Marilyn Jo Percy, 804 Broadway, P.O. Box 71, Lamar 64759
     (417)682-3531

Bates Jim L. McLaughlin, Butler 64730 (816)679-4151

Benton Mrs. Esther Bibb, East Gate Shopping Center, P.O. Box 126, Warsaw 65355 (816)438-7357

Bollinger Mrs. Sally Youngblood, P.O. Box 7, Lutesville 63762 (314)238-2624

Boone Jerry Brewer, 2100 E. Broadway, P.O. Box 997, Columbia 65201 (314)442-6191

Buchanan Charles Roberts, 2305 St. Joseph Ave., St. Joseph 64505 (816)364-2921

Butler Mrs. Clara Hendrix, 209 S. Broadway, P.O. Box 488, Popular Bluff 63901 (314)785-6458

Caldwell Mrs. Lita B. Loch, Hamilton 64644 (816)583-2045

Callaway Mrs. Delia Ehrsam, Rte. 4, 502 Collier Lane, Fulton 65251 (314)642-2238

Camden Mrs. Irene Franklin, Camdenton 65020 (314)346-2249

Cape Girardeau Mrs. Louise Wright, P.O. Box 578, Cape Girardeau 63701 (314)335-3351

Carroll Mrs. Sharon Eiserer, 104 N. Mason St., Carrollton 64633 (816)542-0656

Carter Mrs. Lillian L. Crass, Van Buren 63965 (314)323-4203

Cass Orville Price, Harrisonville 64701 (816)884-3681

Cedar George Woodward, Stockton 65785 (417)276-5113

Chariton Mrs. Elizabeth Baer, Keytesville 65261 (816)288-3293

Christian Mrs. Maude Cook, P.O. Box 304, Ozark 65721 (417)485-7511

Clark Mrs. Helen F. Macomber, 207 N. Johnson St., Kahoka 63445 (816)727-3393

Clay Mrs. Sandra Brooks, 234 W. Shrader St., P.O. Box 176, Liberty 64068 (816)781-8900

Clinton Mrs. Joy Breckenridge, Plattsburg 64477 (816)539-2146

Cole Mrs. Lilliam Shults, 830 E. High St., Jefferson City 65101 (314)751-4688

Cooper John Chipley, 905 Main St., P.O. Box E, Boonville 65233 (816)882-5311

Crawford Franklin Cunningham, P.O. Box 310, Steelville 65565 (314)775-2146

Dade Ronald C. Reiman, 105 Grand St., P.O. Box 27, Greenfield 65661 (417)637-5362

Dallas Mrs. Virginia Owens, P.O. Box 415, Buffalo 65622 (417)345-7651

Daviess James Myers, Gallatin 64640 (816)663-2189

De Kalb Mrs. Rena M. White, Maysville 64469 (816)449-2165

Dent Louis Williamson, 417 E. 4th St., P.O. Box 4900, Salem 65560 (314)729-6931

Douglas Mrs. Pauline Sellers, P.O. Box 187, Ava 65608 (417)683-4817

Dunklin Carltin L. Ewbank, 110 Oakview St., P.O. Box 649, Kennett 63857 (314)888-4606

Franklin Mrs. Sharon Michel, 706 Hwy. 50 W., P.O. Box 312, Union 63084
(314)583-2571

Gasconade Mrs. Orpha Nance, 207 N. 1st St., P.O. Box 545, Owensville 65066
(314)437-3313

Gentry Louis Langford, Albany 64402   (816)726-5524

Greene Miss Jean Heyle, 1258 E. Trafficway, Springfield 65802
(417)862-1781

Grundy Mrs. Leo L. Griffith, 207 E. 10th Ct., P.O. Box 404, Trenton 64683
(816)359-3971

Harrison Mrs. Juanita Packer, P.O. Box 309, Bethany 64424   (816)425-7995

Henry Mrs. Louis Brownfield, 115 E. Grand River St., P.O. Box 7, Clinton
64735   (816)885-5531

Hickory Mrs. Lucille Davis, Hermitage 65668   (417)745-6491

Holt Mrs. Crystal Bohart, P.O. Box 183, Mound City 64470   (816)442-3314

Howard James Woodsmall, 100 E. Davis St., P.O. Box 231, Fayette 65248
(816)248-3324

Howell Mrs. Ruby Pranti, 719 N. Hwy. 63, P.O. Box 67, West Plains 65775
(417)256-7121

Iron H. Elmo Nations, Ironton 63650   (314)546-7463

Jackson J. Joseph Lewis, 615 E. 13th St., Kansis City 64106   (816)274-6011

Jasper Vernon McConnell, 1530 E. 6th St., P.O. Box 1353, Joplin 64802
(417)624-3246

Jefferson Mrs. Mary Jean Wellman, P.O. Box 188, Hillsboro 63050
(314)789-3322

Johnson John Hooper, 708 N. College St., P.O. Box H, Warrensburg 64093
(816)747-6181

Knox Mrs. Bonnie McGlothlin, Edina 63537   (816)397-3245

Laclede Robert F. Rickard, 213 E. Commercial St., Leganon 65536
(417)532-3137

Lafayette Mrs. Margaret L. Gray, 701 S. 13th St., P.O. Box 338, Lexington
64067   (816)259-2294

Lawrence Alfred F. Blair, P.O. Box 228, Aurora 65605   (417)678-4138

Lewis Mrs. Rosemary Taylor, Monticello 63457   (314)767-5284

Lincoln Mrs. Edna Gerlach, 590 Main St., Troy 63379   (314)528-8521

Linn Miss Doris Stuart, 422 E. Brooks St., P.O. Box 343, Brookfield 64628
(816)258-3388

Livingston Mrs. Jeanette Calvird, 921 Jackson St., P.O. Box 685, Chilicothe
64601   (816)646-5770

McDonald Mrs. Barbara Newell, Pineville 64856   (417)223-4331

Macon Ms. Anne Morris, 118 N. Rollins, P.O. Box 469, Macon 63552
(816)385-3191

Madison Mrs. Retta White, 215 E. Main St., P.O. Box 269, Fredericktown
    63645   (314)783-5596
Maries Mrs. Maxine Travis, P.O. Box 127, Vienna 65582   (314)422-3335
Marion Mrs. Linda N. Clark, 411 Broadway, Hannibal 63401   (314)221-8332
Mercer Olin Derry Jr., Princeton 64673   (816)748-3292
Miller Dean Shorter, P.O. Box 354, Eldon 65026   (314)392-5141
Mississippi Mrs. Agnes Cunningham, 220 E. Main St., P.O. Box 69, East Prairie
    63845   (314)649-3593
Moniteau Mrs. Lorna Newby, 601 E. Smith St., P.O. Box 209, California
    65018
Monroe Mrs. Mary W. Keith, Paris 65275   (816)327-4185
Montgomery Mrs. Opal Noell, 113 W. 3rd St., Montgomery City 63361
    (314)564-2258
Morgan James Vogel, Versailles 65084   (314)378-4226
New Madrid Mrs. LaVerne Hadder, 600 Main Street, New Madrid 63869
    (314)748-5536
Newton Robert W. Clifton, 216 N. Washington St., P.O. Box 646, Neosho
    64850   (417)451-3125
Nodaway (vacant), Mary Mart Shopping Center, P.O. Box 439, Maryville
    64468   (816)582-3141
Oregon John W. Barton, Alton 65606   (417)778-7251
Osage Mrs. Jewell Thompson, Linn 65051   (314)897-3113
Ozark Louie A. Wallace, Gainesville 65655   (417)679-4616
Pemiscott Carl Morris, P.O. Box 999, Caruthersville 63830   (314)333-0470
Perry Mrs. Betty M. Bertke, P.O. Box 30, Perryville 63775   (314)547-6501
Pettis Herman Wallace, State Fair Shopping Center, Sedalia 65301
    (816)826-0496
Phelps Jay Hutchinson, 18 Kings Highway, P.O. Box 860, Rolla 65401
    (314)364-2153
Pike Ronald Stanislaus, Bowling Green 63334   (314)324-2243
Platte Mrs. Elsie Wells, Platte City 64079   (816)431-2147
Polk Terry Phillips, P.O. Box A, Bolivar 65613   (417)326-7661
Pulaski Roger Briggs, 601 Hwy. 66 W., Waynesville 65583   (314)774-6491
Putnam Miss Evelyn L. Smith, P.O. Box 308, Unionville 63565   (816)947-2567
Ralls Mrs. Sara Johnson, New London 63459   (314)985-7211
Randolph Mrs. Esther Creed, 223 N. Clark St., Moberly 65270   (816)263-4330
Ray Mrs. Mildred Branaman, Hwy. 13 S., P.O. Box 410, Richmond 64085
    (816)776-2268
Reynolds Hubert Woods, P.O. Box 30, Centerville 63633   (314)648-2341
Ripley Mrs. Bettie Bagwill, 101 Jackson St., P.O. Box 40, Doniphan 63935
    (314)996-2175

St. Charles Mrs. Mildred Peterman, 140 N. Kings Highway, P.O. Box 278, St. Charles 63301 (314)724-8747

St. Clair Samuel Clayton, Osceola 64776 (417)646-8165

St. Francois Alfred W. Ehlert, 409 W. Karsch Blvd., P.O. Box 149, Farmington 63640 (314)756-4578

Ste. Genevieve John Marshall, 795 Market St., Ste. Genevieve 63670 (314)883-5757

St. Louis Sam Crawford, 1260 Andes Blvd., St. Louis 63132 (314)991-4260

Saline Mrs. Beverly S. Olsen, 632 N. Miami St., City Rte. N., P.O. Box 457, Marshall 65340 (816)886-8366

Schuyler Mrs. Bonnie Ketchum, Lancaster 63548 (816)457-3751

Scotland Mrs. Mary Rockhold, Memphis 63555 (816)465-8540

Scott Breman L. Montgomery, P.O. Box 628, Sikeston 63801 (314)471-5194

Shannon Mrs. Thela Winterbottom, Eminence 65466 (314)226-3211

Shelby Mrs. Dorothy Dixon, Shelbyville 63469 (314)633-2550

Stoddard M. Leon Ward, Bloomfield 63825 (314)568-2112

Stone Mr. Vearl Counts, Galena 65656 (417)357-6215

Sullivan Mrs. Marjorie Woods, Milan 63556 (816)265-4295

Taney Mrs. Donna Stuart, Forsyth 65653 (417)546-4728

Texas Robert D. Smith, 507 W. Hwy. 17, Houston 65483 (417)967-4132

Vernon Larry J. Rose, 208 N. Cedar St., Nevada 64772 (417)667-3394

Warren Mrs. Wilma Zeh, 111 W. Main St., Warrenton 63383 (314)456-3307

Washington Mrs. Myra Yount, 108 E. High St., P.O. Box 250, Potosi 63664 (314)438-2121

Wayne Mrs. Neoma G. Mosley, 306 N. 2nd St., P.O. Box 128, Piedmont 63957 (314)223-4236

Webster Mrs. Vera Wallace, Marshfield 65706 (417)468-2208

Worth Mrs. Bonnie Welch, E. 6th and Lyons Sts., P.O. Box E, Grant City 64456 (816)564-3711

Wright Miss Geraldine Hailey, P.O. Box 168, Mountain Grove 65711 (417)926-4142

St. Louis Paul R. Nelson, 4255 W. Pine St., 63108 (314)531-9500

Montana

Reporting Requirements

Persons mandated to report (compulsory) when reasonable cause to believe a child is or has been subjected to abuse or neglect: physician who examines, attends, or treats a person under the age of majority; any nurse, teacher, social worker, attorney, or law enforcement officer, or any other person, who has reason to believe that a child has had a serious injury as a result of abuse or neglect

Permissive: none

Form of report and when made: no procedure specified; "promptly"

To whom report is made: department of social and rehabilitation services, its local affiliate, and the county attorney of the county wherein the child resides

Penalties: none

Immunities: presumption of good faith reporting: civil and criminal immunity, unless demonstration of bad faith or malicious purpose

Child Abuse Legislation

Citation: RCM: §10-1300-1322
Year enacted: 1974
Effective date: not available
Purpose of legislation: mandatory reporting, yes
Reportable age: 0–18 years
Definitions: commission or omission of any act or acts which materially affect the normal physical or emotional development of a youth; any excessive physical injury; sexual assault; failure to thrive, taking into account age and

medical history of youth, shall be presumptive of material effect and nonaccidental

Education/school reports: mandatory reporting, yes
Immunity: yes
Mandatory investigation: yes, no specific provision
Confidentiality of records: yes; penalty: no specific provision
Cooperation with law courts, state agencies: no specific provision
Guardian ad litem: yes
Administrative proceedings, trained personnel, facilities: no specific provision
Dissemination of information: no specific provision

Programs and Agencies

Where to write:

Chief, Social Services Bureau
Department of Social and Rehabilitation Services
Helena 59601

Montana Department of Social and Rehabilitation Services

P.O. Box 1723
Helena 59601
Theodore Carkulis, Director (406)449-3451

Financial Management

Benjamin F. Johns, Assoc. Dir. (406)449-3411

Program Coordination

J. C. Carver, Assoc. Dir. (406)449-3858

Management Systems

Frank Smoyer, Special Asst. (406)449-3859
Thomas H. Mahan, Atty. for the Dept. (406)449-2001
Susan Kirkpatrick, Inf. Off. (406)449-2742

Legal Unit

Henry Flatow, Hearings Ofr. (406)449-2741
Gene McLatchy, Atty. (406)449-2741

Community Services Division

Edward J. Malensek, Adm. (406)449-3467

Social Services Bureau

Norma Cutone, Chief (406)449-3729

Child and Youth Development Bureau

Charles McCarthy, Chief (406)449-3724
Richard Forehand, 4C's Program (406)449-3794

Children and Youth Unit

Clark Welsh, Community Planning Coord. (406)449-3960

Department of Social and Rehabilitation Services Regional Offices

I. Miles City (Carter, Custer, Daniels, Dawson, Fallon, Garfield, McCone,
Phillips, Powder River, Prairie, Richland, Roosevelt, Rosebud, Sheridan,
Treasure Valley, and Wibaux Counties): 708 Palmer, P.O. Box 880, Miles
City 59301   John Konecny, Regl. Rep. (406)232-1385
II. Great Falls (Blaine, Cascade, Chouteau, Glacier, Hill, Liberty, Pondera,
Teton, and Toole Counties): 1818-10th Ave., S., Suite 1, Great Falls 59401
Laulette Hansen, Regl. Rep. (406)452-7837
III. Billings (Big Horn, Carbon, Fergus, Golden Valley, Judith Basin, Mussel-
shell, Petroleum, Stillwater, Sweet Grass, Wheatland, and Yellowstone
Counties): 1211 Grand Avenue, Billings 59101   Boyce Fowler, Regl. Rep.
(406)245-6452
IV. Helena (Beaverhead, Broadwater, Deer Lodge, Gallatin, Granite, Jefferson,
Lewis and Clark, Madison, Meagher, Park, Powell, and Silver Bow Counties):
25 S. Ewing, Rm. 208, Helena 59601   Donald Lee, Regl. Rep.
(406)449-2579
V. Missoula (Flathead, Lake, Lincoln, Mineral, Missoula, Ravalli, and Sanders
Counties): 818 Burlington, Missoula 59801   Gary Walsh, Regl. Rep.
(406)549-2754

County Departments of Public Welfare

Beaverhead Wayne Contway, Dillon 59725   (406)683-2142
Big Horn Mrs. Genevieve Dyche, Hardin 59034   (406)665-1906
Blaine Nancy Neibauer, Chinook 59523   (406)357-3335* (Economic Assis-
tance) and (406)357-3330 (Social Services)
Broadwater Norman Waterman, Townsend 59644   (406)266-3447

Carbon Mrs. Helen Bohnert, Red Lodge 59068   (406)446-1302
Carter Mrs. Betty Mueller, Ekalaka 59324   (406)775-3251
Cascade Harold McLaughlin, P.O. Box 1546, Great Falls 59401
        (406)761-6605* or 0655 (Economic Assistance) 316-1st Ave., N., Great
        Falls 59401   (406)727-4421 (Social Services)
Chouteau Olga Erickson, Ft. Benton 59442   (406)662-5251
Custer Ruth Stephenson, Miles City 59301   (406)232-1247
Daniels Delores Shelton, P.O. Box 794, Scobey 59474   (406)487-2721
Dawson George Shanley, Glendive 59330   (406)365-4314
Deer Lodge Stanley Drazich, Anaconda 59711   (406)563-3448
Fallon Betty Mueller, Baker 59313   (406)778-2512
Fergus Verlin Gaskill, Lewiston 59457   (406)538-9432 or 8411
Flathead Ruth Davis, Kalispell 59901   (406)755-5300
Gallatin Robert Sybrant, Bozeman 59715   (406)587-3193
Garfield Ethel Bond, Jordon 59337   (406)435-2297
Glacier Lowell McGhie, Cut Bank 59427   (406)938-4134; Browning 59471
        (406)338-5131
Golden Verlin Gaskill, Ryegate 59074   (406)568-2231
Granite Frieda Howery, Philipsburg 59858   (406)859-3671
Hill Nancy Neibauer, Havre 59501   (406)265-5481, ext. 42
Jefferson Norman Waterman, Boulder 59632   (406)225-3327
Judith Basin Verlin Gaskill, Stanford 59479   (406)566-2461
Lake Bonnie Mueller, Polson 59860   (406)883-2500
Lewis and Clark Norman Waterman, Helena 59601   (406)442-2020
Liberty Nancy Neibauer, Chester 59522   (406)334-3841
Lincoln William Willard, Libby 59923   (406)293-6249 or 296-2424
McCone Ethel Bond, Circle 59215   (406)485-3425
Madison Emery Smith, Virginia City 59755   (406)843-5361
Meagher Robert Sybrant, White Sulphur Springs 59645   (406)547-3752
Mineral Mrs. Edna Brader, Superior 59872   (406)822-4551
Missoula Elizabeth Johnson, Missoula 59801   (406)543-6641* (Economic
        Assistance) or (406)728-7210 (Social Services)
Musselshell Verlin Gaskill, Roundup 59072   (406)323-2101
Park Robert Sybrandt, Livingston 59047   (406)222-1173
Petroleum Verlin Gaskill, Winnett 59087   (406)429-4555
Philips Delores Shelton, Malta 59538   (406)654-2252
Pondera Rita Christiaens, Conrad 59425   (406)278-5222
Powder River James Petersen, Broadus 59317   (406)436-2621
Powell Frieda Howery, Deer Lodge 59722   (406)846-1092
Prairie Ethel Bond, Terry 59349   (406)637-5570
Ravalli Alice Thane, Hamilton 59840   (406)363-1944
Richland Sharon Rau, Sidney 59270   (406)482-2015

Roosevelt Delores Shelton, P.O. Box 370, Wolf Point 59201   (406)653-1512
  (Economic Assistance); P.O. Box 28, Culbertson 59218   (406)787-5861
  (Social Services); P.O. Box 849, Poplar 59255   (406)768-3911 (Social
  Services)
Rosebud Michael Kennedy, Forsyth 59327   (406)356-2563; Lame Deer 59043
  (406)477-6251
Sanders Norma Jones, Thompson Falls 59873   (406)827-3581
Sheridan Delores Shelton, P.O. Box 413, Plentywood 59254   (406)765-1370
Silver Bow Queenie Lynch, Butte 59701   (406)792-2351* (Economic Assis-
  tance) or (406)792-0436 (Social Services)
Stillwater Diane Altimus, Columbus 59019   (406)322-5331
Sweet Grass Diane Altimus, Big Timber 59011   (806)932-2566
Teton Rita Christiaens, Chouteau 59422   (406)466-5721
Toole Rita Christiaens, Shelby 59474   (406)434-2371
Treasure Michael Kennedy, Hysham 59038   (406)342-2191
Valley Delores Shelton, P.O. Box 272, Glasgow 59230   (406)228-8662 or 8281
Wheatland David Wallace, Harlowton 59036   (406)632-5611
Wibaux Betty Mueller, Wibaux 59353   (406)795-2433
Yellowstone James Greer, Courthouse, Rm. 207, Billings 59101
  (406)248-1691

Nebraska

Reporting Requirements

Persons mandated to report (compulsory) when reasonable cause to believe a child is or has been subjected to abuse or neglect: physician, medical institution, nurse, school employee, social worker, or any other person with reasonable cause to believe that a child or incompetent or disabled person is being abused or neglected

Permissive: none

Form of report and when made: oral, followed by written report; no time requirement

To whom report is made: proper law enforcement agency

Penalties: none

Immunities: none

Child Abuse Legislation

Citation: NRS §28-1501-1508, §43-205.06; 209 (6)
Year enacted: 1974
Effective date: not available
Purpose of legislation: mandatory reporting, yes
Reportable age: "child" includes any incompetent or disabled person who has been subjected to abuse
Definition: anyone who knowingly, intentionally, or negligently causes or permits a minor child, incompetent, or disabled person to be placed in a situation that may endanger his life or health; tortured, cruelly confined, or cruelly punished; deprived of necessary food, clothing, shelter, or care;

left unattended in a motor vehicle if such minor child is 6 years of age or
    younger
Education/school reports: mandatory reporting, yes
Immunity: yes
Mandatory investigation: yes, no specific time frame
Confidentiality of records: no specific provision (however language suggests
    they are confidential); penalty: no specific provision
Cooperation with law courts, state agencies: no specific provision
Guardian ad litem: yes
Administrative proceedings, trained personnel, facilities: no specific provision
Dissemination of information: no specific provision

Programs and Agencies

Where to write:

> Director, Department of Public Welfare
> 1526 K St., 4th Fl.
> Lincoln 68508

Nebraska Department of Public Welfare

> 1526 K St., 4th Fl.
> Lincoln 68508
> Telephone: (402)471-2369
> Eldin J. Ehrlich, Director
> Alan H. Ihms, Dep. Director
> Derald Lembrich, Dep. Director
> Michael D. Lamontia, Exec. Assistant
> E. D. Warnsholz, Gen. Cnsl.

Public Information Office

> Virgin Falloon, Chief

Administrative Support

> Bud Whitmore, Mgr.

Division of Social Services

> 4900 O St.
> Lincoln 68510
> Telephone: (402)471-2983
> Larry Nedrow, Chief

Department of Public Welfare Regional Offices

Region I. (Banner, Box Butte, Cheyenne, Dawes, Deuel, Garden, Kimball, Morril, Scottsbluff, Sheridan, and Sioux Counties): 1030 North St., 2nd Fl., Gering 69341   Delmas Lamberson, Dir. (308)436-2828

Region II. (Arthur, Chase, Dawson, Dundy, Frontier, Gosper, Hant, Hayes, Hitchcock, Hooker, Keith, Lincoln, Logan, McPherson, Perkins, Red Willow, and Thomas Counties): 1019 Jeffers Street, North Platte 69101 Warren Krages, Dir. (308)532-7221

Region III. (Adams, Blaine, Buffalo, Clay, Custer, Franklin, Furnas, Garfield, Greeley, Hall, Hamilton, Harlan, Howard, Kearny, Loup, Merrick, Nuckolls, Phelps, Sherman, Valley, Webster, and Wheeler Counties): P.O. Box 1967, Grand Island 68801   Vernon Smith, Dir. (308)382-0376

Region IV. (Antelope, Boone, Boyd, Brown, Burt, Cedar, Cherry, Colfas, Cuming, Dakota, Dixon, Holt, Keya, Paha, Knox, Madison, Nance, Pierce, Platte, Stanton, Thurston, and Wayne Counties): 118 Norfolk Avenue, Norfolk 68701   Thurman Carpenter, Dir. (402)371-6506

Region V. (Butler, Cass, Fillmore, Gage, Jefferson, Johnson, Lancaster, Nemaha, Otoe, Pawnee, Polk, Richardson, Saline, Saunders, Seward, Thayer, and York Counties): 525 S. 13th St., Lincoln 68608   John Gage, Dir. (402)471-2741

Region VI. (Dodge, Douglas, Sarpy, and Washington Counties): City National Bank Building, Rm. 1120, 405 S. 16th St., Omaha 68102   Philip Caniglia, Dir. (402)554-2021

County Division of Public Welfare

Adams Lawrence L. Morris, Hastings 68901   (402)463-2491
Antelope Mrs. Louise Ruterbories, Neligh 68756   (402)887-4196
Arthur Douglas Cole, Ogallala 69153   (308)284-4698
Banner Mrs. Dianna Bokelman, Harrisburg 69345   (308)436-5265
Blaine Mrs. Shirley Kennedy, Brewster 68821   (308)547-2226
Boone Charlene J. Ludwick, Albion 68620   (402)395-2440
Box Butte Dave N. Ashley, Alliance 69301   (308)762-3360
Boyd Mrs. Vivian I. Kinzie, Butte 68722   (402)775-2551
Brown Mrs. Josephine See, Ainsworth 69210   (402)387-2523
Buffalo Mrs. Arlis Torrey, Kearney 68847   (308)237-5981
Burt Mrs. Dorothy Moore, Tekamah 68061   (402)374-2332
Butler Mrs. Mildred Schroeder, David City 68632   (402)367-3091
Cass Mrs. Beulah Kildare, Plattsmouth 68048   (402)296-3257
Cedar Mrs. William Jean Leise, Hartington 68739   (402)254-3983
Chase Mrs. Juanita O'Neil, Imperial 69033   (308)882-4791
Cherry Mrs. Marcella Mooney, Valentine 69201   (402)376-1790
Cheyenne Virgil Knackstedt, Sidney 79162   (308)254-5891

Clay Donald Mills, Clay Center 68933 (402)762-5465

Colfax Mrs. Evelyn Vanicek, Schuyler 68661 (402)352-5466

Cuming Mrs. Ester Thompson, West Point 68788 (402)372-2340

Custer Mrs. Margaret Hall, Broken Bow 68822 (308)872-6416

Dakota Mrs. Mildred Jorgensen, Dakota City 68731 (402)987-3445

Dawes Mrs. Phyllis Brown, Chadron 69337 (308)432-2952

Dawson Edward Maertens, Lexington 68850 (308)324-4679

Deuel Mrs. Laura Terry, Chappell 69129 (308)874-2203

Dixon Mrs. Doris Anderson, Ponca 68770 (402)755-2291

Dodge Mrs. Donna Stork, Fremont 68025 (402)721-7010

Douglas Michael T. Healey, 1101 S. 42nd St., Omaha 68105 (402)444-7511

Dundy Mrs. Patricia Denny, Benkelman 69021 (308)423-2328

Fillmore Otis Mattox, Geneva 68361 (402)759-3718

Franklin Franklin Reynolds, Franklin 68939 (308)425-6869

Frontier Mrs. Dianna Miller, Curtis 69025 (308)367-8344

Furnas Mrs. Barbara Bates, Beaver City 68926 (308)268-3185

Gage Mrs. Doris Crocker, Beatrice 68310 (402)223-4006

Garden Mrs. Ardis Shepherd, Income Maintenance Technician-in-Charge, Oshkosh 69154 (308)772-3745

Garfield Mrs. Lila Goos, Burwell 68823 (308)346-4620

Gosper Mrs. Dixie Dreher, Elwood 68937 (308)785-2230

Grant Mrs. Sandra Yorges, Hyannis 69350 (308)458-2241

Greeley Mrs. Alta June Cook, Greeley 68842 (308)428-3655

Hall Mrs. Eleanore Brune, Income Maintenance Technician-in-Charge, 118 S. Pine St., Grand Island 68801 (308)381-1000

Hamilton Charles Ponec, Aurora 68818 (402)694-6134

Harlan Mrs. Carol Wynne, Alma 68920 (308)928-2176

Hayes Mrs. Velma Collins, Hayes Center 69032 (308)286-3415

Hitchcock Mrs. Patricia Merrill, Trenton 69044 (308)334-5545

Holt Mrs. Margaret Saunders, O'Neil 68763 (402)336-2750

Hooker Ruth Barneby, Mullen 69152 (308)546-2248

Howard Kenneth Christensen, St. Paul 68873 (308)754-5408

Jefferson Marianne Bailey, Faribury 68352 (402)729-2896

Johnson Mrs. Esther Buethe, Tecumseh 68450 (402)335-4032

Kearney Mrs. Gaynelle Meiner, Minden 68959 (308)832-2329

Keith Douglas Cole, Ogallala 69153 (308)284-2394

Keya Paha Mrs. Josephine See, Ainsworth 69210 (402)387-2523

Kimball Mrs. Diana Bokelman, Kimball 69145 (308)235-4626

Knox Mrs. Loretta Sandoz, Center 68724 (402)271-6220

Lancaster J. G. Lemonds, 2200 St. Marys, Lincoln 68502 (402)475-6221

Lincoln Mrs. Ester Bloom, North Platte 69101 (308)532-5150

Logan Mrs. Judith I. Gewecke, Stapleton 69163 (308)636-2422

Loup Mrs. Lila Goos, Taylor 68879 (308)942-6615

McPherson Mrs. Ethel Pinkerton, Income Maintenance Technician-in-Charge, Tryon 69167 (308)587-2311

Madison Russel Crocker, Norfolk 68701 (402)371-1744

Merrick Mrs. Garnet Broom, Central City 69826 (308)946-3821

Morrill Mrs. Kathleen Ruda, Bridgeport 69336 (308)262-1703

Nance Ms. Dianna Eggli, Fullerton 68638 (308)536-2511

Nemaha Mrs. LaVerne Weers, Auburn 68305 (402)274-4021

Nuckolls Mrs. Charlotte Clabaugh, Nelson 68961 (402)225-2331

Otoe Mrs. Clara Reimers, Nebraska City 68410 (402)873-5443

Pawnee Mrs. Vera Taylor, Pawnee City 68420 (402)852-2973

Perkins Mrs. Gladys Fitzgerald, Grant 69140 (308)352-4962

Phelps Mrs. Jeanene Schwartz, Holdrege 68949 (308)995-8658

Pierce Mrs. LaVern Dickinson, Pierce 68767 (402)329-6675

Platte Carol Obershaw, Columbus 68601 (402)564-4228

Polk Mrs. Lucile Hohnbaum, Osceola 68651 (402)747-5351

Red Willow Mrs. Dorlean Ward, Income Maintenance Technician-in-Charge, McCook 69001 (308)345-3892

Richardson Deryl Reed, Falls City 68355 (402)245-4469

Rock Mrs. Frances Nelson, Bassett 68714 (402)684-3544

Saline Daryl Wusk, Wilber 68465 (402)821-4371

Sarpy Harvey Shoberg, Papillion 68046 (402)339-4290

Saunders Mrs. Leone Liliedahl, Wahoo 68066 (402)443-4252

Scottsbluff Sanley J. Huth, Gering 69341 (308)437-3341

Seward Mrs. Maysel Pederson, Seward 68434 (402)643-2669

Sheridan William F. Reed, Rushville 69360 (308)327-2651

Sherman James Rademacher, Loup City 68853 (308)745-1516

Sioux Mrs. Elizabeth Quintard, Harrison 69346 (308)668-2407

Stanton Mrs. Verna Chamberlain, Stanton 68779 (402)439-2160

Thayer Mrs. Verma Ripley, Hebron 68370 (402)768-6011

Thomas Mrs. Opal Witt, Thedford 69166 (308)645-2258

Thurston Mrs. Winifred Staub, Pender 68047 (402)385-2571

Valley Mrs. Alma M. Nelson, Ord 68862 (308)728-5731

Washington Mrs. Mary Lou Gregory, Blair 68008 (402)426-2329

Nevada

Reporting Requirements

Persons mandated to report (compulsory) when reasonable cause to believe a child is or has been subjected to abuse or neglect: physicians, surgeons, dentists, osteopaths, chiropractors, optometrists, residents and interns, the superintendent or director of any hospital when physician in staff notifies, licensed nurse, attorney, clergyman, social worker, and every person who maintains or is employed by a licensed child care facility or children's camp

Permissive: none

Form of report and when made: oral, followed by written report as soon as possible

To whom report is made: local office of the welfare division of the department of human resources, any county agency authorized by the juvenile court to receive such reports, any police department or sheriff's office

Penalties: misdemeanor for willful violation

Immunities: civil and criminal immunity for good faith report

Child Abuse Legislation

Citation: NRS §200.501-8
Year enacted: 1965
Effective date: July 1, 1965
Purpose of legislation: mandatory reporting, yes
Reportable age: 0-18 years
Definitions: nonaccidental physical or mental injury, sexual abuse, negligent treatment, or maltreatment

Education/school reports: mandatory reporting, yes
Immunity: yes
Mandatory investigation: yes, promptly
Confidentiality of records: yes; penalty: misdemeanor
Cooperation with law courts, state agencies: yes
Guardian ad litem: no specific provisions
Administrative proceedings, trained personnel, facilities: yes
Dissemination of information: no specific provision

Programs and Agencies

Where to write:

> Welfare Division
> Capitol Complex
> 251 Jeanell Drive
> Carson City 89710

Nevada Department of Human Resources

> Capitol Complex
> 505 E. King Street
> Carson City 89710
> Telephone: (702)885-4730
> Roger S. Trounday, Director

Welfare Division

> 251 Jeanell Drive
> Carson City 89710
> Telephone: (702)885-4771
> George E. Miller, Administrator
> Margie Richards, Chief Deputy Attorney General (702)885-4765
> Earl Yamashita, State Plan Coordinator

Service Operations

> James Faehling, Chief

Program Services

> Gloria Handley, Chief

Program Evaluation

> Betty Madison, Chief

Medical Care Services

Minor Kelso, Chief (702)885-4775

Welfare Division District Offices

Carson City Billie Shearer, Capitol Complex, 410 E. John St., Carson City 89710 (702)885-4760

Elko Doris Anderson, 946 Idaho St., Elko 89801 (702)738-7211

Ely Mary McKay, P.O. Box 506, Ely 89301 (702)289-3091

Pioche Agnes Cottino, P.O. Box 128, Pioche 89043 (702)962-5315

Fallon Phyllis Kent, 151 N. Maine St., Fallon 89406 (702)423-3161

Hawthorne Blanche Edison, P.O. Box 1546-9, Hawthorne 89415 (702)945-3602

Henderson Susan Devens, 145 N. Panama St., Henderson 89015 (702)564-5452

Las Vegas Vince Fallon, 700 Belrose St., Las Vegas 89107 (702)648-8550

Reno Jack Abbott, 790 Sutro St., Reno 89502 (702)623-3679

Winnemucca Robert Jackson, 501 Bridge St., Winnemucca 89445 (702)623-3679

Yerington Joanne Grundman, 14 Pacific St., Yerington 89447 (702)463-2171

New Hampshire

Reporting Requirements

Persons mandated to report (compulsory) when reasonable cause to believe a child is or has been subjected to abuse or neglect: any person having reason to suspect that a child has been neglected or abused; physician on staff at hospital or similar institution shall notify director who shall make report

Permissive: none

Form of report and when made: immediate oral, followed as soon as possible by written

To whom report is made: bureau of child and family services of the division of welfare of the department of health and welfare

Penalties: knowing violation is misdemeanor

Immunities: civil and criminal immunity for good faith report

Child Abuse Legislation

Citation: NHRSA §169:37-44; §170-C:8
Year enacted: 1975
Effective date: exact date not available
Purpose of legislation: mandatory reporting, yes
Reportable age: 0-18 years
Definitions: child who has been sexually molested or has had physical, emotional, or other injuries inflicted by other than accidental means.
Education/school report: mandatory reporting, yes
Immunity: civil/criminal, yes
Mandatory investigation: yes, immediately

192

Confidentiality of records: yes; penalty: no specific provision
Cooperation with law courts, state agencies: no specific provision
Guardian ad litem: yes
Administrative proceedings, trained personnel, facilities: no specific provision
Dissemination of information: no specific provision

Programs and Agencies

Where to write: Correspondence regarding SSI/state supplement aid to families with dependent children, food stamps, medical assistance, and Title XX services program should be addressed to the proper district office. Correspondence regarding social information on general assistance clients should be addressed to the overseer of public welfare in the town or city concerned, or to the board of county commissioners in the county concerned. Correspondence regarding the ability of relatives to provide financial support should be addressed to the relatives themselves. Correspondence regarding the interstate placement of children and other child welfare service programs should be addressed to:

> Bureau of Child and Family Services
> Department of Health and Welfare
> 8 Loudon Rd.
> Concord 03301

New Hampshire Department of Health and Welfare

> 8 Loudon Road
> Concord 03301
> Frances E. Whaland, Comm. (603)271-3331
> Norman Champagne, Asst. to the Comm. (603)271-3597

Bureau of Child and Family Services

> Barbara A. Hanus, Chief (603)271-2522

Division of Welfare District Offices

Berlin (Coos County): 227 Main Street, Berlin 03570   Mylo V. Johnson, Dir.
  (603)752-7800
Claremont (Sullivan County): 137 Broad Street, Claremont 03743   Ruth
  Caine, Dir. (603)542-9544
Concord (Merrimack County): 10 Pleasant St. Ext., Concord 03301   Peter
  Selway, Dir. (603)228-1571
Franklin Branch Office: 2 Central St., Franklin 03235   Elizabeth Dunn, Supv.
  (603)934-4700

Conway (Carroll County): Rte. 16, Box 462, North Conway 03860 Irvin A. Grubbs, Sr., Dir. (603)356-5401

Dover (Strafford County): 4 Plaza Dr., Dover 03820 Agatha King, Dir. (603)749-2210

Rochester Branch Office: 40 Winter St., Rochester 03867 Cynthia Libby, Asst. Superv. (603)332-9120

Keene (Cheshire County): 114-116 Main St., Keene 03431 Carl Jacobs, Jr., Dir. (603)357-3510

Laconia (Belknap County): 111 Church St., Laconia 03246 Elizabeth Farmlett, Dir. (603)524--4485

Manchester (Northern Hillsborough County): 66 Lake Ave., Manchester 03101 Dagny Fecht, Dir. (603)668-2330

Peterborough Branch Office: North Bldg. Rte. 202, Peterborough 03458 (vacant) Supv. (603)924-7262

Nashua (Southern Hillsborough County): 223 Main St., Nashua 03060 Richard Chevrefils, Dir. (603)431-6180

Portsmouth (Rockingham County): 600 State St., Portsmouth 03801 Clifton Stickney, Dir. (603)431-6180

Salem Branch Office: 288 N. Broadway, Salem 03079 Preston Mears, Supv. (603)893-8666

Woodville (Grafton County): 45 Central St., Woodsville 03785 Theodore Marston, Dir. (603)747-2786

Lebanon Branch Office: 2 Mascoma St., Lebanon 03766 Richard Kleinfelder, Supv. (603)448-4700

Littleton Branch Office: 141 Main St., Littleton 03561 Richard Kleinfelder, Supv. (603)444-6514

Ashland Branch Office: 10 N. Main St., Ashland 03217 Richard Kleinfelder, Supv. (603)968-7131

New Jersey

Reporting Requirements

Persons mandated to report (compulsory) when reasonable cause to believe a child is or has been subjected to abuse or neglect: any person having reasonable cause to believe that a child has been subjected to abuse

Permissive: none

Form of report and when made: promptly, by telephone or otherwise

To whom report is made: bureau of children's services

Penalties: knowing failure to report when having reasonable cause renders offender a disorderly person, punishable for that offense

Immunities: civil and criminal immunity when acting pursuant to the act

Child Abuse Legislation

Citation: NJSA Chap. 119 of 1974, §9:6-8.23
Year enacted: 1974
Effective date: October 10, 1974
Purpose of legislation: mandatory reporting, yes
Reporting age: 0-18 years
Definitions: physical injury by other than accidental means; causing or creating risk of death, serious or protracted disfigurement, protracted impairment of physical or emotional health, sexual abuse; failure to provide care; substantial or ongoing risk of physical injury or death.
Education/school report: mandatory reporting, yes
Immunity: civil/criminal, yes
Mandatory investigation: permissive hearing

195

Confidentiality of records: yes; penalty: no specific provision
Cooperation with law courts, state agencies: yes
Guardian ad litem: yes
Administrative proceedings, trained personnel, facilities: no specific provision
Dissemination of information: no specific provision

Programs and Agencies

Requests for information concerning foster home placement, residential or institutional placement, adoptions, guardianships, care, protective services, special consultation services, interstate movement of children, homemaker services, family planning services, the provision of congregate meals, and requests for contacts with relatives of children, families, or aged, blind, or disabled individuals under agency supervision, if social evaulation of a situation is desired, should be addressed to:

Division of Youth and Family Services
Department of Institutions and Agencies
P.O. Box 510
Trenton 08625
James G. Kagen, Director (609)292-6920

Development Operations

Nicholas R. Scalera, Adm. (609)292-6920

Bureau of Research, Planning, and Program Development

William Resnick, Chief (609)292-8060

Bureau of Resource and Development

Fred Sigafoos, Chief (609)292-4941

Field Services Operations

Harold Rosenthal, Adm. (609)292-6920

Bureau of Family Services

Richard O'Grady, Chief (609)292-0570

Bureau of Residential Services

(vacant) Chief (609)292-0730

Management Operations

> Jeffrey Weinstein, Adm. (609)292-1790

Bureau of Fiscal Services

> John F. Henry, Chief (609)292-4613

Bureau of Management Services

> Robert Johnston, Chief (609)292-8253

Contract Development and Administration

> (vacant) Adm. (609)292-1870

Bureau of Day Care Services

> Mary Agnes Jennings, Chief (609)292-4623

Division of Youth and Family Services District Offices

Atlantic and Cape May Counties: 18 S. Arkansas Ave., Atlantic City 08401
George Muller, Supv. (609)344-4141

Bergen County: 190 Main St., Hackensack 07601   Dorothy Donaldson, Supv.
(201)487-5380

Burlington County: 50 Rancocas Rd., Mt. Holly 08060   Alan Eddison, Supv.
(609)267-7550

Camden County: 808 Market St., Camden 08102   Norman Chickachop, Supv.
(609)964-4995

Cumberland and Salem Counties: 40 E. Broad St., Bridgeton 08302   Louis P.
Starkweather, Supv. (609)451-3100

Essex County (excluding Newark): 139 Main St., 2nd Fl., Orange 07050   Iola
Fountain, Supv. (201)672-2900

Gloucester County: 818 N. Broad St., Woodbury 08096   Barry Silverstein,
Supv. (609)848-6604

Hudson County: 910 Bergen Ave., Jersey City 07306   Donald Baird, Supv.
(201)653-5750

Hunterdon and Somerset Counties: 73 E. High St., Somerville 08876   Linda
Lieberman, Supv. (201)722-2224

Mercer County: 1901 N. Olden Ave., Trenton 08618   Thomas Frase, Supv.
(609)883-7970

Middlesex County: 78 Carroll Place, New Brunswick 08901   Barbara Happe,
Supv. (201)249-4616

Monmouth County: Family Center, 705 Summerfield Ave., Asbury Park 07712

Allen Feuchtwanger, Jr., Supv. (201)988-4300; Family Center, 279 Broadway, 6th Fl., Longbranch 07740   William Fredericks, Supv.
(201)870-3400; Family Center, 270 Hwy. 35, Middletown 07748   Linda Hodes, Supv. (201)741-5220

Morris County: 3 Schuyler Pl., Morristown 07960   Joan Schroeder, Supv. (201)822-1770

Newark (city of Newark only): 1100 Raymond Blvd., Rm. 412, Newark 07102

Newark Intake Office: Dolly Bonneau, Supv.

Tramburg Supervision Office: Helen Fradkin, Supv.

Alloway Supervision Office: Robert Lease, Acting Supv.

Ocean County: 954 Lakewood Rd., Toms River 08753   Nelson Amey, Supv. (201)244-4300

Passaic County: 370 Broadway, Paterson 07501   Maureen Hinchy, Supv. (201)742-1428

Sussex and Warren Counties: 200 Woodport Rd., P.O. Box 903, Spata 07801   Louis Purcaro, Supv. (201)729-9163

Union County: 1155 Magnolia Ave., Elizabeth 07207   Florine Brown, Supv. (201)289-3333

New Mexico

Reporting Requirements

Persons mandated to report (compulsory) when reasonable cause to believe a child is or has been subjected to abuse or neglect: any licensed physician, resident, or intern examining, attending, or treating a child; any law enforcement officer; registered or visiting nurse; school teacher or social worker acting in her official capacity; or any other person having reason to believe that serious injury has been inflicted upon a child as a result of abuse, neglect, or starvation

Permissive: none

Form of report and when made: immediately, no form specified

To whom report is made: county social services office of the health and social services department in the county where the child lives, the probation services office of that judicial district

Penalties: misdemeanor for failure to report, fine not less than $25 and not more than $100

Immunities: presumption of good faith provides civil land criminal immunity unless rebutted by a showing of bad faith or malicious purpose

Child Abuse Legislation

Citation: NMSA §13-14-14, 13-14-251(G)
Year enacted: 1973
Effective date: April 3, 1973
Purpose of legislation: mandatory reporting, yes
Reporting age: 0–18 years
Definitions: no definition stated

Education school report: mandatory reporting, yes
Immunity: civil/criminal, yes
Mandatory investigation: no specific time frame or provision
Confidentiality of records: no specific provision; penalty: no specific provision
Cooperation with law courts, state agencies: no specific provision
Guardian ad litem: yes
Administrative proceedings, trained personnel, facilities: no specific provision
Dissemination of information: no specific provision

Programs and Agencies

Where to write:

New Mexico Health and Social Services Department
P. O. Box 2348
Santa Fe 87503
Fernando E. C. DeBaca, Exec. Dir. (505)827-2371
Alex Armijo, Adm. for Planning and Mgmt. (505)827-5400
Larry Gordon, Adm. for Health and Environmental Programs (505)827-3164
Charles Lopez, Adm. for Social Welfare Programs (505)827-5151
(vacant) Gen. Cnsl. (505)827-2305

Office of Fiscal and Administrative Services

Max Garcia, Dir. (505)827-5485

Social Services Agency

Richard Cole, Act. Dir. (505)827-2208
Michael Varela, Dep. Dir. (505)827-2208
David Cohen, Legal Cnsl. (505)827-2305

Social Services Agency County Offices

Bernalillo* Marcos Romero, P. O. Box 669, Albuquerque 87102   (505)265-1761
Catron Served by Grant County Office
Chaves* Nancy Harvey, 105 W. 3rd St., Rosewell 88201   (505)623-5131
Colfax Janet Bryan, P. O. Box 368, Ratan 87740   (505)455-2222
Curry Judith Bonem, P. O. Box 423, Clovis 88101   (505)762-7721
Debaca Served by Curry County Office
Dona Ana* Alline Stevens, P. O. Box 790, Las Cruces 88001   (505)542-2807
Eddy* Doris Sturdevant, 701 N. Guadalupe St., Carlsbad 88220   (505)
     887-3576
Grant* Olive Lamgendorf, P. O. Box 311, Silver City 88061   (505)538-2948

Guadalupe Served by San Miguel County Office
Harding Served by Colfax County Office
Hidalgo Served by Grant County Office
Lea* Served by Eddy County Office
Lincoln* Served by Otero County Office
Los Alamos Served by Rio Arriba County Office
Luna Served by Grant County Office
McKinley Beverly Maldonado, P. O. Box Drawer 1300, Gallup 87301   (505)
    863-9556
Mora Served by San Miguel County Office
Otero* Phyllis Morgan, 411 10th St, Alamogordo 88310   (505)437-0030
Quay Served by Curry County Office
Rio Arriba* Larry Lucero, P. O. Box 219, Espanola 87532   (505)753-7191
Roosevelt Served by Curry County Office
Sandoval Served by Bernalillo County Office
San Juan Tom Kerley, P. O. Drawer 1, Farmington 87401   (505)325-7575
San Miguel* Epifania Duran, P. O. Box 1348, Las Vegas 87701   (505)427-6741
Santa Fe* Robert Hayward, 104 S. Capitol St., Santa Fe 87503 (505)827-5422
Sierra William Strouse, P. O. Box 392, Truth or Consequences 87901   (505)
    894-6644
Socorro Served by Sierra County Office
Taos Mary Alexander, P. O. Box 1816, Taos 87571 (505)758-2279
Torrance Served by Valencia County Office
Union Served by Colfax County Office
Valencia Pete Adolph, P. O. Box 435, Belen 87002 (505)864-7432

New York

Reporting Requirements

Persons mandated to report (compulsory) when reasonable cause to believe a child is or has been subjected to abuse or neglect: physician; surgeon; medical examiner; coroner; dentist; osteopath; optometrist; chiropractor; podiatrist; resident; intern; registered nurse; hospital personnel engaged in the admission, examination, care, or treatment of persons; Christian Science practitioner; school official; social services worker; day-care center or other child care or foster worker; mental health professional; peace officer or law enforcement official (both staff and director in agencies may report)

Permissive: any person having reasonable cause to suspect that the child is an abused or maltreated child

Form of report and when made: immediate oral; written, within 48 hours

To whom report is made: to statewide registry, unless appropriate local plan calls for report to local child protective service; written reports shall always be made to the local service; if the child has died, report must be made to the appropriate medical examiner or coroner

Penalties: criminal: class A misdemeanor for willing failure to report; civil: civil liability for all proximate damages caused by knowing and willing failure to report

Immunities: presumption of good faith in making report; civil and criminal immunity for reporters

Child Abuse Legislation

Citation: Tit. 6, L. 1973, Chap. 1039; NYFC Act §241-9
Year enacted: 1973

Effective date: June 23, 1973
Purpose of legislation: mandatory reporting, yes
Reportable age: 0-18 years
Definitions: abused, as defined by family court act; neglected, as defined by family court act; or has had serious physical injury inflicted upon him by other than accidental means
Education/school reports: mandatory reporting, yes
Immunity: yes
Mandatory investigation: yes, 24 hours
Confidentiality of records: yes; penalty: misdemeanor
Cooperation with law courts, state agencies: no specific provision
Guardian ad litem: yes
Administrative proceedings, trained personnel, facilities: yes
Dissemination of information: yes

Programs and Agencies

Where to write:

Division of Services
Department of Social Services
1450 Western Ave.
Albany 12203

New York State Department of Social Services

1450 Western Ave.
Albany 12243
Philip L. Toia, Comm. (518)457-7454
(vacant) Exec. Dep. Comm. (518)457-5224
Sheldon Jaffee, Assoc. Comm. for Admv. Srvs. (518)457-5224
Hugh B. O'Neil, Spec. Asst. to the Comm. (518)457-6894
William Sais, Spec. Asst. to the Comm. for Community Relations, Two
  World Trade Center
  New York 10047 (212)488-2339
Pat Bartlett, Exec. Asst. to the Exec. Dep. Comm. (518)457-6958
Carmen Shang, Cnsl. (518)457-7662

Office of Child Support

Albert Jackson, Dir., Two World Trade Center
New York 10047 (212)488-3803

Bureau of Family Services

  Gregory L. Coler, Dir. (518)457-7261

Day Care Section

  Berta M. Brewster, Dir. (518)457-734⁵

Foster Care/Adoption Center

  Robert Paige, Dir. (518)457-6162

Bureau of Child Protective Services

  James S. Cameron, Dir. (518)457-6287

Board of Social Welfare Area Offices

I.   *Buffalo* (Cattaraugus, Chatauqua, Erie, Genesee, Niagara, Orleans, and
     Wyoming Counties): 125 Main St., Buffalo 14203   (vacant) Area Dir.
     (716)842-4403; Adult Institutions (716)842-4375; Children's Services
     (716(842-4471

II. *Rochester* (Allegheny, Chemung, Livingston, Monroe, Ontario, Schuyler,
     Seneca, Steuben, Wayne, and Yates Counties): 36 Main St. F. Rochester
     14606   Mrs. Rose Marie Dunham, area Dir. (716)454-7870; Adult Institu-
     tions (716)454-7872; Children's Services (716)454-7870

III. *Syracuse* (Broome, Cayuga, Chenango, Cortland, Herkimer, Jefferson, Lewis,
     Madison, Oneida, Onondaga, Oswego, St. Lawrence, Tioga, and Tompkins
     Counties): 333 E. Washington St., Syracuse 13202   Mrs. Rose Marie
     Durham, Area Dir. (315)473-8470; Adult Institutions (315)473-8410;
     Children's Services (315)473-8118

IV. *Albany* Albany, Clinton, Columbia, Delaware, Essex, Franklin, Fulton,
     Greene, Hamilton, Montgomery, Otsego, Rensselaer, Saratoga, Schenectady,
     Schoharie, Warren, and Washington Counties): 74 State St., Albany 12207
     Arthur J. Doring, Area Dir. (518)474-8534: Adult Institutions (518)
     474-4137; Children's Services (518)474-4143

V.   *New York Suburban* (Dutchess, Nassau, Orange, Putnam, Rockland, Suffolk,
     Sullivan, and Westchester Counties): Two World Trade Center, 55th Fl.,
     New York 10047   (vacant), Ass. Exec. Dir. for the Metropolitan Area
     (212)488-7024; Adult Institutions (212)488-3560; Children's Services
     (212)488-4588

VI. *New York City* (Bronx, Kings, New York, Queens, and Richmond Counties):
     Two World Trade Center, 55th Fl., New York 10047   (vacant) Asst. Exec.
     Dir. for the Metropolitan Area (212)488-7024; Adult Institutions (212)
     488-3560; Children's Services (212)488-3485

Local Departments of Social Services

Albany* John J. Fahey, 40 Howard St., Albany 12207 (518)471-5300

Allegany Raymond F. Shear, County Home, Angelica 14709 (716)466-7691

Bronx See below, New York City

Broome Peter Dinitri (Act.) 119 Shenago St., Binghamton 13901 (607)
722-2401

Cattaragus Ronald Hackett, 265 N. Union St., Olean 14760 (716)372-0030

Cayuga Anthony Sylvester, County Office Bldg., 160 Genesee St., Auburn
13021 (315)253-1011

Chautaqua Charles V. Fiorella, Hall R. Clothier Health and Social Service Bldg.,
Mayville 14757 (716)753-7161

Chemung William Liddle, 203-209 William St., Elmira 14901 (607)737-2842

Chenango Stanley J. Kimiecik, Jr., County Office Bldg., Norwich 13815
(607)335-4521

Clinton Richard H. Duquette, 10 Healey Ave., P. O. Box 990, Plattsburg 12901
(518)563-4560

Columbia James R. Van Alstyne, 610 State St., Hudson 12534 (518)828-9411

Cortland S. Margaret Cashel (Act.) 133 Homer Ave. Cortland 13045 (607)
753-9681

Delaware Francis M. Comins, 126 Main St., Delhi 13753 (607)746-2325

Dutchess William J. Eagen Jr., County Office Bldg., 22 Market St., Poughkeepsie
12603 (914)485-4690

Erie* Barry Van Lare, 95 Franklin St., Buffalo 14202 (716)846-7511

Essex Robert E. Laundree, Courthouse, Elizabethtown 12932 (518)873-6301

Franklin Orra A. Langdon, Jr., Courthouse, Malone 12953 (518)483-4770

Fulton William Grandy Foster, County Building, Johnstown 12095 (518)
762-4671

Genesee Miss Beverly J. Crabb, 3837 W. Main Rd., Batavia 14020
(716)343-8786

Greene Miss Estella Canniff, 465 Main St., Catskill 12414 (518)943-3200

Hamilton David Curry (Act.), Courthouse, Lake Pleasant 12108 (518)548-3462

Herkimer Michael John Bush, County Office Bldg., Herkimer 13350
(315)866-3420

Jefferson Mrs. S. Jean Wagoner, 173 Arsenel St., Watertown 13601
(315)785-3141

Kings See below, New York City

Lewis Beryl W. Freeman, Stowe St., Lowville 13367 (315)376-3536

Livingston W. Michael Woodhouse, 4223 Lakeville Rd., Genesee 14454
(716)243-3100

Madison William T. Carlson, Wampsville 13163 (315)366-2211

Monroe James Reed, 111 Westfall Rd., Rochester 14620 (716)442-4000

Montgomery Francis G. Dimond, County Office Bldg., Fonda 12068
(518)853-3491

Nassau Joseph A. D'Elia, Administration Bldg., 900 Ellison Ave., Westbury
  11590 (516)535-2950

New York See below, New York City

Niagara John A. Weber, 100 Davidson Rd., P. O. Box 506, Lockport 14094
  (716)433-2671

Oneida Mrs. Antoinette Hyer, County Office Bldg., 800 Park Ave., Utica 13501
  (315)798-5733

Onondaga John L. Lascaris, Onondaga County Civic Center, 421 Montgomery
  St., Syracuse 13202 (315)425-2985

Ontario George E. Boisvert, 120 N. Main St., Canandaigua 14424
  (315)394-1440

Orange Henry G. Parry, Jr., Quarry Rd., Box Z, Goshen 10924 (914)294-9361

Orleans Jerim Klapper, County Home, Albion 14411 (716)589-5676

Oswego Rupert J. Collins, County Office Bldg., Spring St., Mexico 13114
  (315)963-7271

Otsego Alton E. Sillieto, County Office Bldg., 197 Main St., Cooperstown
  13326 (607)547-9901

Putnam John Sweeney, 2 Mahopac Plaza, Mahopac 10541 (914)628-7403

Queens See below, New York City

Rensselaer* John R. Beaudoin, 133 Bloomingrove Dr., Troy 12180
  (518)283-2000

Richmond See below, New York City

Rockland Noah Weinberg, 250 N. Nyack Rd., West Nyack 10994
  (914)623-1000

St. Lawrence Donald E. Kitchin, Harold B. Smith County Office Bldg., Judson
  St., Canton 13617 (315)379-2100

Saratoga Joseph V. Gemmiti, County Complex Bldg., A, Ballston Spa 12020
  (518)885-5381

Schenectady Richard J. Stazak, 487 Nott St., Schenectady 12308
  (518)382-3400

Schoharie Russel Palmer, Professional Bldg., Schoharie 12157 (518)295-8173

Schuyler Robert O. Bale, Jr., County Office Bldg., Watkins Glen 14891
  (607)535-2789

Seneca Richard S. Dombrowski, County Office Bldg., 118 R.D. 3 Box 179,
  Waterloo 13165 (315)568-9854

Steuben Miss Sara Curtis, County Home, Box 631, Bath 14810 (607)776-7611

Suffolk* James E. Kirby, 10 Oval Dr., P. O. Box 2000, Hauppauge 11787
  (516)348-4004

Sullivan Robert B. Travis, P. O. Box 231, Liberty 12754 (914)292-4900

Tioga Allan J. Eisenberg, Rte. 38, R.D. 3, Box 394, Owego 13827
  (607)687-5000

Tompkins Robert J. Wagner, 108 Green St., E., Ithaca 14850 (607)273-9050

Ulster Bernhardt S. Kramer, County Office Bldg., 244 Fair St., Kingston 12401
  (914)331-9300

Warren   Joseph Nenaldino, County Municipal Center, Lake George 12845
(518)792-9951
Washington Donald R. Reynolds, 6 Church St., Granville 12832 (518)793-8837
Wayne James F. Bellamy, 16 Williams St., Lyons 14489   (315)946-4881
Westchester Charles W. Bates, 150 Grand St., White Plains 10601
(914)682-2471
Wyoming Mrs. Lois Bowling, 466 N. Main St., Warsaw 14569   (716)796-3111
Yates William J. Falvey, County Office Bldg., Court St., Penn Yan 14527
(315)536-4451
New York J. Henry Smith, 250 Church St., New York 10013 (212)553-5465
(Boroughs of Bronx, Brooklyn, Manhattan, Queens, and Richmond (Staten
Island)

North Carolina

Reporting Requirements

Persons mandated to report (compulsory) when reasonable cause to believe a child is or has been subjected to abuse or neglect: Any professional person who has reasonable cause to suspect that any child is an abused child

Permissive: None

Form of report and when made: oral, telephone, or written; no time limit

To whom report is made: director of social services of the county where the child lives or is found

Penalties: none

Immunities: Any person making a report or otherwise participating in the program set up by the act is given civil and criminal immunity in the absence of a showing of malice or lack of reasonable cause.

Child Abuse Legislation

Citation: NCGS 7A-286(7)
Year enacted: 1975
Effective date: Exact date not available
Purpose of legislation: mandatory reporting, yes
Reportable age: 0-18 years
Definitions: physical injury by other than accidental means which causes a substantial risk, death, disfigurement, or impairment of physical health
Education/school reports: mandatory reporting, yes
Immunity: yes
Mandatory investigation: yes, promptly

Confidentiality of records: yes; penalty: no specific provision
Cooperation with law courts, state agencies: no specific provision
Guardian ad litem: no specific provision
Administrative proceedings, trained personnel, facilities: no specific provision
Dissemination of information: no specific provision

Programs and Agencies

Where to write:

Division of Social Services
Department of Human Resources
325 N. Salisbury St.
Raleigh 27611

North Carolina Department of Human Resources

325 N. Salisbury St.,
Raleigh 27611
Telephone: (919)829-4534
Philip J. Kirk, Secy.
Ben W. Aiken, Asst. Secy.
Craig Souza, Chf. Asst.
Bill White, Special Asst.
R.L. Holley, Comptroller
Archie Johnson, M.D., Asst. Secy. for Health Affairs and Dir. Health
  Planning and Resources Development
Frank Thompson, Dir. of Public Information (919)829-4471
Clark Edwards, Dir. Personnel Management Services Division (919)829-2940
Tom Cross, Dir. Administrative Services Division (919)829-4358
Harold M. Manes, Dir., Plans and Programs Division (919)829-2173
J. S. Grimes II, Dir., Information and Referral (919)829-4261
Care Line, information and referral. 1-800-662-7030 (toll-free in N. C.)
Sue Glasby, Head, Children's Services (919)829-7907
Thomas Barnett, Head, PACE in N.C. (919)829-4650
Gary Vassar, Head, Jobs Corps, (919)829-4610
Helen Crisp, Ph.D., Head, Psychological Services (919)829-4458
Mrs. Jacqueline Vogel, Head, Contract Services (919)829-4690

Department of Human Resources Regional Offices

I. Western (Alexander, Allegheny, Ashe, Avery, Buncombe, Burke, Cabarrus,
  Caldwell, Catawba, Cherokee, Clay, Cleveland, Gaston, Graham, Haywood,

Henderson, Iredell, Jackson, Lincoln, McDowell, Macon, Madison, Mecklenburg, Mitchell, Polk, Rowan, Rutherford, Stanley, Swain, Transylvania,
Union, Watauga, Wilkes, and Yancey Counties): Western Carolina Sanitor-
ium, Bldg. 7, Black Mountain 28711

Division of Social Services

Melvin Martin, Dir. (704)669-6479

Division of Health Services

James McCormick, Jr., Dir. (704)669-6445

Division of Mental Health Services

Dr. Gary Greer, Dir. (704)669-8056

Division of Vocational Rehabilitation Services

John Yoder, Dir. (704)669-8080

Division of Services for the Blind

R. L. Clark, Dir. (704)669-6448;
District Office: Cole Bldg., 207 Hawthorne Lane, Charlotte 28204
J. W. Smith, Supv. (704)334-4781

Division of Youth Services

c/o Juvenile Evaluation Center, Swannanoa 28778
Ken Foster, Dir. (704)686-5411

II. *North Central* (Alamance, Caswell, Davidson, Davie, Forsyth, Franklin,
Granville, Guilford, Person, Randolph, Rockingham, Stokes, Surry, Vance,
Warren and Yakin Counties): 720 Colesium Plaza, W. Winston-Salem 27106

Division of Social Services

Albert E. Thompson, Dir. (919)761-2320

Division of Health Services

Robert L. Lichtenhan, Dir. (919)727-2417

Division of Mental Health Services

Dr. Patterson Webb, Dir. (919)761-2375

D ivision of Vocational Rehabilitation Services

C. Page Truitt, Dir. (919)761-2290

Division of Services for the Blind

A. B. Caudle, Dir. (919)722-2445

Division of Youth Services

>   1520 A. Martin St., Suite 110, Winston-Salem 27103
>   Ray Moss, Dir. (919)722-9341

III. South Central (Anson, Bladen, Chatham, Cumberland, Durham, Hartnett, Hoke, Johnston, Lee, Montgomery, Moore, Orange, Richmond, Robeson, Sampson, Scotland, and Wake Counties): Wachovia Bank Bldg., Suite 604, 225 Green St., Fayetteville 28301

Division of Social Services

>   Robert G. Stewart, Dir. (919)323-0717

Division of Health Services

>   Etra Wood, Dir. (919)483-3635

Division of Mental Health Services

>   Dr. Will Adgerton, Dir. (919)323-1252

Division of Vocational Rehabilitation Services

>   Thomas R. Gaines, Dir. (919)323-1119

Division of Services for the Blind

>   Harry L. Wicker, Dir. (919)484-4141; District Office: 410 N. Boylan Ave., P. O. Box 2658, Raleigh 27602   Mrs. Hilda M. Sandlin, Sup. (919) 829-4231

Division of Youth Services

>   Wachovia Bldg., 225 Green St., Suite 1003, Fayetteville 28301   George Hicks, Dir. (919)485-8841

IV. Eastern (Beaufort, Bertie, Brunswick, Camden, Carteret, Chowan, Columbus, Craven, Currituck, Dare, Duplin, Edgecombe, Gate, Green, Halifax, Hertford, Hyde, Jones, Lenoir, Martin, Nash, New Hanover, Northampton, Onslow, Pamlico, Pasquotank, Pender, Perquimans, Pitt, Tyrrell, Washington, Wayne, and Wilson): 404 St. Andrews St., Greenville 27834

Division of Social Services

>   H. Leon Norman, Dir. (919)756-6742

Division of Health Services

>   Jean Lassiter, Dir. (919)756-1343

Division of Mental Health Services

>   Dr. Robert Radcliff, Dir. (919)756-2295

Division of Vocational Rehabilitation Services

Forrest H. Teague, Dir. (919)756-3112

Division of Services for the Blind

Mack V. Worley, Jr., Dir. (919)756-5851; District Office: 601 Carolina
Power and Light Bldg., Corner 4th and Chestnut Streets, Wilmington 28401
Ronald C. Brantly, Sup. (919)763-6241

Division of Youth Services

221 W. 10th St., Suite D, Greenville 27834   Paul Holeman, Dir. (919)
752-3732

County Departments of Social Services

Almance Annie Laurie Burton, P. O. Box 3406, Burlington 27215
Alexander James Berdine, 100 Happy Plains Dr., Taylorsville 28681
Alleghaney Mrs. Rodney F. Busic, P. O. Box 194, Sparta 28675
Anson Charles P. Haskill, P. O. Box 213, Wadesboro 28170
Ashe Frances Tucker, P. O. Box 298, Jefferson 28640
Avery Donald Lee Thompson, P. O. Box 187, Newland 28657
Beaufort Mrs. Betty Agnew P. O. Box 1048, Washington 27889
Bertis Mrs. Mary Whitted, P. O. Box 627, Winsor 27983
Bladen Charles E. Prince, P. O. Box 365, Elizabethtown 28337
Brunswick Joel R. Webb, P. O. Box 368, Southport 28461
Buncombe Mrs. Margaret H. Coman, P. O. Box 7555, Asheville 28807
Burke James A. Blakely, P. O. Drawer 549, Morgantown 28655
Cabarrus Mrs. Frances B. Long, P. O. Box 668, Concord 28025
Caldwell H. Gene Herrell, P. O. Box 930, Lenoir 28645
Camden John B. Spangler (Trainee) P. O. Box 62, Camden 27973
Carteret Robert D. Eason, P. O. Box 329, Beaufort 28516
Caswell Frank Hinson (Trainee), P. O. Box 187, Yanceyville 27379
Catawba Willard C. Blevins, P. O. Box 669, Newton 28658
Chatham Mrs. C.K. Strowd, P. O. Box 488, Pittsboro 27312
Cherokee Vernie O. Ayers, P. O. Box 595, Murphy 28906
Chowan Ronald Huffman, P. O. Box 296, Edenton 27932
Clay (vacant) P. O. Box 137, Hayersville 28904
Cleveland Hal D. Smith, 130 S. Post Rd., Shelby 28105
Columbus Mrs. Alice S. Wright, P. O. Box 112, Whiteville 28472
Craven Jane T. Stephenson, P. O. Box 310, New Bern 28560
Cumberland E. C. Modlin, P. O. Drawer 4384, Fayetteville 28306
Currituck Mrs. Cora Edge, P. O. Box 25, Currituck 27929
Dare Mark Aydlett (In Charge), P. O. Box 667, Manteo 27954
Davidson Doris Gertrude Lopp, P. O. Box 788, Lexington 27292

Davie Donald C. Wall, P. O. Box 446, Mocksville 27028
Duplin Mrs. Millie Brown (In Charge), P. O. Box 439, Kenansville 28349
Durham Thomas W. Hogan, P. O. Box 810, Durham 27702
Edgecombe Mrs. Claudia Edwards, P. O. Box 38, Tarboro 27886
Forsyth Gerald Thorton, P. O. Box 999, Winston-Salem 27102
Franklin Mrs. Jane York, P. O. Box 669, Louisburg 27549
Gaston Ben Carpenter, P. O. Box 10, Gastonia 28052
Gates Mrs. Mary Riddick, P. O. Box 185, Gatesville 27938
Graham Mrs. Christine Corpening, P. O. Box 398, Robinsville 28771
Granville William W. Mullen, P. O. Box 966, Oxford 27565
Greene Rachael Sugg, 103 S. E. 2nd St., Snow Hill 28580
Guilford Wayne Metz, P. O. Box 3388, Greensboro 27402
Halifax Edward L. Garrison, P. O. Box 158, Halifax 27839
Harnett Mrs. Helen Crews, P. O. Box 668, Lilington 27546
Haywood Edgar Israel, P. O. Box 509, Waynesville 28786
Henderson Mrs. Annabella Parks, 246 2nd Ave., Hendersonville 28739
Hertford Margaret NewBern, King St., Winton 27986
Hoke Ben Niblock, P. O. Box 340, Raeford 28376
Hyde William Miller, P. O. Box 237, Swan Quarter 27885
Iredell Mrs. Dorothy Fleming, P. O. Box 1146, Statesville 28677
Jackson Mrs. Edith Jenkins, P. O. Box 96, Sylvia 28779
Johnston Don Morrison, P. O. Box 911, Smithfield 27577
Jones Mrs. Louise Mills (In Charge), P. O. Box 250, Trenton 28585
Lee James E. Coats, P. O. Box 1066, Sanford 27330
Lenoir Mrs. Martha Bovinet, P. O. Box 6, Kingston 28501
Lincoln Mrs. Betty Rhyne, P. O. Box 98, Lincolnton 28092
Macon Mrs. Dorothy Crawford, P. O. Box 149, Franklin 28734
Madison Mrs. Frances Ramsey, P. O. Box 177, Marshal 28753
Martin Rittie Biggs, P. O. Box 809, Williamston 27892
McDowell Michael S. Gibson, P. O. Box 338, Marion 28752
Mecklenburg Edwin Chapin, 301 Billingsley Rd., Charlotte 28211
Mitchell James Griffith, P. O. Box 365, Bakersville 28705
Montgomery Frank Ledbetter, P. O. Drawer N, Troy 27371
Moore Mrs. Walter Cole, P. O. Box 918, Carthage 28327
Nash Mrs. Genera Greene, P. O. Drawer 40, Nashville, 27856
New Hanover Lela Hall, 1020 Rankin St., Wilmington 28401
Northampton James Clark, P. O. Box 157, Jackson 27845
Onslow Edward Sexton, P. O. Box 910, Jacksonville 28540
Orange Thomas Ward, Cameron St., Hillsborough 27278
Pamlico Miss Willie Sutton, P. O. Box 395, Bayboro 28515
Pasquotank Ernest Anderson (Trainee), P. O. Box 159, Elizabeth City 27909
Pender Mrs. Hewell Harrell, P. O. Box 977, Burgaw 28425
Perquimans Edgar White, P. O. Box 316, Hertford 27944

Person Margaret Brite, P. O. Box 770, Roxboro 27573

Pitt Dorothy Bolton, P. O. Drawer 1546, Greenville 27834

Polk Edward Inman, P. O. Drawer 1576, Tryon 28782

Randolph Marion Smith, P. O. Box 1147, Asheboro 27203

Richmond Brent Yount, P. O. Box 545, Rockingham 28379

Robeson Russel Sessions, P. O. Box 1505, Lumberton 28358

Rockingham Glenn Fuqua, P. O. Drawer 120, Reidsville 27320

Rowan Edwin Koontz, 1236 Innes St., Salisbury 28144

Rutherford Robert Jones, P. O. Drawer 100, Rutherfordton 28139

Sampson Robert Gribble, P. O. Box 1105, Clinton 28328

Scotland Daniel Hudgins, 1224 Briggs St., Laurinburg 28352

Stanley John Link, 201 S. 2nd St., Albemarle 28001

Stokes Paul Priddy, P. O. Box 37, Danbury 27016

Surry Carl Brittain, P. O. Box 38, Dobson 27017

Swain Mrs. Freda Livingston (Trainee), P. O. Box 610, Bryson City 28713

Transylvania Alvin Penland, 120 E. Main St., Brevard 28712

Tyrrell James Orrock, P. O. Box 426, Columbia 27925

Union Franklin Wayne Morris, P. O. Box 370, Monroe 28110

Vance Bobby Boyd, 300 S. Garnett St., Henderson 27536

Wake Mrs. Josephine Kirk, P. O. Box 1247, Raleigh 27602

Warren Julian Farrar, 538 W. Ridgeway St., Warrenton 27589

Washington Edwin H. Modlim (Trainee) P. O. Box 664, Plymouth 27962

Watauga Curlee Joyce, Courthouse Annex, Boone 28607

Wayne Floyd Evans, P. O. Box HH, Goldsboro 27530

Wilkes John Ellege (Trainee), P. O. Box 119, Wilkesboro 28679

Wilson Jerry A. Smith, P. O. Box 150, Wilson 27893

Yadkin Mrs. Patty Martin (In Charge), P. O. Box 548, Yadkinville 27055

Yancey Mrs. Ruby Smith (In Charge), P. O. Box 67, Burnsville 28714

North Dakota

Reporting Requirements

Persons mandated to report (compulsory) when reasonable cause to believe a child is or has been subjected to abuse or neglect: physician, nurse, dentist, optometrist, medical examiner or coroner, and other medical or mental health professional, school teacher or administrator, school counselor, social worker, day-care center or any other child care worker, police or law enforcement officer in his/her professional capacity

Permissive: any person having reasonable cause to suspect that a child is abused or neglected

Form of report and when made: oral, immediately; written, within 48 hours if requested

To whom report is made: division of community services of the social service board of North Dakota

Penalties: failure to report is a class B misdemeanor for persons required to report

Immunities: anyone who reports, except alleged violator, is presumed to do so in good faith and is granted full civil and criminal immunity

Child Abuse Legislation

Citation: NDCC §27-20-26, 27-20-48, 50-25.1
Year enacted: 1975
Effective date: July 1, 1975
Purpose of legislation: mandatory reporting, yes
Reportable age: 0-18 years

215

Definitions: nonaccidental serious physical harm, traumatic abuse, neglect, i.e.,
    deprivation
Education/school reports: mandatory reporting, yes
Immunity: yes
Mandatory investigation: yes, promptly
Confidentiality of records: yes; penalty: misdemeanor
Cooperation with law courts, state agencies: yes
Guardian ad litem: yes
Administrative proceedings, trained personnel, facilities: yes
Dissemination of information: no specific provision

Programs and Agencies

Correspondence regarding Title XX social services, Interstate Compact on the
Placement of Children, Interstate Compact on Juveniles, Older Americans Act,
and crippled children's services should be prepared in duplicate and addressed
to:

> Director of Community Services
> Social Services Board
> State Capitol
> Bismarck 58505

Social Service Board of North Dakota

> State Capitol
> Bismarck 58505
> Telephone: (701)224-2310
> T.N. Tangedahl, Exec. Dir.
> Wayne J. Anderson, Legal Cnsl.
> Jon Nelson, Legal Cnsl.
> Mary Jane Low, Info. Specialist
> Mrs. Joan Senzek, Supervisor Child Abuse and Neglect Programs

Community Services Program Operations

> Robert W. Nelson, Adm.

Child Welfare Services

> Donald L. Schmid, Adm. (701)224-2325
> Mrs. Phyllis Wigen, Specialist, Adoptions and Unmarried Parents
> George Robinson, Supv., Day Care
> Sandy Robin, Supv., Foster Care Centers

County Social Service Boards

Adams (vacant), Hettinger, 58639   (701)567-2967
Barnes Don R. Nelson, Valley City 58072   (701)845-2920
Benson Stanley R. Franek, Minnewaukan 58351   (701)473-5302
Billings Alvin E. Cheadle, Beach 58621   (701)872-4121
Bottineau Mrs. Mary Rothmann, Bottineau 58318   (701)228-2930
Bowman James W. Davis, Bowman 58623   (701)523-3285
Burke (vacant), Bowbells 58721   (701)377-2313
Burleigh Richard C. Throndset, P. O. Box 1313, Bismarck 58501   (701)258-5600
Cass Robert E. Barrett, 702 Main Ave., P. O. Box 3106, Fargo 58102
     (701)232-9271
Cavalier Richard K. Mowbray, Langdon 58249   (701)256-2175
Dickey John E. Peterson, Ellendale 58436   (701)349-3272
Divide Bill Brewer, Crosby 58730   (701)965-6521
Dunn Mrs. Mardell Transtom, Killdeer, 58640   (701)764-5385
Eddy (vacant), New Rockford 58356   (701)947-5314
Emmons Arlyn Bjerke, Linton 58552   (701)254-4774
Foster David E. Braaten, Carrington 58421   (701)652-2221
Golden Valley Alvin E. Cheadle, Beach 58621   (701)872-4121
Grand Forks Clarence O. Ohlsen, 118 N. 3rd St., P. O. Box 1695, Grand Forks
     58201   (701)772-8171
Grant (vacant), Carson 58529   (701)622-3564
Griggs (vacant), Cooperstown 58425   (701)797-2127
Hettinger Robert V. Marthaller, Mott 58646   (701)824-2570
Kidder Arlyn Bjerke, Steele 58482   (701)475-2551
LaMoure Clarence R. Daniel, Lamoure 58468   (701)883-4282
Logan Mrs. Ruth S. Wurl, Napoleon 58561   (701)754-2283
McHenry Winston Pottenger, Towner 58788   (701)537-5740
McIntosh Roland Weisenburger, Ashley 58413   (701)288-3343
McKenzie Mrs. Michon Sax, Watford City 58854   (701)842-3661
McLean Royce G. Roberson, Washburn 58577   (701)462-3236
Mercer (Royce G. Roberson, Stanton 58571   (701)745-3384
Morton Thelma Armstrong, Mandan 58554   (701)663-7444
Mountrail Dale Ellis, Stanley 58784   (701)628-2925
Nelson (vacant), Lakota 58344   (701)247-2551
Oliver (vacant), Center 58530   (701)794-3212
Pembina Mrs. Lois Stanislowski, Cavalier 58220   (701)265-4313
Pierce Winston Pottenger, Rugby 58368   (701)776-5818
Ramsey Leonard Michalski, Devils Lake 58301   (701)662-4055
Ransom Clarence R. Daniel, Lisbon 58054   (701)683-5661
Renville Jean A. Connole, Mohall 58761   (701)756-6374
Richland Glen H. Gustafson, Washpeton 58075   (701)642-6619

Rolette Garmann Jorgensen, Rolla 58367 (701)477-3141
Sargent Victor Ball, Forman 58032 (701)724-3291
Sheridan Royce G. Roberson, McClusky 58463 (701)363-2281
Sioux Mrs. Lora L. Siegfried, Ft. Yates 58538 (701)854-2360
Slope James W. Davis, Bowman 58623 (701)523-3285
Stark Mrs. Lynn Jacobson, Dickinson 58601 (701)225-6731
Steele (vacant), Finley 58320 (701)524-2584
Stutsman Stanley Waagen, Jamestown 58401 (701)252-7172
Towner (vacant), Cando 58324 (701)968-3613
Traill Margaret Ralston, Hillsboro 58045 (701)436-5220
Walsh Mrs. Lois Stanislowski, Grafton 58237 (701)352-2951
Ward Daniel P. Richter, 405 3rd Ave., S. E. Minot 58701 (701)852-3552
Wells Edward D. Forde, Fessenden 58438 (701)547-3694
Williams Richard Stewart, Williston 58801 (701)572-6373

Ohio

Reporting Requirements

Persons mandated to report (compulsory) when reasonable cause to believe a child is or has been subjected to abuse or neglect: any attorney, physician, intern, resident, dentist, podiatrist, surgeon, registered or licensed practical nurse, other licensed health-care professional, pathologist or audiologist, coroner, administrator, employee of a certified child care agency or other public or private childrens services agency, school teacher or authority, social worker or spiritual healer acting in his/her official capacity (director shall make report for staff of hospital)

Permissive: anyone having reason to believe that a child has been abused

Form of report and when made: telephone immediately, followed by written report if requested

To whom report is made: the children services board or the county department of welfare exercising the children's services functions, or to a municipal or county peace officer in the county where the abuse has taken place

Penalties: none

Immunities: civil and criminal immunity for those participating in reporting or judicial proceedings under the act

Child Abuse Legislation

Citation: ORC §2151.287; Amended Substitute HB85
Year enacted: 1975
Effective date: November 28, 1975
Purpose of legislation: mandatory reporting, yes

Reportable age: 0–18; 0–21 physically, mentally handicapped
Definitions: victim of sexual activity, endangered; evidence of any physical
    injury or death other than by accidental means; or injury or death which is
    at variance with the history given to it; failure to provide necessary care,
    support, medical attention, and educational facilities.
Education/school report: mandatory reporting, yes
Immunity: civil/criminal, yes
Mandatory investigation: yes, 24 hours
Confidentiality of records: yes; penalty: misdemeanor
Cooperation with law courts, state agencies: yes
Guardian ad litem: yes
Administrative proceedings, trained personnel, facilities: yes
Dissemination of information: no specific provision

Programs and Agencies

Requests for social information must be sent to the appropriate county welfare
department. In children's cases such requests are to be sent to the appropriate
county children's services board or, when one does not exist, to the county
welfare department.

Ohio Department of Public Welfare

    30 E. Broad St., 32nd Fl
    Columbus 43215
    Telephone: (614)466-7987
    Kwegyir Aggrey Dir. (614)466-6282
    Raymond F. McKenna, Asst. Dir. (614)466-6283

Division of Social Services

    Telephone: (614)466-2306
    Mrs. Mildred Madry, Chief

Department of Public Welfare District Offices

Canton Ashland, Belmont, Carroll, Columbiana, Coshocton, Guernsey, Harrison,
    Holmes, Jefferson, Mahoning, Monroe, Morgan, Muskingum, Noble, Rich-
    land, Stark, Tuscarawas, Washington, and Wayne Counties): 117 Walnut
    Ave., N.E. Canton 44702 Carl Albu, Dir. (216)453-7729
Cincinnati (Adams, Brown, Butler, Champaign, Clark, Clermont, Darke, Fayette,
    Greene, Hamilton, Highland, Madison, Miami, Montgomery, Preble, and
    Warren Counties): 100 E. 8th St., Cincinnati 45202 Dante Bernardini, Dir.
    (513)852-3288

Cleveland (Ashtabula, Cuyahoga, Geauga, Lake, Lorain, Medina, Portage, Summit, and Trumbull Counties): Perry-Payne Bldg., Rm. 320, 740 Superior Ave. N.W., Cleveland 44113 Marion Jones, Act. Dir. (216) 579-2937

Columbus (Athens, Delaware, Fairfield, Franklin, Gallia, Hocking, Jackson, Knox, Lawrence, Licking, Meigs, Morrow, Perry, Pickaway, Pike, Ross, Scioto, Union, and Vinton Counties): 30 E. Broad St., 34th Floor, Columbus 43215 Clarence V. Tittle, Dir. (614)466-4456

Toledo (Allen, Auglaize, Crawford, Defiance, Erie, Fulton, Hancock, Hardin, Henry, Huron, Logan, Lucas, Marion, Mercer, Ottawa, Paulding, Puynam, Sandusky, Seneca, Shelby, Van Wert, Williams, Wood, and Wyandot Counties): 4445 Talmadge Rd., 2nd Fl., Toledo 43623 Charles E. Noggle, Dir. (419)472-1153

County Welfare Departments

Adams Mrs. Velma Lee Fletcher, 308 Market St., West Union 45693 (513) 544-2371

Allen Neal E. Sprang, 139 S. Pine St., Lima 45801 (419)228-2621

Ashland Daniel C. Kettering, Ashland County Office Bldg., 110 Cottage St., Ashland 44805 (419)289-0000

Ashtabula John H. Koren, 2036 E. Prospect Rd., Ashtabula 44004 (216) 998-1110

Athens Mrs. Charlotte Balding, 184 N. Lancaster St., P. O. Box 548, Athens 45701 (614)592-4477

Auglaize John C. Wine, Courthouse, Wapakoneta 45895 (419)738-4311

Belmont Thomas A. Williams, 147 W. Main St., P. O. Box 186, St. Clairsville 43950 (614)695-1074

Brown Mrs. Bonnie Swearingen, 303 E. Cherry St., Georgetown 45121 (513)378-6104

Butler William Schaffner, 611 Maple Ave., Hamilton 45011 (513)895-6971

Carroll Robert W. Tasker, 40-2nd St., N. E., P. O. Box 216, Carrollton 44615 (216)627-2571

Champaign Mrs. Jane Throckmorton, 2380 S. Rte. 68, P. O. Box 327, Urbana 43078 (513)652-1346

Clark Ronald E. Rockwell, 529 E. Home Road, Springfield 45503 (513) 399-2720

Clermont Wayne Oney, P. O. Box 96, Rte. 1, Batavia-Stonelick Pike, Batavia 45103 (513)732-2415

Clinton Charles L. Grove, Jr., 32 E. Sugartree St., P. O. Box 631, Wilmington 45177 (513)382-0964

Columbiana Robert H. Stambaugh, 117 E. Washington St., St. Lisbon 44432 (216)424-9551

Coshocton Mrs. Oneita B. Adams, 318 Chestnut St., P. O. Box 88, Coshocton 43812 (614)622-1020

Crawford Richard P. Shackelford, 117 E. Mansfield St., Bucyrus 44820
    (419)562-0015

Cuyahoga Samuel P. Bauer, 220 St. Clair Ave., N.W., Cleveland 44113
    (216)861-7700

Darke Robert Cool, 802 E. 4th St., Greenville 45331   (513)548-2920

Defiance Mrs. Helen L. Weaner, Holiday Plaza, Rte. 2, Defiance 43512
    (419)782-3881

Delaware Mrs. Nancy Ellen Perry, 109 N. Sandusky St., Delaware 43015
    (614)369-8761, ext. 227

Erie Max Hofmeister, 220 Columbus Ave., Sandusky 44870   (419)626-6781

Fairfield Donald L. Dowell, 121 E. Chestnut St., P. O. Box 890, Lancaster
    43130 (614)653-1701

Fayette O. M. Riegel, 119 E. Market St., Washington Courthouse 43160
    (614)335-0350

Franklin Miss Shelia Harshaw, 80 E. Fulton St., Columbus 43215   (614)
    462-4191

Fulton Jerry Collamore, 135 Courthouse Plaza, Wauseon 43567   (419)
    335-5081

Gallia Virgil Cross, 848-3rd Ave., P.O. Box 219, Gallipolis 45631   (614)
    446-3222

Geauga Wellington H. Chapman, 13281 Ravenna Rd., Chardon 44024
    (216)285-9141

Greene Keith Moon, 45 E. 2nd St., Xenia 45385   (513)376-2951

Guernsey Robert E. Cesner, 324 Highland Ave., Cambridge 43725   (614)
    432-2381

Hamilton Seth P. Staples, 628 Sycamore St., Cincinnati 45202   (513)632-6111

Hancock Mrs. Janet R. Myers, 222-224 Broadway, Findlay 45840   (419)
    422-0182

Hardin Mrs. Helene L. Schwemer, Courthouse, Kenton 43326   (419)675-1130

Harrison Mrs. Mildred Burrier, 115 W. Warren St., Cadiz 43907   (614)942-2171

Henry Gerald Donnelly, Courthouse, Napolean 43545   (419)592-0896

Highland Stephen Doorneweerd, 135 N. High St., P. O. Box N, Hillsboro 45133
    (513)393-4278

Hocking Harley Ellinger, 1221 W. Hunter St., P. O. Box 548, Logan 43138
    (614)385-5663

Holmes Mrs. Donna Jean Gallion, 112 W. Jackson St., Millersburg 44654
    (216)674-1816 or 3891

Huron Grant W. Walls, 190 Benedict Ave., P. O. Box 256, Norwalk 44857
    (419)668-8126

Jackson Herbert McCormick, Corner Huron and Gay Sts., P. O. Box 232,
    Jackson 45640 (614)286-4181 or 3122

Jefferson Carl Bello, Exchange Realty Bldg., 428 Market St., Steubenville
    43952 (614)282-0961

Knox Daniel Schneider, 17604 Coshocton Rd., Mt. Vernon 43050 (614) 397-7177 or 392-0056

Lake Miss Jean A. Giebink, 33 Mill St., Painesville 44077 (216)352-8963

Lawrence Jim Steed, 151 Park Ave., P. O. Box 539, Ironton 45638 (614) 532-3324

Licking Russell Payne, 74 S. 2nd St., P. O. Box 458, Newark 43055 (614) 345-6607

Logan Miss Dorothy M. Scott, 224 S. Main St., Bellefontaine 43311 (513) 593-1896

Lorain Gerard Prinz, 226 Middle Ave., 3rd Fl., Elyria 44035 (216)323-5726

Lucas George J. Steger, 437 Michigan St., Toledo 43624 (419)259-2648

Madison Frank Horn, 249 W. High St., London 43140 (614)852-4770

Mahoning Ezell L. Armour, 234 W. Federal St., Youngstown 44503 (216) 747-2051

Marion Don E. Thomas, 125 W. Church St., Marion 43302 (614)383-4941

Medina Mrs. Donna A. Mack, Old Courthouse, 2nd Fl. Medina 44256 (216) 725-6671

Meigs Mrs. Barbara S. Shuler, 175 Race St., P. O. Box 191, Middleport 45760 (614)992-2117

Mercer Morris A. Now, 311 S. Main St., P. O. Box 30, Celina 45822 (419) 586-5106

Miami Paul Noffsinger, 410 N. Elm St., Troy 45373 (513)335-7142

Monroe Richard W. Oehler, 100 Home Ave., P. O. Box 638, Woodsfield 43793 (614)472-1602 or 0067

Montgomery David W. Simmons, 14 W. 4th St., Dayton 45402 (513)224-9114

Morgan James C. Davis, 65 W. Union St., McConnelsville 43756 (614)962-4616

Morrow Mrs. Carol Ann Curl, 27 W. High St., Mt. Gilead 43338 (419)946-6060

Muskingum Ernest Parent, 445 Woodlawn Ave., P. O. Box 1027, Zanesville 43701 (614)454-0161

Noble Ewell Smith, Olive Shopping Center, R.F.D. 4, P. O. Box 185, Caldwell 43724 (614)732-2392

Ottawa Mrs. Esther W. Sutton, 1628 E. Perry St., P. O. Box 548, Port Clinton 43452 (419)732-3128

Paulding Mrs. Sonia V. Peeper, 101 W. Perry St., Paulding 45879 (419) 399-3756

Perry Owen C. Bozeman, 318 S. Main St., New Lexington 43764 (614) 342-3534

Pickaway Miss Pauline E. Roese, 109 E. Mount St., P. O. Box 439, Circleville 43113 (614)474-7589

Pike Harold H. Jenkins, 219 W. Emmitt Ave., Waverly 45690 (614)947-2171

Portage Layton C. Thomas, 230 W. Riddle Ave., Ravenna 44266 (216) 296-3891

Preble Mrs. Elizabeth Gray, Courthouse Annex, Eaton 45320 (513)456-5591

Putnam Mrs. Mildred C. Lanwehr, 211 S. Oak St., P. O. Box 249, Ottawa 45875 (419)523-3893

Richland Miss Ruth N. Strong, 69 S. Walnut St., P. O. Box 188, Mansfield 44901 (419)524-2321

Ross Byron Eby, 133 W. 2nd St., Chillicothe 45601 (614)773-2651

Sandusky Richard Simington, 1809 E. State St., Fremont 43420 (419) 334-3891

Scioto Robert G. Raines, 710 Court St., P. O. Box 1347, Portsmouth 45662 (614)354-6661

Seneca Mrs. Ruth M. O'Neill, R.F.D. 1, P. O. Box 50B, Infirmary Rd., Tiffin 44883 (419)447-5011

Shelby Terry Pellman, 500 E. Court St., Sidney 45365 (513)492-9138

Stark Logan Burd, 209 W. Tuscarawas Ave., Canton 44702 (216)452-4661

Summit Frank J. Birkel, 695 S. Main St., Akron 44311 (216)384-1681

Trumbull James R. Leisy, 1092 University St., N. E., Warren 44481 (216) 372-1104

Tuscarawas Leonard W. Snyder, 154-2nd St., N. E., New Philadelphia 44663 (216)364-7791

Union John A. Popio, 246 W. 5th St., Marysville 43040 (513)642-4901 or 2801

Van Wert Frank H. Stoops, 1052 S. Washington St., P. O. Box 86, Van Wert 45891 (419)238-5430

Vinton Mrs. Helen Garrison, 123 E. Main St., McArthur 45651 (614) 596-4310

Warren Mrs. Susan H. Wilson, 416 South East St., Rm., 120, Lebanon 45036 (513)932-3791

Washington Mrs. Genevieve H. Nuckles, 202 Davis Ave., Marietta 45750 (614)373-5513

Wayne Mrs. Louise D. Anthony, 203 S. Walnut St., Wooster 44691 (216) 264-3362

Williams John W. Hahn, 205 E. High St., Bryan 43506 (419)636-5675

Wood Ellsworth M. Edwards, 545 Pearl St., P. O. Box 47, Bowling-Green 43402 (419)352-7566

Wyandot Lawrence G. Merrick, 122 S. Sandusky Ave., Upper Sandusky 43351 (419)294-3214

County Children's Services Boards

Adams Mrs. Delaner Coomer, 300 N. Wilson Dr., West Union 45693 (513) 544-2511 or 5067

Allen Barry D. Smith, 1000 Wardhill Ave., P. O. Box 419, Lima 45805 (419) 227-8590

Ashtabula Ronald C. Loos, 2036 E. Prospect Rd., Ashtabula 44004 (216)
998-1811

Athens Miss Rowena Sorout, P. O. Box 367, Athens 45701 (614)593-5388

Belmont Robert E. Jacobs, 100 S. Market St., Clairsville 43950 (614)
695-3813

Clinton Miss Brenda Bloom, Courthouse, 3rd Fl., Wilmington 45177 (513)
382-2449

Coshocton Mrs. Lorena Sims, 318½ Chestnut St., Coshocton 43812 (614)
622-2292

Crawford Lawrence W. Dawson, 865 Harding Way W., Galion 44833 (419)
468-3255

Erie Mrs. Marian E. Johnson, County Office Bldg., 1200 Sycamore Line,
Sandusky 44870 (419)626-9440 ext. 241

Fairfield Ms. JoAnn Schaffer, Courthouse, 4th Fl., Lancaster 43130 (614)
653-7911

Franklin Wilbert A. Jansen, 1951 Gantz Rd., Grove City 43123 (614)
276-9061

Gallia Mrs. Gerry Miller, 423-2nd Ave., P. O. Box 468, Gallipolis 45631
(614)446-4963

Greene Mrs. Mary Ann Paloncy, 641 Dayton Xenia Rd., Xenia 45385 (513)
376-2971

Guernsey Mrs. Eloise Anker, Courthouse Annex, Cambridge 43725 (614)
432-7381

Hancock Michael Boutwell, 2515 N. Main St., Findlay 45840 (419)422-8912

Harrison Mrs. Mae I. Arris, P. O. Box 213, Cadiz 43907 (614)942-2877

Highland Mrs. Evelyn Vanzant, Courthouse Annex, 135 N. High St., Hillsboro
45133 (513)393-1071

Hocking Mrs. Eleanor Horwell, Logan Federal Bldg., Rm. 211, 61 N. Market St.,
Logan 43138 (614)385-4168

Jefferson Robert A. Pagnanelli, 240 John Scott Memorial Hwy., Steubenville
43952 (614)264-5515

Lawrence Mrs. Mary E. Marting, c/o Receiving Home, 912 Vernon St., Ironton
45638 (614)532-1176

Logan Michael R. Horton, 128 E. Columbus Ave., Bellefontaine 43311
(513)592-0871

Lorain Thomas W. Porter, 226 Middle Ave., 3rd Fl., Elyria 44035 (216)
323-5776, ext. 333

Lucas Charles H. Klippstein, 2500 River Rd., Maumee 43537 (419)893-4861

Mahoning Mrs. Mary J. Credico, Stambaugh Bldg., Rm. 613, 44 Central Square,
Youngstown 44503 (216)747-2671

Marion Paul M. Rogers, Jr., 1680 Marion-Waldo Rd., Marion 43302 (614)
389-2317

Miami Larry E. Ganger, Miami County Safety Bldg., 201 W. Main St., Troy 45373 (513)335-8341

Montgomery Edward R. Coker, 3501 Merrimac Ave., Dayton 45405 (513) 276-6121

Muskingum Mrs. Donna W. Schaefer, 445 Woodlawn Ave., Zanesville 43701 (614)454-9781

Perry Clifford D. Wilson, 107 W. Brown St., P. O. Box 657, New Lexington 43764 (614)342-3836

Pickaway Oscar Burchfield, P. O. Box 594, Circleville 43113 (614)474-3105

Pike Andrew S. Kohler, P. O. Box 172, Waverly 45690 (614)947-5080

Preble Ray Swank, Jr., R.F.D. 2, Eaton 45320 (513)456-5591

Richland Gerald F. Futty, Richland County Attention Center, 277 Hedges St., Mansfield 44903 (419)524-4004

Ross John T. Smith, 381 Western Ave., Chillicothe 45601 (614)774-1205

Scioto Mrs. Ruth S. Linger, National Bank Bldg., Rm. 724, Portsmouth 45662 (614)354-5659

Shelby Robert J. Borchers, R.R. 3, Sidney 45365 (513)492-5951

Summit David Miller, 264 S. Arlington St., Akron 44306 (216)379-5800

Trumbull Craig H. Neuman, 2296 Reeves Rd., N. E. Warren 44483 (216) 372-2010

Vinton Mrs. Mildred Buehler, c/o Courthouse, McArthur 45651 (614) 594-5033

Warren Roy D. Burchwell, 416 South East St., Rm. 132, Lebanon 45036 (513)932-1855

Washington James R. Coyle, c/o Children's Home, Muskingum Dr., Marietta 45750 (614)373-3485

Wayne George R. Arnold, 521 Beall Ave., P. O. Box 521, Wooster 44691 (216)264-8800

Oklahoma

Reporting Requirements

Persons mandated to report (compulsory) when reasonable cause to believe a child is or has been subjected to abuse or neglect: every physician or sugeon; dentist; licensed osteopath; resident and intern examining, attending, or treating a child under 18 years; every registered nurse performing the same function in the absence of a physician; and every other person having reason to believe that the child has been abused or neglected

Permissive: none

Form of report and when made: oral report optional; written required, no time limit

To whom report is made: county office of the department of institutions, social and rehabilitative services in the county where the abuse occurred

Penalties: misdemeanor to knowingly and willfully fail to promptly report

Immunities: none

Child Abuse Legislation

Citation: ORS Tit. 10, §1109(e); SB 304, Chap. 98
Year enacted: 1975
Effective date: April 30, 1975
Purpose of legislation: mandatory reporting, yes
Reportable age: 0-18 years
Definitions: harm or threatened harm to child's health or welfare through non-accidental injury (physical or mental), sexual abuse, negligent treatment or maltreatment; failure to provide adequate food, clothing, etc.

Education/school report: mandatory reporting, yes
Immunity: civil/criminal, no specific provision
Mandatory investigation: yes, immediately
Confidentiality of records: yes; penalty: misdemeanor
Cooperation with law courts, state agencies: no specific provision
Guardian ad litem: yes
Administrative proceedings, trained personnel, facilities: no specific provision
Dissemination of information: no specific provisions

Programs and Agencies

Where to write:

L. E. Rader, Director
Department of Institutions, Social and Rehabilitative Services
Oklahoma City 73125
Attention: Division of Social Services

Oklahoma Department of Institutions, Social, and Rehabilitative Services

P. O. Box 25352
Oklahoma City 73125
Telephone: (405)521-3646
L. E. Rader, Director (405)521-3646

J. Harry Johnson, Gen. Cnsl., Exec. Asst. and Reimbursement Ofr.
  (405)521-3638
Lyle Coit, Exec. Asst. Institutional Maintenance Construction and Farms
  (405)521-3618
Pauline Mayer, Exec. Asst., Assistance Payments and Services, (405)
  521-3076
Charles McDermott, Comptroller (405)521-3603
Jim McGlasson, Admv. Asst., Operations and Personnel (505)521-3529
W. Kilgore, Admv. Asst., Departmental Services (405)521-3521
George McDonnold, M.D., Admv. Asst., Medical Assistance (405)521-3801
Paul Reed, M.D., Admv. Asst., Medical Hearing Office (405)521-3584
Floyd Moorman, M.D., Admv. Asst., Disability Determination Unit
  (405)525-3366

CW SABD SF WIN Division of Social Services

Telephone: (405)521-3438
Dennis Sharp, Supv.

Whitaker State Children's Home

P. O. Box 98
Pryor 74361
Mitchell Rowe, Superintendent (918)825-3254

Children's Center

P. O. Box 92
Taft 74463
Telephone: (918)682-7841
Harold Wilson, Supt., North Campus
Linzy Wilson, Supt., South Campus

*Department of Institutions Social and Rehabilitative Services County Offices
(AFDC, CCS, CW, FS, GA, MAP, SABD, SF, SSI/S)*

Adair Vol Woods, P. O. Box 72, Stilwell 74960 (918)774-7736
Alfalfa Mrs. Sharon Horton, Courthouse, 1st Fl., Cherokee 73728 (405)
596-3335
Atoka Joe Voto, P. O. Box 159, Atoka 74525 (405)889-3394
Beaver Mike Ross, P. O. Box 306, Beaver 73932 (405)625-3281
Beckham Mrs. Charlotte Nesser, Courthouse, 2nd Fl., Sayre 73662 (405)
928-3348
Blaine Mrs. Allene Barnes, 216 W. A St. Watonga 73712 (405)632-5282
Bryan Jackie Morris, P. O. Box 837, Durant 74701 (405)924-1866
Caddo Mrs. May Franklin, P. O. Box 608, Anadarko, 73005 (406)247-6621
Canadian Gerald Carey, 212 W. Rogers St., El Reno 73036 (405)262-1184
Carter Hazel Seagraves, P. O. Box 398, Ardmore 73401 (405)223-6923
Cherokee Alton Hall, 914 S. College St., Tahlequah 74464 (918)456-2554
or 8441
Choctaw Mrs. Ernestine Pittman, P. O. Box 40, Hugo 74743 (405)326-3325
Cimarron Mrs. Mary Ellsworth, P. O. Box 326, Boise City 73933 (405)
544-2512
Cleveland Mrs. Rebecca Richardson, P. O. Box 516, Norman 73069 (405)
321-1434
Coal Vernon Cauthron, P. O. Box 231, Coalgate 74538 (405)927-2363
Comanche Raul Stinchomb, P. O. Box 328, Lawton 73501 (405)248-6900
Cotton Gary Huckabay, Courthouse, 1st fl., Walters, 73752 (405)875-3331
Craig Dayton Rudick, P. O. Box 279, Vinita 74301 (918)256-3694
Creek Fred Orr, P. O. Box 1068, Sapulpa 74301 (918)224-0213
Custer Carl Henry, P. O. Box 397, Clinton 73601 (405)323-3333
Delaware Winston Dunaway, P. O. Box 368, Jay 74346 (918)253-4213
Dewey Mrs. Docia Powers, P. O. Box 118, Taloga 73667 (405)328-5547

Ellis Mrs. Alma Holt, P. O. Box 215, Arnett 73832 (405)885-3551
Garfield Mildred Chambers, P. O. Box 3628, Enid 73701 (405)233-0234
Garvin Jerry Pile, P. O. Box 100, Pauls Valley 73075 (405)238-2433
Grady Madeline Cook, P. O. Box 1338, Chickasha 73018 (405)224-4517
Grant Mrs. Emmerine Cink, P. O. Box 128, Medford 73759 (405)395-2183
Greer Willie Rogers, P. O. Drawer E. Mangum 73554 (405)782-3657
Harmon Mrs. Lenore Moore, Courthouse, 1st Fl., Hollis, 73550 (405)
688-2727
Harper Mrs. Katherine Ramsey, P. O. Box 355, Buffalo 73834 (405)735-2123
Haskell Robert Folsom, P. O. Box 469, Stigler 74462 (918)967-4658
Hughes Mrs. Oda Weatherred, P. O. Box 550, Holdenville 74848 (405)
379-3357
Jackson Mrs. Margaret Carder, P. O. Drawer G, Altus 73521 (405)482-4333
Jefferson Mrs. Imogene Latham, P. O. Box 97, Waurika 73573 (405)228-2368
Johnston Jake Davidson (Act.), P. O. Box 398, Tishomingo 73460 (405)
371-2293
Kay Thomas Lilly, P. O. Box 210, Newkirk 74647 (405)362-2586
Kingfisher Eugene Harris, Courthouse, 1st Fl., Kingfisher 73750 (405)
375-3864
Kiowa Ed Newall, P. O. Box 660, Hobart 73651 (405)726-3339
Latimer David Claxton, Courthouse, 1st Fl., Wilburton 74578 (918)465-2333
Leflore Bill Suter, P. O. Box 370, Poteau 74953 (918)647-2163
Lincoln Dwain Young, Courthouse, Chandler 74834 (405)258-1680
Logan Ralph Willey, P. O. Box 460, Guthrie 73044 (405)282-4500
Love Odis Hearell, Courthouse Basement, Marietta 73448 (405)276-3383
McClain Eula Lester, Courthouse, 1st Fl., Purcell 73080 (405)527-6511
McCurtain Gary Whelchel, P. O. Box 39, Idabel 74745 (405)286-3326
McIntosh H. E. Cook, P. O. Box 231, Eufaula 74432 (918)689-2524
Major Mrs. Freda Blevins, 118 E. Broadway, Fairview 73737 (405)227-4831
Marshall W. Moore, 403 Main St., Madill 73446 (405)795-3292
Mayes James Watkins, P. O. Box 1088, Pryor 74361 (919)825-4535
Murray Gerald Bradley, 1023 Broadway, Sulphur 73086 (405)622-2186
Muskogee Mrs. Bernice Thompson, P. O. Box 608, Muskogee 74401 (918)
683-3291
Noble Mrs. Deloras Day, P. O. Box 768, Perry 73077 (405)336-2551
Nowata Mrs. Lurline Johnson, P. O. Box 548, Nowata 74048 (981)273-2327
Okfuskee Ernest Fox, P. O. Box 69, Okemah 74859 (918)623-1363
Oklahoma Myrl Hill, P. O. Box 26768, Oklahoma City 73126 (405)424-5818
Okmulgee Dean Craig, P. O. Box 730, Okmulgee 74447 (918)756-3364
Osage John Kenny, 624 Kihekah St., 2nd Fl. Pawhuska 74056 (918)287-3521
Ottawa William Bynun, P. O. Box 640, Miami 74354 (918)542-2836
Pawnee Mrs. Molly Spears, P. O. Box 250, Pawnee 74058 (918)762-2567
Pittsburg Charles Armstrong, P. O. Box 1006, McAlester 74501 (918)423-3066

Pontotoc Ken Townsend, P. O. Box 1627, Ada 74820 (405)332–1070
Pottawatomie Roy Wylie, P. O. Box 1148, Shawnee 74801 (405)273–1831
Pushmataha Mrs. Ellie Jackson, P. O. Box 40, Antlers 74523 (405)298–3363
Roger Mills Donals Estes, P. O. Box M, Cheyenne 73628 (405)497–3393
Rogers Mrs. Betty Willey, P. O. Box 838, Claremore 74017 (918)341–2282
Seminole Mrs. Mabel Carter, P. O. Box 1518, Wewoka 74884 (905)257–3337
Sequoyah Frank Black, P. O. Box 448, Sallisaw 74955 (918)775–4464
Stephens Ted A. Sutton, P. O. Box 1367, Duncan 73533 (405)255–7550
Texas Mrs. Peggy Moore, P. O. Box 379, Guymon 73942 (405)338–8593
Tilman Patsey Bradley, P. O. Drawer 336, Frederick 73542 (405)335–2728
Tulsa Mrs. Nora Nicholson, 444 S. Hudson, Tulsa 74127 (918)585–2011
Wagoner Mrs. Sue Ann Graham, P. O. Box 485, Wagner 74467 (918)485–2162
Washington Mrs. Esther E. Hendrix, P. O. Box 1006, McAlester 74501 (918)423–3066
    336–2655
Washita J. Irwin Barger, P. O. Box 98, Cordell 73632 (405)832–3391
Woods Mrs. Thelma Elmore, P. O. Box 624, Alva 73717 (405)327–2714
Woodward William Ramsey, 1012-7th St., Woodward 73801 (405)256–6091

Oregon

Reporting Requirements

Persons mandated to report (compulsory) when reasonable cause to believe a child is or has been subjected to abuse or neglect: any physician, intern, resident, dentist, school employee, licensed or registered nurse, employee of the department of human resources, employee of county and community mental and social health agencies, peace officer, psychologist, clergyman, social worker, optometrist, chiropractor, certified provider or employee of day-care center, or attorney who in his/her official capacity as a public official has reasonable cause to suspect abuse

Permissive: none

Form of report and when made: Immediate oral

To whom report is made: local office of the children's services division, or to a law enforcement agency within the subject county

Penalties: misdemeanor punishable by fine of $250

Immunities: civil and criminal immunity for good faith reports upon reasonable grounds

Child Abuse Legislation

Citation: ORS Tit. 10, §1109(b); SB 304, Chap. 98
Year enacted: 1975
Effective date: September 13, 1975
Purpose of legislation: Mandatory reporting, yes
Reportable age: 0–18 years
Definitions: nonaccidental physical injury, including any injury which appears

to be at variance with explanation given; maltreatment which leads to physical harm; sexual molestation.

Education/school report: mandatory reporting, yes

Immunity: civil/criminal, yes

Mandatory investigation: yes, 24 hours

Confidentiality of records: yes; penalty: misdemeanor

Cooperation with law courts, state agencies: no specific provision

Guardian ad litem: yes

Administrative proceedings, trained personnel, facilities: no specific provision

Dissemination of information: no specific provision

Programs and Agencies

Where to write: Inquiries regarding requests for social information should be sent directly to the local units rather than to the Department of Human Resources. In case of verification of legal residence, correspondence should be directed to the last local unit in which the person lived (for inquiries directed to Multnomah County, copies are requested)

Oregon Department of Human Resources

Public Service Building
Salem 97310
Telephone: (503)378-3033
Richard A. Davis, Director
Cornelius Bateson, Department Director

Family Services Section

Lois McCarthy, Manager (503)378-3016

Community Resources Section

James McAllister, Manager (503)378-4507

Children's Services Division Regional Offices

Region I. (Multnomah County): 516 Morrison Street, S.E., P. O. Box 14606, Portland 97214 Larry Miller, Manager (503)238-8448

Region II. (Benton, Clatsop, Lincoln, Linn, and Tillamook Counties: Human Resources Center, 850-35th Street, S.W., Corvallis 97330 Robert White, Manager (503)757-4111

Region III; (Marion, Polk, and Yamhill Counties): 680 Cottage Street, N.E., P. O. Box 1027, Salem 97308 Glen Knickerbocker, Manager (503) 378-6325

Region IV. (Lane County): 1102 Lincoln Street, Eugene 97401 Thomas C. Moan, Manager, (503)686-7806

Region V. (Coos, Curry, Douglas, Jackson, and Josephine Counties): 650 Royal Street, No. 7, P. O. Box 459, Medford 97501 Dick Newstrum, Manager (503)776-6095

Region VI. (Crook, Deschutes, Hood River, Jefferson, Klamath, Lake, Sherman, and Wasco Counties): Human Resource Center, 2150 Studio Road, N.E., Bend 97701 John Kerns, Manager (503)389-5511

Region VII. (Baker, Gillian, Grant, Harney, Malheur, Morrow, Umatilla, Union, Wallowa, and Wheeler Counties): 1227-5th Avenue, S.W. Apartment 1 Ontario 97914 Caroline Craig, Manager (503)889-3186

Region VIII. (Clackamas, Columbia, and Washington Counties): 516 Morrison Street, S.E., P. O. Box 14606, Portland 97214 Fred Stock, Manager (503)238-8448

Children's Services Division Branch Offices

Baker County Stan Ludviksen, 1768 Auburn Street, P. O. Box 597, Baker 97814 (503)523-6423

Benton County Emery Gardner, Human Resource Center, 850-35th Street, S.W., Corvallis 97330 (503)752-9966

Clackamas County Robert Smith, 320 Warner-Milne Road, Oregon City 97045 (503)656-0811

Clatstop County Stan Mosley, 818 Commercial Street, P.O.Box 119, Astoria 97103 (503)325-4811

Columbia County Lee Hamilton, 105 South 3rd Street, P.O. Box 807, St. Helens 97051 (503)397-3292

Coos County (vacant), 465 Elrod Street, P.O. Box 59, Coos Bay 97420 (503)269-5961

Crook County Jerry Horn, 450 West 4th Street, P.O. Box 340, Prineville 97754 (503)447-6207

Curry County (vacant), 480 South Ellensburg Street, P.O. Box 887, Gold Beach 97444 (503)247-6666

Deschutes County Jerry Horn, 2150 Studio Road, N.E., P.O. Box 583, Bend 97701 (503)389-5780

Douglas County Thomas Notter, 751 Main Street, S.E., P.O. Box 1730, Roseburg 97470 (503)672-6541

Gilliam County Virginia Rose, Courthouse, P.O. Box 65, Condon 97823 (503)384-2882

Grant County Stan Ludviksen, 135 Ford Road, John Day 97845 (503) 575-0309

Harney County Paula Becks, 450 North Buena Vista Road, P.O. Box 589, Burns 97720 (503)573-6381

Hood River County Ron Nelson, Courthouse, P.O. Box 216, Hood River 97031 (503)386-2962

Jackson County Norma Ford, 650 Royal Avenue, No. 3, P.O. Box 1549, Medford 97501 (503)776-6124

Jefferson County Jerry Horn, 245-4th Street, P.O. Box F, Madras 97741 (503)475-2292

Josephine County Norma Ford, 725-6th Street, N.E., P.O. Box 189, Grants Pass 97526 (503)479-9791

Klamath County Betty Williams, 403 Pine St., P.O. Box 5230, Klamath Falls 97601 (503)884-1302

Lake County Betty Williams, 105 N. G. St., P.O. Box 910, Lakeview 97630 (503)947-3376

Lane County Helen Lilja, Asst. Regl. Mgr., 1102 Lincoln St., Eugene 97401 (503)686-7555; Florence Shepard, Asst. Regl. Mgr. (503)686-7563

Lincoln County Stan Mosley, 119 N. E. 4th St., Newport 97365 (503) 265-8557

Linn County Emery Gardner, 121 E. 1st St., P. O. Box 249, Albany 97321 (503)926-5571

Malheur County Paula Becks, 690 W. Idaho Ave., Ontario 97914 (503) 889-9194

Marion County Arthur Fisher, 680 Cottage St., N.E., P. O. Box 1027, Salem 97308 (503)378-6701

Muntnomah County East: (vacant) 1415-122nd Ave., S.E., P.O. Box 16338 Portland 97216 (503)257-4252; North: Lewis Winchester, Human Resource Center, 7201 N. Interstate, Portland 97217 (503)283-5722; Southeast: Austin Robert, 4506 Belmont St., S.E., Suite 201, Portland 97215 (503)238-8300; West: Austin Robert, 526 S.W. Mill St., P.O. Box 8291, Portland 97207 (503)229-6601; Albina: Roy Odren, 5022 N. Vancouver Ave., Portland 97217 (503)280-6002

Polk County Karen Pierson, 326 Main St., P. O. Box 85, Dallas 97338 (503) 623-8118

Sherman County Served by Wasco County

Tillamook County Stan Mosley, 3600 E. 3rd St., Tillamook 97141 (503) 842-5571

Umatilla County Virginia Rose, State Office Bldg., 700 Emigrant St., S.E. Pendleton 97801 (503)276-6131

Union County Stan Ledviksen, 1901 Adams St., P. O. Box 1984. LaGrande 97850 (503)963-8571

Wallowa County Stan Ludviksen, 215 W. Main St., P.O. Box A, Enterprise
   97828   (503)426-3146
Wasco County Ron Nelson, 110½ E. 2nd St., P. O. Box 498, The Dalles 97058
   (503)298-5136
Washington County Gary Shurtz, 326 Lincoln St., N.E., P. O. Box 315, Hillsboro 97123   (503)648-8951
Wheeler County Virginia Rose, Courthouse, P. O. Box 366, Fossil 97830
   (503)763-2541
Yamhill County Karen Pierson, 703 Gilson St., P.O. Box 682, McMinnville
   97128   (503)472-4634

Pennsylvania

Reporting Requirements

Persons mandated to report (compulsory) when reasonable cause to believe a child is or has been subjected to abuse or neglect: includes, but is not limited to, licensed physician; medical examiner; coroner; dentist; osteopath; optometrist; chiropractor; podiatrist; intern; registered or licensed practical nurse; hospital personnel engaged in admission, examination, care, or treatment of patients; Christian Science practitioner; school employee (including school nurse); social services or day-care worker; any other child care or foster care worker; mental health professional; and peace officer or law enforcement official (directors of hospitals and similar institutions shall report in lieu of staff who shall report to the director)

Permissive: anyone who has reasonable cause to believe that the child is abused

Form of report and when made: immediate oral; written, within 48 hours

To whom report is made: appropriate child protective service; if child dies, report of that fact must be made to the coroner

Penalties: willful failure: summary offense; second or subsequent offense is a third degree misdemeanor

Immunities: civil and criminal immunity for good faith report

Child Abuse Legislation

Citation: PSA Tit. 11, §50-317; Act 124 of 1975
Year enacted: 1975
Effective date: November 26, 1975
Purpose of legislation: mandatory reporting, yes

Reportable age: 0-18 years

Definitions: Serious nonaccidental physical or mental injury, sexual abuse, serious physical neglect.

Education/school report: mandatory reporting, yes

Immunity: civil/criminal, yes

Mandatory investigation: yes, immediately

Confidentiality of records: yes; penalty: misdemeanor

Cooperation with law courts, state agencies: yes

Guardian ad litem: yes

Administrative proceedings, trained personnel, facilities: yes

Dissemination of information: no specific provision

Programs and Agencies

Where to write:

> Child Support Programs
> Department of Public Welfare
> P. O. Box 2675
> Harrisburg 17120

> Director, Bureau of Child Welfare
> Office of Children and Youth
> Department of Public Welfare
> P.O. Box 2675
> Harrisburg 17120

Pennsylvania Department of Public Welfare

> P.O. Box 2675
> Harrisburg 17120
> Telephone: (717)787-2600
> Frank Beal, Secy.
> Edward B. Carskadon, Exec. Asst. (717)787-7101
> Eileen Schoen, Special Asst. (717)783-8741
> Paul Carey, Jr., Gen. Cnsl. (717)787-6398
> Normal Lourie, Exec. Dep. Secy. for Federal Policies and Prgms. (717) 787-3800
> Aldo Colautti, Exec. Dep. Secy. (717)787-3422

Office of Children and Youth

> Jerome Miller, Comm. (717)787-6010

Department of Public Welfare Regional Offices

Southeastern (Bucks, Chester, Delaware, Montgomery, and Philadelphia
Counties): State Office Bldg., Rm. 302, 1400 Spring Garden St., Phila-
delphia 19130 Wilbur Hobbs, Dep. Secy. (215)238-7130
Northeastern (Berks, Bradford, Carbon, Lackawanna, Lehigh, Luzerne, Monroe,
Northampton, Pike, Schulykill, Sullivan, Susquehanna, Tioga, Wayne, and
Wyoming Counties): Chamber of Commerce Bldg., 426 Mulberry St.,
Scranton 18501 Mrs. Kathryn McKenna, Dep. Secy., (717)961-4393
Central (Adams, Bedford, Blair, Cambria, Centre, Clinton, Columbia, Cumber-
land, Dauphin, Franklin, Fulton, Huntingdon, Juniata, Lancaster, Lebanon,
Lycoming, Mifflin, Montour, Northumberland, Perry, Snyder, Somerset,
Union, and York Counties): P. O. Box 2675, Harrisburg 17120 Ford
Thompson, Jr., Dep. Secy. (717)787-8048
Western (Allegheny, Armstrong, Beaver, Butler, Cameron, Clarion, Clearfield,
Crawford, Elk, Fayette, Forest, Greene, Indiana, Jefferson, Lawrence,
McKean, Mercer, Potter, Venango, Warren, Washington, and Westmoreland
Counties): State Office Bldg., Rm. 701m, 300 Liberty Ave., Pittsburgh
15222 Anna Calloway, Dep. Secy. (412)565-5220

County Commissioners' Offices

Adams Courthouse, Gettysburg 17325 (717)334-6781
Allegheny County Office Bldg., Pittsburgh 15219 (412)355-5311
Armstrong Courthouse, Kittanning 16201 (412)542-2741
Beaver Courthouse, Beaver 15009 (412)774-5000
Bedford Courthouse, Bedford 15522 (814)623-1173
Berks Courthouse, Reading 19601 (215)375-6121
Blair Courthouse Annex 2, Hollidaysburg 16648 (814)695-5541
Bradford Courthouse, Towanda 18848 (717)265-9137
Bucks Courthouse, Doylestown 18901 (215)348-2911
Butler Courthouse, Butler 16001 (412)285-4731
Cambria Courthouse, Ebensburg 15931 (814)472-8600
Cameron Courthouse, Emporium 15834 (814)486-2315
Carbon Courthouse, Jim Thorpe 18229 (717)325-3611
Centre Bellfonte 16823 (814)355-5521
Chester Courthouse, West Chester 19380 (215)431-6100
Clarion Courthouse, Clarion 16214 (814)226-9461
Clearfield Courthouse, Clearfield 16830 (814)765-6546
Clinton Courthouse, Lock Haven 17745 (717)748-7779
Columbia Courthouse, Bloomsburg 17815 (717)784-1991
Crawford Courthouse, Meadville 16335 (814)336-1151
Cumberland Courthouse, Carlisle 17013 (717)249-1133
Dauphin Courthouse, Harrisburg 17101 (717)234-7001
Delaware Courthouse, Media 19063 (215)891-2191
Elk Courthouse, Ridgeway 15853 (814)776-1161

Erie Courthouse, Erie 16501   (814)456-8851

Fayette Courthouse, Uniontown 15401   (412)437-4525

Forest Courthouse, Tionesta 16353   (814)755-3537

Franklin Courthouse, Chambersburg 17201   (717)264-4125

Fulton Courthouse, McConnellsburg 17233   (717)485-3691

Greene County Courthouse Bldg., Rm. 404, Waynesburg 15370   (412) 627-7525

Huntingdon Courthouse, Huntingdon 16652   (814)643-3091

Indiana Courthouse, Indiana 15701   (412)465-2661

Jefferson Courthouse, Brookville 15825   (814)849-8031

Juniata Courthouse, Mifflintown 17059   (717)436-6242

Lackawanna Courthouse, Scranton 18503   (717)961-6800

Lancaster Courthouse, Lancaster 17602   (717)397-8201

Lawrence Courthouse, New Castle 16101   (412)658-2541

Lebanon Municipal Bldg., Lebanon 17042   (717)273-8867

Lehigh Courthouse, Allentown 18105   (215)434-9471

Luzerne Courthouse, Wilkes-Barre 18711   (717)823-6161

Lycoming Courthouse, Williamsport 17701   (717)323-9811

McKean Courthouse, Smethport 16749   (814)887-5571

Mercer Courthouse, Mercer 16137   (412)662-3800

Mifflin Courthouse, Lewistown 17044   (717)248-8147

Monroe Courthouse, Stroudsburg 18360   (717)424-5100

Montgomery Courthouse, Norristown 19404   (215)275-5000

Montour Courthouse, Danville 17821   (717)275-1331

Northampton Courthouse, Easton 18042   (215)253-4111

Northumberland Courthouse, Sunbury 17801   (717)286-7721

Perry Courthouse, New Bloomfield 17068   (717)582-2636

Philadelphia Department of Welfare, City Hall Annex, Philadelphia 19107 (215)686-3460

Pike Courthouse, Milford 18337   (717)296-7613

Potter Courthouse, Coudersport 16915   (814)274-8290

Schuylkill Courthouse, Pottsville 17901   (717)622-5570

Snyder Courthouse, Middleburg 17842   (717)837-2724

Somerset Courthouse, Somerset 15501   (814)445-7991

Sullivan Courthouse, Laporte 18626   (717)946-5201

Susquehanna Courthouse, Montrose 18801   (717)278-3878

Tioga Courthouse, Wellsboro 16901   (717)724-1906

Union Courthouse, Lewisburg 17837   (717)524-4461

Venango Courthouse, Franklin 16323   (814)437-6871

Warren Courthouse, Warren 16365   (814)723-7550

Washington Courthouse, Washington 15301   (412)225-0100

Wayne Courthouse, Honesdale 18431   (717)253-4241

Westmoreland Courthouse, Greensburg 15601   (412)834-2191

Wyoming Courthouse, Tunkhannock 18657   (717)836-3200
York Courthouse, York 17401   (717)848-3301

The Pennsylvania County Institution District Act singles out Philadelphia from all other Pennsylvania counties and places responsibility for welfare services other than categorical assistance with the City of Philadelphia Department of Public Welfare and not with the Philadelphia County (City) Commissioners.

Rhode Island

Reporting Requirements

Persons mandated to report (compulsory) when reasonable cause to believe a child is or has been subjected to abuse or neglect: any person (especially physicians) who has reasonable cause to believe that a child has been battered and/or abused

Permissive: same; any person with reasonable cause

Form of report and when made: physician, immediate oral, followed by a written; others, within 24 hours; no form given

To whom report is made: physicians, department of social and rehabilitative services, division of community services, also, to law enforcement agency; others, director of social and rehabilitative services

Penalties: none

Immunities: civil and criminal immunity for reporters and those involved in judicial proceedings under the act for good faith report

Child Abuse Legislation

Citation: HB 6341, §40-11-1-10
Year enacted: 1975
Effective date: July 1, 1975
Purpose of legislation: mandatory reporting, yes
Reportable age: 0-18 years
Definition: any child who has any serious physical injury or injuries which reasonably appear to have been caused by other than accidental means and/or any child suffering from the battered child syndrome.

242

Education/school report: mandatory reporting, no specific provision
Immunity: civil/criminal, yes
Mandatory investigation: yes, no specific time frame
Confidentiality of records: no specific provision; penalty: no specific provision
Cooperation with law courts, state agencies: no specific provision
Guardian ad litem: no specific provision
Administrative proceedings, trained personnel, facilities: no specific provision
Dissemination of information: no specific provision

Programs and Agencies

Requests for information concerning children, including public child placement, legal residence of individual children, interstate placement of children, and adoptive investigations will secure more prompt action if sent directly to:

Assistant Administrator, Child Welfare Services
Division of Community Services
600 New London Ave.
Cranston 02920

Rhode Island Department of Social and Rehabilitative Services

600 New London Ave.
Cranston 02920
Telephone: (401)464-1000
John J. Affleck, Dir. (401)464-2121
James H. Reilly, Dep. Dir. (401)464-2421
Walter J. Breen, Asst. to the Dir. (401)464-2121
Anthony C. Ferri, Chief, Public Information and Public Relations
(401)464-2484

Division of Community Services

Anthony E. Ricci, Asst. Dir. (401)464-2423

Family and Children's Services

Robert F. McCaffrey, Adm. (401)464-2651
Thomas A. McDonough, Asst. Adm., Adult and Specialized Services
(401)464-3071
Joseph J. Dean, Jr., Asst. Adm. Family Services (401)464-3071
Catherine M. Cooney, Asst. Adm., Child Welfare Services (401)464-3471

Committee on Children and Youth

   (vacant), Exec. Secy.

Day Care Services

   100 Fountain St.
   Providence 02903
   Telephone: (401)277-2804
   John E. Anzivino, Chief

Dr. Patrick O'Rourke Children's Center

   610 Mt. Pleasant Ave.
   Providence 02908
   Telephone: (401)831-6700
   Frank A. Spinelli, Supt.

Department of Social and Rehabilitative Services District Offices

Bristol 400 Hope St., Bristol 02809   (401)253-3972
Burrillville Rte. 102, Victory Hwy., P. O. Box 199, Oakland 02858   (401)
   568-3033
Central Falls 580 Broad St., Central Falls 02863   (401)728-2500
Coventry 624 Washington St., Coventry 02816   (401)828-2440
Cranston 804 Dyer St., Valley Falls 02920   (401)722-2880
Cumberland 6 Davis St., Valley Falls 02864   (401)722-2880
East Greenwich Le Baron Dr., East Greenwich 02818   (401)884-7250
East Providence 75 James St., East Providence 02914   (401)438-7500
Johnston 1385 Hartford Ave., Johnston 02919   (401)861-6180
Lincoln 100 River Rd., Lincoln 02865   (401)728-7000
Newport Welfare Center, Elm St., Newport 02840   (401) 849-6000
North Providence 2226 Mineral Spring Ave., North Providence 02908   (401)
   231-2600
Pawtucket 56 High St., Pawtucket 02860   (401)728-2000
Providence 111 Fountain St., Providence 02903   (401)272-2000
Smithfield Town Hall, Esmond 02917   (401)231-6603
South Kingstown Old Town Hall, Wakefield 02879   (401)783-4611
Warren 28 Market St., Warren 02885   (401)245-7387
Warwick 1515 W. Shore Rd., Warwick 02889   (401)739-9530
Westerly Old Town Hall, Westerly 02891   (401)569-2081
West Warwick 152 Washington St., West Warwick 02893   (401)828-0500
Woonsocket 171 Front St., Woonsocket 02895   (401)769-3500

South Carolina

Reporting Requirements

Persons mandated to report (compulsory) when reasonable cause to believe a child is or has been subjected to abuse or neglect: all practitioners of the healing arts and any other person having reasonable cause to believe that a child under the age of 17 years has been subjected to physical abuse or neglect

Permissive: none

Form of report and when made: immediate oral

To whom report is made: county department of social services, or to the county sheriff's office, or chief law enforcement officer in the county where the child is found

Penalties: violation of the provisions of the act results in misdemeanor, and, upon conviction, is punishable by up to $500 and/or six months

Immunities: good faith reporter or participant in judicial proceedings merits civil and criminal immunity

Child Abuse Legislation

Citation: CLSC §20-302.0-302.4
Year enacted: 1974
Effective date: July 9, 1974
Purpose of legislation: mandatory reporting, yes
Reporting age: 0–17 years
Definition: severely battered, physically abused, safety seriously endangered
  unless parental rights are terminated and child be made eligible for adop-
  tion, abandonment, neglect

Education/school report: mandatory reporting, yes
Immunity: civil/criminal, yes
Mandatory investigation: yes, 3 days
Confidentiality of records: no specific provision; penalty: misdemeanor
Cooperation with law courts, state agencies: no specific provision
Guardian ad litem: no specific provision
Administrative proceedings, trained personnel, facilities: no specific provision
Dissemination of information: no specific provision

Programs and Agencies

Where to write:

Department of Social Services
P.O. Box 1520
Columbia 29202
Telephone: (803)758-3244
R. Archie Ellis, Commissioner
Legal Services Division, Frank Potts, Chief (803)758-5847
Individual and Family Services Division, Miss Linda Liverman, Chief
(803)758-2996

Department of Social Services District Offices

District I. (Anderson, Cherokee, Greenville, Oconee, Pickens, and Spartanburg
Counties): P.O. Box 6167, Station B, Greenville 29606 Thomas K. Barnes,
Dir. (803)271-9770

District II. (Abbeville, Aiken, Allendale, Barnwell, Edgefield, Greenwood,
Laurens, McCormick, and Saluda Counties): P.O. Box 177, Johnston
29832 Mrs. Thelma M. Crouch, Dir. (803)275-3242

District III. (Chester, Farfield, Lancaster, Lexington, Newberry, Richland,
Union, and York Counties): 219 N. Congress St., Winnsboro 29180
Redde J. Thames, Dir. (803)635-5566

District IV. (Chesterfield, Darlington, Dillion, Florence, Georgetown, Horry
Marion, Marlboro, and Williamsburg Counties) P.O. Box 510, Florence
29501 George S. Nichols, Jr., Dir. (803)665-4585

District V. (Beaufort, Berkley, Charleston, Colleton, Dorchester, Hampton, and
Jasper Counties): P.O. Box 1174, Walterboro 29488 Harry H. Mills, Jr.,
Dir. (803)549-5508

District VI. (Bamberg, Calhoun, Clarendon, Kershaw, Lee, Orangeburg, and
Sumter Counties): P.O. Box 1508, Sumter 29150 Mrs. Harrianne Dent,
Dir. (803)775-7364

County Departments of Social Services

Abbeville Mrs. Peggy Harrison, P. O. Box 189, Abbeville 29620 (803)
459-5481

Aiken Richard Poor, P. O. Box 687, Aiken 29801 (803)648-4203

Allendale Miss Adeline Kearse, P. O. Box 186, Allendale 29810 (803)
584-2181

Anderson Ken Pryor, P. O. Box 827, Anderson 29622 (803)224-0281

Bamberg Mrs. Wadedelle Moody, P. O. Box 60, Bamberg 29003 (803)
245-2451

Barnwell Mrs. Elizabeth Cherry, P. O. Box 517, Barnwell 29812 (803)
259-3039

Beaufort Franklin Axmann, P. O. Box 1065, Beaufort 29902 (803)524-4922

Berkeley Mrs. Julia Young, P. O. Box 158, Moncks Corner 29461 (803)
899-2157

Calhoun Mrs. Ann Whetstone, P. O. Box 202, St. Matthews 29135 (803)
874-3384

Charleston William Knowles, County Center, Rm. 409, Charleston 29403
(803)723-5541

Cherokee Mrs. Rose Rhyme, P. O. Box 606, Gaffney 29340 (803)489-6026

Chester Mrs. Grace Robertson, P. O. Box 732, Chester 29706 (803)385-2610

Chesterfield Milton Jackson, P. O. Box 269, Chesterfield 29790 (803)
623-2147

Clarendon Mrs. Vera Covington, County Health Center, S. Church St., Manning
29102 (803)435-8139

Colleton Mrs. Elma Rogers, P. O. Box 626, Walterboro 29488 (803)549-5569

Darlington Walter Copeland, P. O. Drawer 557, Darlington 29532 (803)
393-5451

Dillon Alfred Finklea, P. O. Drawer 630, Dillon 29356 (803)774-2435

Dorchester Mrs. Mary Kirby, P. O. Box 906, St. George 29477 (803)563-2321

Edgefield Mrs. Rachel Smith, P. O. Box 644, Edgefield 29824 (803)637-3126

Fairfield James Holcombe, P. O. Box 210, Winnsboro 29180 (803)635-4233

Florence Mrs. Anna Anderson, P. O. Box 5689, Florence 29501 (803)
669-3554

Georgetown Mrs. Clara Waddell, P. O. Drawer P., Georgetown 29440 (803)
546-4333

Greenville Richard Carver, P. O. Box 10249, Greenville 29630 (803)232-8703

Greenwood Mrs. Barbara Lyles, P. O. Box 1069, Greenwood 29646 (803)
229-6674

Hampton Mrs. Iva Mace, County Office Bldg. Hampton 29924 (803)943-3641

Horry Mrs. Joyce Strickland, P. O. Box 388, Conway 29526 (803)365-5556

Jasper Mrs. Eunice McKellar, P. O. Box 1349, Ridgeland 29936 (803)
726-8131

Kershaw Mrs. Kathryn Baxley, P. O. Box 546, Camden 29020 (803)432-7676
Lancaster John Whitehurst, 107 S. French St., Lancaster 29720 (803) 285-6914
Laurens Mrs. Alice Davidson, P. O. Box 947, Laurens 29360 (803)984-4541
Lee Mrs. Virginia Matthews, Courthouse Square, Bishopville 29010 (803) 484-6012
Lexington Mrs. Jennie Alexander, P. O. Box 447, Lexington 29072 (803) 359-4173
McCormick Mrs. Elizabeth Furman, P. O. Box 506, McCormick 29835 (803) 564-6300
Marion Hybert Strickland, P. O. Box 1135, Marion 29571 (803)423-4623
Marlboro Miss Florence McIntyre, P. O. Drawer 120, Bennettsville 29512 (803)479-4071
Newberry Jimmy Alewine, P. O. Box 309, Newberry 29108 (803)276-3611
Oconee J. W. Todd, P. O. Box 511, Walhalla 29691 (803)638-5882
Orangeburg Miss Rebecca Crowell, P. O. Drawer E, Orangeburg 29115 (803) 536-1685
Pickens John Bond, P. O. Box 158, Pickens 29671 (803)878-2451
Richland Benjamin Blocker, 2020 Hampton St., Columbia 29204 (803) 779-4800
Saluda Mrs. Grace Long, P. O. Box 276, Saluda 29138 (803)445-2139
Spartanburg James Thompson, P. O. Box 1747, Spartanburg, 29301 (803) 585-9364
Sumter Marcus Mann, P. O. Box 68, Sumter 29150 (803)773-5531
Union S. Clayburn (Act.), P. O. Box 428, Union 29379 (803)427-8401
Williamsburg Mrs. Owen Cook, P. O. Drawer 389, Kingstree 29556 (803) 354-6034
York Newton Adams, P. O. Box 261, York 29745 (803)684-3551

South Dakota

Reporting Requirements

Persons mandated to report (compulsory) when reasonable cause to believe a child is or has been subjected to abuse or neglect: any physician, surgeon, dentist, osteopath, chiropractor, optometrist, podiatrist, psychologist, social worker, hospital intern or resident, law enforcement officer, teacher, school counselor, school official, nurse, coroner, (hospital staff report to director, who shall in turn make the required official report)

Permissive: any person who suspects or has reason to believe that a child has received physical or emotional injury as a result of abuse or neglect

Form of report and when made: immediate oral

To whom report is made: state's attorney of the county in which the child lives or is present, or the department of social services

Penalties: knowing and willful failure to make required report is a misdemeanor

Immunities: immunity from civil and criminal liability if report is made in good faith

Child Abuse Legislation

Citation: SDCLA §26-8-22, 26-10
Year enacted: 1975
Effective date: exact date not available
Purpose of legislation: mandatory reporting, yes
Reporting age: 0-18 years
Definition: exposure, torture, torment, cruelty, punished willfully; deprivation

249

of necessary food, clothing, shelter, or medical care; physical or emotional abuse

Education/school report: mandatory reporting, yes

Immunity: civil/criminal, yes

Mandatory investigation: yes, no specific time frame

Confidentiality of records: yes; penalty: misdemeanor

Cooperation with law courts, state agencies: no specific provision

Guardian ad litem: yes

Administrative proceedings, trained personnel, facilities: no specific provision

Dissemination of information: no specific provision

Programs and Agencies

The Division of Social Welfare will act as a forwarding center for inquiries pertaining to ADC, Food Stamps, Title XIX programs, and Child Support Enforcement. Letters should be addressed to:

> Division of Social Welfare
> State Office Bldg.
> Illinois St.
> Pierre 57501
> Attn: Inter-Agency Inquiry

South Dakota Department of Social Services

> State Office Bldg.
> Illinois St.
> Pierre 57501
> Telephone: (605)224-3165

Office of Community Services

> Robert Leach, State Prgm. Adm. (605)224-3227

Office of Resource Development

> Wayne Lunder, State Prgm. Adm. (605)224-3195

Tennessee

Reporting Requirements

Persons mandated to report (compulsory) when reasonable cause to believe a child is or has been subjected to abuse or neglect: any person having knowledge of or called upon to render aid to any child who is suffering from or has sustained any mental or physical injury that is such as may be reasonably the result of brutality, abuse, or neglect (director of hospital reports to staff)

Permissive: none

Form of report and when made: oral or otherwise

To whom report is made: judge having juvenile jurisdiction; or to the county office of the department of human services; or to the office of the sheriff or chief law officer in the county

Penalties: knowing failure to report is a misdemeanor punishable by not more than fine of $50.00 and/or three months imprisonment; judge may bind respondent over to grand jury if he pleads innocent

Immunities: presumption of good faith; civil and criminal immunity

Child Abuse Legislation

Citation: TCA Tit. 37, §1201–1212
Year enacted: 1973
Effective date: April 17, 1973
Purpose of legislation: mandatory reporting, yes
Reportable age: 0–18 years
Definition: no specific definition provided
Education/school report: mandatory reporting, yes

Immunity: civil/criminal, yes
Mandatory investigation: yes, promptly
Confidentiality of records: yes; penalty: no specific provision
Cooperation with law courts, state agencies: yes
Guardian ad litem: yes
Administrative proceedings, trained personnel, facilities: no specific provision
Dissemination of information: no specific provision

Programs and Agencies

Inquiries regarding support for dependent children should be addressed to:

> Support Services
> Department of Human Services
> State Office Bldg., Rm. 410
> Nashville 37219

Inquiries about family and children's services which involve referrals for social information, authorization to return dependent minors, and placements which come under the Interstate Compact on the Placement of Children should be directed in triplicate to:

> Virginia Moore, Director of Social Services
> Department of Human Services
> State Office Bldg., Rm. 310
> Nashville 37219

Tennessee Department of Human Services

> State Office Bldg., Rm. 410
> Nashville 37219
> Telephone: (615)741-3241
> Horace Bass, Commissioner
> Mrs. Jeanne M. Bowman, Dep. Comm.
> Warren Causey, Admv. Asst. and Pub. Info.
> James H. Tucker, Admv. Asst.

Social Services

> Mrs. Virginia Moore, Dir. (615)741-2906

Department of Human Services County Offices

Anderson Franklin D. Mee, Clinton 37716 (615)457-3660
Bedford John W. Parker, Jr., Shelbyville 37160 (615)684-4741

Benton James H. Wiseman, Camden 38320 (901)584-4712
Bledsoe Lawrence L. Swafford, Jr., Pikeville 37367 (615)447-2193
Blount Mrs. Sylvia L. Powell, Maryville 37801 (615)982-4531
Bradley Mrs. Nell S. Eldridge, Cleveland 37311 (615)476-8591
Campbell Cade D. Sexton, Jacksboro 37757 (615)562-8466
Cannon Mrs. Donna Nichols, Woodbury 37190 (615)563-4158
Carroll James E. Cantrell, Huntingdon 38344 (901)986-4812
Carter Jack Hensley, Elizabethton 37643 (615)543-3189
Cheatham (vacant), Ashland City 37015 (615)792-5628
Chester Mrs. Lois R. Bell, Henderson 38340 (901)989-5121
Claiborne Mrs. Wilma Beatty, Tazewell 37879 (615)626-5228
Clay Cordell Masters, Celina 38551 (615)243-2621
Cocke Harold E. Cates, Newport 37821 (615)623-6185
Coffee Mrs. Frances Powers, Manchester 37355 (615)728-2986
Crockett William L. Tillman, Alamo 38001 (901)696-5521
Cumberland Mrs. Camilla Thurman, Crossville 38555 (615)484-6410
Davidson Richard Moore, 1616 Church St., Nashville 37203 (615)329-4538
Decatur Gary Hall, Decaturville 38329 (901)852-2981
De Kalb Mrs. Helen Y. Ford, Smithville 37166 (615)597-4725
Dickson Mrs. Marilyn Field, Dickson 37055 (615)446-2893
Dyer Mrs. Willa D. Adams, Dyersburg 38024 (901)285-5901
Fayette Mrs. Francine Zeran, Somerville 38068 (901)465-3637
Fentress J. E. Crouch, Jamestown 37758 (615)879-8105
Franklin Nora Lee Hardin, Winchester 37398 (615)967-0624
Gibson Donald C. Holland, Trenton 38382 (901)855-9451
Giles Mrs. Elizabeth Hewgley, Pulaski 38478 (615)363-4578
Grainger Richard Dalton, Rutledge 37861 (615)828-5251
Greene Mrs. Mary Sue Brakebill, Greeneville 37743 (615)638-6141
Grundy Mrs. Lorene Tittsworth, Tracy City 37387 (615)592-6338
Hamblen Samuel C. Moore, Morristown 37814 (615)586-7142
Hamilton Gary R. Helton, 42 E. 11th St., Chattanooga 37402 (615)266-3181
Hancock William P. Seal, Speedville 37869 (615)733-2761
Hardeman Mrs. Inez Brisendine, Bolivar 38008 (901)658-5545
Hardin Mrs. Lillian S. Shaw, Savannah 38372 (901)925-4968
Hawkins Mrs. Mildred R. Day, Rogersville 38757 (615)272-2606
Haywood Mrs. Pauline Shellabarger, Brownsville 38012 (901)772-1562
Henderson Mrs. Margaret D. Todd, Lexington 38351 (901)968-3652
Henry Jerry M. Cannon, Paris 38242 (901)642-9711
Hickman Rupert Richardson, Centerville 37033 (615)729-4116
Houston Samuel N. Richardson, Erin 37061 (615)289-4105
Humphreys Mrs. Lanelle S. Coleman, Waverly 37185 (615)296-4227
Jackson Miss Linda Rybee, Gainesboro 38562 (615)268-9545
Jefferson Mrs. Mary T. Jarvis, Dandridge 37725 (615)397-3197

Johnson Miss Florence Tucker, Mountain City 37683   (615)727-7704
Knox Mrs. Mary Louise Chambers, 1501-5th Ave., Knoxville 37917   (615)
   546-1530
Lake Raymond H. Goodgine, Tiptonville 38079   (901)253-7271
Lauderdale Larry T. McBride, Ripley 38063   (901)635-4141
Lawrence Mrs. Mildred P. Bassham, Lawrenceburg 38464   (615)762-2231
Lewis Kenny P. Graves, Hohenwald 38462   (615)796-3017
Lincoln Thomas L. Springer, Fayetteville 37334   (615)433-3593
Loudon Mrs. Jessie W. Ridenour, Loudon 37774   (615)458-4616
McMinn Lake Lillard, Athens 37303   (615)745-3984
McNairy Junior Cody, Selmer 38375   (901)645-3516
Macon Mrs.Gwendolyn Howser, Lafayette 37083   (615)666-4041
Madison Mrs. Doris Wilson, Jackson 38301   (901)424-0782
Marion Mrs. Harriet Pair, Jasper 37347   (615)942-3481
Marshall Mrs. Gayle H. Cathey, Lewisburg 37091   (615)359-6251
Maury Mrs. Nancy B. Thomas, Columbia 38401   (615)388-3025
Meigs Mrs. Audrey H. Perry, Decatur 37322   (615)334-5787
Monroe Mrs. Carolyn M. Peck, Madisonville 37354   (615)442-2445
Montgomery Lionel Senseney, Clarksville 37040   (615)645-4531
Moore Ronald C. Spencer, Lynchburg 37352   (615)759-7181
Morgan Mrs. Ruth LaMance, Wartburg 37887   (615)346-6237
Obion Mrs. Frances Latimer, Union City 38261   (901)885-2292
Overton Walter C. Masters, Livingston 38570   (615)823-1285
Perry Mrs. Jessie Tiller, Linden 37096   (615)589-2414
Pickett Charles Jolly, Byrdstown 38549   (615)864-3153
Polk Robert L. Lattimore, Jr., Benton 37307   (615)338-2076
Putnam Lloyd M. Loftis, Cookeville 38501   (615)526-2148
Rhea Mrs. Florence Lace, Dayton 37321   (615)775-2681
Roane Billy R. Leffew, Kingston 37763   (615)376-3491
Robertson Mrs. Lee Oma Wilkinson, Springfield 37172   (615)384-5562
Rutherford Mrs. Wanda Leverette, Murfreesboro 37130   (615)893-3032
Scott Malvin C. Sexton, Huntsville 37756   (615)663-2821
Sequatchie Mrs. Sarah J. Walker, Dunlap 37327   (615)949-3629
Sevier Clyde M. Terry, Sevierville 37862   (615)453-4686
Shelby Mrs. Peggy Edmiston, 170 N. Main St., Memphis 38103   (901)534-6623
Smith Mrs. Mattie Bradley, Carthage 37030   (615)735-9740
Stewart Mrs. Geneva Whitford, Dover 37058   (615)232-5304
Sullivan Darrell Godsey, Blountville 37617   (615)323-5146
Sumner Miss Elizabeth Allen, Gallatin 37066   (615)452-1997
Tipton Mrs. Kaye B. Smith, Covington 38019   (901)476-5223
Trousdale Mrs. Jerry Robinson, Hartsville 37074   (615)374-3513
Unicoi Danny J. Keesecker, Erwin 37650   (615)743-3166
Union Troy Lee Hollaway, Maynardville 37807   (615)992-5261

Van Buren Mrs. Velma Rogers, Spencer 38585 (615)946-2437
Warren Mrs. Jean Marsh, McMinnville 37110 (615)473-2328
Washington Ronald Helsabeck, Johnson City 37601 (615)929-0171
Wayne Mrs. Ethel Bundrant, Waynesboro 38485 (615)722-3431
Weakley Mrs. Martha Smith, Dresden 38225 (901)364-3128
White Mrs. Mildred Thurman, Sparta 38583 (615)836-3275
Williamson Mrs. Mary Brazil, Franklin 37064 (615)794-3593
Wilson Mrs. Joanne H. Smith, Lebanon 37087 (615)444-1670
Knox Mrs. Charles P. Swan, Ft. Hill Bldg., 701 E. Vine Ave., Knoxville 37915
(615)637-0431
Chattanooga Mrs. Maureen Boyd, Warner Park Field House, 1254 E. 3rd St.,
Chattanooga 37404 (615)757-5172
Knoxville (vacant), City Hall Park, Knoxville 37902 (615)523-1621
Memphis Mrs. Shirley Ferlona, City Hall, Rm. 1-B1, 125 N. Main St., Memphis
38103 (901)528-2596
Nashville Mrs. Camilla Caldwell, 25 Middleton St., Nashville 37210 (615)
259-5381
Oak Ridge Joseph A. Mitchell, P. O. Box 1, Oak Ridge 37830 (615)483-5671

Reporting Requirements

Persons mandated to report (compulsory) when reasonable cause to believe a child is or has been subjected to abuse or neglect: any person having cause to believe that a child's physical or mental health or welfare has been or will be adversely affected by abuse or neglect

Permissive: none

Form of report and when made: oral, immediately; written, within five days; anonymous reports, while not encouraged, are accepted and acted upon

To whom report is made: county welfare unit, the county agency responsible for the protection of juveniles, or any local or state law enforcement agency

Penalties: none

Immunities: any person reporting under this act is immune from civil and criminal liability; immunity extends to participation in judicial proceedings; persons reporting in bad faith or with malice are not protected

Child Abuse Legislation

Citation: Family Code Chaps. 10, 11, 34
Year enacted: 1973
Effective date: January 1, 1974
Purpose of legislation: mandatory reporting, yes
Reportable age: child
Definition: no specific definition provided
Education/school report: mandatory reporting, yes
Immunity: civil/criminal, yes

Mandatory investigation: yes, 5 days
Confidentiality of records: no specific provision; penalty: no specific provision
Cooperation with law courts, state agencies: yes
Guardian ad litem: yes
Administrative proceedings, trained personnel, facilities: no specific provision
Dissemination of information: no specific provision

Programs and Agencies

Where to write: Communications regarding requests for social information and interstate placement of children and inquiries concerning AFDC, Medicaid, and child welfare should be sent directly to:

Division of Special Services
Department of Public Welfare
John H. Reagen Bldg.
Austin 78701

Texas Department of Public Welfare

John Reagan Bldg.
Austin 78701
Telephone: (512)475-3555
Raymond W. Vowell, Comm. (512)475-5777
Jerome D. Chapman, Jr., Dep. Comm. (512)475-2795
Jack Blanton, Exec. Asst. (512)475-2506

Social Services Branch

Burton F. Raiford, Asst. Dep. Comm. (512)475-6561
Clifton Martin, Chief Adm. (512)475-6713

Social Services Program Support Division

Kenneth Pennington, Adm. (512)475-6561

Program Evaluation and Review Division

Robert Reeves, Adm. (512)475-6561

Program and Policy Development Division

John Lindell, Adm. (512)475-6713

State Contracts Division

    Charles Martin, Adm. (512)475-6561

Program Management Division

    Dennis Sullivan, Adm. (512)475-5991

Department of Public Welfare Regional Offices

Region I. Nathan Martin, P. O. Box 10528, Lubbock 74908 (817)797-4311
Region II. Hazel Baylor, 5150 El Paso Dr., El Paso 79905 (915)779-7790
Region III. James Covey, 410 N. 13th St., Edinburgh 78539 (512)383-5344
Region IV. Raymond Cheves, 101 S. Santa Rosa Dr., San Antonio 78298
    (512)533-3161
Region V. Joe Villarreal, 9910 Homestead Rd., Houston 77016 (713)631-6800
Region VI. June Klein, 215 Franklin St., Beaumont 77701 (713)838-3721
Region VII. Lloyd S. Sterling, 901 Kaufman St., Paris 75460 (214)784-3395
Region VIII. Tom Cragen, Old Courthouse, Dallas 75202 (214)741-7811
Region IX. J. W. Keith, 711 W. 7th St., Ft. Worth 76102 (817)335-5171
Region X. Homer Rodriguez, 3000 S. Hwy. IH-35, Austin 78704 (512)
    475-6914

Local Public Welfare Agencies

Angelina P. O. Box 211, Lufkin 75901
Armstrong P. O. Box 425, Panhandle 79068
Bell See below, Temple City
Brazoria Angelton 77515
Brazos County Courthouse, Bryan 77801
Cameron P. O. Box 431, Brownsville 78520
Carson P. O. Box 425, Panhandle 79068
Coleman P. O. Box 938, Coleman 76834
Crane Crane 79731
Dallas 4917 Harry Hines Blvd., Dallas 75235
Dawson 309 N. Houston, Lamesa 79331
Deaf Smith Courthouse, Hereford 79045
Denton County Courthouse Annex, Denton 76201
Ector Courthouse, Odessa 79761
Ellis County Family Welfare Association, Courthouse Basement, Wasahachie
    75165
El Paso County General Assistance Agency, 145 N. Raynolds Blvd., El Paso
    79905
Fisher P. O. Box 395, Roby 79543
Ft. Bend Richmond 77469
Galveston County Courthouse Annex, Galveston 77550
Gray Courthouse, 1st Fl. Pampa 79065

Guadalupe Courthouse, Seguin 78155
Harris 1225 Elder St., Houston 77007
Hidalgo P. O. Box 607, Edinburg 78539
Howard Courthouse, Rm. 201, Big Spring 79720
Hutchinson P. O. Box 697, Borger 79007
Jefferson North Jefferson County Welfare Department, 345 Franklin St.,
     Beaumont 77701; Supervisor, South Jefferson County Welfare Department,
     246 Dallas Ave., Pt. Arthur 77640
Klegerg P. O. Box 1106, Kingsville 78363
Lamar Supervisor, King's Daughters City-County Welfare Department, City Hall,
     Paris 75460
Lamb Courthouse, Littlefield 79339
Lubbock City-County Welfare Department, County Office Bldg., Rm. 100,
     P. O. Box 1554, Lubbock 79408
McLennan 201 W. Waco Dr., Rm. 209, Waco 76701
Matagorda P. O. Box 337, Blessing 77419
Midland Courthouse Annex, Rm. 606, 218 Illinois St., Midland 79701
Montgomery Supervisor, P. O. Box 292, Conroe 77301
Moore County Health and Welfare Agency, P. O. Box 794, Dumas 79029
Navarro Executive Secretary, Family Service Association, 409 Beaton St., P. O.
     Box 1415, Corsicana 75110
Nolan Courthouse, Sweetwater 79556
Nueces Welfare Division, County Department of Public Health and Welfare,
     1810 Howard St., P. O. Box 1540, Corpus Christi 78403
Orange 701 N. 2nd St., Orange 77630
Potter Crossroads Motel, Rm. 49, Amarillo 79101
San Patricio Courthouse, Sinton 78387
Scurry 1921-25th St., Synder 79549
Smith 110 S. Spring St., P. O. Box 4298, Tyler 75701
Tarrant 200 Bluff St., Ft. Worth 76102
Taylor Executive Secretary, Pecan St., Abilene 79602
Terry Courthouse, Brownfield 79316
Tom Green San Angelo City-County Welfare Dept., 122 W. 1st St., San Angelo
     76901
Travis 624 Pleasant Valley Rd., Austin 78702
Val Verde City-County Welfare Department, 200 Griner St., Del Rio 78840
Webb P. O. Box 1234, Laredo 78040
Wichita Supervisor, 100 Jefferson St., Wichita Falls 76304
Wilbarger Courthouse, Vernon 76384
Winkler County Courthouse, P. O. Box 275, Kermit 79745
Corpus Christi Department of Public Health and Welfare. P. O. Box 49, Corpus
     Christi 78403
San Antonio Department of Welfare, 426 South Laredo St., San Antonio 78207
Temple Family Welfare Society, 701 E. Central St., Temple 76501

Utah

Reporting Requirements

Persons mandated to report (compulsory) when reasonable cause to believe a child is or has been subjected to abuse or neglect: any person who knows or reasonably suspects that a child's health or welfare has been, or appears to have been, harmed as a result of abuse or neglect (director of hospital or similar institution makes reports for staff)

Permissive: none

Form of report and when made: oral report as soon as possible; may follow with written (permissive)

To whom report is made: local city police or county sheriff, or office of the division of family services

Penalties: knowing or willful violation is a misdemeanor

Immunities: good faith report engenders civil and criminal immunity and extends to judicial proceedings

Child Abuse Legislation

Citation: UCA §55-16-6, 7; 55-10-89, 96, 111
Year enacted: 1965
Effective date: May 11, 1965; July 1, 1965
Purpose of legislation: mandatory reporting, yes
Reportable age: 0-18 years
Definition: harm, threatened harm, nonaccidental physical or mental injury, sexual abuse, negligent treatment, or maltreatment; failure to provide adequate food, clothing, and shelter.

Education/school report: mandatory reporting, yes
Immunity: civil/criminal, yes
Mandatory investigation: yes, no specific time frame
Confidentiality of records: yes; penalty: misdemeanor
Cooperation with law courts, state agencies: no specific provision
Guardian ad litem: yes
Administrative proceedings, trained personnel, facilities: no specific provision
Dissemination of information: no specific provision

Programs and Agencies

Social service inquiries, except adoption cases and requests for interstate placement of children, should be sent directly to the appropriate division of family services district office. Inquiries pertaining to social service policies should be sent to:

> Division of Family Services
> Department of Social Services
> 333 S. 200 East
> Salt Lake City 84111

Inquiries relating solely to the willingness and financial ability of relatives to assist should be sent directly to the relatives. Inquiries regarding adoption cases and requests for interstate placements of children should be directed in duplicate to:

> Assistant Director, Program Services
> Division of Family Services
> 333 S. 200 East
> Salt Lake City 84111

Utah Department of Social Services

> State Capitol, Rm. 104
> Salt Lake City 84114
> Telephone: (801)533-5331
> Paul S. Rose, Exec. Dir.
> D. D. Williams, Dep. Exec. Dir.

Division of Family Services

> 333 S. 200 East
> Salt Lake City 84111
> Telephone: (801)533-5031
> Evan E. Jones, Jr., Dir.

Social Services Branch

Lloyd H. Nelson, Dep. Dir. (801)533-5094

Program Services

William S. Ward, Asst. Dir. (801)533-5041

Support Services

Heber Mehr, Asst. Dir. (801)533-5094

Manpower Planning and Development

Bayard M. Taylor, Dir. (801)533-5048

Division of Family Services District Offices

District I. (Box Elder, Cache, and Rich Counties): 129 N. 100 West, Logan 84231   Glen Winslow, Dir. (801)752-2511

District IIA. (Davis, Morgan, and Weber Counties): 320 Healy St., Ogden 84402 Marguerite Horton, Dir. (801)399-1131

District IIB. (Salt Lake and Tooele Counties): 3195 S. Main St., Salt Lake City 84115   Sam N. Anton, Dir. (801)486-1811

District III. (Summit, Utah, and Wasatch Counties): 260 W. 300 North Provo 84601   Floy Taylor, Dir. (801)373-6154

District IV. (Juab, Millard, Piute, Sanpete, Sevier, and Wayne Counties): 180 N. 100 East, Professional Plaza, Suite E. Richfield 84701   Clair Cowley, Dir. (801)896-5439

District V. (Beaver, Garfield, Iron, Kane, and Washington Counties): 1552 W. 200 North Cedar City 84720   Kirt Soderquist, Dir. (801)586-3841

District VI. (Daggett, Duchesne, and Uintah Counties): 671 W. 100 North, Vernal 84078   Jerry Jackson, Dir. (801)789-4884

District VIIA. (Carbon, Emery, and Grant Counties): Courthouse, Main and 100 East, Price 84501   Evelyn Roberts, Dir. (801)637-3305

District VIIB. (San Juan County): 110 E. Center St. Blanding 84511   Bruce Shumway, Dir. (801)678-2247

Vermont

Reporting Requirements

Persons mandated to report (compulsory) when reasonable cause to believe a child is or has been subjected to abuse or neglect: any physician, osteopath, chiropractor, physician's assistant, resident or intern in any hospital in the state, registered or licensed practical nurse, medical examiner, dentist, or police officer with reasonable cause to believe that any child has been abused or neglected

Permissive: psychologist, school teacher, day-care center worker, school principal or guidance counselor, mental health professional, social worker, probation officer, or clergyman who has reasonable cause to believe that a child is being abused or neglected

Form of report and when made: oral report, followed in one week by written

To whom report is made: commissioner of social and rehabilitative services or his designee

Penalties: knowing and willful violation of duty to report subject to fine of not more than $100

Immunities: all reporters (mandatory and permissive) who do so in good faith receive civil and criminal immunity, extending to judicial proceedings

Child Abuse Legislation

Citation: VSA Tit. 13, Chap. 27; Tit. 33, §653(a)
Year enacted: 1973
Effective date: July 1, 1974
Purpose of legislation: mandatory reporting, yes

Reportable age: under age of majority

Definition: nonaccidental physical injury where health, life, development, welfare is in jeopardy; neglect, abandonment.

Education/school report: mandatory reporting, permissive

Immunity: civil/criminal, yes

Mandatory investigation: yes, 72 hours

Confidentiality of records: yes; penalty: fine of $500 or less

Cooperation with law courts, state agencies: no specific provision

Guardian ad litem: yes

Administrative proceedings, trained personnel, facilities: no specific provision

Dissemination of information: no specific provision

Programs and Agencies

Inquiries relating to child welfare services, including adoption services, protective services, and foster care of children, should be addressed to:

Director, Division of Social Services
Department of Social and Rehabilitation Services
81 River St.
Montpelier 05602

Vermont Agency of Human Services

79 River St.
Montpelier 05602
Telephone: (802)828-2471
Thomas Davis, Secy.

Office of Child Development

81 River St.
Montpelier 05602
Rolland Gerhart, Jr., Dir. (802)828-3433

Division of Social Services

Allen R. Ploof, Dir. (802)828-3433

Division of Social Services District Offices

Barre Nevia Campi, Barre 05641   (802)828-3401
Bennington Mrs. Claire O'Leary, Bennington 05201   (802)442-8541

Brattleboro Mrs. Elaine M. Willingham, 4 Park Pl., Brattleboro 05301 (802) 257-1381

Burlington Mrs. Marion Paris, 80 St. Paul St., Burlington 05401 (802) 863-2331

Hartford Virginia Soule, White River Junction 05001 (802)295-3063

Middlebury Mrs. H. Ann Clark, 97 MacDonough Dr., Vergennes 05491 (802) 388-4011

Morrisville Carolyn Russell, Morrisville 05661 (802)888-4206

Newport John Goddard, Newport 05855 (802)334-6504

Rutland Dorothy Walker, Rutland 05701 (802)775-3346

St. Albans Anna Neville, St. Albans 05478 (802)524-9531

St. Johnsbury Edgerton Elliott, St. Johnsbury 05819 (802)748-3148

Springfield Helen Pierce, 197 Union St., Sprinfield 05156 (802)885-5791

Virginia

Reporting Requirements

Persons mandated to report (compulsory) when reasonable cause to believe a child is or has been subjected to abuse or neglect: physician, resident, intern, nurse, social worker, probation officer, school employee, full- or part-time child care employee, Christian Science practitioner, mental health professional, or law enforcement official in his official capacity

Permissive: any person

Form of report and when made: immediate oral

To whom report is made: local branch of the state department of welfare; if an employee of the department is suspected of being the abuser, the report shall be filed with juvenile and domestic relations district court for that county

Penalties: fine of not more than $500 for first failure to report; subsequent failures to be fined between $100 and $1000

Immunities: immunity from civil and criminal liability provided in absence of malicious intent

Child Abuse Legislation

Citation: VCA §16.1-173(f), 63.1-248.12
Year enacted: 1975
Effective date: June 1, 1975
Purpose of Legislation: mandatory reporting, yes
Reportable age: 0-18 years
Definition: nonaccidental physical or mental injury; risk of death, disfigurement,

impairment; neglect or refusal to provide necessary health care; abandonment;
sexual abuse
Education/school report: mandatory reporting, yes
Immunity: civil/criminal, yes
Mandatory investigation: yes, immediately
Confidentiality of records: yes; penalty: misdemeanor
Cooperation with law courts, state agencies: yes
Guardian ad litem: yes
Administrative proceedings, trained personnel, facilities: yes
Dissemination of information: yes

Programs and Agencies

Where to write: Communications regarding social information and ability of
relatives to provide financial support should be sent in duplicate directly to the
appropriate local public welfare agency. In instances where the appropriate
county or city cannot be determined, the Virginia Department of Welfare will
serve as the referral agency. If inquiries to local units do not bring about satis-
factory solutions after a reasonable amount of correspondence, the Department
will, upon request, review the situation.

Virginia Department of Welfare

   8007 Discovery Dr.
   P. O. Box K-176
   Richmond 23288
   William L. Lukhard, Comm. (804)786-8571
   (vacant), Dep. Comm. (804)786-8571
   Herbert A. Krueger, Special Asst. to the Comm. (804)786-8521
   John Arupp, Asst. Atty. Gen. and Compact Adm. (804)786-2071

Division of Social Services

   Henry L. Gunn III, Dir. (804)786-8986

Bureau of Service Programs

   Mrs. Helen Binns, Chf. (804)786-8986

Department of Welfare Regional Offices

Lynchburg (Amelia, Amherst, Appomattox, Bedford, Brunswick, Buckingham,
   Campbell, Charlotte, Cumberland, Halifax, Lunenburg, Mecklenburg, Notto-

way, and Prince Edward Counties: Cities of Bedford, Lynchburg, and South
Boston): 2600 Memorial Ave., Suite 301, Lunchburg 24501   Frederick D.
Fraley, Adm., (804)847-1254

Northern Virginia (Arlington, Caroline, Culpepper, Fairfax, Fauquier, King
George, Loudoun, Madison, Orange, Prince William, Rappahannock, Spotsylvania, and Stafford Counties; Cities of Alexandria, Fairfax, Falls Church,
Fredericksburg, and Manassas): Marcoin Bldg., Suite 202, 150 S. Washington St., Falls Church 22046   Mrs. Illa S. Young, Adm. (703)534-5054

Richmond (Charles City, Chesterfield, Dinwiddie, Essex, Gloucester, Goochland,
Greensville, Hanover, Henrico, King and Queen, King William, Lancaster,
Mathews, Middlesex, New Kent, Northumberland, Powhatan, Prince George,
Richmond, Surry, Sussex, and Westmoreland Counties; Cities of Colonial
Heights, Emporia, Hopewell, Petersburg, and Richmond): 5021 Brook Rd.,
2nd Fl., Richmond 23227   Miss Mary S. Hale, Adm. (804)786-2342

Roanoke (Allegany, Botetourt, Craig, Floyd, Franklin, Giles, Henry, Mont-
gomery, Patrick, Pittsylvania, Pulaski, and Roanoke Counties; Cities of Clifton
Forge, Covington, Danville, Martinsville, Radford, and Roanoke): 920 S.
Jefferson St., Roanoke 24016   Odell W. Gray, Adm. (703)245-4991

Southwest (Bland, Buchanan, Carroll, Dickenson, Grayson, Lee, Russell, Scott,
Smyth, Tazewell, Washington, Wise, and Wythe Counties: Cities of Bristol,
Galax, and Norton): P. O. Box 268, Abington 24210   James D. Crockett,
Adm. (703)628-5172

Tidewater (Accomack, Isle of Wight, James City, Northampton, Southampton,
and York Counties: Cities of Chesapeake, Franklin, Hampton, Newport
News, Norfolk, Portsmouth, Pouquoson, Suffolk, Virginia Beach, and
Williamsburg): Pembroke Office Park, Pembroke Four Office Bldg., Suite
300, Virginia Beach 23462   Horace H. Selby, Adm. (804)490-1681

Valley (Albermarle, Augusta, Bath, Clarke, Fluvanna, Frederick, Greene,
Highland, Louisa, Nelson, Page, Rockbridge, Rockingham, Shenandoah, and
Warren Counties: Cities of Buena Vista, Charlottesville, Harrisonburg,
Lexington, Staunton, Waynesboro, and Winchester): P. O. Box 350, Verona
24482   A. Jackson Ridder, Adm. (703)885-0318

Local Public Welfare Agencies

Accomack Marietta M. Eichelberger, Dir., Dept. of Social Services, County
Office Bldg., P. O. Box 35, Accomac 23301   (804)787-1530

Albemarle Karen L. Morris, Dir., Dept. of Social Services, 409 8th St., N. E.
Charlottesville 22901   (804)295-0102

Alleghany Barbara B. Hammond, Dir., Dept. of Social Services, 117 E. Prospect
St., Covington 24426   (703)962-4966

Amelia Barbara Sirry, Dir., Dept. of Social Services, Court St., P. O. Box 255,
Amelia 23002   (804)561-2681

Amherst Virginia R. Burks, Dir., Dept. of Social Services, Court Ave., P. O. Box 414, Amherst 24521 (804)946-7475

Appomatox Hazel R. Mann, Dir., Dept. of Social Services, Courthouse Square Morton Lane, P. O. Box 326, Appomattox 24522 (804)352-7125

Arlington Ray C. Goodwin, Chief, Division of Social Services, Dept. of Human Resources, 2300 S. 9th St., P. O. Box 4310, Arlington 22204 (703)558-2203

Augusta Barbara Scott, Supt., S. Augusta St., County Bldg., Staunton 24401 (703)885-1531

Bath Mrs. Harriet W. Asbury, Soc. Wrkr.-in-Charge, P. O. Box 5, County Bldg., Warm Springs 24484 (703)839-2721

Bedford Catherine L. Creasy, Supt., Courthouse, P. O. Box 377, Bedford 24523 (703)586-2777

Bland Sadie M. Bane, Dir., Dept. of Social Services, Courthouse, Bland 24315 (703)688-3722

Botecourt Mary Mullis, Dir., Dept. of Social Services, Courthouse Annex, P. O. Box 163, Fincastle 24090 (703)473-8210

Brunswick Livie C. Trice, Dir., Dept. of Social Services, 228 Main St., P. O. Box 165, Lawrenceville 23868 (804)848-2412

Buchanan Curtis Deel, Dir., Dept. of Social Services, Main St., P. O. Box 674, Grundy 24614 (703)935-2237

Buckingham Braxton Apperson, Sr., Soc. Wrkr.-in-Cjharge, County Office Bldg., P. O. Box 155, Buckingham 23921 (804)969-4551

Campbell Cilla Brown, Supt., Courthouse Square, P. O. Box 126, Rustburg 24588 (804)332-5161, ext. 190

Caroline Robert G. Kassebaum, Dir., Courthouse Annex, P. O. Box 493, Bowling Green 22427 (804)633-5464

Carroll Love W. Cox, Dir., Dept. of Social Services, Carter Bldg., Maine St., P. O. Box 68, Hillsville 24343 (703)728-2351

Charles City Connie Andrews, Dir., Courthouse Green, P. O. Box 98, Charles City 23030 (804)829-2401, ext. 35

Charlotte Margaret H. Bradner, Supt., Treasurer's Office, P. O. Box 128, Charlotte Courthouse 23923 (804)542-5352

Chesterfield Lucy V. Corr, Dir., Dept. of Social Services, Social Services Bldg., Rte. 10, Chesterfield 23832 (804)748-1304

Clarke Gay Mason Allen, Dir., Dept. of Social Services, 21 S. Church St., P. O. Box 109, Berryville 22611 (703)955-1378

Craig Sarah B. Graham, Dir., Dept. of Social Services, New Castle 24127 (703) 864-6131

Culpeper Robert H. Reitmeier, Dir., Dept. of Social Services, County Office Bldg., Culpeper 22701 (703)825-1251

Cumberland Elsie B. McGavock, Supt., Beasley Bldg., Rte. 60, P. O. Box 145, Cumberland 23040 (804)492-4146

Dickenson Roy F. Rose, Dir., Dept. of Social Services, Brush Creek Rd., P. O. Box 417, Clintwood 24228 (703)926-3661

Dinwiddie King B. Talley, Dir., Dept. of Social Services, Dinwiddie Mall, P. O. Box 146, Dinwiddie 23841 (804)469-3741

Essex Ella H. Durham, Dir., Dept. of Social Services, Courthouse Office Bldg., P. O. Box 1004, Tappahannock 22560 (804)443-3561

Fairfax Edward W. Sterling, Dir., Dept. of Social Services, 4041 University Dr., Fairfax 22030 (703)938-5300

Fauquier Nancy B. Price, Dir., Carter Hall, 31 Winchester St., Warrenton 22186 (703)347-2316

Floyd Maude B. Shelor, Supt., Courthouse Bldg,, Main St., P. O. Box 314, Floyd 24091 (703)745-4166

Fluvanna Charles S. Nation III, Dir., Dept. of Social Services, County Bldg., Palmyra 22963 (804)589-8221

Franklin George P. Stone, Jr., Dir., Dept. of Social Services, County Office Bldg., E. Court St., Rocky Mount 24151 (703)483-9247

Frederick Roberta A. James, Supt., 117 W. Boscawen St., Winchester 22601 (703)662-4666

Giles Jesse W. Johnson, Dir., Dept. of Social Services, 211 Main St,, Narrows 24124 (703)726-2341

Gloucester Robbie E. Blackwell, Dir., Dept. of Social Services, Main St., P. O. Box 186, Gloucester 23061 (804)693-2671

Goochland Lois F. Rollins, Dir., Dept. of Social Services, County Office Bldg., P. O. Box 61, Goochland 23063 (804)556-2794 or 784-5510

Grayson Carol A. Brunty, Dir., Dept. of Social Services, County Office Bldg., P. O. Box 434, Independence 24348 (703)773-2452

Greene James B. Keenan, Dir., County Bldg., P. O. Box 117, Stanardsville 22973 (804)985-2318

Greensville Samuel E. Bush, Jr., Dir., Dept. of Social Services, 418 S. Main St., P. O. Box 32, Emporia 23847 (804)634-6576

Halifax Mary W. Faris, Supt., Dept. of Social Services, Courthouse Square, P. O. Box 666, Halifax 24588 (804)476-2354

Hanover Nannette M. Silverthorne, Dir., Dept. of Social Services, 405 Air Park Rd., Suite G, Ashland 23055 (804)798-4788

Henrico Mildred G. Davis, Supt., 4912 W. Marshall St., Richmond 23230 (804)359-4411

Henry Frances D. Beam, Dir., Dept. of Social Services, Kings Mountain Rd., P. O. Box 788, Collinsville 24078 (703)632-6373

Highland Constance G. Waggy, Dir., Courthouse, Monterey 24465 (703) 468-2230

Isle of Wight Linda A. Bean, Dir., Dept. of Social Services, Isle of Wight 23397 (804)357-3191

James City Frederick Scherberger III, Dir., Dept. of Social Services, E.O.C. Bldg., Forge Rd. P. O. Box 308, Toana 23168 (804)564-3314

King and Queen Patrick L. McKeever, Dir., Dept. of Social Services, Courthouse Annex, King and Queen Courthouse 23085 (804)785-2963

King George Patrica N. Combs, Dir., Dept. of Social Services, Rte. 610, Box 126, King George 22485 (703)775-3544

King William Ben Owen, Dir., County Office Bldg., King William 23086 (804) 769-3752

Lancaster Marian Farley, Supt., P. O. Box 978, White Stone 22578 (804) 435-1191

Lee Lucy W. McNiel, Supt., Main St., P. O. Box 146, Jonesville 24263 (703) 346-1181

Loudoun Joan Linhardt, Dir., Dept. of Social Services, 137A A. Catoctin Circle, Leesburg 22075 (703)777-2660, ext. 60

Louisa Hunter S. Bowles, Supt., Courthouse Bldg., P. O. Box 425, Louisa 23093 (703)967-1320

Lunenburg Avoy S. Glover, Supt., Lunenburg Courthouse, Lunenburg 23952 (804)696-2134

Madison Elmer B. Gray, Jr., Dir., Dept. of Social Services, N. Court Square, P. O. Box 176, Madison 22727 (703)948-5521

Mathews Barbara D. Walters, Dir., Dept. of Social Services, P. O. Box 394, Rte. 14, Mathews 23109 (804)725-7192

Mecklenburg Jeanne H. Trent, Dir., Dept. of Social Services, County Office Bldg., 132-133 E. Washington St., P. O. Box 400, Boydton 23917 (804) 738-6606

Middlesex Kathryn F. Fitchett, Dir., Dept. of Social Services, County Office Bldg., P. O. Box 118, Saluda 23149 (804)758-5311

Montgomery Jean Bourne, Dir., Dept. of Social Services, 215 Roanoke St., P. O. Box 31, Christiansburg 24073 (703)382-8501 or 9181

Nelson Paul B. Mays, Dir., Dept. of Social Services, Health Dept. Bldg., P. O. Box 357, Lovingston 22949 (804)263-2831

New Kent Louise A. Walls, Dir., Dept. of Social Services, New Kent Courthouse, Rte. 249, New Kent 23124 (804)966-2903

Northampton Allen D. Richardson, Dir., Dept. of Social Services, P. O. Box 207, Courthouse, Eastville 23347 (804)678-5153

Northumberland Sarah H. Cowart, Dir., Dept. of Social Services, Traylor Office Bldg., P. O. Box 296, Heathsville 22473 (804)580-3477 or 3721

Nottoway Shirley R. Eaton, Dir., Dept. of Social Services, Courthouse, Nottoway 23955 (804)645-9429

Orange Alan F. Courtney, Supt., Madison Rd., P. O. Box 646, Orange 22960 (703)672-1155

Page: Roberta D. Ruffner, Supt., County Office Bldg., S. Court St., Luray 22835 (703)743-6568

Patrick Barbara Swofford, Senior Eligibility Wrkr.-in-Charge Dept. of Social Services, Blue Ridge St., P. O. Box 498, Stuart 24171 (703)694-3328

Pittsylvania Harry E. Land, Dir., Dept. of Social Services, P. O. Drawer E., 21 N. Main St., Chatham 24531 (804)432–2041

Powhatan Dennis B. Draper, Jr., Dir., Dept. of Social Services, Courthouse, P. O. Box 98, Powhatan 23139 (804)598–4227

Prince Edward Ruth J. Jones, Dir., Courthouse, P. O. Drawer 628, Farmville 23901 (804)392–3113

Prince Goerge Grace M. Lee, Dir., Dept. of Social Services, County Bldg., P. O. Box 68, Prince George 23875 (804)733–5897

Prince William Richardo Perez, Dir., Dept. of Social Services, Iron Bldg., 9127 Euclid Ave., Manassas 22110 (703)361–4131

Pulaski Cornelia B. Bevins, Dir., Dept. of Social Services, 143 3rd St., N.W., Pulaski 24301 (703)980–8888

Rappahannock M. Elizabeth Huntin, Supt., P. O. Box 87, Washington 22747 (703)675–3613

Richmond Elizabeth K. Rhodes, Supt., Chesapeake Bldg., 106 W. Richmond Rd., P. O. Box 35, Warsaw 22572 (804)333–4089

Roanoke Betty Lucas, Supt., 510 College Ave., P. O. Box 31, Salem 24153 (703)389–0811

Rockbridge Betty J. McClure, Dir., Social Services Dept., Main and Preston St., P. O. Box 1065, Lexington 24450 (703)463–7143

Rockingham Ben B. Arrington, Supt., 4 S. Main St., Harrisonburg 22801 (703)434–9973 or 2425

Russell Roger L. Duff, Dir., Dept. of Social Services, Health Dept. Bldg., P. O. Box 1207, Lebanon 24266 (703)889–3031

Scott Jimmy L. Osborne, Supt., P. O. Box 205, Gate City 24251 (703) 386–6031 or 3631

Shenandoah Mary U. Haines, Dir., 236 S. Main St., Woodstock 22663 (703) 459–3736

Smyth Virgil J. Miller, Dir., Supt. of Social Services, Hull Bldg., 554 S. Main St., Marion 24354 (703)783–8148

Southampton Gwen G. Vick, Dir., Dept. of Social Services, Welfare Bldg., Rte. 35 N., P. O. Box 405, Courtland 23837 (804)653–2523

Spotsylvania Alice L. Aldrich, Dir., Dept. of Social Services, County Courthouse, P. O. Box 45, Spotsylvania 22553 (703)582–6381

Stafford Kate G. Woods, Supt., Stafford Courthouse, P. O. Box 7, Stafford 22554 (703)659–4101

Surry Carol G. Thompson, Dir., P. O. Box 263, Surry 23883 (804)294–3239 or 3182

Sussex Louise T. Wilson, Dir., Dept. of Social Services, County Courthouse Bldg., P. O. Box 1336, Sussex 23884 (804)246–5061

Tazewell Harold D. French, Dir., Dept. of Social Services, Main St., P. O. Box 149, Tazewell 24651 (703)988–2521

Warren Ann P. Carbaugh, Dir., 912 Warren Ave., P. O. Box 506, Front Royal 22630 (703)635–3430

Washington Gary D. Meade, Dir., Dept. of Social Services, 203 Court St.,
S. E. Abingdon 24210 (703)628-6071

Westmoreland William D. McDonnall, Dir., Dept. of Social Services, Bank Bldg.,
P. O. Box 302, Montross 22520 (804)493-6353

Wise Basil G. Jennings, Dir., Dept. of Social Services, Welfare Bldg., Water St.,
P. O. Box 888, Wise 24293 (703)328-8056

Wythe Dorothy G. Jordan, Dir., Dept. of Social Services, County Office Bldg.,
275 S. 4th St., Wytheville 24382 (703)228-5493

York Elizabeth H. Copland, Dir., Social Service Bureau, Ballard St., P. O.
Drawer 572, Yorktown 23690 (804)887-5647

Virgin Islands

Programs and Agencies

For verification of legal residence, authorization to return, interstate placement of children, and request for social information address:

Commissioner, Department of Social Welfare
P. O. Box 539, Charlotte Amalie
St. Thomas 00801

Division of Social Services

P. O. Box 539, Charlotte Amalie St. Thomas 00801
Mrs. Alice Benjamin, Dir.
Mrs. Nieta Battiste, WIN Coord.

Washington

Reporting Requirements

Persons mandated to report (compulsory) when reasonable cause to believe a child is or has been subjected to abuse or neglect: any practitioner of the healing arts (broadly defined), professional school personnel, registered or licensed nurse, social worker, psychologist, pharmacist, or employee of the department of social and health services who has reasonable cause to believe that a child has suffered abuse or neglect

Permissive: any other person who has reasonable cause to believe that a child has suffered abuse or neglect

Form of report and when made: immediate oral, followed by written if requested

To whom report is made: local law enforcement agency, or department of social health services

Penalties: failure to report as required is punishable as a misdemeanor

Immunities: reporting or testifying results in immunity from prosecution arising out of that reporting or testifying under any law of the state

Child Abuse Legislation

Citation: WRCA Chap. 217, 1975 §26.44(8)
Year enacted: 1975
Effective date: September 8, 1975
Purpose of legislation: mandatory reporting, yes
Reportable age: 0–18 years
Definition: nonaccidental injury, sexual abuse, negligent treatment or mal-

treatment, death, cruelty; child or mentally retarded person deprived of
right to conditions of minimal nurture, health, and safety.
Immunity: civil/criminal, yes
Education/school report: mandatory reporting, yes
Mandatory investigation: yes, no specific time frame
Confidentiality of records: yes; penalty: misdemeanor
Cooperation with law courts, state agencies: no specific provision
Guardian ad litem: yes
Administrative proceedings, trained personnel, facilities: no specific provision
Dissemination of information: no specific provision

Programs and Agencies

Inquiries concerning services to blind and deaf children, mentally retarded,
epileptic, mental patients, importation and deportation of mental patients,
mental institutions, retarded children's programs, Interstate Compact on Mental
Health, inmates of juvenile correctional institutions, Interstate Compact on
Juveniles, Interstate Compact on Adults, and Interstate Compact on Dependent
Children should be addressed to:

> Director, Division of Community Services
> Department of Social and Health Services
> P.O. Box 1788, MS412
> Olympia 98504

Washington Department of Social and Health Services

> Mail Stop 440
> Olympia 98504
> Telephone: (206)753-7039
> Milton Burdman, Secy. (206)753-3395
> Cheri Gonyaw. Exec. Asst. (206)753-0607
> (vacant). Dep. Secy., (206)753-6050
> Don Wolgamott, Admv. Asst. (206)753-1159
> Richard Mattsen, Senior Asst. Atty. Gen. (206)753-3397

Division of Community Services

> Neil Peterson, Dir. (206)753-1054

Department of Social and Health Services Regional Offices

Region I. (Adams, Chelan, Douglas, Ferry-Grant, Lincoln, Okanogan, Pend

Orielle, Spokane, Stevens, and Whitman Counties): 711 N. Lincoln,
Spokane 99201 Bernard Nelson, Adm. (509)456-4487
Region II. (Asotin-Benton, Columbia, Franklin, Garfield, Kittitas, Walla Walla,
and Yakima Counties): P.O. Box 2505, Yakima 98902 George Brock,
Adm. (509)453-5639
Region III. (Island, San Juan, Skagit, Snohomish, and Watcom Counties):
1509-32nd St., Everett 98201 Maurice Anderson, Adm. (206)259-7244
Region IV. (King County): 2009 Minor Ave. E., Seattle 98102 Ralph Dunbar,
Adm. (206)464-6250
Region V. (Kitsap and Pierce Counties): P. O. Box 1397, Tacoma 98491
James Anderson, Adm. (206)593-2300
Region VI. (Challam, Clark, Cowlitz, Grays, Harbor, Jefferson, Klickitat, Lewis,
Mason, Pacific, Skamania, Thurston, and Wahkiakum Counties): P. O. Box
239, Chehalis 98532 Robert Quant, Adm. (206)748-6616

Department of Social and Health Services Local Offices

Region I

Colfax Lionel D. Moes, P. O. Box 149, Colfax 99111 (509)397-4326
Colville W. Richard Philpott, Rte. 3, Colville 99114 (509)684-5261
Ephrata Bonnie Sinnard, P. O. Box 638, Ephrata 99823 (509)754-2427
Omak Gregory Works, P. O. Box Y, Omak 98841 (509)826-0082
Spokane (vacant), P. O. Box 2868, Spokane 99220 (509)456-3100
Wenatchee (vacant), P. O. Box 398, Wenatchee 98801 (509)663-8171

Region II

Clarkston Stanley Patterson, 720 6th St., Clarkston 99403 (206)758-5537
Ellensburg Kenneth Wilson, P. O. Box 366, Ellensburg 98926 (509)925-9834
Pasco Dwayne Upp, P. O. Box 931, Pasco 99301 (509)545-2247
Toppenish Ed Keegan, P. O. Box 470, Toppenish 98948 (509)865-2805
Walla Walla Jean Benson, P. O. Box 517, Walla Walla 99362 (509)527-4364
Yakima Robert Lolcama, P. O. Box 1809, Yakima 98907 (509)248-4680

Region III

Anacortes John Troutner, P. O. Box 568, Anacortes 98221 (206)293-2176
Bellingham Dean Rutledge, P. O. Box 639, Bellingham 98225 (206)676-2005
Everett Ralph Renner, P. O. Box 598, Everett 98206 (206)259-8484
Mountlake Terrace Betty Ross, 21309-44th Ave. W., Mountlake Terrace 98043
(206)775-5555
Mt. Vernon John Troutner, P. O. Box 310, Mt. Vernon 98273 (206)429-3126
Oak Harbor John Troutner, P. O. Box PP, Oak Harbor 98277 (206)675-5928

Region IV

Bellevue Darby Brown, 15027 Main St., Bellevue 98007 (206)641-3290
Burien Daniel Peyton, 149 S. 140th St., Burien 98166 (206)464-7116
Federal Way Thomas Gilmore, P. O. Box 3438, Federal Way 98002 (206)
    838-2474
Kent John Mathewson, P. O. Box 848, Kent 98031 (206)872-6300
Seattle Capitol Hill, Joyce Hopson, 720-25th St., Seattle 98122 (206)
    464-7250
King North Joe Quaranta, 1231 N. Allen Pl., Seattle 98103 (206)545-6500
Rainier Glen Wonders, 2809-26th Ave., S., Seattle 98144 (206)464-7225

Region V

Bremerton Mary Ryse, 4810 Arsenal Way, Bremerton 98310 (206)478-4995
Puyallup Frances Leif, 1004 E. Main Ave., Pyallup 98371 (206)848-5521
Tacoma: Hilltop, Michael Healy, 1210-6th Ave., Tacoma 98405 (206)
    593-2958
Pacific Center Glen Mcilraith, 9201 Pacific Ave., Tacoma 98444 (206)
    593-2556
Tacoma Avenue Eugene V. Zinck, 1301 Tacoma Ave., S., Tacoma 98402
    (206)593-2711

Region VI

Aberdeen Ralph Mackey, P. O. Box 189, Aberdeen 98520 (206)532-0962
Cathlamet (vacant) P. O. Box 38, Cathlamet 98612 (206)795-3226
Chehalis Barbara Bartram, P. O. Box 359, Chehalis 98532 (206)748-8803
Goldendale Willis Green, P. O. Box 185, Goldendale 98620 (509)773-5835
Kelso (vacant), P. O. Box 120, Kelso 98626 (206)425-4610
Olympia Dean Gregorius, P. O. Box 1816, Olympia 98507 (206)753-5983
Pt. Angeles Conrad Graham, 716 S. Chase St., Pt. Angeles 98362 (206)
    452-2377
Pt. Townsend Conrad Graham, P. O. Box 554, Pt. Townsend 98368 (206)
    385-0200
Shelton Irvin McArthur, P. O. Box 519, Shelton 98548 (206)426-5511
South Bend Roy Livengood, P. O. Box 5, South Bend 98586 (206)875-5583
Stevenson Willis Green, P. O. Box 326, Stevenson 98648 (509)427-5611
Vancouver Ron Morrison, P. O. Box 751, Vancouver 98660 (206)696-6111
White Salmon Willis Green, P. O. Box 126, White Salmon 98672 (509)
    493-1012

West Virginia

Reporting Requirements

Persons mandated to report (compulsory) when reasonable cause to believe a child is or has been subjected to abuse or neglect: physician or surgeon, intern, doctor of the hearling arts examining, attending, or treating a child under the age of 18 years; any registered or visiting nurse; school teacher; social worker acting in her official capacity as such having reason to believe that the child has injuries as a result of abuse or neglect (director of hospital or similar institution shall report for staff)

Permissive: none

Form of report and when made: must be reduced to writing as soon as practicable

To whom report is made: nearest office of the department of welfare, and to the prosecuting attorney of the county in which the injury occurred, or, if unknown, the county in which the child was found

Penalties: none

Immunities acting in good faith results in civil and criminal immunity, extending to judicial proceedings

Child Abuse Legislation

Citation: Art. 6A, §49-6A-1-4
Year enacted: 1975
Effective date: not available
Purpose of legislation: mandatory reporting, yes
Reportable age: 0-18 years

Definition: no specific definition provided
Education/school report: mandatory reporting, yes
Immunity: civil/criminal, yes
Mandatory investigation: yes, no specific time frame
Confidentiality of records: no specific provision; penalty: no specific provision
Cooperation with law courts, state agencies: no specific provision
Guardian ad litem: no specific provision
Administrative proceedings, trained personnel, facilities: no specific provision
Dissemination of information: no specific provision

Programs and Agencies

Inquiries relating to interstate placement of children should be directed to:

Division of Social Services
Department of Welfare
1900 Washington St., E.
Charleston 25303

West Virginia Department of Welfare

State Office Bldg.
1900 Washington St., E.
Charleston 25305
Telephone: (304)348-2400
Thomas R. Tinder, Comm.
Susan M. Harman, Admv. Asst. to the Comm.
Virgil L. Conrad, Dep. Comm., Operations
Paige Skaggs, Jr., Dep. Comm. Administration
Alvin M. Thacker, Dir., Adm. Review

Division of Social Services

Dorothy E. Allen, Asst. Comm.
(304)348-7980

TRIP Program

Roy E. Payton, Asst. Comm.
(304)348-3780

Federal-State Relations

Harley R. Hedge, Coord.

Department of Welfare Area Offices

I. Wheeling (Brooke, Hancock, Marshall, and Ohio Counties): 407 Main St., Wheeling 26003   Henry M. Ruppenthal III, Adm. (304)232-4411

II. New Martinsville (Tyler and Wetzel Counties): 331 Main St., New Martinsville 26155   Ted Tuel, Adm. (304)455-2490

III. Fairmont (Monongalia and Marion Counties): 310 Gaston Avenue, Fairmont 26554   (Adna Irl Thomas, Adm. (301)363-3261

IV. Romney (Hampshire and Mineral Counties): 239 W. Birch Lane, Romney 26757   Lloyd E. O'Brein, Jr., Adm. (304)822-3821

V. Martinsburg (Berkeley, Jefferson, and Morgan Counties): 615 W. King St., P. O. Box 1247, Martinsburg 25401   Dorothy R. Weller, Adm. (304) 267-2966

VI. Parkersburg (Wirt and Wood Counties): 327-6th St., Parkersburg 26101   John M. Kaltenecker, Adm. (304)428-8251

VII. Harrisville (Pleasants and Ritchie Counties): 121 E. Main St., Harrisville, 26362   Maynard G. Snodgrass, Adm. (304)643-2934

VIII. Clarksburg (Doddridge and Harrison Counties): 431 W. Pike St., Clarksburg 26301   Betty Jo Jones, Adm. (304)624-7541

IX. Grafton (Barbour, Preston, and Taylor Counties): 5 Harmon Center, Grafton 26354   Joseph P. Gennette, Adm. (304)265-3820

X. Elkins (Pocahontas, Randolph, and Tucker Counties): 227-3rd St., Elkins 26241   Robert L. Cochran, Adm. (304)636-3700

XI. Moorefield (Grand, Hardy, and Pendleton Counties): 427 S. Main St., Moorefield 26836   Gary L. Butts, Adm. (304)538-2391

XII. Huntington (Cabell and Mason Counties): 533-4th Ave., Huntington 25701   Edward L. Henderson, Adm. (304)529-6281

XIII. Spencer (Jackson and Roane Counties): P. O. Box 159, Spencer 25276   Richard L. Rector, Adm. (304)927-2830

XIV. Grantsville (Calhoun and Gilmer Counties): 101 Main St., Grantsville 26147   Earl M. Nicholson, Adm. (304)354-6118

XV. Weston (Lewis and Upshur Counties): 31 Main St., Weston 26452   D. Brad Shaffer, Adm. (304)269-4472

XVI. Hamlin (Lincoln and Putnam Counties): P. O. Box 468, Hamlin 25523   Vincent Anderson, Adm. (304)755-1926

XVII. Charleston (Kanawha County): 601 Morris St., Charleston 25301   John E. Burdette II, Adm. (304)345-1200

XVIII. Sutton (Braxton and Clay Counties): 301 Main St., Sutton 26601   Robert Lemaster, Act. Adm. (304)765-7346

XIX. Summersville (Nicholas and Webster Counties): 998 Arbuckle Rd., Summersville 26651   Paul E. Girod, Adm. (304)872-1921

XX. Wayne (Wayne County): Rte. 2., State Rte. 37, E., P. O. Box 8, Wayne 25570   Carl K. Little, Jr., Adm. (304)272-5153

XXI. Logan (Boone and Logan Counties): P. O. Box 387, Logan 25601   Edsel Aliff, Adm. (304)752-4440

XXII. Fayetteville (Fayette County): 211 W. Maple Ave., Fayetteville 25840 Jack Tanner, Adm. (304)574-0143

XXIII. Lewisburg (Greenbrier and Monroe Counties): Lewisburg 24901 Stanley Newton, Adm. (304)645-2222

XIV. Williamson (Mingo County): P. O. Box 1820, Williamson 25661   Ellis M. Brown, Adm. (304)235-3400

XV. Beckley (Raleigh County): 220½ S. Valley Dr., Beckley 25801   David W. Rogers, Adm. (304)252-5381

XVI. Welch (McDowell and Wyoming Counties): 331 Court St., Welch 24801 Robert Kent, Adm. (304)436-4175

XVII. Princeton (Mercer and Summers Counties): P. O. Box 349, Princeton 24720   Vivian T. Baumgardner, Adm. (304)425-8744

Wisconsin

Reporting Requirements

Persons Mandated to report (compulsory) when reasonable cause to believe a child is or has been subjected to abuse or neglect: physician, surgeon, nurse, hospital administrator, dentist, social worker, or school administrator having reasonable cause to believe that a child has a physical injury or other abuse inflicted on him/her by nonaccidental means

Permissive: none

Form of report and when made: immediately by telephone or otherwise, followed by the written report within 48 hours

To whom report is made: A county child welfare agency specified in section 48.56(1), or the sheriff of the county, or the local police department

Penalties: anyone knowingly and willfully violating this section by failing to file a report as required may be fined not more than $100 and/or imprisoned for not more than six months

Immunities: acting in good faith in reporting or participating in judicial proceeding results in civil and criminal immunity that might be imposed otherwise

Child Abuse Legislation

Citation: WSA §48.25.5, 48.981
Year enacted: 1975
Effective date: October 10, 1965
Purpose of legislation: mandatory reporting, yes
Reportable age: 0–18 years
Definition: no specific definition provided

Education school report: mandatory reporting, yes
Immunity: civil/criminal, yes
Mandatory investigation: yes, immediately
Confidentiality of records: yes; penalty: no specific provision
Cooperation with law courts, state agencies: yes
Guardian ad litem: yes
Administrative proceedings, trained personnel, facilities: yes
Dissemination of information: no specific provision

Programs and Agencies

Inquiries relating to specific cases involving public assistance and requests for social information should be sent directly to the county social services office in duplicate. Correspondence concerning state policy on aid to dependent children, medical assistance, and interstate transfer of minors will be handled by the Division of Family Services. Address inquiries to:

Frank Newgent, Administrator
Division of Family Services
State Office Bldg., Rm. 300
1 W. Wilson St.
Madison 53702

The Division of Family Services advises that correspondence it receives pertaining to the fields of service of other divisions will be forwarded to the proper agency. All inquiries should be sent in duplicate with additional copies if more than one investigation is desired.

Wisconsin Department of Social and Health Services

State Office Bldg., Rm. 663
1 W. Wilson St.
Madison 53702
Telephone: (608)266-3681
Manuel Carballo, Secy. (608)266-3681
Fred W. Hinkle, Dep. Secy. (608)266-3681

Division of Family Services

State Office Bldg., Rm. 300
1 Wilson St.
Madison 53702
Telephone: (608)266-3035

Frank Newgent, Adm. (608)266-3035
Bernard Stumbras, Dep. Div. Adm. Operations (608)266-3039
Robert H. Lizon, Dep. Div. Adm., Planning and Development (608)
266-3036

SSI Planning

Carl Martin, Coord. (608)266-8760

Bureau of Program Planning and Development

Lowell Trewartha, Dir. (608)266-2850

Division of Family Services Regional Offices

Green Bay (Brown, Calumet, Door, Fond du Lac, Green Lake, Kewaunee,
Manitowoc, Marinette, Marquette, Menominee, Oconto, Outagamie,
Shawano, Sheboygan, Waupaca, Waushara, and Winnebago Counties):
1181 Western Ave., Green Bay 54935   (414)494-9641
Fond du Lac District: 485 S. Military Rd., Fond du Lac 54935   (414)922-6810
Eau Claire (Barron, Buffalo, Chippewa, Clark, Crawford, Dunn, Eau Claire,
Jackson, La Crosse, Monroe, Pepin, Pierce, Polk, St. Croix, Trempealeau, and
Vernon Counties): 718 W. Clairemont Ave., Eau Claire 54701   (715)
836-6151
La Crosse District: 250 Mormon Coulee Rd., La Crosse 54601   (608)
788-1000
Madison (Columbia, Dane, Dodge, Grant, Green, Iowa, Jefferson, Lafayette,
Richland, Rock, and Sauk Counties): 1206 Northport Dr., Madison 53704
(608)249-0441
Milwaukee (Kenosha, Milwaukee, Ozaukee, Racine, Walworth, Washington, and
Waukesha Counties): 819 N. 6th St., Milwaukee 53203   (414)224-4501
Rhinelander (Adams, Ashland, Bayfield, Burnett, Douglas, Florence, Forset,
Iron, Juneau, Langlade, Lincoln, Marathon, Oneida, Portage, Price, Rusk,
Sawyer, Taylor, Vilas, Washburn, and Wood Counties): 819 N. 6th St.,
Milwaukee 53203   (414)224-4501
Schiek Plaza 54501   (715)683-3405
Ashland District: 100-2nd St., W., Ashland 54806   (715)682-3405
Wisconsin Rapids District: 1681-2nd Ave., S., Wisconsin Rapids 54494
(715)423-4305

County Social Services Offices

Adams Richard Holt, 149 N. Main St., P.O. Box C, Adams 53901   (608)
339-3356

Ashland Edwin Hallen, Courthouse, Rm. 102, Ashland 54806 (715)682-2761

Barron Ira M. Culter, Courthouse, Rm. 338, Barron 54812 (715)537-5691

Brown William R. Miller, 300 S. Adams St., Green Bay 54301 (414)432-9221

Buffalo Jerome W. Benson, Courthouse Annex, Alma 54610 (608)685-4412

Burnett Thomas E. Keith, Community Bldg., P. O. Box 45, Webster 54893
(715)866-3091

Calumet Florence Woelfel, Courthouse, Chilton 53014 (414)849-2361

Chippewa John D. Thurman, County Hwy. 1, P. O. Box 520, Chippewa Falls
54279 (715)723-5583

Clark Gary Johnston, Courthouse, P. O. Box 190, Neillsville 54456 (715)
743-3148

Columbia Robert W. Andrews, Administration Bldg., P. O. Box 134, Portage
53901 (608)742-2191

Crawford Kenneth L. Arneson, 111 W. Dunn St., P. O. Box 60, Prairie du
Chien 53821 (608)326-2491

Dane Jerry McCartney, 1202 Northport Dr., Madison 53704 (608)249-5351

Dodge Donald W. Nolter, Administration Bldg., P. O. Box 204, Juneau 53039
(414)386-2777

Door John Michalski, Courthouse, P. O. Box 478-479, Sturgeon Bay 54235
(414)743-5511

Douglas John L. Barrett, Courthouse, Superior 54880 (715)394-0241

Dunn Douglas Larson, Courthouse, Menomonie 54751 (715)232-1116

Eau Claire Maurice G. Miller, Courthouse, Eau Claire 54701 (715)839-4747

Florence Duanne A. Foltz, Courthouse, P. O. Box 7, Florence 54121 (715)
528-3296

Fond du Lac Marvin E. Diedrich, 63 Western Ave., Fond du Lac 54935 (414)
921-1451

Forest Mary Barge (Act.), Courthouse, P. O. Box 9, Crandon 54520 (715)
478-3321

Grant Peter Brayko, 111 Jefferson St., P. O. Box 111, Lancaster 53813 (608)
723-2138

Green Robert P. Ransom, Argyle Rd., P. O. Box 296, Monroe 53566 (608)
325-4155

Green Lake Alfred L. Olesen, Courthouse, Green Lake 54941 (414)294-6566

Iowa Michael Tiber, 101 Leffler St., P. O. Box 98, Dodgeville 53533 (608)
935-3324

Iron Lawrence Samardich, Courthouse, Hurley 54534 (715)561-3636

Jackson Marshall H. Graff, Courthouse, P. O. Box 227, Black River Falls 54615
(715)284-4301

Jefferson Thomas F. Yonash, Courthouse, Rm. 111, Jefferson 53549 (414)
674-2500

Juneau David I. Hasselquist, Courthouse, P. O. Box 39, Mauston 53948 (608)
843-1751

Kenosha Paul D. Hickey, 714-52nd St., P. O. Box 336, Kenosha 53140 (414) 654-3591

Kewaunee Giles Hanson, Courthouse, Kewaunee 54216 (414)388-3777

La Crosse Malcolm J. Johnson, 400 N. 4th St., P. O. Box C, La Crosse 54602 (608)785-0100

Lafayette William T. McGreane, 700 N. Main St., Darlington 53530 (608) 776-4066

Langlades James C. Kroller, Courthouse, P. O. Box 158, Antigo 54409 (715) 623-3724

Lincoln Curtis Moe, 107 Scott St., Merrill 54452 (715)536-5568

Manitowoc Kenneth Tate, 926 S. 8th St., Manitowoc 54420 (414)682-8261

Marathon Richard W. Delap, 302 Grand Ave., Wausau 54401 (715)842-3216

Marinette John Gustafson, Courthouse, P. O. Box 46, Marinette 54143 (715) 732-0191

Marquette Robert Ransom, Courthouse, P. O. Box 413, Montello 53949 (414) 297-2177

Menominee Dale Druckery, Courthouse, Keshena 54135 (715)799-3324

Milwaukee Edwin Mundy, Dept. of Institution, 8731 Watertown Plank Rd., Milwaukee 53226

Milwaukee Arthur Silverman, 1220 W. Vliet St., Milwaukee 53205 (414) 289-6897

Monroe John P. Wieczorek, Dept. of Public Welfare, 114 W. Oak, P. O. Box 207, Sparta 54656 (608)269-6791

Oconto Steven A. Clifton, Courthouse, P. O. Box 299, Oconto 54153 (414) 834-5322

Oneida Paul Spencer, Courthouse, P. O. Box 400, Rhinelander 54501 (715) 362-5695

Outagamie James E. Stampp, Courthouse, Appleton 54912 (414)739-0361

Ozaukee Lawrence A. Neve, Courthouse, Rm. 335, P. O. Box 307, Pt. Washington 53074 (414)377-6400

Pepin Donald G. Melstrom, 200-3rd Ave., P. O. Box 69, Durand 54736 (715) 672-8941

Pierce Dale Menstrom, Courthouse, P. O. Box 668, Ellsworth 54011 (715) 273-4334

Polk Patricia G. Kallsen, Municipal Bldg., P. O. Box 216, Balsom Lake 54810 (715)485-3133

Portage Raymond L. Bartkowiak, Courthouse, Stevens Point 54481 (715) 346-3691

Price Alex F. Hardxinski, Courthouse, Phillips 54555 (715)339-2425

Racine Edwin Affolter, 425 Main St., P. O. Box 606, Racine 53403 (414) 636-3301

Richland Lewis Koehn, 323 S. Central Ave., Richland Center 53581 (608) 647-2128

Rock Judy Bablitch, 306 W. Milwaukee St., Janesville 53545   (608)756–418
Rusk Thomas R. Lovely, Jr., Courthouse, Ladysmith 54848   (715)532–5536
St. Croix Robert Sanden, 904 3rd St., P. O. Box 31, Hudson 54016   (715) 386–5581
Sauk Wesley M. Rohrer, Courthouse, P. O. Box 24, Babraboo 53913   (608) 356–4866
Sawyer Robert R. Van Roy, Courthouse, P. O. Box 192, Hayward 54843 (715)634–4806
Shawano Earl G. Lundmark, Courthouse, Shawano 54166   (715)526–6178
Sheboygan John E. Lubbers, Courthouse Annex, Rm. 114, P. O. Box 610, Sheboygan 53081   (414)458–4681
Taylor Bruce Willett, Courthouse, Medford 54451   (715)748–4135
Trempealeau Du Wayne A. Mickelson, Courthouse, Whitehall 54733   (751) 538–4301
Vernon Richard Q. Scott, 113 W. Court St., Viroqua 54665   (608)637–2135
Vilas Edward Chess, Courthouse, Eagle River 54521   (715)479–4436
Walworth Edward J. Leveille, County Trunk NN, P. O. Box 46, Elkhorn 53121 (414)723–5580
Washburn Clyde G. Stouffer, Community Bldg., P. O. Box 250, Shell Lake 54871   (715)468–7878
Washington Donald V. Ryd, 320 S. 5th Ave., P. O. Box 476, West Bend 53095 (414)338–0081
Waukesha Joseph R. Himden, Courthouse, 500 Riverview Dr., Waukesha 53186 (414)544–4421
Waupaca Dennis D. Wendt, 1402 Royalton St., P. O. Box 72, Waupaca 54981 (715)258–8551
Waushara August K. Pagel, Courthouse Annex, P. O. Box 310, Wautona 54982 (414)787–2219
Winnebago Norman L. Whitford, 448 Algoma Blvd., P. O. Box 2646, Oshkosh 54901   (414)233–1300
Wood Phillip J. Lukowicz, Courthouse, Wisconsin Rapids 54494   (715) 421–1010
—— 604 E. 4th St., Marshfield 54449   (715)384–3158

Wyoming

Reporting Requirements

Persons mandated to report (compulsory) when reasonable cause to believe a child is or has been subjected to abuse or neglect: any physician, surgeon, dentist, osteopath, chiropractor, podiatrist, intern, resident, nurse, druggist, pharmacist, laboratoy technician, school teacher or administrator, social worker, or any other person having reasonable cause to believe that a child under the age of 18 years is or has been the subject of child abuse (director of hospital or similar institution shall make report for staff)

Permissive: none

Form of report and when made: oral immediately, followed by written if requested.

To whom report is made: department of health and social services, division of public assistance and social services, in the county where the examination was conducted or the child was observed.

Penalties: none

Immunities: persons reporting or participating in judicial proceedings in good faith are immune from civil or ciminal liability that might otherwise arise.

Child Abuse Legislation

Citation: WSA §14-28.7-28.13; 14-115.17, 115.23
Year enacted: 1971
Effective date: May 21, 1971
Purpose of legislation: mandatory reporting, yes
Reportable age: 0-18 years

Definition: skin bruising, bleeding, malnutrition, sexual molestation, burns, bone fractures, subdural hematoma, soft tissue swelling, failure to thrive unjustified death.
Education/school report: mandatory reporting, yes
Immunity: civil/criminal, yes
Mandatory investigation: yes, immediately
Confidentiality of records: no specific provision; penalty: no specific provision
Cooperation with law courts, state agencies: no specific provision
Guardian ad litem: yes
Administrative proceedings, trained personnel, facilities: no specific provision
Dissemination of information: no specific provision

Programs and Agencies

Where to Write:

Correspondence should be sent directly to the county departments of public assistance and social services regarding the following: aid to families with dependent children, general assistance, medical assistance, verification of residence, authorization to return, and requests for social information.

Wyoming Department of Health and Social Services

> Hathaway Bldg.
> Cheyenne 82002
> Telephone: (307)777-7657
> Harvey Peterson, Coord.
> Craig Newman, Special Asst. Atty. Gen.
> Bert D. Morrison, Dir., Administrative Services
> James E. Rusch, Personnel Ofr.
> Tom Miyamoto, Dir., Finance and Accounting

Division of Public Assistance and Social Services

> Telephone: (307)777-7561
> Richard G. Weathermon, Asst. Adm. of Soc. Srvs.

Staff Development

> Mrs. Grace P. Riley, Dir.

County Departments of Public Assistance and Social Services

Albany Michael R. Beaver, Laramie 82070   (307)745-7324
Big Horn Charles W. Shannon, Greybull 82426   (307)765-4494

Campbell Robert Kuchera, Gillette 82716 (307)682-7277

Carbon E. Raymond Ring, Jr., Rawlins 82301 (307)324-3428

Converse Mrs. Anna S. Ballard, Douglas 82633 (307)358-3138

Crook Mrs. Alice Hawken, Sundance 82729 (307)283-2014

Fremont Nat Belser, Lander 82520 (307)332-4038

Goshen William C. Brown, Torrington 82240 (307)532-2191

Hot Springs Mrs. Lee Ola Ingle, Thermopolis 82443 (307)864-2158

Johnson Mrs. Helen M. Clark, Admv. Asst., Buffalo 82834 (307)684-7281;
    Mrs. Mary Paine, District Director (Johnson and Sheridan Counties),
    Sheridan 82801

Laramie Mrs. Edith K. Howard, Eligibility Unit, 2000 Carey Ave., Cheyenne
    82002 (307)777-7641; Social Service Unit, 2006 Carey Ave., Cheyenne
    82002 (307)777-7721

Lincoln Mrs. Joan Beachler, Kemmerer 83101 (307)877-6670

Natrona Guy Noe, 142 N. Kimball St., P. O. Box 560, Casper 82610 (307)
    234-9305

Niobrara Robert W. Miller, Lusk 82225 (307)334-2153

Park Joseph D. Nies, Cody 82414 (307)587-2204, ext. 44

Platte Mrs. Jill E. Holloway, Wheatland 82201 (307)322-3790

Sheridan Mrs. Maty Paine, District Dir. (Johnson and Sheridan Counties) and
    Mrs. Denise Brewer, Admv. Asst., Sheridan 82801 (307)672-2404

Sublette Mrs. Madge M. Funk, Pinedale 82941 (307)367-4371

Sweetwater Louise M. Groh, Rock Springs 82901 (307)362-5639

Teton: Mrs. E. Helen Lang, Jackson 83001 (307)733-2907

Uinta Earl D. Gardner, Evanston 82930 (307)789-2756

Washakie Mrs. Janice L. Akins, Worland 82401 (307)347-6181

Weston George Butler III (Act.), Newcastle 82701 (307)746-4657

Canada: Department of National Health and Welfare

Canada provides income maintenance, social services, and health care programs to its citizens through the Department of National Health and Welfare in conjunction with the provices and municipalities. Programs are supported by a combination of federal, provincial, and municipal funding. Regional offices are located in the provinces to operate programs for the Income Security, Developmental Programs (New Horizons), Fitness and Amateur Sport, Field Operations, and Medical Services Branch Offices.

Income maintenance programs are administered in Canada by the Income Security Programs unit of the Department of National Health and Welfare.

Social services in Canada are administered by the Social Services Programs Branch of the Department of National Health and Welfare's Welfare unit under a Deputy Minister of Welfare. For child abuse and neglect purposes, the Family Planning Program makes grants to public and nongovernmental organizations to support family planning services and demonstration projects and to provide information and consultation services.

Department of National Health and Welfare

Office of the Minister
Brooke Claxton Bldg.
Ottawa, Ontario K1A OK9
Telephone: (613)996-4950
Marc Lalonde, Minister (613)996-5461
Bruce Rawson, Dep. Minister, Welfare (613)992-5320
Jean Lupien, Dep. Minister, Health (613)996-8147
J. Q. McCrindell, Act. Asst. Dep. Minister, Administration (613)996-1622
B. J. Iverson, Asst. Dep. Minister, Social Services Programs (613)996-2741

Social Services Program Branch Regional Offices

Alberta Thelma Chandler, Financial Bldg., Rm. 203, Edmonton T5J OB4
(403)425-7580

British Columbia Patricia Fulton, 1525 W. 8th Ave., Main Fl., Vancouver (604)
      732-4303
Manitoba L. Forest, 460 Main St., Suite 202, Winnipeg R3B 1B6
New Brunswick B. Bourgeois, 1222 Main St., 2nd Fl., Moncton E1C 1H6
      (506)858-2484
Newfoundland J.C. Melloy, 127 Water St., P.O. Box 5580, St. John's A1C 5W4
      (709)753-1761
Northwest Territories See Alberta
Nova Scotia P. Stehelin, Halifax Insurance Bldg., 5670 Spring Garden Rd.,
      Halifax B3J 1H6   (902)426-2741
Ontario J. Allman, 1243 Islington Ave., Toronto M8X 1Y9   (416)239-3973
Prince Edward Island G. Fraser, Dominion Bldg., 97 Queen St., Charlottetown
      C1A 4A9   (902)892-6587
Quebec C. Douville, 685 Cathcart St., 3rd Fl., Montreal H3B 1M7   (514)
      238-7306
Saskatchewan J. Zakreski, Brent Bldg., Rm. 101, 2505 11th Ave., Regina S4P
      0K6   (306)525-8149
Yukon See Alberta

Health Protection Branch Regional Offices (Field Operations Directorate)

Central D. A. Gray, Federal Bldg., Rm. 310, 269 Main St., Winnipeg R3C 1B2
      (204)985-3004
Maritimes G. S. Chalmers (Act.), Ralston Bldg., 1557 Hollis St., Halifax B3J
      2R7   (902)426-5770
Ontario J. R. Elliott (Act.), 2301 Midland Ave., Scarborough M1P 4R7   (416)
      291-4231
Pacific A. J. Sandbrook, Customs Bldg., Rm. 601, 1001 Pender St., Vancouver
      V6E 2M7   (604)544-3359
Quebec P. Mottet, 1001 St. Laurent St., W., Longueil J4K 1C7   (514)283-5497

Medical Services Branch Regional Offices

Alberta Dr. J. Kirkbride, 501 Chancery Hall, Edmonton T5J 2C3   (403)
      425-6901
Atlantic Dr. L. R. Hirtle, Ralston Bldg., 1557 Hollis St., Halifax B3J 1V6
      (403)425-6901
British Columbia Dr. G. C. Butler, 814 Richards St., 4th Fl., Vancouver V6B
      3A9   (604)544-3235
Manitoba Dr. A. Schwartz, 303 Main St., Winnipeg R3C 0H4   (204)985-4171
Northwest Territories Dr. F. J. Cavill, Baker Centre, 14th Fl., Edmonton T5J
      1H2   (403)425-5690
Ontario Dr. K. Butler, 370 Catherine St., Ottawa K1A 0L3   (613)995-6361

Quebec Dr. M. Savoie, 515 Ste. Catherine St. W., P.O. Box 638, Station B, Montreal H3B 1B4   (514)283-4774

Saskatchewan Dr. C. A. Bentley, 500 Derrick Bldg., 2431 11th Ave., Regina S4P 0K4   (306)569-5413

Yukon R. E. Avison, 212 Main St., Suite 200, Whitehorse Y1A 2O1   (403) 667-6321

Alberta

Department of Social Services and Community Health

10820-98th Ave.
Edmonton T5K 0C8
Telephone: (403)427-2734
Hon. Helen Hunley, Minister (403)427-2606
Stanley Mansbridge, Chf. Dep. Minister (403)427-6448

Public Information

Jon White, Dir. (403)427-4801

Social Services

D. M. Stolee, Dep. Minister (403)427-6424

Child Welfare

O. M. Melsness, Dir. (403)427-6370

Department of Social Services and Community Health Regional Offices

Athabasca K. Scheffler, Box 179, Athabasca T0G 0B0   (403)675-2243

Barrhead E. Kost-Santo, Box 700, Barrhead T0G 0E0   (403)674-3351

Blairmore H. Enry, Box 474, Blairmore T0K, 0E0   (403)562-2856

Bonnyville L. A. Arcand, Box 990, Bonnyville T0A 0L0   (403)826-3324

Brooks P. W. Pritchard, Box 1029, Brooks T0J 0J0   (403)362-5551

Calgary G. Brannan, Regl. Dir., Executive Place Bldg., 727 6th Ave., S.W., Rm. 101, Calgary T2P 0V1   (403)267-7111; C. Bracken, 406 16th Ave., N.W., Calgary T2M 0J2   (403)261-7111; L. Thompson, Executive Place Bldg., 727 6th Ave., S.W., Rm. 101, Calgary T2P 0V1   (403)261-7111; F. K. Wood, Alberta Place, 4th Fl., 1520 4th St., S.W., Calgary T2R 1H5 (403)261-7111

Camrose J. Wiuff, The Fairgrounds, Box 1497, Camrose T4V 1Y8   (403) 672-4411

Drumheller T. Aman, Box 2079, Drumheller T0J 0Y0 (403)823-5740

Edmonton B. P. Reichwein, Regl. Dir., 10010 105th St., Rms. 21 and 22, Main Fl., Edmonton (403)429-6761; D. Anholt, 11713 82d St., Edmonton T5B 2V9 (403)474-6424; E. Schwarzat, 10455 80th Ave., Edmonton T6E 1V1 (403)427-2763; R. Blewett, Centennial Mall, 170th St., and Stony Plain Rd., Edmonton T5P 4B5 (403)487-3440; R. Howell, West-10, 11016 127th St., Edmonton T5M 0T2 (403)452-6193

Edson B. B. Simmonds, Box 98, Edson T0E 0P0 (403)723-3343

Ft. McMurray D. Gleming, Box 5656, Ft. McMurray T9H 3G6 (403)743-2291

Grande Cache C. McLeod, Box 240, Grande Cache T0E 0Y0 (403)827-3335

Grande Prairie D. W. Merchant, 10014 99th St., Grande Prairie T8V 3N4 (403)532-2100

Hanna R. Zimmer, Box 998, Hanna T0J 1P0 (403)854-4451

High Level K. Jardine, Mail Bag 400, High Level T0H 1Z0 (403)926-3791

High Prairie G. M. Henderson, Box 849, High Prairie T0G 1E0 (403)523-3303

Lac La Biche W. F. Boman, Box 420, Lac La Biche T0A 2C0 (403)623-4821

Lethbridge B. Rechner, 314 Houghton Bldg., 515 7th St., S., Lethbridge T1J 2G9 (403)329-5290

Medicine Hat F. E. Lockwood, 631 Prospect Dr., S.W., Rm. 152, Medicine Hat T1A 4C2 (403)527-6615

Olds G. Rowe, Box 520, Olds T0M 1P0 (403)226-8200

Peace River R. Scotney, Box 1860, Peace River T0H 2X0 (403)624-4850

Red Deer J. Campbell, 4740 Ross St., Red Deer T4N 1X2 (403)343-5439

Rocky Mountain House G. Zuidwyk, Box 909, Rocky Mountain House T0M 1T0 (403)845-3394

Slave Lake E. M. Gromek, Box 70, Slave Lake T0G 2A0 (403)849-2281

Smoky Lake A. B. Cooper, Box 518, Smoky Lake T0A 3C0 (403)656-3662

Stettler C. Baergen, Postal Bag 600, Stettler T0C 2L0 (403)742-4481

St. Paul J. Trefanenko, Box 1452, St. Paul T0A 3A0 (403)645-4475

Vegreville J. Gullion, Box 840, Vegreville T0B 4L0 (403)632-3361

Vermilion A. Allarie, Box 1228, Vermilion T0G 4M0 (403)853-2811

Wainwright L. Heinemann, Box 699, Wainwright T0B 4P0 (403)842-3347

Wetaskiwin A. Nobert, Provincial Bldg., 5201 50th Ave., Wetaskiwin T9A 1Y4 (403)352-3306

Whitecourt G. Fernhout, Box 749, Whitecourt T0E 2L0 (403)778-3808

Local Preventive Social Services Directors

Athabasca Miss Marcella Blais, Box 90, Athabasca T0G 0B0 (403)675-2623

Banff Bertram Dyck, Box 1835, Banff T0L 0C0 (403)762-4426

Barons Eureka John Boon, Box 328, Coaldale T0K 0L0 (403)345-3388 or (403)345-3934

Barrhead Gavin Farmer, Stutchbury Bldg., Barrhead T0G 0E0 (403)674-3441

Blairmore Allen Wilcke, P. O. Box 326, Blairmore T0K 0E0 (403)562-2331

Bonnyville Grieg Miles, Box 1665, Bonnyville T0A 0L0 (403)826-2120

Calgary Mr. S. E. Blakely, P. O. Box 2100, Calgary T2P 2M5 (403)268-5111

Camrose Bonnie Hutchinson, 5402-48A Ave., Camrose T4V 0L3 (403) 672-4446

Claresholm Art Vandenberg, P. O. Box 1000, Claresholm T0L 0T0 (403) 235-3381

Drumheller Leroy Angle, Box 2549, Drumheller T0J 0Y0 (403)823-5195

Edmonton D. K. Wass, C. N. Tower, 6th Fl., Edmonton T5J 0K1 (403) 425-5917

Elk Point Don Robertson, Box 340, Elk Point T0A 1A0 (403)724-3800

Ft. McMurray John Harper, 9924 MacDonald Ave., Ft. McMurray T9H 1S6 (403)743-2241

Ft. Saskatchewan Vera Radio, 10005 102d St., Ft. Saskatchewan T8L 2C5 (403)998-2266

Grande Cache Ted Tymchuk, Community Srvs. Dir., Box 300, Grande Cache T0E 0Y0 (403)827-3362 or 2296

Grande Prairie Timothy Leslie-Spinks, 10306 102nd St., Grande Prairie T8V 2W3 (403)532-1055

High Level Robert Turner, P. O. Bag 400, High Level T0H 1Z0 (403)926-3791

High Prairie Richard McDonald, Box 999, High Prairie T0H 1E0 (403) 523-4147

Lac La Biche Rick Sloan, Box 756, Lac La Biche T0A 2C0 (403)623-4463

Lacombe Paul Olson, Box 1179, Lacombe T0C 1S0 (403)782-6638

Leduc (County) Gordon Bligh, 4301 50th St., Leduc T9E 2X3 (403) 986-2251

Leduc (Town) Robert Mitchell, Civic Centre, Box 187, Town of Leduc, Leduc T9E 2X1 (403)986-2004

Lethbridge Tom Hudson, Supt. of Social Planning, Community Services Dept., 1020 20th St., S., Lethbridge T1K 2C8 (403)329-4877

Medicine Hat Anthony G. Tobin, 631 Prospect Dr., S.W., Medicine Hat T1A 4C2 (403)527-7781

Peace River Barry Ellis, Box 1062, Peace River T0H 2X0 (403)624-2574

Pincher Creek Brian Chambers, Municipal Office, 753 Kettles St., P.O. Box 1513, Pincher Creek T0K 1W0 (403)627-3925

Provost Dennis Maier, Box 449, Provost T0B 3S0 (403)753-2556

Red Deer Mr. W. H. Irvine, City of Red Deer, Red Deer T4H 3T4 (403) 347-4421

Slave Lake Lorne Larson, Box 858, Slave Lake (403)849-2281, ext. 33

Smoky River 130, Gerald Nicolet, P. O. Box 210, Falher T0H 1M0 (403) 837-2014

St. Albert Charles Gale, Town of St. Albert, St. Albert T8N 0G2 (403) 459-6601

Stettler Mrs. Jean Gilbert, Box 2097, Stettler T0C 2C0   (403)742-3214

St. Paul Deanna Easthope, Box 248, St. Paul T0A 3A0   (403)645-4482

Vegreville Mrs. Lillian Whittier, Box 809, Vegreville T0H 4L0   (403)632-3966

Vermilion River Neil Proctor, 4925 49th Ave., Lloydminister S9V 0T6   (403) 825-4100

Wainwright Gail LaHaye, P. O. Box 1391, Wainwright T0H 4P0   (403) 842-4731

Wetaskiwin Jeff Arnold, 5101 50th Ave., 1, Wetaskiwin T9A 0S5   (403) 352-6023

Westlock Dwayne Macaulay, Municipal Bldg., Box 1266, Westlock T0G 0L0 (403)342-3079

Wolf Creek-Pembina Harold Wynne, Box 216, Wildwood T0E 2M0   (403) 325-3782

County of Strathcona Jim Common, 2011 Brentwood Blvd., Sherwood Park (403)467-5571

Cold Lake/Grande Centre Warren Johnston, Box 361, Cold Lake T0A 0V0 (403)639-3298

British Columbia

Department of Human Resources

Parliament Bldgs.
Victoria V8V 1X4
Hon. William N. Vander Zalm, Minister (604)387-3602
J. A. Sadler, Dep. Minister (604)387-3121
E. L. Northup, Assoc. Dep. Minister (604)387-3122
Bob Eliott, Adm. Asst. to the Assoc. Dep. Minister (604)387-5459
G. Wood, Chief Technical Negotiator, Canada Assistance Plan (604) 387-3134

Community Services

R. J. Burnham, Exec. Dir.
R. K. Butler, Asst. Exec. Dir. (Vancouver) (604)872-8154
Martin M. Cook, Comptroller (604)387-5521
David Niven, Asst. Comptroller (604)387-5594

Child Welfare Division

Parliament Bldgs.
Victoria V8W 3A2

J. V. Belknap, Supt. and Dir., Family and Children Services (604)387-3121
J. J. Allman, Dep. Supt. (604)387-3211
Mrs. I. G. Preddy, Dep. Supt. (604)387-3123
Mrs. J. Brown, Dep. Supt., 33 E. 8th Ave., Vancouver (604)872-8154
  (serving lower mainland area)

Family Services

J. J. Allman, Coord. (604)387-3211

Adoption and Child Care Services

Mrs. I. G. Preddy, Coord. (604)387-3123

Residential and Treatment Programs for Children

Parliament Bldgs.
Victoria V8V 1X4
R. F. Cronin, Dir. (604)387-3126

Department of Human Resources Regional Offices

III. Monagan G. A. Reed, 3205 32nd St., Rm. 209, Vernon V1T 5M7
  (604)542-4034
IV. Nootenays T. Prysiazniuk, 385 Baker St., Nelson V1L 4H6 (604)
  352-2211, local 219/309
V. Prince George T. T. Hoogstraten, Courthouse, Prince George; 1488 4th Ave.,
  Rm. 277, Prince George V2L 3I7
VI. Fraser Valley A. E. Bingham, 33820 S. Fraser Way, Abbotsford (604)
  859-8214
VII. Prince Rupert Bulkley Valley Mrs. M. Greening, 4642 Lazelle Ave., 4,
  Terrace V8G 1S6 (604)638-1151
VIII. North and South Peace River R. E. Phillips, 1017B 105th Ave., Dawson
  Creek V1G 2B9 (604)782-5931, local 279
IX. Kamloops Mainline Geoff Eggleton, Tranquille, Tranquille (604)
  376-3361, local 203
X. Vancouver Island North of Malahat Miss I. R. Woodward, 435 Trunk Rd.,
  Suite 205, Duncan V9L 2P8 (604)746-6183, local 265 and 268
XI. Victoria and Area J. A. Mollberg, 1627 Fort St., Victoria V8R 1H8 (604)
  598-5121 or 387-3735
XII. Fraser South T. Pollard, 5766 176A St., Surrey
XIII. Fraser North K. Levitt, 1111 Austin, Suite 4, Coquitlam V3K 3P4
XIV. West Coast S. Abma, 800 Cassiar St., Rm. 211, Vancouver V5K 4NG

Department of Human Resources District Offices

Region III

Grand Forks G. D. McPherson, P. O. Box 460, Courthouse, V0H 1H0   (604) 442-8124

Kalowna L. T. Wace, 1400 St. Paul St., Kelowna V1Y 2E6   (604)763-8407

Oliver G. D. McPherson, P. O. Box 459, Courthouse, Oliver V0H 1T0   (604) 498-3461

Penticton Miss J. Bennest, 152 Main St., Penticton V2A 5A6   (604)492-5629

Vernon S. E. Kerslake, Courthouse V1T 4W5   (604)545-1376

Region IV

Castlegar R. W. Gattinger, 280 Columbia Ave., Rm. 3, Castlegar, V1N 1G4 (604)365-3322

Cranbrook C. H. Moorhouse, Courthouse, Cranbrook V1C 2P2   (604) 489-2311, local 223/4

Creston E. K. Hurd, 228 10th Ave., N., P. O. Box 1180, Creston V0B 1G0 (604)428-2246

Fernie C. H. Moorhouse, 60 2nd Ave., P. O. Box 790, Fernie V0B 1M0 (604)423-4484

Invermere G. C. Fagan, P. O. Box 730, Invermere V0A 1K0   (604)342-6867

Kimberley G. C. Fagan, 250 Howard St., Kimberley V1A 2G7   (604)427-4831

Nelson W. B. English, 310 Ward St., Nelson V1L 5S4   (604)352-2211, local 215

New Denver R. W. Gattinger, P. O. Box 27, New Denver V0G 1S0   (604) 358-2225

Trail B. R. Earthy, 1504 Cedar Ave., Trail V1R 4C6   (604)368-3371

Region V

Ft. St. James T. D. Clark, Box 1300, Ft. St. James V0J 1P0   (604)996-8604 or 7410

Mackenzie D. C. Millar, Wronski Bldg., Rm. 200, Mackenzie   (604)997-3966

100 Mile House N. Gill, 272 5th St., P. O. Box 730, 100 Mile House V0K 2E0 (604)395-2207

Prince George Central City Mr. J. McCunn, 1717 3rd Ave., Rm. 109, Prince George V2L 3G7   (604)563-1751

Prince George/Hart Highway D. C. Millar, 6437 Hart Hwy., Prince George (604)962-9227

Prince George-North West/Spruceland D. C. Millar, 1717 3rd Ave., Rm. 316, Prince George   (604)563-1751

Prince George/South East Mr. J. Eredics, 1717 3rd Ave., Rm. 109, Prince George (604)563-1751

Prince George/South West Mr. P. Clugston, 1717 3rd Ave., Rm. 109, Prince George (604)563-1751

Quesnel W. Prokop, 350 Barlow Ave., Rm. 316, Quesnel V2J 2C1 (604) 992-5555
Vanderhoof T. D. Clark, 1757 Stewart St., P.O. Drawer 830, Vanderhoof (604)567-2234
Williams Lake N. M. Gill, 540 Borland St., Williams Lake V2G 1R5 (604) 392-6261, local 317

Region VI

Abbotsford W. Teichroeb, 33780 Laurel St., Rm. 103, Abbotsford V2S 1X5 (604)853-2246
Chilliwack H. S. Basi and D. A. Livingstone, Courthouse, Chilliwack V2P 4L8 (604)795-7223
Hope H. Basi, P. O. Box 1537, Hope V0X 1L0 (604)869-5662
Maple Ridge Mrs. M. Clarke (Act.), 22438 119th Ave., Maple Ridge V2X 2Z4 (604)463-4157
Mission Mrs. I. M. Harris, 33070 5th Ave., Mission V2V 1V6 (604)826-6237
Langley N. E. Proznick, 20189 56th Ave., Rm. 202, Langley V3A 3Y6 (604) 534-4167

Region VII

Burns Lake D. G. Beddows, Federal Bldg., 2nd Fl., Box 302, Burns Lake V0J 1E0 (604)692-3118
Houston Mr. D. G. Beddows, Box 800, Houston V0J 1Z0 (604)845-2294
Kitimat D. Anonby, City Centre, Rm. 282, Kitimat V8C 1T6 (604)632-6134
Prince Rupert C. C. Dow and M. N. Vinge, 222 5th St., Prince Rupert V8J 3S4 (604)627-1391
Queen Charlotte City M. N. Vinge, P. O. Box 279, Queen Charlotte (604) 559-4558
Smithers D. G. Beddows, 3793 S. Alfred Ave., P. O. Box 848, Smithers V0J 2N0 (604)847-4411, local 246
Terrace D. Anonby, 4506 Lakelse Ave., Government Bldg., Terrace (604) 635-2283

Region VIII

Chetwynd Mrs. V. E. Goodrich, Box 360, Chetwynd V0C 1J0 (604)788-9241
Dawson Creek Mrs. V. E. Goodrich and H. I. Kovacs, Provincial Government Bldgs., 1201 103rd Ave., Dawson Creek (604)782-5931, local 288
Ft. St. John C. N. Sacuta, 9711 100th Ave., Rm. 114, Ft. St. John V1J 1Y2 (604)785-8011, local 258
Ft. Nelson D. C'Allesandro, P. O. Box 566, Ft. Nelson (604)774-6185

Region IX

Cache Creek J. Friend, P. O. Box 218, Cache Creek V0K 1H0 (604)457-6271

Golden K. A. Rutczynski, Courthouse, P. O. Box 930, Volden V0A 1H0 (604) 344-5219

Kamloops G. Wellwood, 1800 Tranquille Hwy., Rm. 32, Brock Mall, Kamloops V2B 3L9 (604)376-6242

Lilooet J. Friend, Courthouse, Box 196, Lilooet V0K 1V0 (604)256-4277

Merritt J. Friend, 2090 Coutlee Ave., P. O. Box 370, Merritt V0K 2B0 (604) 378-4248

Revelstoke K. A. Rutczynski, 108 1st St., W., P. O. Box 462 Revelstoke V0E 2B0 (604)837-5166

Salmon Arm K. A. Rutczynski, Samara Bldg., Box 220, Salmon Arm V0E 2T0 (604)832-2178

Region X

Alert Bay Mrs. Donna May, P. O. Box 10, Alert Bay (604)974-5943

Campbell River G. R. Callander, 1170 Island Hwy., Campbell River V9W 4E4 (604)287-8861

Courtenay J. A. Melville and Mrs. C. E. Whittaker, Cumberland Rd., Courthouse, Rm. 218, Courtenay V9N 5M6 (604)334-2411

Duncan L. Ohlmann, 238 Government, 4th Fl., Duncan V9L 2P8 (604) 746-6183, local 225

Nanaimo D. E. Dunn and Mrs. R. A. Weston, 80 Charny St., Nanaimo V9R 5H2 (604)753-0231

Parksville D. E. Dunn, 194 Morrison Ave., P. O. Box 480, Parksville V0R 2S0 (604)248-6134

Port Alberni Terry MacFadden, 3039 4th Ave., Port Alberni (604)723-9401

Port Hardy Mrs. C. E. Whittaker, P. O. Box 730, Port Hardy V0N 2P0 (604) 949-7500

Powell River J. A. Melville 6953 Alberni St., Powell River V8A 2B8 (604) 485-285

Region XI

Downtown Blanshard K. D. Matheson, 1820 Blanshard, Blanshard V8T 4J1 (604)387-5044

Esquimalt Mrs. D. Bocsik, 939 Esquimalt Rd., Esquimalt V9A 3M7 (604) 387-6381

Fairfield Mrs. G. Lundy, 1520 Fairfield Rd., Fairfield V8T 1G1 (604) 387-5117

Fernwood-Glanstone J. Shields, 2002 Fernwood Rd., Fernwood V8T 2Y9 (604)387-6971

Gordon Head-Shebourne E. Nowotniak, 3750 Shelbourne St., Suite C Shelbourne V8P 4H4 (604)477-1811

James Bay R. G. Leach, 435 Simcoe St., James Bay V8T 1L6 (604)388-6291

Oak Bay Mrs. B. Dane, 1627 Fort St., Oak Bay V8R 1H8 (604)598-5121

Saanich D. H. McLaughlin, 780 Vernon Ave., Saanich V8X 2W6 (604) 385-4451

Sidney and Islands D. H. McLaughlin, 2440 Sidney V8L 1Y6 (604)656-3941

Sooke-Langford M. Thomas (Act.), 2820 Bryn Maur Rd., Langford V9B 3T4 (604)478-5516

Tillicum-Gorge G. K. Webb, 85 Burnside Rd., W., Tillicum-Gorge V9A 1B6 (604)387-3716

Victoria West Mrs. D. Bocsik, 965 Alston St., Victoria West V9A 3S5 (604) 388-4281

Region XII

Delta E. J. Lautard, 4918 Delta St., P.O. Box 99, Delta V4K 3N5 (604) 946-9581

Richmond Mrs. B. Armstrong, Social Services Dept., 694 No. 3 Rd., Richmond V6Y 2C1 (604)273-8411

Surrey W. Schneider, Social Services Dept., 10693 135 A St., P. O. Box 207, Surrey V3T 4W9 (604)581-3334

White Rock L. R. Voth, 1185 Centre St., White Rock V4K 4C8 (604) 531-5505

Region XIII

Burnaby C. C. McKenzie (Adm.), 6161 Gilpin St., Burnaby V5G 4A3 (604) 294-7700; General Information (604)294-7988

Coquitlam J. B. Thomson (Adm.), Social Welfare Dept., 640 Poirier St., Coquitlam V3J 6B1 (604)939-9242

New Westminster City A. Jones (Adm.), Social Service Dept., 55 6th St., New Westminster V3L 2Z4 (604)522-9766

Port Coquitlam G. F. Schramm, 2563 1A Lougheed Hwy., Port Coquitlam V3B 1B4 (604)941-3491

Port Moody G. F. Schramm, 2802 St. John's St., Port Moody V3H 2C1 (604)939-2421

Region XIV

Bella Coola J. C. A. Nuyens (Wrkr.), Box 80, Mathews Bldg., Cliff St., Bella Coola V0T 1C0 (604)799-5443

North Vancouver E. P. Murphy (Adm.), Social Service Dept., 107 W. 20th St., North Vancouver V7M 1Y3 (604)985-8721

Manitoba

Department of Health and Social Development

185 Carlton St., Rm. 200

Winnipeg R3C 3J1
Telephone: (204)946-7207
Hon. Laurent L. Desjardins, Minister (204)946-7329
T. Tulchinsky, M.D., Dep. Minister (204)946-7349 or 7435
R. D. Johnstone, Assoc. Dep. Minister (204)946-7694
R. S. Hikel, Asst. Dep. Minister (204)944-2117
D. F. McLean, Asst. Dep. Minister (204)775-9761
R. Travener, M.D., Chf. Med. Cnslt. and Provincial Psychiatrist   (204)
    946-7788 or 7785

Personal Services Branch

831 Portage Ave.
Winnipeg R3G 0N6
Telephone: (204)775-9761
Dr. J. Ryant, Exec. Dir.

Child and Family Services Section

Rev. C. Greene, Dir.

Community Service Operations Division Regional Offices

Central J. Robson, 170 Saskatchewan Ave. W., Portage la Prairie R1N 3B9
    (204)857-6891
Eastman J. Ross, 250 1st St., Beausejour R0E 0C0   (204)268-1411
Interlake J. Gow, 337A Main St., Selkirk   (204)482-7922
Norman J. Karpan, Box 2550, The Pas R9A 1M4   (204)623-6411
Parklands E. Everett, 707 3rd St. S.W., Dauphin R7N 1R8   (204)638-3840
Thompson M. Draper, 871 Thompson Dr. S., Thompson (204)778-7371
Westman C. Hutchinson, 340 9th St., Brandon R7A 6C2   (204)728-7000
Winnipeg W. Werbeniuk, 189 Evanson St., Winnipeg R3G 0N9   (204)786-7971

New Brunswick

Department of Social Services

P.O. Box 6000
Fredericton E3B 5H1
Telephone: (506)453-2313
Hon. Leslie I. Hull, Minister (506)453-2313
Raymond P. Campbell, Dep. Minister (506)453-2590
William D. Chapman, Exec. Secy., Interdepartmental Committee on Mental
    Retardation (506)453-3633

Special Care Services Division

Robert J. Macdonald, Exec. Dir. (506)453-2955

Day Care Services

Jean-Eudes Levesque, Supv. (506)453-2001 or 2006

Department of Social Services Regional Offices

I. Moncton Bruce Roberts, P. O. Box 5001, Moncton (506)858-2601
II. St. John Gerald Hickey, P. O. Box 5001, St. John (506)658-2450
III. Fredericton Mrs. Flora Jeane Kennedy, P. O. Box 5001, Fredericton
IV.Edmundtson Marcel Arseneau, P. O. Box 5001, Edmunston (506)
735-4725
V. Bathurst Theophile Gagnon, Regional Office, Rm. 102, P. O. Box 5001,
Bathurst (506)548-8953

Department of Social Services District Offices

Region I: Moncton

Moncton John Meahan, P. O. Box 5001, Moncton (506)858-2631
Dorchester Miline Taylor, P. O. Box 5001, Dorchester (506)379-2411
Richibucto Donald Daigle, P. O. Box 5001, Richibucto (506)523-4471

Region II: St. John

St. John (vacant), P. O. Box 5001, St. John (506)658-2541
Sussex Archibald Smith, P. O. Box 5001, Sussex (506)433-3070
St. Stephan Headley Way, P. O. Box 5001, St. Stephan (506)466-4260

Region III: Fredericton

Fredericton Phil Thompson, P. O. Box 5001, Fredericton (506)454-1531
Woodstock Raymond Walker, Woodstock (506)328-3335
Minto Jane Asher, Office Mgr., P. O. Box 5001, Minto (506)327-3374
Perth-Andover Glen Yeomans, P. O. Box 5001, Perth-Andover (506)273-2059

Region IV: Edmundtson

Edmundtson Paul LeClerc, P. O. Box 5001, Edmundtson (506)735-4725
Campbelton Armand LeCouffe, P. O. Box 5001, Campbelton (506)753-7694
Grand Falls Alexandre Godbout, P. O. Box 5001, Grand Falls (506)473-1830
Kedgwick Jacques Nadeau, P. O. Box 5001, Kedgwick (506)284-2927

Region V: Bathurst

Bathurst Bernard Paulin, P. O. Box 5001, Bathurst (506)546-9951
Newcastle Gerard Doucet, P. O. Box 5001, Newcastle (506)622-2800

Caraquet Alfred Paulin, P. O. Box 5001, Caraquet (506)727-3447
Tracadie Hilarion Coughlin, P. O. Box 5001, Tracadie (506)395-3391
Shippegan Gerard Robichaud, P. O. Box 5001, Shippegan (506)336-8469

Newfoundland

Department of Social Services

Confederation Bldg.
St. John's A1C 5T7
Hon. R. C. Brett, Minister (709)737-3580
H. V. Hollett, Dep. Minister (709)737-3582
G. Pope, Asst. Dep. Minister (709)737-3585

Child Welfare and Corrections Division

Frank Simms, Dir. (709)737-2668

Field Services Division Regional Offices

Central T. L. Wiseman, Provincial Government Bldg., Grand Falls A2A 1W9
    (709)489-5771
Eastern Calvin Payne, Provincial Government Bldg., Harbour Grace A0A 2M0
    (709)596-5054, ext. 41
Labrador Reginald Gabriel, Happy Valley A0P 1E0 (709)896-3306
St. John's Jerome Quinlan, Provincial Government Bldg., Harvey Rd., St. John's
    A1C 5Y6 (709)737-3450
Western John Jenniex, Provincial Government Bldg., Corner Brook A2H 6J8
    (709)639-9111, ext. 308

Field Services Division District Offices

Central Region

Baie Verte Charles Feltham, Box 278, Baie Verte A0K 1B0 (709)532-8024
Fogo Thomas Hanlon, Box 10, Fogo A0G 2B0 (709)266-2238
Gander Earle Crocker, Box 383, Gander A1V 1W8 (709)256-3341
Glovertown William Cook, Box 70, Glovertown A0G 2L0 (709)533-2404
Grand Falls Freeman Pope, Provincial Government Bldg., Grand Falls A2A 1W9
    (709)489-5771, ext. 351
Harbour Breton Michael Griffin, Box 116, Harbour Breton A0H 1P0 (709)
    885-2279
Lewisporte Selby Moss, Box 190, Lewisporte A0G 3A0 (709)535-2614
Milltown Fred Powell, Milltown A0H 1W0 (709)882-2610
Springdale John Jenkins, Box 580, Springdale A0J 1T0 (709)673-3713

Twillingate Malcolm J. Earle, Box 338, Twillingate A0G 4M0   (709)884-2413
Wesleyville Hardy Chippett, Box 13, Wesleyville A0G 4R0   (709)536-2421

Eastern Region

Arnold's Cove Reginald Bowering, Box 100, Arnold's Cove A0B 1A0   (709)
   463-2626
Bay L'Argent Andrew Moriarity, Provincial Government Bldg., Harbour Grace
   A0A 2M0   (709)596-2207
Bay Roberts Eugene Bennett, Box 149, Bay Roberts A0A 1G0   (709)
   786-2151
Bonavista Louis Lecoure (act.), Box 521, Bonavista A0C 1B0   (709)
   468-2461
Clarenville Fred Gosse, Box 220, Clarenville A0E 1J0   (709)466-2495
Grand Bank Edwin Layden, Box 100, Grand Bank A0E 1W0   (709)832-1460
Harbour Grace Irvin Piercey, Box 580, Harbour Grace A0A 2M0   (709)
   596-5054, Ext. 38
Heart's Content Robert Wheadon (Act.), Box 1, Heart's Content A0E 1Z0
   (709)583-2880
Marystown Michael Pickett, Box 458, Marystown A0E 2M0   (709)279-2130
Placentia Thomas McDonald, Box 4, Placentia A0B 2Y0   (709)226-2132
St. Mary's John Higgins, Box 42, St. Mary's A0B 3B0   (709)525-2020
Whitbourne William Dyke, Box 88, Whitbourne A0B 3K0   (709)759-2270

Labrador Region

Cartwright Charles Conway, Cartwright A0K 1V0   (709)896-2256
Nain Michael Dunphy, Nain A0P 1L0   (709)282-6871 (radio)
Mary's Harbour Harry Decker, Mary's Harbour A0K 3P0   (709)896-2446
Wabush George Savoury, Wabush A0R 1B0   (709)282-6651

St. John's Region

Bay Bulls Theobald Delaney, Box 100, Bay Bulls A0A 1C0   (709)334-2551
Bell Island Reginald Earle, Box 1313, Bell Island A0A 1H0   (709)488-3376
Fermeuse Jean Vallis (Act.), Fermeuse A0A 2C0   (709)363-2450
Long Pond Samuel Atkins, Box 400, Long Pond A0A 2Y0   (709)834-2831
St. John's Terrence Haire, Box 4040, St. John's A1C 5Y6   (709)737-3452

Western Region

Bonne Bay Max Seaward, Box 130, Bonne Bay A0K 1P0   (709)453-2249
Burgeo Albert S. Barnes, Box 74, Burgeo A0M 1A0   (709)886-3353
Corner Brook Henry Anthony, Corner Brook A2H 6J8   (709)639-9111,
   ext. 300
Channel Peter Hamlyn, Box 38, Channel A0M 1C0   (709)695-2633
Deer Lake Eugene Smith, Box 809, Deer Lake A0K 2E0   (709)635-2123

Englee Calvin Chaulk, Box 99, Englee A0K 2J0 (709)866-2774
Flower's Cove John Beaufield, Box 9, Flower's Cove A0K 2N0 (709)456-2431
Forteau Patrick Fowler, Forteau A0K 2P0
Port Saunders Gerald W. Power, Box 10, Port Saunders, A0K 4H0 (709)
    861-3507
St. Anthony Maximus King, St. Anthony A0K 4S0 (709)454-2542
Stephenville Peter Godfrey, Box 360, Stephenville A2N 2Z5 (709)643-2185
Stephenville Crossing Redvers Gosse, Box 130, Stephenville Crossing A0N 2C0
    (709)646-2912

Northwest Territories

Department of Social Development

Government of the Northwest Territories
Yellowknife X0E 1H0
Telephone: (403)873-7119
K. J. Torrance, Dir.
Gordon Stangues, Asst. Dir.

Special Services Division

Ms. T. Usher, Coord.
Telephone: (403)873-7312

Department of Social Development Regional and District Offices

Inuvik D. Belzeil, Inucik (403)979-7222
Frobisher Bay D. D. Macers, Frobisher Bay X0A 1HA (403)979-5261
Fort Smith D. Wiedeman, Fort Smith (403)872-2023
Keewatin D. Noseworthy, Rankin Inlet (403)645-2747
Cambridge Bay Miss Kay Minor, Cambridge Bay (403)983-2145
Yellowknife Mrs. P. Bruce, Yellowknife X0E 1H0 (403)873-2711

Nova Scotia

Department of Social Services

P.O. Box 696
Halifax B3J 2T7
Hon. William MacEachern, Minister (902)424-4304
Dr. F. R. MacKinnon, Dep. Minister (902)424-4325

Family and Child Welfare Division

D. H. Johnson, Adm. (902)424-4282
Kevin Burns, Dir. (902)424-3202

Department of Social Services Regional Offices

Cape Breton (Pt. Hawkesbury District) Provincial Bldg., Suite 7, Sydney
A. S. Kyte, Regl. Adm. (902)562-5507
Central (Lunenburg and Queens Districts) F. W. Robinson Bldg., 374 Main St.,
P. O. Box 188, Kentville B4N 3W7 Douglas M. Penney, Regl. Adm.
(902)678-6176
Halifax (Dartmouth and Sackville Districts) P. O. Box 696, Halifax, Mrs. Joan
MacKinnon, Regl. Adm. (902)424-4170
North Shore (Antigonish, Colchester, and Cumberland Districts) P. O. Box 488,
New Glasgow, R. C. Purdy, Regl. Adm. (902)755-3010
Western (Annapolis, Digby, and Shelburne Districts) P. O. Box 460, Yarmouth,
Douglas Raymond (902)742-7871

Department of Social Services District Offices

Annapolis Donald Lefurgey, P. O. Box 39, Amherst (902)532-2334
Antigonish A. G. MacKenzie, Provincial Bldg., James, P. O. Box 1687, Anti-
gonish (902)863-3213
Colchester Harvey MacArthur, Regional Health Center, Willow St., Truro
(902)895-6336
Cumberland Donald Russell, 24 Crescent Ave., P. O. Box 399, Amherst (902)
667-3336
Dartmouth Duncan Rosnok, P. O. Box 665, Dartmouth (902)424-4158
Digby Gerald Walsh, P. O. Box 399, Digby (902)245-2951
Lunenburg Malcolm Burrill, 224 Dufferin St., P. O. Box 170, Bridgewater
(902)543-2411
Pt. Hawkesbury Gordon MacMaster, Pt. Hawkesbury (902)625-0660
Queens Donald Burns, P. O. Box 1360, Liverpool (902)354-3422
Sackville Trevor Townsend, P. O. Box 192, Sackville (902)865-5911
Shelburne Michael Johnston, P. O. Box 9, Barrington (902)637-2335

Children's Aid Societies

Annapolis County D. A. Lefurgey, Family and Children Services, Annapolis
Royal
Cape Breton A. S. Kyte, Children's Aid Society, Sydney
Colchester County Harvey MacArthur, Children's Aid Society, 58 Willow St.,
P. O. Box 950, Truro B2N 5O1 (902)895-6336

Cumberland County Donald Russell, Family and Children Services, Amherst
Halifax Karl Marshall, Children's Aid Society, P. O. Box 65, Halifax
Hants County J. R. Whalen, Family and Children Services, Kentville
Kings County Douglas M. Penney, Family and Children's Services, Kentville
Lunenburg County Malcolm Burrill, Family and Children's Services, Bridge-
    water
Pictou County R. C. Purdy, Children's Aid Society, New Glasgow
Queens County Donald Burns, Family and Children's Services, Liverpool
Shelburne County Michael Johnston, Children's Aid Society, Barrington
Yarmouth County Douglas Raymond, Family and Children's Services, Yarmouth

Ontario

Ministry of Community and Social Services

> Hepburn Block, Parliament Bldg.
> Queen's Park
> Toronto M7A 1E9
> Hon. James Taylor, Minister (416)965-2341
> Miss D. Crittenden, Dep. Minister (416)965-2344

Social Resources

> J. G. Anderson, Asst. Dep. Minister (416)965-0515

Children's Protective and Preventive Services Branch

> J. K. Macdonald, Dir., (416)965-0176

Ministry of Community and Social Services Regional Offices

Northern Dr. C. J. Williams, 127 Cedar St., Sudbury (416)674-7543
Southern Harry Williams, Hepburn Block, 4th Fl., Queen's Park, Toronto
    M7A 1E9 (416)965-9505

Ministry of Community and Social Services County Offices

Addington Served by Lennox County Office
Brant Larry E. Loving, Box 845, Brantford N3T 2J0 (519)759-3330
Bruce D. Verrips, Box 480, Walkerton N0G 2V0 (519)881-0431
Dufferin R. D. Wood, 53 Zina St., Orangeville L9W 1E5 (519)941-6991
Dundas Served by Stormont County Office
Elgin R. E. Bell, Courthouse, St. Thomas N5R 2T2 (519)631-1570
Essex Murray Smith, 360 Fairview St., W., Essex N0R 1E0 (519)776-6441

Glengarry Served by Stormont County Office

Grey J. Nolan, Box 9, Owen Sound N4K 5P1   (519)376-7324

Hastings Reginald Tucker, County Administration Bldg., Pinnacle St., Rm. 4, Belleville K8N 3A9   (613)968-7668

Huron John A. MacKinnon, Courthouse, Goderich N7A 1M2   (519)524-2186

Lambton R. L. Provencher, Box 3021, Sarnia N7T 7N3   (519)337-3265

Lanark R. Elgersma, P. O. Box 37, Perth K7H 3E2   (613)267-4200

Lennox A. Dawson, P. O. Box 190, Napanee K0K 2E3   (613)354-3364

Northumberland A. E. Martin, County Bldg., 860 Williams St., Cobourg K9A 3A9   (416)372-6846

Oxford G. H. MacKay, 86 Light St., Box 397, Woodstock N4S 7Y3   (519) 537-3428

Perth James Henry, 380 Hibernia St., Box 487, Stratford N5A 5W3   (519) 273-2131

Prescott D.A. Davidson, P.O. Box 303, L'Orignal K0H 1K0   (613)675-4642

Prince Edward Mrs. Evelyn Beaumont, County Bldg., Shire Hall, Drawer 1550, Picton K0K 2T0   (613)476-2842

Russell Served by Prescott County Office

Simcoe Gordon Tucker, Simcoe County Bldg., Midhurst L0L 1X0   (705) 726-9300, ext. 244

Stormont E. P. Thompson, Box 605, Cornwall K6H 5T3   (613)933-7909

Victoria T. A. Costello, 42 Victoria Ave., N., P. O. Box 247, Lindsay K9V 4G2 (705)324-9114

Wellington A. D. MacLennan, Box 43, Guelph N1H 6J6   (519)821-2270

Ministry of Community and Social Services Indian Bands Offices

Alderville Mrs. Louise Simpson, P.O. Box 12, Roseneath K0K 2X0   (416) 352-2011

Batchawana Miss Judy Lesage, 236 Frontenac St., Sault Ste. Marie, P6B 2A3 (705)253-1219

Bay of Quinte Douglas S. Brant, R.R. 1, Deseronto K0K 1X0   (613)968-5701

Big Grassy Ms. Geraldine Archie, Morson P0W 1J0   (807)724-7643

Big Island Mrs. Elsie Handorgan, 510 Victoria Ave., Ft. Frances P9A 2C4 (807)274-7643

Brunswick House P. G. Schaak, 208 Walnut St., Sudbury P3C 1L7   (703) 675-2411

Cape Crohar Mrs. Jacqueline Solomon, R.R. 5, Wiarton N0H 2T0   (519) 534-1689

Caribou Lake Cornelius Benson, Weagamow Lake P0V 2Y0   (no telephone)

Cat Lake Mrs. Kanacia Mezzetay, Cat Lake Via, Central Patricia P0V 1K0 (no telephone)

Chapleau P. G. Schaak, 208 Walnut St., Sudbury P3C 1L7   (705)673-0411

Christian Island Mrs. Annette Sunday, Band Council Office, Christian Island Via, Penetang L0K 1P0

Constance Lake Mrs. Jane Cheechoo, Calstock P0L 1B0

Couchiching Chuck McPherson, P. O. Box 723, Ft. Frances P9A 3N1 (807) 274-9607

Curve Lake Mrs. Kathleen Taylor, Curve Lake K0L 1R0 (705)657-8833

Dokis Mrs. Nicole Restoule, Monetville P0M 2K0 (705)763-2200

Eagle Lake Ms. M. Napish, Eagle River, P0V 1S0 (807)755-5662

Ft. Hope George Nate, Eabamet Lake P. O. Via, Nakina P0T 1L0

Ft. William Mrs. Catherine Collins, Box 786, Postal Station F, Thunder Bay P7C 4W6 (807)623-9543

Garden River Mrs. Doreen Lesage, R.R. 4, Site 5, Box 7, Saute Ste. Marie P6A 5K9 (705)248-2333

Georgina Island H. B. MacDonald, 80 Bayview Ave., Newmarket L3Y 4W9 (416)895-5166

Gibson William Rennie, Box 327, R.R. 1, Bala P0C 1A0 (705)762-3343

Golden Lake Joe Cooco, Golden Lake, P. O. K0J 1X0 (613)625-2800

Grand River Arthur W. Anderson, Council House, Oshroken N0A 1M0 (519) 445-2201

Grassy Narrows Steve Fobister, Grassy Narrows P0K 1B0

Henry Inlet Thomas Green, 76 Church St., Parry Sound P2A 1Z1 (705) 746-5851

Hiawatha Mrs. June Robinson, R.R. 2, Keene, K8L 2G0 (705)295-4421

Islington B. Bigblood, Whitedog P0X 1P0 (807)224-2400

Kettle Point S. Wolfe, Band Office, R.R. 2, Forest N0N 1J0 (519)873-5428

Lac La Croix A. Potson, P. O. Box 747, Ft. Frances P9A 3N1

Long Lake 58 Miss Julie Patabon, Longlac P0T 2A0 (807)876-2618

Long Lake 77 Mrs. Celia Echum, P. O. Box 185, Longlac P0T 2A0 (807) 876-2691

Martin Falls (vacant), Ogoki Post Via, Nakina

Matachewan G. D. Balls, 91 Duncan Ave., P.O. Box 757, Kirkland Lake P2N 3K3 (705)567-4300 or 5262

Mattagami P. G. Schaak, 208 Walnut St., Sudbury P3C 1L7 (705)675-2411

Mississauges Mrs. M. Chiblow, Box 1229, Blind River P0R 1B0 (705) 356-7998

Moose Deer Point Mrs. Beatrice Sandy, Box 81, Mactier P0C 1H0

Moose Factory W. Chum, P. O. Box 219, Moose Factory P0L 1W0 (705) 658-4619

Naicatchewenin R. Morriseau, R.R. 1, Devlin P0W 1C0 (807)486-3407

New Credit Mrs. Anne Laforme, R.R. 6, Hagersville N0A 1H0 (416)768-5590

Nicickousemenecaning A. Potson, P. O. Box 747, Ft. Frances P9A 3N1

Nipissing D. Beaucage, R.R. 1, Sturgeon Falls P0H 2G0 (705)753-2050

Northwest Angle 33 Ms. C. Sandy, Via Angle Inlet, Minnesota 56711 (U.S.A.)

Northwest Angle 37 (vacant), Box 232, Sioux Narrows P0X 1N0
Osnaburgh (vacant), Osnaburgh House
Parry Island G. Tabobondung, Box 253, Parry Sound P1A 2X4 (705)746-2531
Pic Heron Mrs. Myra Michano, Heron Bay P0T 1R0 (807)229-0240
Pikangikum (vacant), Pikangikum
Rainy River Mrs. Jean Bombay, P. O. Box 292, Emo P0W 1E0 (807)482-2479
Rama Gordon Simcoe, Rama Rd., P. O. L0K 1T0 (705)325-3611
Rat Portage and Dallas W. Skead, P. O. Box 88, Kenora P9N 3X1 (807)
    468-5541
Rocky Bay Mrs. Diana Hardy, MacDiarmid P0T 2B0
Sabaskong L. Indian, Nestor Falls P0X 1K0 (807)484-5245
Sarnia Mrs. H. Williams, R.R. 4, Sarnia N7T 7H5 (519)344-5371
Saugeon Gary Mason, Chippewa Hill P. O. N0H 1H0 (519)797-2218
Scugog Ronald Edgar, R.R. 3, Port Perry L0B 1N0 (416)985-2631
Seine River A. Potson, P. O. Box 747, Ft. Frances P9A 3N1
Serpent River Frank Lewis, Cutler P0P 1B0 (705)844-2418
Shawanga Roger Jones, R.R. 1, Nobel P0G 1G0 (705)366-2269
Sheguiandah Fred Fineday, Sheguiandah P. O. P0P 1W0 (705)368-2887
Sheshegwaning Lloyd Sampson, Sheshegwaning P.O. P0R 1X0 (705)283-3297
Shoal Lake 39 S. Mandamin, Kejick P.O. P0X 1E0 (807)733-2560
Shoal Lake 40 John Redsky, Kejick, P.O. P0X 1E0 (807)733-2315
Spanish River Mrs. Mary Toulouse, P.O. Box 158, Massey P0P 1K0 (705)
    865-5287
Sucker Creek Mrs. Georgena Nahwegahbow, Little Current P0P 1K0 (705)
    368-2228
Thames (Chippewas) Mrs. Marcia Dockstater, R.R. 1, Muncey N0L 1Y0 (519)
    264-1528
Thames (Muncey) Mrs. Christine Dolson, R.R. 1, Muncey N0L 1Y0 (519)
    289-5396
Thames (Oneidas) Mrs. Charity Doxtater, R.R. 2, Southwold N0L 2G0
    (519)652-3244
Thames (Moravians) Mrs. E. Hopkins, R.R. 3, Thamesville N0P 2K0 (519)
    692-4341
Wabigoon Ms. S. Shabequay, Dinorwic P0V 1P0 (807)938-6450
Walpole Island Mrs. J. Bird, R.R. 3, Wallaceburg N8A 4K9 (519)627-1481
Watha Served by Gibson Office
West Bay Miss F. Roy, West Bay P0P 1S0 (705)377-5367
Whitefish Bay John Namaypoke, Pawitik P.O. P0X 1L0 (807)226-5411
Whitefish Lake Mrs. Linda Pehtahtegoose, Naughton P.O. P0M 2M0 (705)
    692-3423
Whitefish River Miss Pauline Andrews, Birch Island P0P 1A0 (705)285-4335
Wikwemikong Richard Flamand, P.O. Box 2, Wikwemikong P0P 2J0 (705)
    859-3122

Prince Edward Island

Department of Social Services

P.O. Box 2000
Charlottetown C1A 7N8
Telephone: (902)892-5421
Hon. Catherine Callbeck, Minister
John Eldon Green, Dep. Minister
Ralph G. Dumont, Dir. of Administration
Robert B. Doherty, Dir. of Personnel

Field Services Division

Joseph E. Kiley, Dir.
Telephone: (902)892-5421

Department of Social Services Regional Offices

Charlottetown Marie MacDonald, 188 Prince St., Charlottetown (902) 892-1261
O'Leary Ron Irnie, West Prince Regional Services Center, O'Leary (902) 859-2400
Souris Stephen McQuaid, Eastern Kings Regional Services Center, Souris (902)687-3022
Summerside Carol Anne Newson, 237 Water St., Summerside (902)436-7294
Montague Stephen McQuaid, Main St., Montague (902)838-2992

Quebec

Department of Social Affairs

1075 Ste. Foy Rd.
Quebec City
Hon. Claude E. Forget, Minister (418)643-3160
Jacques Brunet, M.D., Dep. Minister (418)643-6462
Julien Giasson, Minister of State (418)643-2260
Jean-Caulade LaFleur (418)643-6451

Social Aid Division

Jean-Guy Houde, Assoc. Dep. Minister

Saskatchewan

Department of Social Services

2240 Albert St.
Regina S4P 2Y3
Hon. Herman H. Rolfes, Minister (306)565-3663
Frank J. Bogdasavich, Dep. Minister (306)565-3491

Social Services Branch

Don Cameron, Dir. (306)565-3641

Social Services Branch Regional Offices

Malfort W. M. Sanderman, 104 McLeod Ave., E., Malfort S0E 1A0 (306)
752-2701
Nipawin K. M. Burke, Supv., Box 1360, Nipawin S0E 1E0 (306)862-4629
Moose Jaw G. J. Peterson, 60 Fairford St., W., Moose Jaw S6H 1V1 (306)
693-3657
North Battleford R. R. E. Hunks, Provincial Bldg., Rm. 206, 1146 102nd St.,
North Battleford S9A 1G1 (306)445-6194
Meadow Lake S. W. Krahenbil, Supv., Box 1000, Meadow Lake S0L 1Z0
(306)236-5641
Prince Albert V. R. Wiebe, 101 15th St., E., Prince Albert S6V 0X5 (306)
763-7444
Qu'Appelle J. D. Fraser, 2402 2nd Ave., Regina S4R 1A6 (306)565-3502
Regina D. B. Exner, 1308 Winnipeg St., Regina S4R 1J7 (306)565-3691
Saskatoon L. E. Brierley, S.G.T. Bldg., Rm. 300, 101 Pacific Ave., N.,
Saskatoon S7K 1W9 (306)653-0550
Swift Current E. H. Gilchrist, 340 Chaplin St., W., Swift Current S9H 0E9
(306)773-9386
Kinderfley Ian Casswell, Supv., Box 1658, Kinderfley S0L 1S0 (306)463-2033
or 2595
Weyburn Miss D. W. Moore, 50 3rd St., N., Weyburn S4H 0V9 (306)842-4644
Estevan R. J. Reiter, Supv., 1134 4th St., Estevan S4A 0W7 (306)634-3646
Yorkton B. Strong, 72 Smith St., Yorkton S3N 2Y4 (306)783-3666

Local Unit Offices

Moose Jaw E. C. Dawkins, Moose Jaw City Social Services Dept., 304 City Hall,
Moose Jaw S6H 3J8 (306)693-3621
Prince Albert Les Talbot, Prince Albert City Social Service Dept., 1521 6th Ave.
W., Prince Albert S6B 5K2 (306)764-5291

Yukon Territory

Department of Health, Welfare, and Rehabilitation

P.O. Box 2703
White Horse
Florence Whyard, Exec. Committee Member, (403)667-5428

Social Welfare Branch

Telephone: (403)667-6211
M. Van der Veen, Dir.
J. O'Bryne, Admv. Ofr.

Child Welfare

M. Van der Veen, Dir.
(vacant), Asst. Dir.

Field Service

J. Robeson, Supv.

Metropolitan Area

W. Gladman, Supv.

Special Placements

M. Kehoe, Supv.

Geriatric Services

M. Taggart, Supv.

Social Welfare Branch Area Offices

Faro and Ross River David Hovland, Faro-number pending
Mayo Miss Kathy Haubrich, Box 9, Mayo   (403)996-2283
Watson Lake Ajmal Kahn, Box 305, Watson Lake   (403)996-2232

Bibliography

The following code is used here to designate selected subject categories for all entries.

A. General—Definitions and Characteristics of Child Abuse and Neglect
B. Law—Legislation—Enforcement
C. Parenthood—Family Relations
D. Treatment—Parent
E. Treatment—Child
F. Social and Cultural Aspects
G. Education
H. Prevention

Example:

123. Billingsley, A. "A Study of Child Neglect and Abuse." *University of California School of Social Welfare,* Berkeley, California, 1965. **A**
123. Citation Number
     Billingsley, A . . . Citation
     A   Subject

Bibliography

1. Ackerman, N. "Preventive Implications of Family Research." In G. Caplan, *Prevention of Mental Disorders in Children.* New York: Basic Books, 1961. **C, H.**

2. Ackerman, N. *The Psychodynamics of Family Life.* New York: Basic Books, 1958. **C.**

3. Adams, P. et al. *Children's Rights: Towards the Liberation of the Child.* New York: Praeger, 1972. **B.**

4. Adelson, L. "Homicide by Pepper." *Journal of Forensic Science* 9 (1964): 391-395. **D.**

5. ——. "Homicide by Starvation." *Journal of the American Medical Association* 186 (1963):458. **D.**

6. ——. "Slaughter of the Innocents—A Study of Forty-Six Homicides in Which The Victims Were Children." *New England Journal of Medicine* 264 (1961):1345-1349. **A.**

7. ——. "The Battered Child." *Journal of the American Medical Association* 222 (1972):159-161. **A.**

8. Ainsworth, M. "The Effects of Maternal Deprivation: A Review of Findings and Controversy in the Context of Research Strategy." *Deprivation of Maternal Care: A Reassessment of Its Effects.* Public Health Papers No. 14, Geneva, Switzerland: World Health Organization, 1962. **A.**

9. Aldous, J. "Children's Perceptions of Adult Role Assignment: Father-Absence, Class, Race and Sex Influences." *Journal of Marriage and the Family* 34 (1972):55-65. **C, F.**

10. Aldrich, C. "Impact of Community Psychiatry on Casework and Psychotherapy." *Smith College Studies in Social Work* 38 (February 1968):109. **E, H.**

11. Alexander, H. "The Social Worker and the Family." In C. Kempe and R. Helfer, *Helping the Battered Child and His Family.* Philadelphia and Toronto: J.B. Lippincott, 1972. **C, H.**

12. Alexander, J. "How Psychologists Can Help Stop Child Abuse." *Journal of Clinical Child Psychology* 5 (1976):13-14. **E.**

13. Allen, A. "Maltreatment Syndrome in Children." *Canadian Nurse* 62 (1966):40–42. **A.**

14. Allen, A., and A. Morton. *This is Your Child: The Story of the National Society for the Prevention of Cruelty to Children.* London: Routledge and Kegan Paul Ltd., 1961. **A.**

15. Allen, H., et al. "The Battered Child Syndrome. 1. Medical Aspects." *Minnesota Medicine* 51 (1968):1793–1799. **A.**

16. ——. "The Battered Child Syndrome. 2. Social and Psychiatric Aspects." *Minnesota Medicine* 52 (1969):155–156. **A, C.**

17. ——. "The Battered Child Syndrome. 3. Legal Aspects." *Minnesota Medicine* 52 (1969):345–347. **B.**

18. ——. "The Battered Child Syndrome. 4. Summary." *Minnesota Medicine* 52 (1969):539–540. **A.**

19. Allott, R. "The District Attorney." In C. Kempe and R. Helfer, *Helping the Battered Child and His Family.* Philadelphia and Toronto: J.B. Lippincott, 1972. **B, C, D, E.**

20. Altman, D., and R. Smith. "Unrecognized Trauma in Infants and Children." *Journal of Bone and Joint Surgery* 42 (1960): 407. **A.**

21. Alvy, K. "On Child Abuse: Values and Analytic Approaches." *Journal of Clinical Child Psychology* 4 (Spring 1975):36–37. **A.**

22. ——. "Preventing Child Abuse." *American Psychology* 30 (September 1975):921–928. **H.**

23. America. "Battered Child Cases." *America,* April 25, 1964, p. 559. **A.**

24. ——. "Battered Child Syndrome." *America,* February 18, 1967, p. 236. **A.**

25. Annual of the American Academy. "Prevention of Cruelty to Children." *Annual of the American Academy* 26 (November 1905):774–777. **H.**

26. American Academy of Pediatrics. *A Descriptive Study of Nine Health Based Programs in Child Abuse and Neglect.* Evanston, Illinois: American Academy of Pediatrics, 1974. **A, H.**

27. ——. "The Battered Child Syndrome." Committee on Infant and Preschool Child Maltreatment of Children. *Pediatrics* 50 (July 1972):160–162. **A, H.**

28. ——. "Maltreatment of Children: The Physically Abused Child." Committee on Infant and Pre-school Children. *Pediatrics* 37 (1966):377–380. **A, H.**

29. American Humane Association. *A National Symposium on Child Abuse.* Denver, Colorado: Children's Division, American Humane Association, 1972. **A.**

30. ——. *Child Protective Services—A National Survey.* Denver, Colorado: Children's Division, American Humane Association, 1967. **B, H.**

31. ——. *Guidelines for Legislation to Protect the Battered Child.* Denver, Colorado: Children's Division, American Humane Association, 1963. **B.**

32. ——. *1. Guidelines for Schools.* Denver, Colorado: Children's Division, American Humane Association, 1961. **G.**

33. ———. *In the Interest of Children: A Century of Progress.* Denver, Colorado: Children's Division, American Humane Association, 1966. **H.**

34. ———. *Position Statement on Proposals for Mandatory Reporting of Suspected Inflicted Injuries on Children.* Denver, Colorado: American Humane Association, 1962. **A, B, D.**

35. ———. *Protecting the Battered Child.* Denver, Colorado: Children's Division, American Humane Association, 1962. **D, H.**

36. ———. *Protecting the Child Victim of Sex Crimes.* Denver, Colorado: Children's Division, American Humane Association, 1965. **A.**

37. ———. *Protecting the Child Victim of Sex Crimes Committed by Adults.* Denver, Colorado: Children's Division, American Humane Association, 1969. **A.**

38. ———. *Psychiatric Implications of Physical Abuse of Children in Protecting the Battered Child.* Denver, Colorado: American Humane Association, 1962. **D.**

39. ———. *Report of National Agencies Workshop on Child Protective Services,* Part 1. Denver, Colorado: Children's Division, American Humane Association, 1957. **A, H.**

40. ———. *Report of National Agencies Workshop on Child Protective Services,* Part 2. Denver, Colorado: Children's Division, American Humane Association, 1957. **A, H.**

41. ———. *Review of Legislation to Protect the Battered Child.* Denver, Colorado: American Humane Association, Undated. **B.**

42. ———. *Second National Symposium on Child Abuse.* Denver, Colorado: Children's Division, American Humane Association, 1973. **A**

43. ———. *Speaking Out for Child Protection.* Denver, Colorado: Children's Division, American Humane Association, 1973. **A, H.**

44. ———. *Special Issue of Child Welfare on Protective Service.* Denver, Colorado: American Humane Association, 1963. **A, H.**

45. ———. *The Fundamentals of Child Protection.* Denver, Colorado: Children's Division, American Humane Association, 1955. **D.**

46. ———. *The Masters on Case, Neglected Children—Constructive Use of the Juvenile Courts.* Denver, Colorado: American Humane Association, Undated. **B.**

47. ———. *The Nancy Smith Case, Neglected Child—Unmarried Mother.* Denver, Colorado: American Humane Association, Undated. **B.**

48. American Medical Association. *Physical Abuse of Children—Suggested Legislation.* Chicago, Illinois: American Medical Association, 1965. **B.**

49. American Public Welfare Association. *Preventive and Protective Services to Children, A Responsibility of the Public Welfare Agency.* Chicago, Illinois: American Public Welfare Association, 1958. **D, H.**

50. American School Board Journal. "What Would You Do If . . a High School Girl Reported a Case of Sexual Child Abuse?" *American School Board Journal* 162 (July 1975):12, 16. **G.**

51. Amiel, S. "Child Abuse in Schools." *Northwest Medicine* 71, 11 (1972): 808. **G.**

52. Anderson, J., et al. "Attitudes of Nova Scotia Physicians to Child Abuse." *Nova Scotia Medical Bulletin* 52 (1973):185-189. **A.**

53. Andrews, J. "The Battered Baby Syndrome." *Illinois Medical Journal* 122 (November 1962):494. **A.**

54. Anthony, E. "A Clinical and Experimental Study of High-Risk Children and Their Schizophrenic Parents." In A. Kaplan, *Genetic Factors in Schizophrenia.* Springfield, Illinois: Thomas, 1971. **C, D.**

55. ——. "A Clinical Evaluation of Children with Psychotic Parents." In S. Chess and A. Thomas, *Annual Progress in Child Psychiatry and Child Development.* New York: Brunner-Mazel, 1970. **A, C, D.**

56. ——. "A Group of Murderous Mothers." *Acta Psychotherapy,* Supplement 7 (1959):1-6. **C.**

57. ——. "Mothers with Murderous Obsessions." In E. Anthony and T. Benedek, *Parenthood: Its Psychology and Psychopathology.* Boston, Massachusetts: Little, Brown, 1969. **C.**

58. ——. "The Effect of Maternal Psychosis on Children." In E. Anthony and T. Benedek, *Parenthood: Its Psychology and Psychopathology.* Boston, Massachusetts: Little, Brown, 1969. **C.**

59. Aptekar, H. *Anjea: Infanticide, Abortion, and Contraception Savage Society.* New York: William Godwin, 1931. **A, F.**

60. Areen, J. "Intervention Between Parent and Child—Reappraisal of States Role in Child Neglect and Abuse Cases." *Georgetown Law Journal* 63 (1975):887-937. **B, D.**

61. Arnold, G., and J. Hard. "Child Protection: A Suggested Role for Members of the Wyoming State Bar." *Land and Water Law Review* 9 (1974): 187-208. **B, C, H.**

62. Aron, J., et al. "Occular Symptoms Observed in Silverman's Syndrome (Battered Child Syndrome)," *Annales d'Oculistique* 203 (June 1970): 533-546. **D.**

63. Arnold, M., and V. Miller. *Termination of Parental Rights.* Denver, Colorado: Children's Division, The American Humane Association, Undated. **B, C.**

64. Asch, S. "Crib Deaths: Their Possible Relationship to Post-Partum Depression and Infanticide." *Journal of the Mt. Sinai Hospital* 35 (1968):214-220. **A.**

65. Asken. M. "Medical Psychology—Psychology's Neglected Child." *Professional Psychology* 6 (1975):155-160. **D.**

66. Astley, R. "Multiple Metaphyseal Fractures in Small Children." *British Journal of Radiology* 26 (1953): 577. **A.**

67. Atkinson, R., et al. *The Battered Child Syndrome,* Unpublished thesis for Master's Degree in Social Work, University of British Columbia, 1965. **A.**

68. Auerbach, M., et al. "The Abused Child in Washington, D.C., June 1, 1963–November 30, 1964." Master's thesis, Howard University School of Social Work, June 1965. **F.**

69. Avery, J. "The Battered Child: A Shocking Problem." *Mental Hygiene* 57 (1973):40–43. **A.**

70. Babow, I., and R. Babow. "The World of the Abused Child: A Phenomenological Report." *Life-Threatening Behavior* 4 (Spring 1974):32–42. **A.**

71. Badner, G. "Child Abuse Cases Increase: Pennsylvania." *Pennsylvania School Journal* 124 (October 1975):20–22. **B.**

72. Bain, K., et al. "Child Abuse and Injury." *Military Medicine* 130 (1965): 747–762. **A.**

73. Bain, K. "The Physically Abused Child—Commentary." *Pediatrics* (June 1963). **A.**

74. Bakan, D. *Slaughter of the Innocents.* San Francisco: Jossey-Bass, 1971. **D.**

75. Baker, D., et al. "Special Trauma Problems in Children." *Radiology Clinic of North America* 4 (1966):289–305. **B, D.**

76. Baker, H. "A Question of Witness." *Nursing Times* 67 (1971):691–694. **A, D.**

77. Bakin, H. "Loneliness in Infants." *American Journal of Diseases in Children* 63 (1942):30–40. **A.**

78. ———. *Slaughter of the Innocents: A Study of the Battered Child Phenomenon.* San Francisco: Jossey-Bass, 1971. **A.**

79. Bakwin, H. "Multiple Skeletal Lesions in Young Children Due to Trauma." *Journal of Pediatrics* 40 (1956):7–16. **A.**

80. ———. "Report of the Meeting of the American Humane Society." *Newsletter of the American Academy of Pediatrics* 13, 8 (September-October 1962):3. **C.**

81. Baldwin, A., J. Kalhorn, and F. Breese. "The Appraisal of Parent Behavior." *Psychological Monographs: General and Applied* 299 (1949). **C.**

82. Baldwin, J., and J. Oliver. "Epidemiology and Family Characteristics of Severely Abused Children." *British Journal of Preventive and Social Medicine* 29 (1975):205–221. **C.**

83. Bandler, L. "Casework—A Process of Socialization: Gaines, Limitations, Conclusions." In E. Pavenstedt, *The Drifters: Children of Disorganized Lower-Class Families.* New York: Little, Brown, 1967. **H.**

84. Barbero, G. and E. Shaheen. "Environmental Failure to Thrive: A Clinical View." *Journal of Pediatrics* 71 (1967):639–644. **A.**

85. Barbero, G., et al. "Malidentification of Mother-Baby-Father Relationships Expressed in Infant Failure to Thrive." In *The Neglected Battered Child Syndrome.* New York: Child Welfare League of America Inc., 1963. **A, C, E.**

86. Bard, M. "Training Police as Specialists in Family Crisis Intervention." In G. Sager, and H. Kaplan. *Progress in Group and Family Therapy.* New York: Brunner/Mazel, 1972. **B.**

87. Barmeyer, G., et al. "Traumatic Periostitis in Young Children." *Journal of Pediatrics* 38 (1951):184–190. **A.**

88. Barnes, G., R. Chabon, and L. Hertzber. "Team Treatment for Abusive Families." *Social Casework* 55 (1974):600–611. **E.**

89. Barnett, B. "Battered Babies." *Lancet* 2 (1970):567–568. **A.**

90. ———. "Violent Parents." *Lancet* 2 (1971):1208–1209. **C.**

91. Baron, M., et al. "Neurologic Manifestations of the Battered Child Syndrome." *Pediatrics* 45 (1970):1003–1007. **A.**

92. Barta, R., and N. Smith. "Willful Trauma to Young Children: A Challenge to the Physician." *Clinical Pediatrics* 2 (1963):545–554. **A.**

93. Bates, B., ed. *Research, Demonstration, and Evaluation Studies: Fiscal Year 1974.* Office of Child Development, Department of Health, Education, and Welfare, Washington, D.C., 1974. **H.**

94. Batinich, M. "How School Can Aid the Abused Child: Principal's Role Central in Protecting Children." *Chicago School Journal* 46 (November 1964):57–62. **G.**

95. Bean, J. "The Parents' Center Project: A Multiservice Approach to the Prevention of Child Abuse." *Child Welfare* 277 (May 1971). **G, H.**

96. Bechtold, M. "Silent Partner to a Parent's Brutalities." *School and Community* 52 (November 1965):33. **C.**

97. ———. "That Battered Child Could Be Dead Tomorrow." *Instructor* 77 (April 1968):20. **C.**

98. Becker, T. *Child Protective Services and the Law.* Children's Division, The American Humane Association, Denver, Colorado, 1969. **B, H.**

99. Becker, T. *Due Process in Child Protective Proceedings-Intervention on Behalf of Neglected Children.* American Humane Association, Denver, Colorado. **B, H.**

100. Bell, C., and W. Mlyniec. "Preparing for a Neglect Proceeding: A Guide for the Social Worker." *Public Welfare* 26 (Fall 1974). **A.**

101. Bell, D., W. Graham, and F. White. "Recommendation for Court-Appointed Counsel in Child Abuse Proceedings." *Mississippi Law Journal* 46 (1975):1072–1095. **B.**

102. Bell, G. "Parents Who Abuse Their Children." *Canadian Psychiatry Association Journal* 18 (June 1973):223–228. **C.**

103. Bell, N., and E. Vogel. "The Emotionally Disturbed Child as tne Family Scapegoat." In *A Modern Introduction to the Family.* New York: New York Press, 1968. **A, C.**

104. Bellucci, M. "Group Treatment of Mothers in Child Protection Cases." *Child Welfare* 51 (1972):110–116. **E, H.**

105. Belzer, R. "Child vs. Parent: Erosion of the Immunity Rule." *The Hastings Law Journal* 19 (1967):201–222. **B.**

106. Benedek, E. "Child Custody Laws: Their Psychiatric Implications." *American Journal of Psychiatry* 192 (1972):326–328. **B.**

107. Bennett, F. "The Condition of Farm Workers, 1968." In L. Ferman, et al.,

Poverty in America. Ann Arbor, Michigan: University of Michigan Press, 1968. **G.**

108. Bennie, E. and A. Sclare. "The Battered Child Syndrome." *American Journal of Psychiatry* 125 (1969):975-979. **A.**

109. Benstead, J. "Infantile Subdural Haematoma." *British Medical Journal* 3 (1971):114-115. **A.**

110. Berant, M., et al. "A Pseudo Battered Child: Scurvy and the Battered Child." *Clinical Pediatrics (Philadelphia)* 5 (1966):230-237. **A.**

111. Bergman, A., and R. Haggerty. "The Emergency Clinic: A Study of its Role in a Teaching Hospital." *American Journal of Disabled Children* 104 (1962):36. **D.**

112. Berlow, L. "Recognition and Rescue of the Battered Child." *Hospitals* 41 (1967):58-61. **H.**

113. Bern, J. "Battered Child, the Family and the Community Agency." *California State Bar Journal* 44 (1969):557. **C, D, H.**

114. Besharov, D. "Building a Community Response to Child Abuse and Maltreatment." *Children Today* 4 (September-October 1975):5, 2-4. **D.**

115. Besner, A. "Economic Deprivation in Family Patterns." In M. Sussman, *Sourcebook on Marriage and the Family.* Houghton Mifflin Company, 1968. **C.**

116. Bezzeg, E., et al. "The Role of the Child Care Worker in the Treatment of Severely Burned Children." *Pediatrics* 50 (October 1972):617-624. **D.**

117. Bhattacharya, A. "Multiple Fractures." *Bulletin Calcutta Sch. Trop. Med.* 14 (1966):111-112. **A.**

118. Bhattacharya, A., et al. "Battered Child Syndrome: A Review with a Report of Two Siblings." *Indian Pediatrics* 4 (1967):186-194. **A.**

119. Bialestock, D. "Letter: Custody of Children." *Medical Journal of Australia* 2 (1973):1128. **A.**

120. Biermann, G., and H. Hausler. *Kindeszuchtigung und Kindesmisshandlung: eine Dokumentation."* Reinhardt (1969):161-164. **A, F.**

121. Bilainkin, G. "Children in Peril." *Contemporary Review* 201 (1962):67-68. **A.**

122. Billingsley, A. "Agency Structure and the Commitment to Service." *Public Welfare* 24 (1966):246-251. **A, G.**

123. Billingsley, A. "A Study of Child Neglect and Abuse." University of California School of Social Welfare. Berkeley, California, 1965. **A.**

124. Billingsley, A., and J. Giovannoni. *Children of the Storm.* New York: Harcourt, Brace, Jovanovitch, 1972. **A.**

125. Birch, H. and L. Belmont. "The Problem of Comparing Home Rearing vs. Foster-home Rearing in Defective Children." *Pediatrics* 28 (1961):956. **C, H.**

126. Bird, H. "Battered Babies: A Social and Medical Problem." *Nursing Times* 69 (1973):1552-1554. **A.**

127. Birrell, J. "Where Death Delights to Help the Living. Forensic Medicine-

Cinderella?" *Medical Journal of Australia* 1 (February 7, 1970):253-261.
A.

128. Birrell, R., and J. Birrell. "The Maltreatment Syndrome in Children: A Hospital Survey." *Medical Journal of Australia* 23 (1968):1023-1029.
A, F.

129. Bishop, F. "Children at Risk." *Medical Journal of Australia* 1 (1971):623-628. **A.**

130. Biship, J. "Helping Neglectful Parents." *Annual American Academy* 355 (September 1964):82-89. **E.**

131. Biship, J., B. Burton, and W. Bourke. *An Intensive Casework Project in Child Protective Services.* Denver, Colorado: American Humane Association. **B, H.**

132. Bivibo, N. "Battered Child Syndrome." *The East African Medical Journal* 49 (1972):934-938. **A.**

133. Bleiberg, N. "The Neglected Child and the Child Health Conference." *New York Journal of Medicine* 65 (1965):1880-1885. **A.**

134. Bloch, E. "Feelings That Kill." *Psychoanalysis Review* 52 (1965). **A.**

135. Bloch, H. "Dilemma of Battered Child and Battered Children." *New York State Journal of Medicine* 73 (1973):799-801. **A.**

136. Block, M. "Child Abuse: What Can We Do To Stop It?" *Forecast for Home Economists* 19 (March 1974): F24-6+. **H.**

137. Bloomberg, W., Jr. "A City for Children: the Year 2005." *Childhood Education* 48 (January 1972):4, 170-174. **H.**

138. Blout, J. "Radiologic Seminar CXXXVII: The Battered Child." *The Journal of the Mississippi State Medical Association* 15 (1974):136-138.
A.

139. Blue, M. "The Battered Child Syndrome From a Social Work Viewpoint." *Canadian Journal Public Health* 56 (1965):197-198. **A, C, E, H.**

140. Blumberg, M. "When Parents Hit Out." *Twentieth Century* 173 (1964-65):39-44. **A.**

141. ——. "Psychopathology of the Abusing Parent." *American Journal of Psychotherapy* 28 (1974):21-29. **C.**

142. Boardman, H. "A Project to Rescue Children from Inflicted Injuries." *Social Work* 7 (1962):43-51. **H.**

143. ——. "Who Insures the Child's Right to Health?" *Child Welfare* 42 (1963):120-124. **A, B.**

144. Boardman, H., et al. *The Neglected Battered Child Syndrome: Role Reversal in Parents.* Denver, Colorado: Child Welfare League of America, 1963. **A.**

145. Boehm, B. "Protection Services for Neglected Children." In Alfred Kadushin, *Child Welfare Services: A Sourcebook.* New York: Macmillan, 1970. **H.**

146. ——. "Protective Services for Neglected Children." *Social Work Practice.* Columbus, Ohio: National Conference on Social Welfare, 1967. **A, D.**

147. ——. "The Community and the Social Agency Define Neglect." *Child Welfare* 453 (November 1964). **A.**

148. Boisvert, M. "The Battered Child Syndrome." *Social Casework* 475 (October 1972). **A.**

149. Bolz, W. "The Battered Child Syndrome." *Delaware Medical Journal* 39 (1967): 176-180. **A.**

150. Bonem, G., and P. Reno. "By Bread Alone and Little Bread." *Social Work* 13 (1968): 5-12. **A.**

151. Bongiovi, J., et al. "Pancreatic Pseudocyst Occurring in the Battered Child Syndrome." *Journal of Pediatric Surgery* 4 (1969):220-226. **A.**

152. Borgman, R. "Intelligence and Maternal Inadequacy." *Child Welfare* 48 (1969):301-304. **A, C.**

153. Boulanger, J. "Depression in Childhood." *Canadian Psychiatry Association Journal* (Special Supplement) 11 (1966):S309-S313. **A.**

154. Bourke, W. "Developing An Appropriate Focus in Casework with Families in Which Children are Neglected." *Dissertation Abstracts International* 31 (October 1970):1891. **E.**

155. Bowen, D. "The Role of Radiology and the Identification of Foreign Bodies at Post Mortem Examination." *Journal of Forensic Sciences* 6 (1966):28-32. **D.**

156. Bower, E. "K.I.S.S. and Kids: A Mandate for Prevention." *American Journal of Orthopsychiatry* 42 (July 1972):556-565. **H.**

157. Bowlby, J. *Child Care and the Growth of Love,* 2d ed. Baltimore: Penguin Books, 1965. **A, C.**

158. ——. *Maternal Care and Mental Health,* 2d Ed. Monograph Series No. 2. Geneva, Switzerland: World Health Organization, 1952. **A, C.**

159. ——. "Processes of Mourning." *International Journal of Psychoanalytic Psychotherapy* 42 (July–October 1961):317. **A.**

160. Brandeis University Papers in Social Welfare. *Nationwide Survey of Legally Reported Physical Abuse in Children.* Publication No. 15. Brandeis University, 1968. **B.**

161. Brandwein, H. "The Battered Child: A Definite and Significant Factor in Mental Retardation." *Mental Retardation* 11 (October 1973):5, 50-51. **D.**

162. Branigan, E., et al. "An Exploratory Study of the Neglected-Battered Child Syndrome." Ph.D. dissertation, Boston College School of Social Work, 1964. **A.**

163. Bratu, M., et al. "Jejunal Hematoma, Child Abuse, and Felson's Sign." *Connecticut Medicine* 34 (1970):261-264. **A.**

164. Braun, I., E. Braun, and C. Simonds. "The Mistreated Child." *California Medicine* 99 (1963):98-103. **A.**

165. Brem, J. "Child Abuse Control Centers: A Project for the Academy?" *Pediatrics* 45 (1970):894-895. **H.**

166. Brenneman, G. "Battered Child Syndrome." *Alaska Medicine* 10 (1968): 175-178. **A.**

167. Breslow, L. "Proposals for Achieving More Adequate Health Care for Children and Youth." *American Journal of Public Health* (Supplement) 60 (April 1970):106–122. **B, G.**

168. Brett, D. "The Battered and Abused Child Syndrome." Ph.D. dissertation, University of California, Berkeley, 1966. **A.**

169. Brieland, D. "Protective Services and Child Abuse." *Social Service Review* 40 (1966):4, 369–377. **A, H.**

170. British Medical Association. *Cruelty to and Neglect of Children.* Report of a Joint Committee of the British Medical Association and the Magistrates' Association. London, England: British Medical Association, 1956. **A.**

171. British Medical Journal. "Battered Babies." *British Medical Journal* 3 (1969):667–668. **A.**

172. British Medical Journal. "Cruelty to Children." *British Medical Journal* 5372 (1963):1544–1545. **A.**

173. ——. "Deliberate Injury to Children." *British Medical Journal* 4 (1973): 61–62. **A.**

174. ——. "Non-accidental Injury to Children." *British Medical Journal* 4 (1973):96–97. **A.**

175. ——. "Deliberate Injury of Children." *British Medical Journal* 4 (1973): 61–62. **A.**

176. ——. "Non-Accidental Injury in Children." *British Medical Journal* 4 (1973):656–660. **A.**

177. ——. "The Battered Baby." Committee on Accidents in Childhood, *British Medical Journal* 5487 (1966):601–603. **A.**

178. ——. "Welfare of Children." *British Medical Journal* 5360 (September 28, 1963):761–762. **A.**

179. Broadhurst, D. "Project Protection: A School Program." *Children Today* 4 (May–June 1975):22–25. **G, H.**

180. ——. "School Program to Combat Child Abuse: Montgomery County, Maryland." *Education Digest* 41 (October 1975):20–23. **G, H.**

181. Broadhurst, D., and M. Howard. "More About Project Protection." *Childhood Education* 52 (November–December 1975):67–69. **H.**

182. Brody, S. *Patterns of Mothering.* New York: International University Press, 1956. **C.**

183. Broeck, E. "Extended Family Center: A Home Away From Home For Abused Children And Their Parents." *Children Today* 3 (March 1974):2–6. **D, E.**

184. Brown, B. "Assault and Battery in Childhood." *Canadian Association of Medical Students and Interns Journal* 24 (1965):18. **A.**

185. Brown, H. "Background and Promise: Juvenile Courts and the Gault Decision." *Children* 15 (1968):87–89. **B.**

186. Brown, J. and R. Daniels. "Some Observations on Abusive Parents." *Child Welfare* 47 (1968):89–94. **C.**

187. Brown, M., and M. Pappas. "Eight Children with Suspected Inflicted Injury. A Follow-up Pilot Study." Master's thesis, University of Southern California School of Social Work, Los Angeles, June 1965. **D.**

188. Brown, R. "Battered Child." *Medical Trial Technique Quarterly* 20 (1974): 272-281. **B, D.**

189. Brown, R., and E. Fox. "Medical and Legal Aspects of the Battered Child Syndrome." *Chicago-Kent Law Review* 50 (1973):45-84. **A, B, D.**

190. Browndale International. "Reaching Out." Program Needed to Aid Battered Babies and Their Parents. *Involvement.* Ontario, Canada: Browndale International, January–February 1973. **H.**

191. Browne, K. "Willful Abuse of Children." *Nebraska Medical Journal* 50 (1965):598-599. **A.**

192. Bryand, H, et al. "Physical Abuse of Children—An Agency Study." *Child Welfare* (March 1963):125. **A.**

193. Buell, B. *Is Prevention Possible?* National Conference on Social Welfare, San Francisco, May 25, 1959. **H.**

194. Buell, B., et al. "Reorganizing to Prevent and Control Disordered Behaviour." *Mental Hygiene* 42 (April 1958):155-194. **D, H.**

195. Buglass, R. "Parents With Emotional Problems." *Nursing Times* 67 (1971): 1000-1001. **C.**

196. Buist, N. "Letter: Deliberate Injury of Children." *British Medical Journal* 4 (1973):739. **A.**

197. ——. "Violent Parents." *Lancet* 1 (January 1, 1972):36. **C.**

198. Bullard, D., Jr., et al. "Failure to Thrive in the 'Neglected' Child." *American Journal of Orthopsychiatry* 37 (1967):680-690. **A, C.**

199. Bullerdickcorey, E., C. Miller, and F. Widlake. "Factors Contributing to Child Abuse." *Nursing Research* 24 (4):293-295, 1975. **A.**

200. Burke, K. "Evidentiary Problems of Proof in Child Abuse Cases—Why Family and Juvenile Courts Fail." *Journal of Family Law* 13 (1973):819-852. **B.**

201. Burland, C., et al. "Child Abuse: One Tree in the Forest." *Child Welfare* 585 (November 1973). **A.**

202. Burlingham, D. and A. Freud. *Infants Without Families.* New York: International Universities Press, 1944. **A, C.**

203. Burns, A., et al. *Child Abuse and Neglect in Suffolk County.* London, England: Edmond Publishing Company; o.p. **F.**

204. Burns, R. "The Battered Child Syndrome." *Louisiana State Medical Society* 115 (1963):332-334. **A.**

205. Burt, M., and R. Balyeat. "New System for Improving Care of Neglected and Abused Children." *Child Welfare* 53 (1974):167-179. **D, H.**

206. Burt, R. "Protecting Children From Their Families and Themselves: State Laws and the Constitution." *Journal of Youth and Adolescence* 1 (1972): 91-111. **B, C, D, E.**

207. Burton, L. *Vulnerable Children.* New York: Schocken, 1968. **A.**

208. Buttenwieser, H. "Children Are Not Chattels." *Trial Law Quarterly* 8 (1972):28-29, 36. **A, B.**

209. Bwibo, N. "Battered Child Syndrome." *East African Medical Journal* 48 (1971):56-61. **A.**

210. ———. "Battered Child Syndrome." *East African Medical Journal* 49 (1972):934-938. **A.**

211. Bynum, A. "A Report on the Battered Child—Indiana, 1966." *Journal of the Indiana Medical Association* 60 (April 1967):469. **A, F.**

212. Caffey, J. "Infantile Cortical Hyperostosis." *Journal of Pediatrics* 29 (November 1946):541-559. **D.**

213. ———. *Journal of Pediatric X-Ray Diagnosis,* 2d. ed. Chicago: Year Book Publishers, 1950. **D.**

214. ———. "Multiple Fractures in the Long Bones of Infants Suffering From Chronic Subdural Hematoma." *American Journal of Roentgenology* 56 (1946):163-173. **D.**

215. ———. "On the Theory and Practice of Shaking Children. Its Potential Residue Effects of Permanent Brain Damage and Mental Retardation." *American Journal of Diseased Children* 124 (1972):161-169. **A.**

216. ———. "The Parent-Infant Traumatic Stress Syndrome." *American Journal Roentgenology Radium Therapy Nuclear Medicine* 114 (1972):218-229. **D.**

217. ———. "The Whiplash Shaken Infant Syndrome: Manual Shaking by the Extremities with Whiplash-Induced Intracranial and Intraocular Bleedings, Linked with Residual Permanent Brain Damage and Mental Retardation." *Journal of Pediatrics* 54 (October 1974):396-403. **D.**

218. ———. "Significance of the History in the Diagnosis of Traumatic Injury to Children." *Journal of Pediatrics* 67 (1965):1008-1014. **A.**

219. ———; "Some Traumatic Lesions in Growing Bones Other than Fractures and Dislocations: Clinical and Radiological Features." *British Journal of Radiology* 30 (1957):225-238. **D.**

220. ———. "Traumatic Cupping of the Metaphyses of Growing Bones." *American Journal of Roentgenology* 108 (1970):451-460. **D.**

221. Caldwell, Bettye M. "The Effects of Psychosocial Deprivation on Human Development in Infancy." *Merrill-Palmer Quarterly of Behavior and Development* 16 (1970):260. **A.**

222. Calef, V. "The Hostility of Parents to Children: Some Notes on Infertility, Child Abuse and Abortion." *International Journal of Psychoanalytic Psychotherapy* 1 (1972):76-96. **C.**

223. California State Health and Welfare Agency. *California Child Day Care Licensing Task Force: Report and Recommendations.* Office of Educational Liaison, California State Health and Welfare Agency, Sacramento, May 31, 1975. **G.**

224. California Law Review. "California Legislative Approach to Problems of Willful Child Abuse." *California Law Review* 54 (1966):1805. **B.**

225. Calkins, C., et al. "Children's Rights: An Introductory Sociological Over-View." *Peabody Journal of Education* 50 (1973):89-109. **A, B, F.**

226. Callaghan, K., et al. "Practical Management of the Battered Baby Syndrome." *Medical Journal of Australia* 1 (1970):1282-1284. **H.**

227. Cameron, I. and L. Rae. *Atlas of the Battered Child Syndrome.* N.Y.: Longman Publishing Company, 1975. **F.**

228. Cameron, J., H. Johnson, and F. Camps. "Battered Child Syndrome." *Medicine, Science and the Law* 6 (1966):2-21. **A, B, D.**

229. Cameron, J.M. "The Battered Baby." *Nursing Mirror and Midwives Journal* 134 (1972):32-38. **A.**

230. ———. "The Battered Child Syndrome." *Practitioner* 209 (1972):302-310. **A.**

231. Cameron, J.S. "Role of the Child Protective Organization." *Pediatrics* 51 (Supplement 4):793-795, 1973. **B, D, E, H.**

232. Canadian Medical Association Journal. "Battered Babies." *Canadian Medical Association Journal* 101 (1969):98. **A.**

233. Canadian Welfare Council "Action Against Child Abuse." *Canadian Welfare Council* 50 (1974):22-23. **H.**

234. ———. "Child Abuse." *Canadian Welfare Council* 51 (1975):15-16. **A.**

235. ———. "Child Protection in Canada." Ottawa: Canadian Welfare Council, 1, 1954. **A, H.**

236. Carter, J. "Battered Children." *British Journal of Social Work* 5 (1975): 370-372. **A.**

237. Cary, A., and M. Reveal. "Prevention and Detection of Emotional Disturbances in Preschool Children." *American Journal of Orthopsychiatry* 37 (1967):719-724. **A, H.**

238. Casgrove, J. "Management and Follow-Up of Child Abuse." *Journal of Medical Societies of the State of New Jersey* 69 (1972):27-30. **H.**

239. Caskey, O., and I. Richardson. "Understanding and Helping Child Abusing Parents." *Elementary School Guidance and Counseling* (March 1975): 196-207. **E.**

240. Castle, R., and A. Kerr. "A Study of Suspected Child Abuse." National Society for the Prevention of Cruelty to Children, London, 1972. **H.**

241. Catholic Lawyer. "Child Abuse: Another Attempt at Solving the Problem." *Catholic Lawyer* 13 (1967):331. **A, B, D, H.**

242. Caulfield, E. *The Infant Welfare Movement in the Eighteenth Century.* New York: Paul Hoeber, 1931. **A.**

243. Centre D'etude de la Delinquance Juvenile. *Child Victims of Bad Treatment.* Brussels: *Centre D'etude de la Delinquance Juvenile,* 1971. **A, F.**

244. Chabon, M., et al. "The Problem of Child Abuse: A Community Hospital Approach." *Maryland State Medical Journal* 22 (1973):50-55. **A, H.**

245. Chandra, R. "The Battered Child." *Indian Journal of Pediatrics* 35 (1968): 365. **A.**

246. Chaneles, S., and D. Brieland. *Sexual Abuse of Children: Implications for Casework.* Denver, Colorado: Children's Division, The American Humane Association, 1967. **A.**

247. Chase, H., and H. Martin. "Undernutrition and Child Development." *New England Journal of Medicine* 282 (1970):933-939. **A.**

248. Chase, N. "Child is Being Beaten." *New Republic,* November 22, 1975, pp. 28-30. **A.**

249. Cheney, K. *A Suggested Statute and Policy for Child Welfare Protective Services in Connecticut.* A Report for the Legislature (State of Connecticut), May 1964. **B.**

250. ——. "Safeguarding Legal Rights in Providing Protective Services." *Children* 13 (1966):86-92. **B.**

251. Cherry, B., et al. "Obstacles to the Delivery of Medical Care to Children of Neglecting Parents." *American Journal of Public Health* 61 (1971): 568-573. **D, H.**

252. Chess, S., and A. Thomas. *Annual Progress in Child Psychiatry and Child Development.* New York: Brunner-Mazel, 1968. **A.**

253. ——. "The Abused Child." In S. Chess and A. Thomas, *Annual Progress in Child Psychiatry and Child Development.* New York: Brunner-Mazel, 1968. **A.**

254. Chesser, E. *Cruelty to Children.* New York: Philosophical Library, 1952. **A.**

255. Child Welfare League of America. *Child Welfare League of America Standards for Child Protective Service—1960.* New York: Child Welfare League of America (Revised, 1973). **A.**

256. ——. *Child Protective Service. A Bibliography of CWLA Publications 1960-1972.* New York: Child Welfare League of America, 1972. **H.**

257. ——. *Child Welfare Research: Summaries of Research Conducted at the Child Welfare League of America.* New York: Child Welfare League of America, 1969. **H.**

258. ——. *The Neglected Battered-Child Syndrome: Role Reversal in Parents.* New York: Child Welfare League of America, July, 1963. **A.**

259. Childhood Education. "Protecting Children: Freeing Them from Mental and Physical Abuse: Symposium." *Childhood Education* 52 (November 1975):58-75. **A.**

260. Children. "Identification of Abused Children." *Children* 10 (September–October 1963):180-184. **A.**

261. Children and Family Services. *Illinois Child Abuse Act: A Survey of the First Year.* Children and Family Services, Division of Planning, Research and Statistics, Springfield, Illinois, November 1966. **A.**

262. Children's Hospital Medical Center. "Draft Report of Phase I of the

Family Development Study." Children's Hospital Medical Center, Boston, Massachusetts, September 1974. **A, C.**

263. Children Today. "Child-Abuse Problem." *Children Today* 17 (July 1973): 32. **A.**

264. ———. "Working with Abusive Parents. A Parent's View—An Interview with Jolly K." *Children Today* 4:6-9. **E.**

265. Children's Aid Society of Metropolitan Toronto. "A Child Protection Service on a 24-Hour, 365-Day Basis." *Our Children* (1), 1968-69. Children's Aid Society of Metropolitan Toronto. **H.**

266. Children's Bureau. *The Abused Child: Principles and Suggested Language on Reporting the Physically Abused Child.* Washington, D.C.: U.S. Government Printing Office, 1962. **A, B.**

267. ———. *Bibliography on the Battered Child.* Clearinghouse on Research in Child Life. Washington, D.C.: U.S. Government Printing Office, 1969. **A.**

268. ———. *The Child Abuse Reporting Laws—A Tabular View.* Washington, D.C.: U.S. Government Printing Office, 1966. **B**

269. Chilton, R. "Family Disruption, Delinquent Conduct and the Effect of Subclassification." *American Sociological Review* 37 (1972): 93-99. **A, C.**

270. Christenson, D., and J. Fuerst. *Child Abuse Alternatives and You.* St. Paul, Minnesota: SEP Consultants, Inc., 1974. **H.**

271. Christian Century. "Helping Physicians Protect Children: Illinois Law to Exempt Physicians from Libel Suits by Parents." *Christian Century* 82 (April 28, 1965):516. **B, C.**

272. Christy, D., and N. Paget. *Innovative Approaches in Child Protective Services.* Denver, Colorado: Children's Division, American Humane Association. **H.**

273. Ciano, M. "Ohio's Mandatory Reporting Statute for Cases of Child Abuse." *Western Reserve Law Review* 18 (1967):1405-1413. **B.**

274. Citizens' Board of Inquiry into Hunger and Malnutrition in the United States. "Hunger U.S.A.: A Report." Washington, D.C.: New Community Press, 1968. **A.**

275. Citizen's Committee for Children of New York. *Child Abuse (A Positive Statement).* New York: Citizen's Committee for Children of New York, March 1964. **A.**

276. Clinical Pediatrics. "The Intricacies of Violence Against Children in American Society." *Clinical Pediatrics* 10 (1971):557-558. **A.**

277. Clarke, D., and J. Koluchova. "Severe Deprivation in Twins: A Case Study." *Journal of Child Psychology and Psychiatry* 13 (June 1972):103-114. **A.**

278. Class, N. "Neglect, Social Deviance and Community Actions." *National Probation and Parole Association Journal* 6 (January 1960):17-23. **A, H.**

279. Cleveland-Marshall Law Review. "Acting in Loco Parentis as a Defense to Assault and Battery." *Cleveland-Marshall Law Review* 16 (1967):39. **B, C, D.**

280. Coburn, D. "Child-Parent Communications: Spare the Privilege and Spoil the Child." *Dickinson Law Review* 74 (1970):599-633. **B.**

281. Cochrane, W. "The Battered Child Syndrome." *Canadian Journal of Public Health* 56 (1965):193-196. **A.**

282. Cohen, M., R. Mulford, and E. Philbrick. *Neglecting Parents—A Study of Psychosocial Characteristics.* Denver, Colorado: American Humane Association, 1964. **A, E.**

283. Cohen, M., et al. "Psychologic Aspects of the Maltreatment Syndrome of Childhood." *Journal of Pediatrics* 69 (1966):279-284. **A.**

284. Cohen, S., and A. Sussman. "Incidence of Child Abuse in United States." *Child Welfare* 54 (1975):432-443. **A, F.**

285. Cohn, A., et al. "Evaluating Innovative Treatment Programs." *Children Today* 4 (May–June 1975):10-12. **H.**

286. Colclough, I. "Victorian Government's Report on Child Abuse, A Re-investigation." *Medical Journal of Australia* 2 (1972):1491-1497. **A.**

287. Coleman, R., and S. Provence. "Developmental Retardation (Hospitalism) in Infants Living in Families." *Journal of Pediatrics* 19 (1957):285-292. **A, C.**

288. Coleman, W. "Occupational-Therapy and Child Abuse." *American Journal of Occupational Therapy* 29 (1975):412-417. **E.**

289. Coles, R. *Children of Crisis: Migrants, Sharecroppers, Mountaineers,* Vol. II. Boston: Little, Brown, 1971. **A.**

290. ——. "Terror-Struck Children." *The New Republic,* May 30, 1964. **A.**

291. Collins, C. "On the Dangers of Shaking Young Children." *Child Welfare* 53 (March 1974):143-146. **D.**

292. Collins, J. "The Role of the Law Enforcement Agency." In R. Helfer and C. Kempe, *The Battered Child.* Chicago and London: University of Chicago Press, 1968. **B.**

293. Colorado State Department of Public Welfare Library. "Innocent By-standers—Abused and Neglected Children." *The Library,* 1967. **A.**

294. Colorado State Department of Social Services. "Abused and Neglected Children." *The Library Counselor,* Colorado State Department of Social Services, 27: #4, Fall, 1972.

295. Colorado State Department of Social Services Library. "What Are We Doing to Defend Them? Abused and Neglected Children." *Library Counselor* 27 (1972). **D.**

296. Columbia Journal of Law and Social Problems. "An Appraisal of New York's Statutory Response to the Problem of Child Abuse." *Columbia Journal of Law and Social Problems* 7 (1971):51-74. **B.**

297. ——. "Representation in Child-Neglect Cases: Are Parents Neglected?" *Columbia Journal of Law and Social Problems* 4 (1968): 230-254. **B.**

298. Columbia Law Review. "Child Neglect: Due Process for the Parent." *Columbia Law Review* 70 (1970):465. **B.**

299. Congress of the United States, Senate, Committee on Labor and Public Welfare, *Child Abuse Prevention and Treatment Act,* 1973. **B.**

300. ———. *Child Abuse Prevention and Treatment Act,* 1974. **B.**

301. Connecticut Law Review. "Emotional Neglect in Connecticut." *Connecticut Law Review* 5 (1972):100. **B, F.**

302. ———. "Post-Commitment Custody of Neglected Children." *Connecticut Law Review* 4 (1971):143. **B, F.**

303. Connell, J. "The Devil's Battered Children." *Journal of the Kansas Medical Society* 64 (1963):385–391. **A.**

304. Constable, H., and B. Gans. "Unnecessary X-rays?" *British Medical Journal* 1 (1970):564. **C.**

305. Cooke, Lena, et al. *Round the Clock Coverage in Child Protective services.* Denver, Colorado: American Humane Association. **D, H.**

306. Cooksey, C. "The Battered Child—Louisiana's Response to the Cry." *Loyola Law Review* 17 (1970–71):372–394. **A.**

307. Corbett, J. "A Psychiatrist Reviews the Battered Child Syndrome and Mandatory Reporting Legislation." *Northwest Medicine* 63 (1964):920–922. **A, B.**

308. Cornell Law Review. "Domestic Relations—Appointment of Counsel for the Abused Child—Statutory Schemes and the New York Approach." *Cornell Law Review* 58 (1972):177. **B.**

309. ———. "New York's Child Abuse Laws: Inadequacies in the Present Statutory Structure." *Cornell Law Review* 55 (1970):298. **B.**

310. Cosgrove, J. "Management and Follow-up of Child Abuse." *The Journal of the Medical Society of New Jersey* 69 (1972):27–30. **A, D.**

311. Costin, L., ed. "Children's Guardianship." In *Child Welfare: Policies and Practices.* New York: McGraw Hill, 1972. **C, H.**

312. ———. "Protecting Children from Neglect and Abuse." In *Child Welfare: Policies and Practices.* New York: McGraw Hill, 1972. **H.**

313. ———. "The Child and the Court." In *Child Welfare: Policies and Practices.* New York: McGraw Hill, 1972. **B, D.**

314. Cotnam, H. "The Battered Child Syndrome or The Maltreatment Syndrome in Children." *Canadian Association of Medical Students and Interns Journal* 24 (Octover 1965):12. **A.**

315. Coughlin, B. "The Rights of Children." *Child Welfare* 47 (1968):133–142. **A, B.**

316. Council of State Governments. "Physical Abuse of Children: Suggested State Legislation." *Council of State Governments* 24 (1965):66–68. **B.**

317. Court, J. "Battering Parents." *Social Work London* 26 (1969):20–24. **C.**

318. ———. "The Battered Child." *Medical Social Work* 22 (1969):11–22. **A.**

319. ———. "The Battered Child Syndrome: The need for a multi-disciplinary approach." *Nursing Times* 67 (1971):659–661. **H.**

320. ———. "Some Reflections on Non-accidental Injury to Young Children." *Social Work Service* (December 1973). **A.**

321. Court, J., and A. Kerr. "The Battered Child Syndrome. 2. A Preventable Disease." *Nursing Times* 67 (1971):695-697. **A, H.**

322. Courter, E. "Physicians Must Co-operate in Child Abuse Cases." *Michigan Medicine* 72 (1973):361-362. **A, B, H.**

323. Cremin, B. "Battered Baby Syndrome." *South African Medical Journal* 44 (1970):1044. **A.**

324. Criswell, H. "Why Do They Beat Their Child?" *Human Needs* 1 (March 1973):5-7. **C.**

325. Cromwell, J., and E. Perkins. "The Battered Child—Dilemmas in Management." *Medical Social Work* 22 (1969):160-168. **H.**

326. Crumrine, J., and J. Cruz. "Two A Day?" *Economist* 254 (March 29, 1975):27-28. **A.**

327. Cunningham, P., M. Gebel, and A. Richter. "Treatment Methods with Child Abusers—Experience Survey." *Smith College Studies in Social Work* 43 (1972):56-57. **E.**

328. Curphey, T. "The Battered Child Syndrome. Responsibilities of the Pathologist." *California Medicine* 102 (1965):102-104. **D.**

329. Curran, W. "The Revolution in American Criminal Law: Its Significance for Psychiatric Diagnosis and Treatment." *American Journal of Public Health* 58 (1968):2209-2216. **B, D.**

330. Currents in Public Health. "Report of a Meeting on Physical Abuse of Infants and Young Children." *Currents in Public Health* II (9), 1962. **A.**

331. ——. "The Battered Child Syndrome." *Currents in Public Health* 2 (October 1962):1. **A.**

332. Currie, J. "A Psychiatric Assessment of the Battered Child Syndrome." *South African Medical Journal* 44 (1970):635-639. **A.**

333. Curtis, G. "Violence Breeds Violence Perhaps?" *American Journal of Psychiatry* 120 (1963):386-387. **A.**

334. Cushing, G. "Work of Societies for the Prevention of Cruelty to Children Essential in the Prevention of Crime." *Conference of Charitable Foundations* 1906:106-111. **B, H.**

335. D'Agostino, P. "Dysfunctioning Families and Child Abuse: The Need for an Inter-agency Effort." *Public Welfare* 30 (1972):14-17. **C, H.**

336. D'Ambrosio, R. *No Language But A Cry.* Garden City, New Jersey: Doubleday, 1970. **A.**

337. Dale, B. "Willful Child Abuse and State Reporting Statutes." *University of Miami Law Review* 23 (1969):283. **B.**

338. Dalton, K. "Children's Hospital Admissions and Mother's Menstruation." *British Medical Journal* 2 (1970):27. **D.**

339. Danckwerth, E. "Techniques of Child Abuse Investigations." *Police Chief* 43 (1976):62-64. **B.**

340. Daniel, G. "Child-Abusers: Parents Anonymous Organization." *PTA Magazine* 68 (September 1973):32-35. **E.**

341. Darity, W., and C. Turner. "Research Findings Related to Sterilization: Attitudes of Black Americans." *American Journal of Orthopsychiatry* 44 (1974):184-185. **F, H.**

342. David, C. "Use of Confrontation Technique in Battered Child Syndrome." *American Journal of Psychotherapy* 28 (1974):543-552. **E.**

343. David, L. "The Shocking Price of Parental Anger." *Good Housekeeping,* March 1964, pp. 181-186. **C.**

344. Davie, R., N. Butler, and H. Goldstein. *From Birth to Seven.* New York: Longman, 1972. **A.**

345. Davies, J., and J. Jorgensen. "Battered but Not Defeated: The Story of an Abused Child and Positive Casework." *Child Welfare* 101 (February 1970). **A.**

346. Davis, K. "Extreme Social Isolation of a Child." *American Journal of Sociology* 45 (1940):554-565. **A.**

347. ———. "Final Note on a Case of Extreme Isolation." *American Journal of Sociology* 52 (March 1974):432-437. **A.**

348. Davoren, E. "Foster Placement of Abused Children." *Children Today* 4 (May-June 1975):41. **C, D.**

349. ———. "The Role of the Social Worker." In R. Helfer and C. Kempe, eds., *The Battered Child.* Chicago and London: University of Chicago Press, 1968. **B, D, E, H.**

350. ———. "Working with Abusive Parents: A Social Worker's View." *Children Today* 4 (May-June 1975):2. **E.**

351. Day Care Council. *Children at Risk: The Growing Problem of Child Abuse.* New York: Day Care Council of New York, 1972. **A.**

352. Debenham, A. "Cruelty and Neglect." In A. Debenham, *Innocent Victims,* Sydney, Australia: Edwards and Shaw, 1969. **A.**

353. DeCourcy, P., and J. DeCourcy. *A Silent Tragedy: Child Abuse in the Community.* Pt. Washington, New York: Alfred, 1973. **A.**

354. DeFrancis, V. *Accent on Prevention.* Denver, Colorado: American Humane Association, 1975. **H.**

355. ———. "Child Abuse—Preview of a Nationwide Survey." Presented at National Conference on Social Welfare. Denver, Colorado: American Humane Association, May 1963. **A.**

356. ———. "Child Abuse—The Legislative Response." *Denver Law Journal* 44 (1967):3. **B.**

357. ———. *Child Abuse Legislation: Analysis of Reporting Laws in the United States.* Part I. Denver, Colorado: Children's Division, American Humane Association, 1966. **B.**

358. ———. *Child Abuse Legislation in the 1970s.* Denver, Colorado: Children's Division, American Humane Association, 1970. **B.**

359. ———. *Child Protective Services—A National Survey.* Denver, Colorado: Children's Division, American Humane Association, 1974. **D, H.**

360. ———. *Child Protective Services in the United States.* Denver, Colorado: Children's Division, American Humane Association, 1956. **D.**

361. ———. "Child Protective Services—1967." *Juvenile Court Judges Journal* 19 (1968):24. **B, D, E, H.**

362. ———. *Children Who Were Helped—Through Child Protective Services.* Denver, Colorado: Children's Division, American Humane Association, 1970. **A.**

363. ———. *Community Cooperation for Better Child Protection.* Denver, Colorado: Children's Division, American Humane Association. 1972. **D, H.**

364. ———. *Guidelines for Legislation to Protect the Battered Child.* Denver, Colorado: Children's Division, American Humane Association, 1975. **D, H.**

365. ———. *Interpreting Child Protective Services.* Denver, Colorado: Children's Division, American Humane Association, 1975. **B.**

366. ———. *Let's Get Technical, The "Why and What" of Child Protective Services.* Denver, Colorado: Children's Division, American Humane Association, 1968. **D, H.**

367. ———. *No Substitute for Child Protection.* Denver, Colorado: Children's Division, American Humane Association, 1965. **C, D.**

368. ———. *Preview of a Nationwide Survey, 1963.* Denver, Colorado: Children's Division, American Humane Association, 1964. **A.**

369. ———. *Protecting the Child Victim of Sex Crimes Committed by Adults.* Denver, Colorado: Children's Division, American Humane Association, 1969. **D, H.**

370. ———. *Protective Services and Community Expectations.* Denver, Colorado: Children's Division, American Humane Association, 1969. **D, H.**

371. ———. *Review of Legislation to Protect the Battered Child: A Study of Laws Enacted in 1963.* Denver, Colorado: Children's Division, American Humane Association, 1964. **C.**

372. ———. *Speaking Out for Child Protection.* Denver, Colorado: Children's Division, American Humane Association, 1973. **D, H.**

373. ———. *Special Skills in Child Protective Services.* Denver, Colorado: Children's Division, American Humane Association, 1973. **D, H.**

374. ———. *Termination of Parental Rights—Balancing the Inequities.* Denver, Colorado: Children's Division, American Humane Association, 1969. **B, D, E, H.**

375. ———. *The Court and Protective Services.* Denver, Colorado: Children's Division, American Humane Association, 1972. **B, D, H.**

376. ———. *The Fundamentals of Child Protection.* Denver, Colorado: Children's Division, American Humane Association, 1955. **D, H.**

377. ———. "The Status of Child Protective Services: A National Dilemma." In C. Kempe and R. Helfer, *Helping the Battered Child and His Family.* Philadelphia and Toronto: J.B. Lippincott, 1972. **D, E, H.**

378. ———. The Battered Child—A Role for the Juvenile Court, The Legislature

and the Child Welfare Agency." *Juvenile Court Judges Journal* 14 (1963). **B, D.**

379. ——. "Protecting the Child Victim of Sex Crimes Committed by Adults." *Federal Probation* 35 (1971):15. **D.**

380. ——. "Parents Who Abuse Children." *P.T.A. Magazine* 58 (3):16-18, November 1963. **C.**

381. ——. "Laws for Mandatory Reporting of Child Abuse Cases." *State Government* 39 (1):8-13, Winter 1966. **B.**

382. DeFrancis, V., and E. InNemy. "Child Abuse: Does It Stem fron Nation's Ills and Its Culture." *New York Times,* August 16, 1971, p. 16. **B.**

383. DeFrancis, V., and B. Oviatt. *The Status of Child Protection—A National Dilemma.* Denver, Colorado: Children's Division, American Humane Association, 1968. **G.**

384. DeFrancis, V., et al. *Marshalling Community Services on Behalf of the Abused Child.* Denver, Colorado: Children's Division, American Humane Association, 1966. **A, D, H.**

385. ——. "Preventing Maltreatment of Children: a Symposium." *Public Welfare,* July 1966, p. 228. **A.**

386. Degas, R., et al. "Silverman's Syndrome, So-Called Battered Child Syndrome (A Case)." *(Paris) Bulletin de la Societé Francaise de Dermatologie et de Syphiligarie* 78 (1971):288-289. **G.**

387. Delaney, D. "The Physically Abused Child." *World Medical Journal* 13 (September–October 1966):145. **A.**

388. Delaney, J. "The Battered Child and the Law." In C. Kempe and R. Helfer, *Helping the Battered Child and His Family.* Philadelphia and Toronto: J.B. Lippincott, 1972. **B, D.**

389. Delassel, C. "Children Abandoned in Paris in 18th Century." *Annales-Economies Societes Civilizations,* 30 (1975):187-218. **F.**

390. Delnero, H., et al. "The Medical Center Child Abuse Consultation Team." In C. Kempe and R. Helfer, *Helping the Battered Child and His Family.* Philadelphia and Toronto: J.B. Lippincott, 1972. **A, D, E, H.**

391. Delsordo, J. "Protective Casework for Abused Children." *Children* 10 (1963):213-218. **H.**

392. Dembitz, N. "Child Abuse and the Law—Fact and Fiction." *Record of the Association of the Bar of the City of New York* 24 (1969):613. **B.**

393. Dennis, J. "Child Abuse and the Physician's Responsibility." *Post-Graduate Medicine* 35 (1964):446. **A, B, D.**

394. Densen-Gerber, J., and C. Rohns. "Drug-addicted Parents and Child Abuse." *Contemporary Drug Problems* 2 (1973):683-695. **C.**

395. Denver Post. *Plain Talk About Child Abuse.* Denver, Colorado: Children's Division, American Humane Association, 1972. **A.**

396. Denzine, N. "Children and Their Caretakers." *Transaction/Social Science and Modern Society* 8 (1971): 62. **C.**

397. ———. "Wednesday's Child." *Transaction/Social Science and Modern Society* 8 (1971):28. **A.**

398. DePaul Law Review. "Privileged Communication—Abrogation of the Physician-Patient Privilege to Protect the Battered Child." *DePaul Law Review* 15 (1966):453. **A, B, D.**

399. Deutsch, M. "The Disadvantaged Child and the Learning Process." In L. Ferman, *Poverty in America.* Ann Arbor, Michigan: University of Michigan Press, 1961. **A.**

400. DeWees, P. "The Role of the Family Doctor in the Social Problem of Child Abuse: Comments on New Legislation Affecting the Legal Immunity of Physicians." *North Carolina Medical Journal* 27 (August 1966):385-388. **D.**

401. Diggle, G., et al. "Child Injury Intensive Monitoring System" *British Medical Journal* 3 (1973):334-336. **H.**

402. Dine, M., and S. Stark. "Slaughter of the Innocents." *Journal of American Medical Association,* 223 (1973):81-82. **A, C.**

403. Dine, M. "Tranquilizer Poisoning: An Example of Child Abuse." *Pediatrics* 36 (1965):782-785. **A, C.**

404. Dodge, P. *Medical Implications of Physical Abuse of Children in Protecting the Battered Child.* Denver, Colorado: Children's Division, American Humane Association, 1962. **D.**

405. Doll, P. "Medical Professional Secrecy and Protection of Martyred Childhood." (Law No. 71-446 of the 15th June 1971.) *(Paris) Medecine Legal et Dammage Corporel* 4 (July–September 1971):217-221. **B.**

406. Donovan, T. "The Legal Response to Child Abuse." *William and Mary Law Review* 11 (1970):960-987. **B.**

407. Donnon, S., et al. "Suspected Child Abuse: Experience in Guy's Hospital Accident and Emergency Department." *Guy's Hospital Report* 121 (1972):295-298. **A.**

408. Downs, W. "Juvenile Courts and the Gault Decision." *Children* 15 (1968): 90-96. **B.**

409. ———. "The Meaning and Handling of Child Neglect—A Legal View." *Child Welfare* (March 1963). **B.**

410. Doxiadis, S. "Mothering and Frederick II." *Clinical Pediatrics* 9 (1970): 565. **A.**

411. Drews, K. "The Child and His School." In C. Kempe and R. Helfer, *Helping the Battered Child and His Family.* Philadelphia and Toronto: J.B. Lippincott, 1972. **G.**

412. Driscoll, P. "Child Abuse Legal Aspects of the Physician's Duty." In *Trial and Tort Trends of 1967.* New York: Bobbs-Merrill, 1961. **B.**

413. Dublin, D., and R. Lourie. "Agency Action and Interaction in Cases of Child Abuse." *Social Casework* 52 (1971):164. **H.**

414. Duncan, E. "Recognition and Protection of Families Interests in Child Abuse Proceedings." *Journal of Family Law* 13 (1973):103-118. **B.**

415. Duncan, G., et al. "Etiological Factors in First-Degree Murder." *Journal of the American Medical Association* 168 (13):1755-1758, November 29, 1958. **A**.

416. Duncan, G., and J. Duncan. "Murder in the Family: A Study of Some Homicidal Adolescents." *American Journal of Psychiatry* 127 (May 1971):1498-1502. **C**.

417. Dunsted, C., R. Oppenheimer, and J. Lindsay. "Aspects of Bonding Failure: The Psychopathology and Psychotherapeutic Treatment of Families of Battered Children." *Developmental, Medicine and Child Neurology* 16 (August 1974):447-456. **E**.

418. Duquesne Law Review. "Abused Child: Problems and Proposals." *Duquesne Law Review* 8 (1969-1970):136-160. **A, B, H**.

419. ———. "Dependent-Neglect Proceedings: A Case for Procedural Law Process." *Duquesne Law Review* 9 (1971):651. **B**.

420. ———. "Infants-Child Neglect Proceeding." *Duquesne Law Review* 11 (1973):735. **A, B**.

421. Dynes, R., et al. *Social Problems; Dissensus and Deviations in an Industrial Society.* New York: Oxford University Press, 1964. **A**.

422. Eads, W. "Child Protection." *Stanford Law Review* 21 (1968-1969): 1129-1155. **D, H**.

423. Earl, H. "Ten Thousand Children Battered and Starved, Hundreds Die." *Today's Health* 43 (September 1964):24-31. **A**.

424. Easson, W., and R. Steinhiber. "Murderous Aggression by Children and Adolescents." *Archives of General Psychiatry* 4 (1961):47. **A**.

425. Ebbin, A., et al. "Battered Child Syndrome at the Los Angeles County General Hospital." *American Journal of Disabled Children* 118 (1969): 660-667. **A**.

426. Ebeling, N., and Hill, D. *Child Abuse.* New York: Publishing Science Company, 1975. **A**.

427. Eckert, W. "Slaughter of the Innocents." *Journal of Florida Medical Association* 54 (1967):256. **A**.

428. Economist. "One Problem, Two Answers." *Economist* 255 (May 3, 1975): 31. **A**.

429. Education Commission of the States. "Child Abuse and Neglect: Model Legislation for the States." Children's Bureau, Department Health, Education, Welfare, Washington, D.C., Report 7, Early Childhood Report 9, July 1975. **B**.

430. Eger, H., and A. Popeck. "The Abused Child: Problems and Proposals." *Duquesne Law Review* 8 (1969-1970):136-160. **B**.

431. Eighmie, D. "Legislation: Child Abuse." *Journal of the International Association of Pupil Personnel Workers* 16 (March 1972):2, 98-99. **B**.

432. Eisenberg, L. "The Sins of the Fathers: Urban Decay and Social Pathology." *American Journal of Orthopsychiatry* 32 (1962):5-17. **F**.

433. Eisenstein, E., et al. "Jejunal Hematoma: An Unusual Manifestation of the Battered-Child Syndrome." *Clinical Pediatrics* 4 (1965):436–440. **A**.

434. Elbin, A., et al. "Battered Child Syndrome at Los Angeles County General Hospital." *American Journal of Disabled Children* 118 (1969):660. **A**.

435. Elmer, E. "Abused Children and Community Resources." *International Journal of Offender Therapy* 11 (1967):16–23. **D, F, H**.

436. ——. "Abused Children Seen in Hospitals." *Social Work* 5 (1960):98–102. **A**.

437. ——. "Child Abuse: A Symptom of Family Crisis." In E. Pavenstedt and V. Bernard, *Crises of Family Disorganization Programs to Soften their Impact on Children.* New York: Behavioral Publications, 1971. **A, C**.

438. ——. "Child Abuse: The Family's Cry for Help." *Journal of Psychiatry Nursing* 5 (1967):322–341. **A, E**.

439. ——. "Children in Jeopardy: A Study of Abused Minors and Their Families." Reviewed in *Child Welfare* (May 1969):305. **C**.

440. ——. "The Fifty Families Study: Summary of Phase I, Neglected and Abused Children and Their Families." Children's Hospital of Pittsburgh, July 26, 1965. **C**.

441. ——. "Studies of Child Abuse and Infant Accidents." In J. Segal, *Mental Health Program Reports* 58–59, 5 DHEW No. (HSM) 72–9042 Washington, D.C.: Superintendent of Documents, U.S. Government Printing Office, 1971. **A**.

442. ——. "Identification of Abused Children." *Children* 10 (1963): 180–184. **A**.

443. ——. "Hazards in Determining Child Abuse." *Child Welfare* 45 (1966): 28–33. **A**.

444. ——. *Fifty Families: A Study of Abused and Neglected Children and Their Families.* Pittsburgh, Pa.: University of Pittsburgh School of Medicine, June 1965. **C**.

445. ——. "Failure to Thrive. Role of the Mother." *Pediatrics* 40 (1960:711–725. **A, C**.

446. Elmer, E., et al. "Developmental Characteristics of Abused Children." *Pediatrics* 40 (1967):596–602. **A**.

447. Elmore, J., et al. "The Nurse's Role in the Care of the Battered Child: Panel Discussion." *Clinical Proceedings of the Children's Hospital, D.C.* 24 (1968):364, 374. **D**.

448. Elonen, A., and S. Swarensteyn. "Sexual Trauma in Young Blind Children." *New Outlook for the Blind* 69 (December 1975):440–442. **D**.

449. Emlen, A. "Daycare For Whom?" In A. Schorr, *Children and Decent People.* New York: Basic Books, 1974. **D**.

450. Enzer, N., and J. Stackhouse. "A Child Guidance Clinic Approach to the Multi-Problem Family." Paper presented at National Conference on Social Welfare June 1966. **C, D, E**.

451. Erickson, H., G. Justis, and J. Lacour. *Public Welfare Responsibility for Child Protective Services.* Denver, Colorado: Children's Division, American Humane Association. **H.**
452. Erwin, D. "The Battered Child Syndrome." *Medicology Bulletin* 130 (1964):1-10. **A.**
453. Etaugh, C. "Effects of Maternal Employment on Children: A Review of Recent Research." *Merrill-Palmer Quarterly,* 20(71):98, 1974. **C.**
454. Evans, P. "Infanticide." *Proceedings of the Royal Society of Medicine* 61 (December 12, 1968):1296, 1298. **A.**
455. Evans, S., et al. "Failure to Thrive. A Study of 45 Children and Their Families." *Journal of the American Academy of Child Psychiatry* 11 (1972):440-457. **A, C.**
456. Everett, M., et al. "The Battered Child Syndrome: The Tasmanian Approach." *Medical Journal of Australia* 2 (1973):735-737. **A.**
457. Fairburn, A. "Small Children at Risk." *Lancet* 1 (1973):199-200. **A.**
458. Fairburn, A., and C. Hunt. "Caffey's Third Syndrome—A Critical Evaluation." *Medical Science and the Law* 4 (1964):123-126. **A.**
459. Fairlie, C. "Post-Commitment Custody of Neglected Children." *Connecticut Law Review* 4 (1971):143-153. **H.**
460. Family Court of the State of New York. *Statistical Report for the Month of December.* Family Court of the State of New York, City of New York, 1963. **B.**
461. Fanai, F. "Course and Prognosis of Child Neglect. Follow-up Studies of Juveniles with Disturbed Social Behaviour." *Psychiatria Clinica (Basel)* (1969):1-13. **D.**
462. Fanshel, D. "Child Welfare." In H. Maas, *Five Fields of Social Service: Reviews of Research.* New York: National Association of Social Workers, 1966. **H.**
463. Fanshel, D., and E. Shinn. *Dollars and Sense in the Foster Care of Children: A Look at Cost Factors.* New York: Child Welfare League of America, 1972. **A, D.**
464. Feinstein, H., et al. "Group Therapy for Mothers with Infanticidal Impulses." *American Journal of Psychiatry* 120 (1964):882-886. **E.**
465. Felder, S. "Lawyers View of Child Abuse." *Public Welfare* 29 (1968): 181. **B.**
466. Fenby, T. "The Work of the National Society for the Prevention of Cruelty to Children." *International Journal of Offender Therapy and Comparative Criminology,* 16 (1972):201-205. **D.**
467. Ferenczi, S. "The Unwelcome Child and His Death-Instinct." *International Journal of Psychoanalysis* 10 (1929):127. **A.**
468. Ferguson, D., et al. *Child Abuse in New Zealand.* Wellington, A.R. Shearer, Government Printer, 1972. **F.**
469. Ferguson, W. "Battered Child Syndrome: Attorney General's Opinion

Regarding the Reporting of Such Occurrences." *Journal of the Kansas Medical Society,* 65 (February 1964):67–69. **B.**

470. Ferro, F. "Combatting Child Abuse and Neglect." *Children Today* 4 (May-June, 1975):inside front cover. **B.**

471. ——. "Protecting Children: The National Center on Child Abuse and Neglect." *Childhood Education* 52:2 (November, December, 1975): 63–66. **B.**

472. Ficarra, B. "Pioneer Laws for Child Protection." *International Journal of Law and Science* 7 (1970):68–71. **B.**

473. Finberg, L. "A Pediatrician's View of the Abused Child." *Child Welfare* 44 (January, 1965):41–43. **A, D, E.**

474. Findley, I. "The Care of Destitute Children: Some Nineteenth Century Practices in Australia." *Medical Journal of Australia* 1 (1972):1142–1146. **A, E.**

475. Fiser, R., et al. "Congenital Syphilis Mimicking the Battered Syndrome. How Does One Tell Them Apart?" *Clinical Pediatrics* 11 (1972):305–307. **A, E.**

476. Fisher, G., and R. McGrath. *The Abusers.* New York: Mott Media, 1975. **A.**

477. Fisher, S. "Skeletal Manifestations of Parent-Induced Trauma in Infants and Children." *Southern Medical Journal* 51 (1958):956–960. **A, C.**

478. Fitzgerald, C. "Characteristics of Families Referred for Child Abuse." Abstracted in *Smith College Studies in Social Work* (November, 1966) p. 39, thesis. **A, C.**

479. Flammang, C. *The Police and the Underprotected Child.* Springfield, Illinois: Thomas Publishers, 1971. **B.**

480. Flato, C. "Parents who Beat Children." *Saturday Evening Post* 235 (October 6, 1962):30. **C.**

481. Fleck, S. "Child Abuse." *Connecticut Medicine* 36 (1972):337. **A.**

482. Fleming, G. "Cruelty to Children." *British Medical Journal* 2 (1967):421–422. **A.**

483. Flynn, W. "Frontier Justice: A Contribution to the Theory of Child Battery." *American Journal of Psychiatry* 127 (September, 1970):375–379. **B.**

484. Fontana, V., and S. Nichamin. "Battered Child Syndrome and Brain Dysfunction." *Journal of the American Medical Association* 223 (1973): 1390–1391. **A.**

485. Fontana, V. "Child Abuse: A Tragic Problem." *Parents Magazine* 48 (March, 1973): 20. **A.**

486. Fontana, V. "Factors Needed for Prevention of Child Abuse and Neglect." *Pediatrics* 46 (1970):318–319. **H.**

487. ——. "Further Reflections on Maltreatment of Children." *New York Journal of Medicine* 68 (1968):2214–2215. **A, C.**

488. ———. "Letter: Battered Children." *New England Journal of Medicine* 289: 1044. **A.**

489. ———. "Physical Abuse of Children." *Pediatrics* 45 (1970):509-510. **A.**

490. ———. "Prevent the Abuse of the Future." *Trial* 10 (May, 1974):14+. **H.**

491. ———. "Preventing Maltreatment of Children: An Insidious and Disturbing Medical Entity." *Public Welfare* 24 (1966):235-239. **A, B, C.**

492. ———. "Recognition of Maltreatment and Prevention of Battered Child Syndrome." *Pediatrics* 38 (1967):1078. **A.**

493. ———. *Somewhere a child is crying. Maltreatment—causes and prevention.* New York: Macmillan Publishing Company, 1973. **A, D, E, H.**

494. ———. "The Battered Child—1973. When to Suspect Child Abuse." *Medical Times* 101 (1973):116-120. **A, B.**

495. ———. "The Battered Child." *Crime and Delinquency* 16 (1970):120-122. **A.**

496. ———. "The Diagnosis of the Maltreatment Syndrome in Children." *Pediatrics* 51 (1973):780-782. **A, H.**

497. ———. *The Maltreated Child: The Maltreatment Syndrome in Children.* Springfield, Illinois, Charles C. Thomas, 1974. **A.**

498. ———. *The Maltreated Child: the maltreatment Syndrome in Children.* 2d ed. Springfield, Illinois, Charles C. Thomas, 1975. **A.**

499. ———. The Maltreatment Syndrome in Children." *Hospital Medicine* 1971. **A.**

500. ———. "The Neglect and Abuse of Children." *New York Journal of Medicine* 64 (1964):215-224. **A, B.**

501. ———. "We Must Stop the Vicious Cycle of Child Abuse." *Parents Magazine* 50 (December, 1975):8. **G, H.**

502. ———. "When to Suspect Parental Assault." *Resident and Staff Physicians* (August, 1973):48-52. **A, D, H.**

503. ———. "Which Parents Abuse Children?" *Medical Insight* 3:16-21, 1971. **C, D, H.**

504. Fontana, V., and D. Donovan, R. Wong. "The Maltreatment Syndrome in Children." *The New England Journal of Medicine* 269 (1963):1389-1394. **A.**

505. Forer, L. "Rights of Children: the Legal Vacuum." *American Bar Association Journal* 55 (1969):1151. **B.**

506. Foresman, L. "Homemaker Service in Neglect and Abuse: I. Strengthening Family Life." *Children* 10 (1963):213-218. **A, C;**

507. Forrer, S. "Battered Children and Counselor Responsibility." *School Counselor* 22 (January, 1975):161-165. **A, G, H.**

508. Forrest, T. "The Family Dynamics of Maternal Violence." *Journal of the American Academy of Psychoanalysis* 2 (1974):215-230. **C.**

509. Foster, F., R. McPartla, D. Kupfer, and E. Elmer. "Psychomotor Activity in Accident Prone and Battered Children—an 8 Year Follow Up." *Psychosomatic Medicine* 37 (1975):89. **C, E.**

510. Foster, H., and D. Freed. "Battered Child Legislation and Professional
     Immunity." *American Bar Association Journal* 52 (1966):1071. **B.**

511. Foster, H., and D. Freed. "The Battered Child: Whose Responsibility . . .
     Lawyer or Physician." *Trial* 3 (1967):33-37. **A, B.**

512. Foster, J. "Bill of Rights for Children." *Family Law Quarterly* 6 (1972):
     343. **A, B.**

513. Fowler, E. "The Physician, The Battered Child, and the Law." *Pediatrics*
     31 (August, 1963):488. **A, B.**

514. Francis, H. "Child Health—Points of Concern." *Public Health* 81 (1967):
     246-249. **E.**

515. Francis, V., and C. Lucht. "Child Abuse Legislation in 1970's." *International Journal of Offender Therapy* 19 (1975):108. **B.**

516. Franklin, A. *Concerning Child Abuse.* New York: Longman Publishers,
     1975. **A.**

517. Franklin, A. "The Tunbridge Wells Study Group on Non-Accidental
     Injury to Children. Report and Resolutions." In *Social Work Service,*
     July, 1974. **A, B.**

518. Franklin, L. "An Exception to Use of the Physician-Patient Privilege in
     Child Abuse Cases." *University of Detroit Law Journal* 42 (1964):88-94.
     B.

519. Fraser, B. *Child Abuse and Neglect: Alternatives for State Legislation.*
     Education Commission of the States, Denver, Colorado, Report #6 in the
     Early Childhood Task Force, December, 1973. **B.**

520. ——. "Momma Used to Whip Her . . . . The Tragedy of Child Abuse."
     Compact (March–April, 1974):10-12. **C.**

521. ——. "Pragmatic Alternative to Current Legislation Approaches to Child
     Abuse." *American Criminal Law Review* 12 (1974):103-124. **B, H.**

522. ——. "Towards a More Practical Central Registry." *Denver Law Journal*
     51 (1975):509-528. **B.**

523. Fraser, F. "Child Abuse in Nova Scotia." *Dalhousie Law School* 1973.
     Funded by the Office of the Secretary of State, Laidlow Foundation, the
     Vanier Institute for the Family and the Nova Scotia Department of Welfare. **A.**

524. Frauenberger, G., and E. Lis. "Multiple Fractures Associated with Subdural Hematoma in Infancy." *Pediatrics* 6 (1950):890. **A, E.**

525. Fray, P. "Crimes and Offenses by Primitive Reactivity." *Annales Medico-Psychologiaue* 1 (May, 1970):701-718. **A.**

526. Freedman, C. "Children's Petition of 1969 and Its Sequel." *British Journal
     of Educational Studies* 14 (May, 1966):216-223. **B.**

527. Freedman, D., et al. "On the Role of Coenesthetic Stimulation in the
     Development of Psychic Structure." *Psychoanalytic Quarterly* 37 (1968):
     418-438. **A.**

528. Fried, R., and M. Mayer. "Socio-Emotional Factors Accounting for

Growth Failure in Children Living in an Institution." *Journal of Pediatrics* 33 (October, 1948):444-456. **F.**

529. Friedman, M. "Traumatic Periostitis in Infants and Children." *Journal of the American Medical Association* 166 (1958):1840-1845. **A, E.**

530. Friedman, S., and C. Morse. "Child Abuse—5 Year Follow-up of Early Case Finding in Emergency Department." *Journal of Pediatrics* 54 (1974): 404-410. **A, E.**

531. Friedman, S. "The Need for Intensive Follow-up of Abused Children." In C. Kempe and R. Helfer (eds.) *Helping the Battered Child and His Family*. Philadelphia: J.B. Lippincott, 1972. **A, E.**

532. Friedrich, W., and J. Boriskin. "Ill-Health and Child Abuse." *Lancet* 1 (1976):649-650. **A.**

533. Friendly, D. "Ocular Manifestations of Physical Child Abuse." *Transactions of the American Academy of Phythamology Otolaryngology* 75 (1971): 318-332. **A, E.**

534. Frommer, E., et al. "Antenatal Identification of Women Liable to Have Problems in Managing Their Infants." *British Journal of Psychiatry* 123 (1973):149-156. **A, D, E.**

535. Fruchtl, G., and A. Brodeur. "Battered Child." *Catholic World* 209 (July, 1969):156-159. **A.**

536. Fulk, D. "The Battered Child." *Nursing Forum* 3 (1964):10-26. **A.**

537. Galdston, R. "Dysfunctions of Parenting: The Battered Child, The Exploited Child." In J. Howells, *Modern Perspective of International Child Psychiatry*. New York: Oliver and Boyd, 1968. **A, C.**

538. ——. "Observations on Children Who Have Been Physically Abused and Their Parents." *American Journal of Psychiatry* 122 (1965):440-443. **A, C.**

539. ——. "Preventing the Abuse of Little Children: The Parents' Center Project for the Study and Prevention of Child Abuse." *American Journal of Orthopsychiatry* 45 (April 1975): 372-381. **H.**

540. ——. "The Burning and Healing of Children." *Psychiatry* 35 (February 1972):57-66. **D.**

541. ——. "Violence Begins at Home. Parents' Center Project for Study and Prevention of Child Abuse." *Journal of American Academy of Child Psychiatry* 10 (1971):336-350. **C.**

542. Galliher, K. "Termination of the Parent-Child Relationship: Should Parental I.Q. Be An Important Factor?" *Law and the Social Order* (1973): 855-879. **B, C.**

543. Ganley, P. "The Battered Child: Logic in Search of Law." *San Diego Law Review* 8 (1971):364-403. **A, B.**

544. Gans, B. "Battered Babies—How Many Do We Miss?" *Lancet* 1 (1970): 1286-1287. **A.**

545. ——. "Unnecessary X-Rays?" *British Medical Journal* (1970):564. **D.**

546. Garbarino, J. "Preliminary Study of Some Ecological Correlates of Child Abuse—Impact of Socioeconomic Stress on Mothers." *Child Development* 47 (1976):178–185. **G.**

547. Garber, C. "Eskimo Infanticide." *Scientific Monthly* 64 (February 1947): 99. **A.**

548. Gardner, J. "Abused Child." *McCalls* September 1967, pp. 96–97 ff. **A.**

549. Geiser, R. *The Illusion of Caring: Children in Foster Care.* Boston' Beacon Press, 1973. **A, C.**

550. Geismar, L. "555 Families: A Social-Psychologicsl Study of Young Families in Transition." *Transaction* (1973). **A, F.**

551. Geismar, L., and M. LaSorte. "Factors Associated with Family Disorganization." *Marriage and Family Living* (1963):479–481. **A, C.**

552. ——. *Understanding the Multi-Problem Family: A Conceptual Analysis and Exploration in Early Identification.* New York: Association Press, 1964. **A, C.**

553. Gelles, R. "A Psychosocial Approach to Child Abuse." *Nursing Digest II* (April 1974):52–59. **A.**

554. ——. "Child Abuse as Psychopathology: A Sociological Critique and Reformation." *American Journal of Orthopsychiatry* 43 (1973):611–621. **A, F.**

555. ——. "Demythologizing Child-Abuse." *Family Coordinator* 25 (1976): 135–141. **A.**

556. ——. "Determinants and Effects of Violence in the Family." In Wesley R. Burr, et al., *Contemporary Theories About the Family,* 1976. **C.**

557. ——. "The Social Construction of Child Abuse." *American Journal of Orthopsychiatry* 45(3):363–371, April 1975. **A, F.**

558. ——. *The Violent Home: A Study of Physical Agression Berween Husbands and Wives."* Beverly Hills: Sage Publications, 1972. **C.**

559. George, G. "Spare the Rod: a Survey of the Battered Child Syndrome." *Forensic Science* 2 (1973):129–167. **A.**

560. Gibbens, T., and A. Walker. *Cruel Parents.* Institute for the Study and Treatment of Delinquency, 1956. **C.**

561. Gibbons, T. "Female Offenders." *British Journal of Hospital Medicine* 6 (1971):279–282, 285–286. **A.**

562. Gibson, C., et al. "Letter: Battered Child Syndrome." *Medical Journal of Australia* 2 (1973):1073. **A.**

563. Gil, D. "A Sociocultural Perspective on Physical Child Abuse." *Child Welfare* 50 (1971):389–395. **F.**

564. ——. "A Sociocultural Perspective on Physical Child Abuse." *Child Welfare* 50 (1971):389–395. **F.**

565. ——. "Child Abuse—Intervention and Treatment." *Social Science and Medicine* 9 (1975):683–684. **D, F.**

566. ——. "Child Abuse Prevention Act." *Journal of Clinical Child Psychology* 11 (1973):7–10. **B, H.**

567. ——. *Epidemiologic Study of Child Abuse-Research in Progress.* Florence Heller Graduate School for Advanced Studies in Social Welfare, Brandeis University, 1965. **H.**

568. ——. *First Steps in a Nationwide Study of Child Abuse.* Social Work Practice 1966. New York: Columbia University Press, 1966. **A.**

569. ——. *Legally Reported Child Abuse: A Nationwide Survey.* Social Work Practice 1968. New York: Columbia University Press, 1968. **B.**

570. ——. *Nationwide Survey of Legally Reported Physical Abuse of Children.* Waltham, Massachusetts: Brandeis University, 1968. **B.**

571. ——. "Physical Abuse of Children. Findings and Implications of a Nationwide Survey." *Pediatrics* 44 (Supplement):857–864, 1969. **A.**

572. ——. "Physical Abuse of Children." *Pediatrics* 45 (1970):510–511. **A.**

573. ——. "Unraveling Child Abuse." *American Journal of Orthopsychology* 45 (1975):346–356. **A, F.**

574. ——. *Violence Against Children.* Cambridge, Massachusetts: Harvard University Press, 1970. **A.**

575. ——. "Violence Against Children." *Journal of Marriage and the Family.* 33 (1971):637–657. **A.**

576. ——. "Violence Against Children." *Pediatrics* 49 (1972):641. **A.**

577. ——. "Violence Against Children—Physical Child Abuse in the United States." *Social Case* 52:536. **A.**

578. ——. "Violence Against Children—Physical Child Abuse in the United States." *Social Service Review* 45:514. **A.**

579. ——. "What Schools Can Do About Child Abuse." *American Education* 5 (1969):2–4. **G.**

580. ——. "Incidence of Child Abuse and Demographic Characteristics of Persons Involved." In R. Helfer and C. Kempe, eds., *The Battered Child.* Chicago and London: University of Chicago Press, 1968. **A.**

581. ——. *Testimony of Dr. David G. Gil, Brandeis University, at Hearings of United States Senate Subcommittee,* March 26, 1973. **B.**

582. Gil, D., et al. *Nationwide Epidemiologic Study of Child Abuse, Progress Report.* Waltham, Massachusetts: Brandeis University, 1967. **A.**

583. ——. "Public Knowledge, Attitudes, and Opinions About Physical Abuse in the United States, No. 14." In *Social Welfare.* Waltham, Massachusetts: Florence Heller Graduate School for Advanced Studies in Social Welfare, Brandeis University, September 1967. **F.**

584. Gillespie, R. "The Battered Child Syndrome: Thermal and Caustic Manifestations." *Journal of Trauma* 5 (1965):523–534. **A.**

585. Ginsburg, L. "Social Problems in Rural America." *Social Work Practice.* New York: Columbia University Press, 1969. **F.**

586. Ginsburg, L., and P. Elliott. "Human Behavior and the Social Environment; The Effects of Social Deprivation on Personality." In A.R. Roberts, *Childhood Deprivation.* Springfield, Illinois: Charles C. Thomas, 1972. **F.**

587. Giovannoni, J. "Parental Mistreatment: Perpetrators and Victims." *Journal of Marriage and the Family* 33 (1971):649-657. **C.**

588. Giovannoni, J., and A. Billingsley. "Child Neglect Among the Poor: A Study of Parental Adequacy in Families of Three Ethnic Groups." *Child Welfare* (April 1970):196. **A, F.**

589. Giovannoni, J., et al. "Child Protective Services." Unpublished manuscript, 1969. **D.**

590. Glaser, H., et al. "Physical and Psychological Development of Children with Early Failure to Thrive." *Journal of Pediatrics* 73 (1968):690-698. **A, C.**

591. Glazier, A., ed. *Child Abuse: A Community Challenge.* New York: Henry Stewart, 1971. **A.**

592. Gluckman, L. "Cruelty to Children." *New Zealand Medical Journal* 67 (1968):155-159. **A.**

593. Godfrey, J. "Trauma in Children." *Journal of Bone and Joint Surgery* 46 (1964):422-447. **D.**

594. Goldacre, P. "Registering Doubt." *Times Educational Supplement* 3135 (July 4, 1975):20-21. **A,B.**

595. Goldberg, G. "Breaking the Communication Barrier: The Initial Interview With an Abusing Parent." *Child Welfare* 54 (April 1975):274-282. **E.**

596. Goldfarb, W. "Emotional and Intellectual Consequences of Psychologic Deprivation in Infancy: A Revaluation." In P. Koch and M. Zubin, *Psychopathology of Childhood.* New York: Grune and Stratton, 1955. **A.**

597. Goldney, R. "Abusing Parents. Legal and Therapeutic Aspects." *Medical Journal of Australia* 2 (1972):597-600. **B, D, E.**

598. Goldstein, J., A. Freud, and A. Solnit. *Beyond the Best Interests of the Child.* New York: The Free Press, 1973. **A, H.**

599. Goldston, R., et al. "Pediatric Hospitalization as Crisis Intervention." *American Journal of Psychiatry* 129 (1972):721-725. **H.**

600. Goldston, R. "Violence Begins at Home. The Parent Centre Project for the Study and Prevention of Child Abuse." *Journal of the American Academy of Child Psychiatry* 10 (1971):336-350. **C, E, H.**

601. Golub, S. "The Battered Child: What the Nurse Can Do." *Registered Nurse* 31 (1968):42-45. **D.**

602. Good Housekeeping. "Battered Child." *Good Housekeeping,* May 1974. **A.**

603. Goode, W. "Force and Violence in the Family." *Journal of Marriage and the Family,* 33 (1971):624-636. **A, C.**

604. Goodpastor, G., and K. Angel. "Child Abuse and Law—California System." *Hastings Law Journal* 26 (1975):0181-1125. **B.**

605. Gordon, A. "A Child is Being Beaten." *Physician's Management* (June (1965):22-24. **A.**

606. Gorham, C. "Not Only the Stranger—A Study of the Problem of Child Molestation in San Diego, California." *Journal of School Health* 36 (1966): 341-345. **A, F.**

607. Gornall, P., S. Ahmed, A. Jolleys, and S. Cohen. "Intro-abdominal Injuries in the Battered Baby Syndrome." *Archives of Disease in Childhood* 47 (1972):211-217. **C.**

608. Gornall, P., et al. "Intra-abdominal Injuries in the Battered Child Syndrome." *Pediatrics* 50 (1972):160-162. **A.**

609. Gottesman, R. *Child Abuse: A Teacher's Responsibility to Report.* National Organization on Legal Problems of Education, Topeka, Kansas, 1975. **G.**

610. Gottlieb, D., ed. *Children's Liberation.* Englewood Cliffs, New Jersey: Prentice-Hall, 1973. **A.**

611. Gould, R., and P. Matthews. "Toward Prevention of Child Abuse." *Children* 11 (March–April 1964). **A, H.**

612. Grantmyre, E. "Trauma X—Wednesday's Child." *Nova Scotia Medical Bulletin* 52 (1973):29-31. **D.**

613. Gray, J. "Hospital Based Battered Child Team." *Hospitals* 47 (1973):50-52. **A, H.**

614. ———. "Looking at the Battered Baby Syndrome." *Time,* April 21, 1964. **A.**

615. Green, A. "Psychiatric Study and Treatment of Abusing Parents." Paper presented at the 122nd Annual Convention of the AMA, June 1973. **E.**

616. ———. "Self-destructive Behavior in Physically Abused Schizophrenic Children; Report of Cases. *Archaelogical General Psychiatry* 19 (1968): 171-179. **A, F.**

617. Green, A., et al. "Child Abuse: Pathological Syndrome of Family Interaction." *American Journal of Psychology* 131 (August 1974):882-886. **C.**

618. ———. "Reactions to the Threatened Loss of a Child: A Vulnerable Child Syndrome." *Pediatrics* 34 (1964):58-66. **A.**

619. Green, D. "Parent and Child—Child Beating—Recent Legislation Requiring Reporting of Physical Abuse." *Oregon Law Review* 45 (1966):114-123. **B.**

620. ———. "Sizing Up the Small Child." *Postgraduate Medicine* 50 (October 1971):103-109. **D.**

621. Green, K. "Diagnosing the Battered Child Syndrome." *Maryland Medical Journal* 14 (1965):83-84. **A.**

622. ———. "The Abused Child." *Maryland Medical Journal* 15 (1966):47-49. **A.**

623. Greengard, J. "The Battered Baby Syndrome." *American Journal of Nursing* 64 (1964):98-100. **A.**

624. ———. "The Battered Child Syndrome." *Medical Science* 15 (1964):82-91. **A.**

625. ——. "Child Abuse: Second Look After State Legislation." *Medical Science* 18 (1967):32. **A, B.**

626. Greenland, C. *Child Abuse in Ontario.* Toronto: Ministry of Community and Social Services, 1973. **A.**

627. Gregg, G. "Physician, Child-Abuse Reporting Laws, and Injured Child. Psychosocial Anatomy of Childhood Trauma." *Clinical Pediatrics* 7 (1968): 720-725. **B, D.**

628. Gregg, G. "Infant Trauma." *American Family Physician* 3 (May 1971): 101-105. **D.**

629. Gregg, G., et al. "Infant Injuries: Accident or Abuse?" *Pediatrics* 44 (1969):434-439. **A.**

630. Gretton, J. "When No One is Minding the Children." *Times Educational Supplement* 3056 (December 21, 1973):4. **A.**

631. Griffiths, D. "Epiphysical Injuries in Babies." *British Medical Journal* 2 (1963):1558-1561. **A.**

632. Griffiths, D., and F. Moynilan. "Multiple Epiphysial Injuries in Babies (Battered Child Syndrome)." *British Medical Journal* 4 (1963):1558-1561. **D.**

633. Griswold, B., and A. Billingsley. "Psychological Functioning of Parents Who Mistreat Their Children and Those Who Do Not." Unpublished manuscript, 1967. **C.**

634. Groff, R., and F. Grant. "Chronic Subdural Hematoma: Collective Review." *Internation Abstracts of Surgery* 74 (1942):9-20. **A.**

635. Grow, L. *Requests for Child Welfare Services: A Five-Day Census.* Children's Bureau, Department of Health, Education, and Welfare, Washington, D.C., July 1969. **H.**

636. Grumet, B. "Plaintive Plaintiffs: Victims of the Battered Child Syndrome." *Family Law Quarterly* 4 (1970):296. **B.**

637. Guandola, V., et al. "The Battered Child Syndrome." *Clinical Proceedings of the Children's Hospital of the District of Columbia* 23 (May 1967): 139-160. **A.**

638. ——. "Grand Rounds: The Battered Child Syndrome." *Clinical Procedures, Children's Hospital, D.C.* 23 (1967):139-160. **A.**

639. Guarnaschelli, J., et al. "Fallen Fontanelle (Coids de Mollara)." *Journal of the American Medical Association* 222 (1972):1545-1546. **A.**

640. Gunn, A. "The Neglected Child." *Nursing Times* 66 (1970):946-947. **A.**

641. ——. "Wounds of Violence." *Nursing Times* 63 (1967):590-592. **A.**

642. Guthkelch, A. "Infantile Subdural Haematoma and its Relationship to Whiplash Injuries." *British Medical Journal* 2 (1971):430-431. **A.**

643. Gwinn, J., et al. "Radiological Case of the Month." *American Journal of Disadvantaged Children* 109 (1965):457-458. **D.**

644. ——. "Roentgenographic Manifestations of Unsuspected Trauma in

Infancy." *Journal of the American Medical Association* 176 (1961): 926-929. **D.**

645. Haas, L. "Injured Baby." *British Medical Journal* 5462 (1965):645. **A.**

646. Hagebak, R. "Disciplinary Practices in Dallas Contrasted with School Systems with Rules Against Violence Against Children." *Journal of Clinical Child Psychology* 2 (Fall 1973):14-16. **G.**

647. Hall, G. "Battered Child Reporting Laws—Mediolegal Considerations." *The Doctor and the Law*, Wyeth Labs, June 1966. **B.**

648. Hall, M. "The Right to Live." *Nursing Outlook* 15 (1967):63-65. **A.**

649. Haller, J., Jr., et al. "Trauma Workshop Report: Trauma in Children." *Journal of Trauma* 10 (1970):1052-1054. **A.**

650. Halliwell, R. "Time Limited Work with a Family at Point of Being Prosecuted for Child Neglect." *Case Conference* 15 (1969):343-348. **E.**

651. Halter, J., and S. Friedman. "Principles of Management in Child Abuse Cases." *American Journal of Orthopsychiatry* (January 1968):127. **A.**

652. Hamlin, H. "Subgaleal Hematoma Caused by Hair-Pull" (Letter). *Journal of the American Medical Association* 204 (1968):339. **A.**

653. Hammel, C. "Preserving Family Life for Children." *Child Welfare* 48 (1969):591, 594; *Abstract for Social Workers* 7 (1969):846. **C, H.**

654. Hancock, C. *Children and Neglect . . . Hazardous Home Conditions.* Bureau of Family Services, Welfare Administration, U.S. Department of Health, Education, and Welfare, Washington, D.C.: U.S. Government Printing Office, 1963. **A, C.**

655. ——. *Digest of a Study of Protective Services and the Problem of Neglect of Children in New Jersey.* State Board of Child Welfare, 1958. **F, H.**

656. ——. *Services for Children Who Need Protection: A Manual for Caseworkers in Public Assistance Agencies.* Washington, D.C., Department of Health, Education, and Welfare, Welfare Administration, Bureau of Family Services, 1964. **F.**

657. Hansen, D., and R. Hill. "Families Under Stress." In H. Christensen, *Handbook of Marriage and the Family.* New York: Rand McNally, 1964. **A, C.**

658. Hansen, R. "Child Abuse Legislation and the Interdisciplinary Approach." *American Bar Association Journal* 52 (1966):734. **B.**

659. ——. "Doctors, Lawyers, and the Battered Child Law." *Journal of Trauma* 5 (1965):826-830. **A, B, D.**

660. ——. "Legal Implications of the Battered Child Syndrome." *Nebraska Medical Journal* 50 (1965):595-597. **B.**

661. ——. "Suggested Guidelines for Child Abuse Laws." *Journal of Family Law* 7 (1967):61-65. **B.**

662. Harcourt, B., et al. "Ophthalmic Manifestations of the Battered Baby Syndrome." *British Medical Journal* 3 (1971):398-401. **A.**

663. Harper, F. "The Physician, the Battered Child and the Law." *Pediatrics* 31 (1963):899-902. **A, B, D.**

664. Harrington, M. *The Other America.* New York: MacMillan, 1962. **F, H.**

665. Harris, M. "Discussion on the Battered Child Syndrome." *Australian Journal of Forensic Sciences* 3 (1970): 277. **A.**

666. Harris, R. "Social Security and Public Welfare—Invalidity of Public Welfare Regulation Requiring Parent to Cooperate With District Attorney in Obtaining Child Support from Abandoning Parent." *Oklahoma Law Review* 25 (1972):438-444. **B.**

667. Harrison, P. *Never Enough—75 Years with the Children's Aid Society of Ottawa.* Ottawa: Children's Aid Society, 1968. **A.**

668. Harrison, S. "Child Abuse Control Centers: A Project for the Academy?" *Pediatrics* 45 (1970):895. **H.**

669. Hart, M. Child Abuse and Neglect: A Report on the Status of the Research U.S. Department of Health, Education, and Welfare, Washington, D.C., 1974. **A, B, H.**

670. Hart, W. "The Law Concerning Abuse of Children." *Journal of South Carolina Medical Association* 61 (1965):391. **B.**

671. Hartley, A. "Identifying the Physically Abused Child." *Texas Medicine* 65 (1969):50-55. **A.**

672. Harvard Education Review. *The Rights of Children.* Cambridge, Massachusetts: Harvard Educational Review, 1974. **B.**

673. Haselkorn, F. "Mothers-at-Risk: The Role of Social Work in Prevention of Morbidity in Infants of Socially Disadvantaged Mothers." Adelphi University School of Social Work, 1966. Thesis. **E, H.**

674. Hass, L. "Injured Baby." *British Medical Journal* 2 (1965):645. **A, C.**

675. Hatfield, A. "Affectional Deprivations and Child Adjustment." In A. Roberts, *Childhood Deprivation.* Springfield, Illinois: Charles C. Thomas, 1974. **D.**

676. Havens, L. "Youth, Violence and the Nature of Family Life." *Psychiatric Annals* 2(2):18-29, 1972. **C.**

677. Haward, L. "Some Psychological Aspects of Pregnancy." *Midwives Chronicle* 83 (1969):199-200. **A.**

678. Hawkes, C. "Craniocerebral Trauma in Infancy and Childhood." *Clinical Neurosurgery* 11 (1964):66-75. **A.**

679. Haynes, G., R. Davie, et al. *National Childrens Bureau Tenth Annual Review.* London, England: The Bureau, 1973. **A.**

680. Hazlewood, A. "Child Abuse: The Dentist's Role." *New York Dentist Journal* 36 (1970):289-291. **A, B, D.**

681. Hecheater, D., et al. "What Can the Schools Do About Child Abuse?" *Todays Education* 57 (September 1968):43-44. **G.**

682. Heins, M. "Child Abuse—Analysis of a Current Epidemic." *Michigan Medicine* 68 (1969):887-891. **A.**

683. ——. "From Us–Doctors View of Child Abuse." *Canadian Welfare* 50 (1974):13-15. **D.**

684. Helfer, R. "A Plan for Protection: The Child Abuse Center." *Child Welfare* 49 (1970):486–494. **H.**

685. ——. "Guidelines for the Emergency Care of the Battered Child." In S. Spitzer and W. Oaks *Emergency Medical Management.* New York: Grune and Stratton, 1971. **D.**

686. ——. "Physicians Told How to Deal with Child Abuse." *Journal of the American Medical Association* 211 (1970):35. **A, D, H.**

687. ——. "Seven Guidelines in Child Abuse Cases." *Resident and Staff Physician* (August 1973):57–58. **H.**

688. ——. "The Battered Child–1973. What to do When the Evidence Hardens." *Medical Times* 1011 (1973):127–128. **H.**

689. ——. "The Center for the Study of Abused and Neglected Children." In C. Kempe and R. Helfer, *Helping the Battered Child and His Family.* Philadelphia: J.B. Lippincott, 1972. **H.**

690. ——. *The Diagnostic Process and Treatment Programs.* National Center for Child Abuse and Neglect, Department of Health, Education, and Welfare, Washington, D.C., 1975. **E.**

691. ——. "The Etiology of Child Abuse." *Pediatrics* 51 (1973):777–779. **A.**

692. ——. "The Responsiblity and Role of the Physician." In R. Helfer and C. Kempe, *The Battered Child.* Chicago: University of Chicago Press, 1968. **A, B, D.**

693. ——. "Why Most Physicians Don't Get Involved in Child Abuse Cases." *Children Today* 4 (May–June 1975):28–33. **D.**

694. Helfer, R., and C. Kempe, eds. *The Battered Child.* Chicago: University of Chicago Press, 1968. **A.**

695. ——. "The Child's Need for Early Recognition, Immediate Care and Protection." In *Helping the Battered Child and His Family.* Philadelphia: J.B. Lippincott, 1972. **H.**

696. ——. "The Consortium: A Community-Hospital Treatment Program." In *Helping the Battered Child and His Family.* Philadelphia: J.B. Lippincott, 1972. **D, E, H.**

697. ——. "Physical Abuse of Children." *Pediatrics* 46 (1970):651–652. **A.**

698. ——. "The Battered Child Syndrome." *Advances in Pediatrics* 15 (1968): 9-27. **A.**

699. Helpern, F. "Sudden Deaths at Home of Infants Under One in Apparent Good Health." Presented to the Congress of the French Speaking International Association of Legal Medicine, Montpellier, France, October 1968. **A.**

700. Helus, Z. "Theoretical and Empirical Contributions to Research Concerning Neglected Child." *Ceskoslovenska Psychologie* 16 (1972):88–91. **A.**

701. Henderson, R. "Environmental Predictors of Academic Performance of

Disadvantaged Mexican-American Children." *Journal of Consulting and Clinical Psychology* 38 (1964)297. **B, H.**

702. Hendriksen, D. "Battered Child: Florida Mandatory Reporting Statute." *University of Florida Law Review,* 18:503-511, 1965. **G, H.**

703. Hepner, R., and N. Maiden. "Growth Rate, Nutrient Intake and 'Mothering' as Determinants of Malnutrition in Disadvantaged Children." *Nutrition Reviews* 29 (1968):219-223. **A, C.**

704. Hepworth, P. "Looking at Baby Battering: Its Detection and Treatment." *Canadian Welfare* 49 (1973):13-15. **A, D, H.**

705. ———. *Services for Abused and Battered Children (Personal Social Services in Canada: A Review),* Volume 3. The Canadian Council on Social Development, 1975. **D.**

706. Herbert, D. "Family-Education-Rights-and-Privacy-Act of 1974 vs. Child Abuse Reporting Laws—Teachers Dilemma." *Juvenile Justice* (1974). **B, G.**

707. Herre, E. Aggressive Casework in a Protective Services Unit." *Social Casework* 46 (1965):358-362. **F.**

708. Herrmann, K. *I Hope My Daddy Dies, Mister.* New York: Dorrance, 1975. **C.**

709. Hessel, S. "Rights of Parents and Children." *New England Journal of Medicine* 283 (1970):156. **B.**

710. Hetzer, H. *"Die Forschungsstelle des Vereins zum Schutz der Kinder vor Ausnutzung und Misshandlung." Mschr. Krim Biol.* 28 (1973):87. **A.**

711. Hicks, J. "Sudden Infant Death Syndrome and Child Abuse." *Pediatrics* 52 (1973):147-148. **A, D.**

712. Hill, D. "Child Abuse" *Publishing Science* (1975). **A.**

713. Hill, E. "Child Neglect, Maltreatment and Trauma: Three Views." Presented at Training Center in Youth Developement, Law-Medicine Institute, Boston University, November 13, 1964. **A.**

714. Hiller, H "Battered or Not—A Reappraisal of Metaphyseal Fragility." *American Journal Roentgenol, Radium Thermal Nuclear Medicine* 114 (1972):241-246. **D.**

715. Hiller, R. "The Battered Child—A Health Visitor's Point of View." *Nursing Times* 65 (1969):1265-1266. **A.**

716. Hinton, C., and J. Sterling. "Volunteers Serve as an Adjunct to Treatment for Child-Abusing Families." *Hospital and Community Psychiatry* 26 (1975):136-137. **E, H.**

717. Hoel, H. "The Battered Child." *Minnesota Medicine* 46 (1963):1001. **A.**

718. Hoffman, M. "From Baby Farms to Yo-Yo Children." *(London) Times Educational Supplement,* July 4, 1975. **A.**

719. Hofstra "Constitutional Law—Neglect Proceedings—Due Process—Equal Protection—Indigent Parent(s) must be Advised of the Availability of Free Legal Counsel." *Hofstra Law Review* 1 (1973):324-331. **B.**

720. Hogan, M. "The Eye of the Battered Child." *Archives of Opthalmology* 72 (1972):231-233. **A.**

721. Holder, A. "Child Abuse and the Physician." *Journal of the American Medical Association* 222 (1972):517-518. **A, B, D.**

722. Holland, C. "Examination of Social Isolation and Availability to Treatment in Phenomenon of Child Abuse." *Smith College Studies in Social Work* 44 (1973):74-75. **D.**

723. Holland, M. "Children at Risk." *New Statesman* 86 (November 16, 1973): 721-722. **A.**

724. Hollingshead, A. "Class Differences in Family Stability." In S. Einsenstadt, ed., *Comparative Social Problems.* New York: The Free Press, 1970. **C, F.**

725. Holmes, S., C. Barnhart, L. Cantoni, and E. Reymer. "Working With Parent in Child Abuse Cases." *Social Casework* 56 (1975):3-12. **E.**

726. Holter, J., and S. Friedman. "Child Abuse: Early Case Findings in the Emergency Department." *Pediatrics* 42 (1968):128. **D.**

727. ———. "Etiology and Management of Severely Burned Children: Psychosocial Considerations." *American Journal of Diseases of Children* 118 (1968):680-686. **D.**

728. ———. "Child Abuse: Early Case Finding in the Emergency Department." *Pediatrics* 42 (1968):128-138. **A, F.**

729. Holter, J., et al. "Principles of Management in Child Abuse Cases." *American Journal of Orthiphychrity* 38 (1968):127-136. **H.**

730. Hopkins, J. "The Nurse and the Abused Child." *Nurse Clinics of North America* 5 (1970). **D.**

731. Horn, P. "Child-Battering Parent: Sick But Slick." *Psychology Today,* December 1974. **C.**

732. Hornbein, R. "Social Workers Orientation to the Use of Authority in Initiating and Maintaining a Social Casework Relationship with Parents Who Abuse and Parents Who Neglect Their Children." Doctoral dissertation, University of Denver, Ann Arbor, Michigan: University Microfilms, No. 72-32, 079, 1972. **F.**

733. Horwitz, F. "Grieving Mother Fights Back: Work of H. Semier." *McCalls,* March 1974. **C.**

734. Hoshino, G., and G. Yoder. "Administrative Discretion in the Implementation of Child Abuse Legislation." *Child Welfare* 52 (1973):414-424. **B.**

735. Housden, L. *The Prevention of Cruelty to Children.* New York: Philosophical Library, 1965. **H.**

736. Howard Law Journal "Child Abuse and the Law: A Mandate for Change." *Howard Law Journal* 18 (1973):200-219. **B.**

737. Hudson, J. "How to Set Up a No-Budget Battered Child Program." *Journal of Medical Society New Jersey* 70 (1973):441-442. **A, H.**

738. Hudson, P. "The Doctor's Handy Guide to Chronic Child Abuse." *Journal Medical Society New Jersey* 70 (1973):851-852. **A, B, D.**

739. Hughs, R. "Clinics Parent—Performance Training Program for Child Abusers," *Hospital and Community Psychiatry* 25 (1974):779. **E.**

740. Hyman, C. "Letter: I.Q. of Parents of Battered Babies." *British Medical Journal* 4 (1973):739. **C.**

741. Hyman, I., and K. Schreiber. "Selected Concepts and Practices of Child Advocacy in Schools Psychology." *Psychology in Schools* 12 (January 1975):50–58. **H.**

742. Illinois Education News. "Teacher's Role in Reporting Child Abuse." *Illinois Education News* 3 (1974):8–9. **G.**

743. Illinois Medical Journal. "Battered Child Law Takes Effect July." *Illinois Medical Journal* 127 (1965):570–571. **B.**

744. ——. "Doctors and Hospitals Must Report Child Abuse: Recent Supreme Court Ruling Doesn't Invalidate State Law." *Illinois Medical Journal* 140 (1971):41. **A, B, D.**

745. ——. "Report Suspected Abuse." *Illinois Medical Journal* 141 (1973):587. **A, B, D.**

746. Indiana Law Journal. "Parent's Right to Counsel in Dependency and Neglect Proceedings." *Indiana Law Journal* 49 (1973):167–180. **B.**

747. Ingraham, F., and J. Heyl. "Subdural Hematoma in Infancy and Child-hood." *Journal of the American Medical Association* 112 (1939):198–204. **A.**

748. Intellect. "Aid to Abused and Neglected Children." *Intellect* 102 (1974): 415. **D.**

749. ——. "Child Abuse Prompts Plan for State Legislative Action." *Intellect* 102 (1974):283–284. **B.**

750. ——. "Massive Child Neglect, Delinquency and Drug Abuse." *Intellect* 101 (1973):412+. **A.**

751. ——. Parents Anonymous and Child Abuse: Self-Help Group for Abusers." *Intellect* 103 (November, 1974):76–77.

752. Ireland, W. "A Registry on Child Abuse." *Children* 13 (1966):113–115. **B, H.**

753. Irwin, T. *To Combat Child Abuse and Neglect.* Public Affairs Committee, Incorporated, N.Y. May 1974. **H.**

754. Issacs, J. "The Law and the Abused and Neglected Child." *Pediatrics* 51 (1973):783–792. **B.**

755. ——. "The Role of the Lawyer in Child Abuse Cases." In C. Kempe and R. Helfer, eds. *Helping the Battered Child and His Family.* Philadelphia: J.B. Lippincott, 1972. **A, B, C.**

756. Issacs, S. "Emotional Problems in Childhood and Adolescents: Neglect, Cruelty and Batterings." *British Medical Journal* 3 (1972):224–226. **A.**

757. ——. "Neglect, Cruelty and Battering." *British Medical Journal* 3 (1972): 224–226. **A, C.**

758. ——. "Physical Ill-Treatment of Children." *Lancet* 1 (1968):37–39. **A, C.**

759. Jackson, J. "Child Abuse Syndrome: The Cases We Miss." *British Medical Journal* 2 (1972):756–757. **A, B, D.**

760. Jacobziner, H. "Rescuing the Battered Child." *American Journal of Nursing* 64 (1964):92-97. **H.**

761. James, J. "Child Neglect and Abuse." *Maryland State Medical Journal* 21 (1972):64-65. **A.**

762. Jeffers, C. *Living Poor.* Ann Arbor, Michigan: Ann Arbor Publishers, 1967. **F.**

763. Jenkins, A., and E. Norman. *Filial Deprivation and Foster Care.* Columbia University Press, 1972. **C.**

764. Jenkins E. "New York Society for the Prevention of Cruelty to Children." *Annals of American Academy* 31 (March 1908):492-494. **H.**

765. Jenkins, R. "Deprivation of Parental Care as a Contributor to Juvenile Delinquency." In A. Roberts, ed., *Childhood Deprivation.* Springfield, Illinois: Charles C. Thomas, 1974. **C.**

766. Jenkins, R., E. Nureddin, and I. Shapiro. "Children's Behavior Syndromes and Parental Responses." *Genetic Psychology Monogram* 74 (1966): 261-329. **A, C.**

767. Jenkins, R., et al. "Interrupting the Family Cycle of Violence." *Journal of the Iowa Medical Society* 60 (1979):85-89. **E, H.**

768. Jenkins, R. "The Psychopathic or Antisocial Personality," *Journal of Nervous and Mental Disease* 131 (1960):318-334. **A.**

769. Jenkins, S., and M. Sauber. *Severe Neglect of Abuse in Paths to Child Placement.* Community Council of Greater New York, New York, 1966. **C, H.**

770. Jennett, B. "Head Injuries in Children." *Developmental Medicine and Child Neurology* 14 (April 1972):137-147. **D.**

771. Jensen, R. "Behavior-Modification Program to Remediate Child-Abuse." *Journal of Clinical Child Psychology* 5 (1976):30-32. **E.**

772. Jeter, H. *Children, Problems, and Service in Child Welfare Programs.* Washington, D.C.: United States Government Printing Office, 1963. **H.**

773. Johnson, B., et al. "Injured Children and Their Parents." *Children* 15 (1968):147-152. **A, C.**

774. Johnson, C. *Child Abuse: Public Welare Agency-Juvenile Court Relationships.* United States Department of Health, Education, and Welfare, Social and Rehabilitation Service, Washington, D.C., April 1974. **B.**

775. Johnson, C. "Child Abuse: Some Findings from the Analysis of 1172 Reported Cases." United States Department of Health, Education, and Welfare, Social Rehabilitation Service, Washington, D.C., February 1975. **A.**

776. Johnson, M. "Symposium: The Nursing Responsibilities in the Care of the Battered Child." *Clinical Proceedings of the Childrens Hospital D.C.* 24 (1968):352-353. **D.**

777. Johnson, R. "The Child-Beaters: Sick But Curable," *The National Observer* March 24, 1973. **C, F.**

778. Johnson, T., and A. Holder. "Child Abuse and the Physician." *Journal of the American Medical Association* 222 (1972):517–518. **A, C, D.**

779. Jones, H. "Multiple Traumatic Lesions of the Infant Skeleton," *Stanford Medical Bulletin* 15(3):259–273, 1957. **D.**

780. Joos, T. "Child Abuse: A Different Point of View." *Pediatrics* 45 (1970): 511. **A.**

781. Jordan, B. *Poor Parents: Social Policy and the Cycle of Deprivation.* N.Y.: Routledge and Kegan, 1974. **C, F.**

782. Jorgense, J. "Battered, But Not Defeated—Story of an Abused Child and Positive Casework." *Child Welfare* 49:101. **A.**

783. Journal of the American Dentist Association. "Child Abuse Reporting Laws." *Journal of the American Dentist Association* 75 (1967):1070. **B.**

784. ——. "From the States. Legislation and Litigation." *Journal of the American Dentist Association* 75 (1967):1081–1082. **B.**

785. Journal of the American Medical Association. "Battered Child Legislation." *Journal of the American Medical Association* 188 (April 27, 1964): 386. **B.**

786. ——. "Battered Child Syndrome and Brain Dysfunction." *Journal of the American Medical Association* 223 (1973):1390. **A.**

787. ——. Editorial (No Title). *Journal of the American Medical Association* 176 (1961):942. **A.**

788. ——. "Slaughter of the Innocents." *Journal of the American Medical Association* 223 (1972):81–82. **A.**

789. ——. "The Battered Child Syndrome" (Editorial). *Journal of the American Medical Association* 181 (1962):42. **A.**

790. ——. "Unsuspected Trauma." *Journal of the American Medical Association* 176 (1961):942. **A.**

791. Journal of the Canadian Dentist Association. "Our Children's Keepers." *Journal of the Canadian Dentist Association* 37 (1971):245. **A, D.**

792. Journal of the Iowa State Medical Society. "The Child Abuse Problem in Iowa. The Extent of the Problem and a Proposal for Remedying It," *Journal of the Iowa Medical Society* 115 (October 1963):322–324. **F.**

793. Journal of the Louisiana State Medical Society. "Battered Child Law." *Journal of the Louisiana State Medical Society* 119317 (August 1967). **B.**

794. ——. "The Battered Child Syndrome," *Journal of the Louisiana State Medical Society* 115 (September 1963):322–324. **A.**

795. Journal of the Medical Society of New Jersey. "Medical Management of Child Abuse." *Journal of the Medical Society of New Jersey* 69 (1972): 551–553. **H.**

796. Journal of the National Education Association. "The Abused Child." *Journal of the National Education Association* 63 (1974):40–43. **A.**

797. Journal of the South Carolina Medical Association. "Neglected or Physically Abused Children." *Journal of the South Carolina Medical Association* 60 (1964):309–315. **A.**

798. Journal of the Tennessee Medical Association. "The Battered Child Syndrome." *Journal of the Tennessee Medical Association* 64 (1971): 346-347. **D.**

799. ———. "TMA X-Ray of the Month." *Journal of the Tennessee Medical Association* 66 (1973):1053-1056. **A, C.**

800. Joyce, W., E. Haynes, and T. Gardner. "Child Molested At Home." *Instructor* 79 (May 1970):35. **A.**

801. Joyner, E. "The Battered Child." *New York Journal of Medicine* 26 (1970):383-385. **A.**

802. ———. "Child Abuse: The Role of the Physician and the Hospital." *Pediatrics* 51 (1973):799-803. **A, B, D.**

803. ———. "M.D. Responsibility for the Protection of the Battered Child." *New York Journal of Medicine* 27 (1971):59-61. **A, B, D.**

804. Justice, B., and D. Duncun. "Life Crisis as a Precursor to Child Abuse." *Public Health Report* 91 (1976):110-115. **A.**

805. Justice, R., and B. Justice. "Work With Child Abuse." *Transaction Analysis Journal* 5 (1975):38-41. **E.**

806. ———. "The Abusing Family." New York: Human Science Press, 1976. **C.**

807. Kadushin, A. *Child Welfare Services.* New York: Macmillan, 1967. **A, H.**

808. Kahn, A. *Planning Community Services for Children in Trouble.* New York: Columbia University Press, 1963. **H.**

809. Kahn, A., S. Kamerman, and B. McGowan. *Child Advocacy: Report of a National Baseline Study.* New York: Columbia University School of Social Work, 1972. **D, H.**

810. Kahn, J. "Uses and Abuses of Child Psychiatry—Problems of Diagnosis and Treatment of Psychosocial Disorders." *British Journal of Medical Psychology* 44:229. **A.**

811. Kalisch, B. "What Are Hospitals Doing About Child Abuse? Report of a Nationwide Survey." *Hospital Topics* 52 (June 1974):21-24. **D.**

812. Kamerman, S. "Cross-National Perspectives on Child Abuse and Neglect." *Children Today* 4 (May-June 1975):34-40. **F.**

813. Kansas Law Review. "Parent Accused of Child Beating May Not Claim the Doctor-Patient Privilege to Prevent Medical Testimony." Opinion No. 63-80, Dated September 24, 1963, and Signed by W.M. Ferguson, Attorney General. *Kansas Law Review* 12 (1964):467-469. **B.**

814. Kaplan, M. "Deaths of Young Studied by City." *New York Times,* May 5, 1962. **A.**

815. Karlsson, A. "The Battered Child Syndrome in Iceland." *Nord. Psychiatr. Tidsokr.* 25 (1971):112-118. **A.**

816. Katz, S. *When Parents Fail: The Law's Response to Family Breakdown.* Boston, Beacon Press, 1972. **B, C.**

817. Katz, S., et al. "Child Neglect Laws in America." *Family Law Quarterly* (Spring 1975); also published as *Child Neglect Laws in America.* Chicago: American Bar Association, 1976. **B.**

818. Kaufman, F. "The Battered Child and the Law." *Canadian Association of Medical Students and Interns Journal* 24 (1965):26. **A, B.**

819. Kaufman, I. "Discussion of Physical Abuse of Children." Paper presented at National Conference on Social Welfare, New York, May 31, 1962. **A.**

820. ———. "Psychiatric Implications of Physical Abuse of Children." *Protecting the Battered Child.* Denver Children's Division American Humane Association, 1962. **A**

821. ———. "The Contribution of Protective Services." *Child Welfare* 36 (February 1957). **D.**

822. Kearns, H. "Battered Baby Syndrome, Concerned People Mobilize Against 'Shocking Injustice' " *Montreal Star* 53 (July 18, 1970). **A, H.**

823. Keller, O. "Hypothesis for Violent Crime." *American Journal of Correction* 37 (March 1975):7. **A.**

824. Kelly, F. "Role of the Courts." *Pediatrics* 51 (1973):796-798. **B.**

825. Kellum, B. "Infanticide in England in the Later Middle Ages," *History of Childhood Quarterly* 1 (1974):367-389. **F.**

826. Kempe, C. "A Practical Approach to the Protection of the Abused Child and Rehabilitation of the Abusing Parent." *Pediatrics* 51 (1973):804-812. **D, E, H.**

827. ———. "Pediatric Implications of the Battered Baby Syndrome." *Archives of Diseased Children,* 46 (1971):28-37. **A.**

828. Kempe, C. "Some Problems Encountered by Welfare Departments in the Management of the Battered Child Syndrome." In R. Helfer and C. Kempe, eds., *The Battered Child.* Chicago: University of Chicago Press, 1968. **D.**

829. ———. "The Battered Child and the Hospital." *Hospital Practice* (1969). **A, D, H.**

830. ———. "The Battered Child Syndrome." *Journal of the American Medical Association* 181 (1962):17-24. **A.**

831. Kempe, C., and R. Helfer, eds. *Helping the Battered Child and His Family.* Philadelphia: J.B. Lippincott, 1972. **C, E, F.**

832. ———. "Innovative Therapeutic Approaches." In *Helping the Battered Child and His Family.* Philadelphia and Toronto: J.B.Lippincott, 1972. **C, D, E, H.**

833. ———. *The Battered Child,* 2nd ed. Chicago: University of Chicago Press, 1974. **A.**

834. Kempe, C., and H. Silver. "The Problem of Parental Criminal Neglect and Severe Physical Abuse of Children." *American Journal of Diseases of Children* 98 (1959):528. **A, B.**

835. Kennedy, R. *Nonpenetrating Injuries of the Abdomen.* Springfield, Illinois: Charles C. Thomas, 1960. **A.**

836. Kenton, C. *Child Abuse,* National Library of Medicine Literature Search No. 73-28, January 1970, July 1973. United States Department of Health, Education, and Welfare, Public Health Service, Bethesda, Maryland. **A.**

837. Kibby, R., L. Sanders, S. Creaghan, and E. Tyrrek. "Abused Child—Need for Collaboration." *Thrust* 4 (1975):11-13. **A.**

838. Kiffney, G. "The Eye of the Battered Child." *Archives of Ophthal.* 72 (1964):231. **A.**

839. Kim, T., et al. "Pseudocyst of the Pancreas as a Manifestation of the Battered Child Syndrome. Report of a Case." *Medical Annual* 36 (1967): 664-666. **A.**

840. Kirchner, S., et al. "X-Ray of the Month. Child Abuse." *Journal of the Tennessee Medical Association* 66 (1973):1053-1054. **D.**

841. Klein, M., et al. "Low Birth Weight and the Battered Child Syndrome. *American Journal of Diseased Children* 122 (1971):15-158. **A.**

842. Kleinfeld, F. "The Balance of Power Among Infants, Their Parents and the State." *Family Life Quarterly* 409 (1970):434. **B, C.**

843. Klibanoff, E. "Child Advocacy in Action: Massachusetts' Office for Children." *Childhood Education* 52 (November–December 1975):70-72. **H.**

844. Kline, D., and M. Hopper. *Child Abuse: An Integration of the Research Related to Education of Children Handicapped as a Result of Child Abuse.* (Final Report) Department of Health, Education, and Welfare, Bureau of Education for the Handicapped, Washington, D.C., January 1975. **D.**

845. Koel, B. Failure to Thrive and Fatal Injury as a Continuum. *American Journal of Diseased Children* 118 (1969):567. **A, C.**

846. Kogelschatz, J., P. Adams, and D. Tucker. "Family Styles of Fatherless Households." *American Academy of Child Psychiatry Journal* 11:365-383. **C.**

847. Koluchova, J. "Severe Deprivation in Twins: A Case Study." *Journal of Child Psychology and Psychiatry* 13 (June 1972):107-114. **A.**

848. Komarovsky, M. "Blue Collar Marriage." In Roach, et al. *Social Stratification in the United States.* Englewood Cliffs, New Jersey: Prentice-Hall, 1969. **F.**

849. Komisaruk, R. "Clinical Evaluation of Child Abuse-Scarred Families: A Preliminary Report." *Juvenile Court Judges Journal* 17 (1966):66. **A, C.**

850. Kraus, J., and J. Smith. "Relationship of 4 Types of Broken Home to Some Neglected Parameters of Juvenile Delinquency." *Australian Journal of Social Issues* 8 (1973):52-57. **C.**

851. Kreech, F. "Adoption Outreach." *Child Welfare* 52 (1973):669-675. **B, H.**

852. Krieger, I. "Food Restriction as a Form of Child Abuse in Ten Cases of Psychosocial Deprivation Dwarfism." *Clinical Pediatrics (Philadelphia)* 13 (1974):127-133. **A.**

853. Kreisler, L., and P. Straus. "The Perpetrator of Cruelty Upon Young Children. A Psychological Approach," *Archives Francaises de Pediatrie* 28 (1971):249-265. **C.**

854. Krige, H. "The Abused Child Complex and Its Characteristic X-Ray Find-
     ings." *South Africa Medical Journal* 40 (1966):490-493. **D.**

855. Kristal, H., and F. Tucker. "Managing Child Abuse Cases." *Social Work* 20
     (1975):392-395. **D.**

856. Kroeger, N. *A Survey of Physically Abused Children Known to Select
     Hospitals and Health Agencies in the Chicago Area, 1964.* Publication No.
     4008, Welfare Council of Metropolitan Chicago, 1964. **A.**

857. Kromrower, G. "Failure to Thrive." *British Medical Journal* (November
     28, 1964):1377-1380. **A.**

858. Krywulak, W., et al. "The Physically Abused Child." *Manitoba Medical
     Review* 47 (1967):472-475. **A.**

859. Kunstadter, R., et al. "The 'Battered Child' and the Celiac Syndrome."
     Illinois Medical Journal 132 (1967):267-272. **A.**

860. Kushnick, T., et al. "Syndrome of the Abandoned Small Child." *Clinical
     Pediatrics, (Philadelphia)* 9 (1970):356-361. **A.**

861. Lakin, M. "Personal Factors in Mothers of Excessively Crying (Colicky)
     Infants." *Society for Research in Child Development* 22 (1957):7-48. **C.**

862. Lampard, F., et al. "Nanook of Eskimo Point." *Nursing Times* 65 (1969):
     1472-1473. **D.**

863. Lancet. "Assaulted Children." *Lancet* 1 (March 7, 1964):543-544. **A.**

864. ———. "Battered Babies." *Lancet* 320 (August 8, 1970):7667. **A.**

865. ———. "Question Time: Battered Babies." *Lancet* 2 (1970):1248. **A.**

866. ———. "Violent Parents." *Lancet* 2 (1971):1017-1018. **C.**

867. Langer, M. "New Year's Resolution: No More Corporal Punishment."
     Teacher 90 (January 1973):5. **G, H.**

868. Langer, W. "Infanticide: A Historical Survey." *History of Childhood
     Quarterly* 1 (1974):353-367. **A.**

869. Langshaw, W. "The Battered Child," *Australian Journal of Forensic
     Sciences* 3 (1970):260. **A.**

870. Lansky, L. "An Unusual Case of Childhood Chloral Hydrate Poisoning."
     American Journal of Diseased Children 127 (1974):275-276. **A.**

871. LaPresti, J. "The Abused 'Battered Child'." *Clinical Proceedings of the
     Hospital, D.C.* 24 (1968):351-352. **A.**

872. Lascari, A. "The Abused Child." *Journal of the Iowa Medical Society* 62
     (1972):229-232. **A.**

873. Laskin, D. "Editorial: The Battered Child Syndrome." *Journal of Oral
     Surgery* 31 (1973):903. **A.**

874. Lauer, B. "Battered Child Syndrome: Review of 130 Patients with Con-
     trols." *Pediatrics* 54 (July 1974): 67-70. **D.**

875. Laury, G., et al. "Mental Cruelty and Child Abuse," *Psychiatric Quarterly*
     (Supplement) 41 (1967):203-254. **A.**

876. Laury, G. "The Battered-Child Syndrome: Parental Motivation, Clinical
     Aspects." *New York Academy of Medicine* 46 (1970):676-685. **A, C.**

877. Leaverton, D. "The Pediatrician's Role in Maternal Deprivation," *Clinical Pediatrics* 7(6):340–343, June 1968. **D.**

878. Leavitt, J. "The Battered Child," *The Instructor* 75 (March 1966):50. **A.**

879. ———. *The Battered Child: Selected Readings.* New York: General Learning Press, 1974. **A.**

880. Leavitt, J., and B. Baldwin. "Battered Child–Selected Readings." *Social Service Review* 49 (1975):465–466. **A.**

881. Leavitt, J., and E. Plank. "Battered Child–Selected Readings." *Young Children* 31 (1975):82. **A.**

882. Le Bourdais, E. "Look Again. Is It Accident or Abuse?" *Canadian Hospitals* 69 (1972):27–30. **A.**

883. Lebrun, F. "Illegitimate Births and Abandoned Children in Anjou During 18th Century." *Annales-Economies Societes Civilisations* 27 (November 1972):1183–1189. **F.**

884. Leger, L. "To Protect Abused Children, Are Physicians Forced to Report the Cases? An Ambiguity to Clear Up." *Presse Medicale (Paris)* 79 (May 29, 1971):1261. **B.**

885. Leibsker, D. "Privileged Communications–Abrogation of the Physician-Patient Privilege to Protect the Battered Child." *DePaul Law Review* 15 (1966):453–461. **A, B, C, F.**

886. Leiken, S., et al. "Clinical Pathological Conference: The Battered Child Syndrome." *Clinical Proceedings of the Childrens Hospital (Washington)* 19 (1963):301–306. **A.**

887. Leivesley, S. "The Maltreated Child–A Cause for Concern." *Medical Journal of Australia* 1 (1972):935–936. **A.**

888. Le Masters, E. "Parenthood As Crises." In M. Sussman, ed., *Sourcebook in Marriage and the Family.* Boston: Houghton Mifflin, 1968. **C.**

889. Leonard, M., et al. "Failure to Thrive in Infants." *American Journal of Diseases of Children* 3 (1966):600–612. **C.**

890. Leserman, S. "There's A Murderer in My Waiting Room." *Medical Economics* 41 (August 24, 1964):62–71. **C.**

891. Levenstein, P. and R. Sunley. "An Effect of Stimulating Verbal Interaction Between Mothers and Children Around Play Materials." *American Journal of Orthopsychiatry* 37 (1967):334–335. **C, D, E.**

892. Levine, A. "Child Neglect: Reaching the Parent." *The Social and Rehabilitation Record* 1 (1974):26–33. **A, C, D.**

893. Levine, L. "The Solution of a Battered Child Homicide by Dental Evidence: Report of Case." *Journal of American Deititstry Association* 87 (1973):1234–1236. **E.**

894. Levitan, S. "Alternative Income Support Programs." In H. Miller, ed., *Poverty–American Style* New York: Prentice Hall, 1966. **A, C.**

895. Lewis, D., D. Balla, M. Lewis, R. Gore, and M. Gore. "Treatment of Adopted Versus Neglected Delinquent Children in Court Problem of

Reciprocal Attachment." *American Journal of Psychiatry* 132 (1975): 142-145. **D, E.**

896. Lewis, H. "Parental and Community Neglect: Twin Responsibilities of Protective Services." *Children* 16 (1969):114-118. **C, D. F.**

897. Lewis, H., et al. *Designing More Effective Protective Services—Intervening in the Recurrent Cycle of Neglect and Abuse of Children,* Philadelphia, Pa. 19104. Research Center, University of Pennsylvania School of Social Work, June 1967. **G, H.**

898. Lewis, M., et al. "Some Psychological Aspects of Seduction, Incest, and Rape in Childhood." *Journal of the American Academy of Child Psychiatry* 8 (1969):606-619. **G, H.**

899. Libia, D. "Protection of the Child Victims of a Sexual Offense in the Criminal Justice System." *Wayne Law Review* 15 (1969):977. **B.**

900. Life. "Cry Rises from Beaten Babies." *Life,* June 14, 1963. **A.**

901. ———. "Mother Confines Three To House For Ten Years." *Life,* August 29, 1960. **A, C.**

902. Light, R. "Abused and Neglected Children in America: A Study of Alternative Policies." *Harvard Educational Review* (Special Issue) 43 (November 1973):481-704. **A.**

903. Lindenthal, J., et al. "Public Knowledge of Child Abuse: Newark, New Jersey." *Child Welfare* 54 (July 1975):521-523. **A.**

904. Lloyd-Roberts, G. "The Diagnosis of Injury of Bones and Joints in Young Babies." *Proceedings of the Royal Society of Medicine* 61 (1968):1299-1300.

905. Lobsenz, N. "One Woman's War Against Child Abuse; SCAN Volunteers." *Good Housekeeping,* July 1975. **H.**

906. Looff, D. *Appalachia's Children: The Challenge of Mental Health.* Lexington: University Press of Kentucky, 1971. **D.**

907. Loomis, W. "Management of Children's Emotional Reaction to Severe Body Damage (Burns)." *Clinical Pediatrics (Philadelphia)* 9 (June 1970): 362-367. **D.**

908. Lord, E., and D. Weidfeld. "The Abused Child." In A. Roberts, ed., *Childhood Deprivation.* Springfield, Illinois: Charles C. Thomas, 1974. **A.**

909. Lorr, M., and R. Jenkins. "Patterns of Maladjustment in Children." *Journal of Clinical Psychology* 9 (1953):16-19. **A.**

910. Lovens, H., and J. Rako. "Community Approach to Prevention of Child Abuse." *Child Welfare* 54 (1975):83-87. **H.**

911. Low, C. "The Battering Parent, the Community and the Law." *Applied Social Studies (Oxford)* 3:65-80. **B, C.**

912. Lowry, T., and A. Lowry. "Abortion as a Preventive for Abused Children." *Psychiatric Opinion* 8 (1971):19-25. **H.**

913. Loyola Law Review. "Battered Child—Louisiana's Response to the Cry." *Loyola Law Review* 17 (1970-1971):372. **B.**

914. Lukianowicz, N. "Attempted Infanticide." *Psychiatria Clinica* 5 (1972): 1-16. **D.**

915. ——. "Battered Children." *Psychiatry Clinic* 4 (1971):257-280. **A.**

916. ——. "Parental Maltreatment of Children." *British Journal of Social Psychiatry* 3 (1969):189-195. **B.**

917. Lux, B. "A Dentist's Eye-View of Delinquency." *Dental News* 6 (1969):7. **A, B, D.**

918. Lynch, A. "Child Abuse in the School-age Population: Philadelphia." *Journal of School Health* 45 (March 1975):141-148. **G.**

919. Lystad, M. "Violence at Home: A Review of the Literature." *American Journal of Orthopsychiatry,* 45 (April 1975):328-345. **A, C.**

920. Maas, H., et al. *Children in Need of Parents.* New York: Columbia University Press, 1959. **C.**

921. MacDonald, J. "The Threat to Kill." *American Journal of Psychiatry* 120 (1963):125-130. **A.**

922. Mackler, S., et al., "Diagnosis and Treatment of Skeletal Injuries in the Battered Child Syndrome." *Southern Medical Bulletin* 58 (1970):27-32. **D.**

923. MacLeod, C. "Parent to Child: Legacy of Battering." *Nation* 218 (June 8, 1974):719-722. **A, C.**

924. Maginnis, E, E. Pevchik, and N. Smith. "A Social Worker Looks at Failure to Thrive." *Child Welfare* 46 (1967):335-338. **A, D.**

925. Mahler, M. "On Child Psychosis and Schizophrenia: Autistic and Symbiotic Infantile Psychoses." In R. Eissler, et al. *The Psychoanalytic Study of the Child,* Vol. VII. New York: International University Press, 1964. **D.**

926. ——. "The Battered Child. Unpublished thesis, Dalhousie Law School, 1968. **A.**

927. Majlath, G. "On the Veracity of Injured Juveniles and on the General Possibilities of Drawing up an Adequate Psychological Expertise in Cases of Deprivation and Incest." *Pszichological Tanuimanvok* 11 (1968):623-640. **D.**

928. Malone, C. "Safety First: Comments on the Influence of External Danger in the Lives of Children of Disorganized Families." *American Journal of Orthopsychiatry* 36 (January 1966):6-12. **A, C.**

929. Mant, A. "The Battered Baby Syndrome." *Medical Legislative Bulletin* 188 (1963):1-8. **A.**

930. Marer, J. "Development of the Law of "The Battered Child Syndrome'." *Nebraska Medical Journal* 51 (1966):368-372. **B.**

931. Marie, J., et al. "Hemotoma Sousdural Due Nourrisson Associe a Des Fractures des Membres." *Sem Hop Paris* 30 (1954):1757. **A.**

932. Marker, G., and P. Friedman. "Rethinking Children's Rights." *Children Today* 2 (November–December 1973):8-11. **B.**

933. Manitoba Law Review. "Child Neglect." *Manitoba Law Review* 3 (1968): 31. **A, B.**

934. Martin, D. "The Growing Horror of Child Abuse and the Undeniable Role of the Schools in Putting an End to It." *American School Board Journal* 160 (November 1973):51–55. **G.**

935. Martin, H. "Antecedents of Burns and Scalds in Children." *British Journal of Medical Psychology (London)* 43 (March 1970):39–47. **D.**

936. ——. "The Child and His Development." In C. Kempe and R. Helfer, eds., *Helping the Battered Child and His Family.* Philadelphia: J.B. Lippincott, 1972. **A, C.**

937. Maryland Community Coordinated Child Care Committee. *A Maryland State Plan for Coordinated Child Development Services.* Maryland State Department of Employment and Social Services, Baltimore, 1974. **D, H.**

938. Maurer, A. "The Eight Amendment, 'Cruel and Unusual': Interpretations and Psychological Applications." *Clinical Child Psychology* 5 (Spring 1976):16. **B.**

939. Maxwell, I. "Assault and Battery of Children and Others." *Nova Scotia Medical Bulletin* 45 (1966):105–107. **A.**

940. McCaghy, C. "Drinking and Deviance Disavowal: The Case of Child Molesters." *Social Problems* 16 (1968):43–49. **A.**

941. McCloskey, K. "Cases Notes. California Cases. Torts: Parental Liability to a Minor Child for Injuries Caused by Excessive Punishment." *Hastings Law Journal* 11 (1960):335–337. **B.**

942. ——. "Torts: Parental Liability to a Minor Child For Injuries Caused by Excessive Punishment." *Hastings Law Journal* 11 (February 1960):335–340. **B.**

943. McCoid, A. "Battered Children and Other Assaults on the Family." *Minnesota Law Review* 50 (1965):1. **A, B.**

944. McConville, B. "The Effects of Bereavement on the Child." In A. Roberts, ed., *Childhood Deprivation.* Springfield, Illinois: Charles C. Thomas, 1974. **A.**

945. McCort, J., et al. "Visceral Injuries in Battered Children." *Radiology* 82 (1964):424–428. **D.**

946. McCrea, R. *Humane Movement.* New York: Consortium Press (reprint of 1910), 1969. **H.**

947. McDermott, J. "Divorce and Its Psychiatric Sequelae in Children." *Archives of General Psychiatry* 23 (November 1970):421. **A.**

948. McFerran, J. "Parents' Groups in Protective Services." *Children* 5 (November–December 1958):223–228. **D, E.**

949. McGeorge, J. "Sexual Assault on Children." *Medicine, Science and the Law* 4 (1964):245. **A.**

950. McHenry, T., B. Girdang, and E. Elmer. "Unsuspected Trauma with Multiple Skeletal Injuries During Infancy and Childhood." *Pediatrics* 31 (1963):903–908. **D.**

951. McKenna, J. "Cases Study of Child Abuse—Former Prosecutors View." *American Criminal Law Review* 12 (1974):165-178. **B.**

952. McKown, C., H. Verhulst, and J. Crotty. "Overdose Effects and Danger from Tranquilizing Drugs." *Journal of the American Medical Association* 185 (1963):425. **D.**

953. McRae, K., C. Ferguson, and R. Lederman. "The Battered Child Syndrome." *Canadian Medical Association Journal* 108 (1973):859-866. **A.**

954. Meacham, W. F. "The Neurosurgical Aspects of the Battered Child." *Southern Medical Bulletin* 58 (1970):33-36. **D.**

955. Medical Journal Editorial. *Medical Journal* 66 (June 1967):394. **A.**

956. Medical Journal of Australia. "Whiplash Injury in Infancy." *Medical Journal of Australia* 2 (1971):456. **A, D.**

957. Medical Society of the County of New York. "Symposium on Child Abuse." Medical Society of the County of New York, New York University Medical Center, June 15, 1971. **A.**

958. Medical World News. "Use the Rod, Spoil the Child." *Medical World News,* October 27, 1961. **A.**

959. Medvecky, J., and J. Kafka. "Psychiatric Aspects of Neonaticide Committed by Mothers." *Ceskoslovenska Psychiatrie* 68 (February 1972): 16-22. **A.**

960. Meier, E. "Child Neglect." In N. Cohen, ed. *Social Work and Social Problems.* New York: National Association of Social Workers, 1964. **A, F.**

961. Meinick, B., and J. Hartley. "Distinctive Personality Attributes of Child-Abusing Mothers." *Journal of Consulting and Clinical Psychology* 33 (1969):746-749. **C.**

962. Melson, E. "Interpreting, Testing and Proving Neglect." In *Case-Worker and Judge in Neglect Cases.* New York: Child Welfare League of America, 1956, (1970). **B.**

963. Menninger Clinic, Bulletin of, "The Reporting of Child Abuse." *Bulletin of Menninger Clinic* 28 (1964):271-272. **B.**

964. Meredith, M. "Developing a Personal Theory of Child Development in High School." *Behavioral and Social Science Teacher* 2 (Spring 1975): 50-53. **G.**

965. Merill, E. "Physical Abuse of Children." Paper presented at National Conference on Social Welfare, New York, May 31, 1962. **A.**

966. ——. "Physical Abuse of Children: An Agency Study." In V. DeFrancis, ed., *Protecting the Battered Child.* Denver, Colorado: American Humane Association, 1962. **D.**

967. ——. "Reporting of Abused or Battered Children." *Journal Maine Medical Association* 56 (1965):119-120. **B.**

968. Merill, E., I. Kaufman, P. Dodge, and A. Schoepfer. *Protecting the Battered Child.* Denver, Colorado: American Humane Association, 1970. **H.**

969. Meyers, A., et al. "Hospital Combats Neglected Health Crisis." *Hospitals, Journal of the American Hospital Association* 48 (September 1, 1974): 46–49. **D.**

970. Meyers, S. "Maternal Filicide." *American Journal of Diseases of Children* 120 (1970):534. **C.**

971. ——. "The Child Slayer. A 25-year Survey of Homicides Involving Pre-adolescent Victims." *Archives of General Psychiatry* 17 (1967):211–213. **D.**

972. Michael, M. "Follow-up Study of Abused Children Reported from University Hospitals." *Journal of the Iowa Medical Society* 62 (1972):235–237. **A.**

973. ——. "The Battered Child." *Iowa Journal of Social Work* 3 (1970):78–83. **A.**

974. Midonick, M., D. Bedharov, and L. Arthur. "Children, Parents and Courts—Juvenile Delinquency, Ungovernability and Neglect." *Family Law Quarterly* 7 (1973):129–131. **B.**

975. Miller, A. "On Therapeutic Technique Regarding the So-Called Narcissistic Neuroses." *Psych (Stuttgart)* 25 (1971):641–668. **E.**

976. Miller, D. "Fractures Among Children. Parental Assault as Causative Agent." *Minnesota Medicine* 42 (1959):1209–1213. **D.**

977. ——. "Fractures Among Children. II. Some Practical Principles of Treatment of Common Fractures." *Minnesota Medicine* 42 (1959):1414–1425. **C, D.**

978. Miller, J. "Ecology of Child Abuse Within A Military Community." *American Journal of Orthopsychiatry* 41:675. **A.**

979. Miller, M. "Community Action and Child Abuse." *Nursing Outlook* 17 (1969):44–46. **D, H.**

980. Miller, M., and J. Fay. "Emergency Child Care Service: The Evaluation of a Project." *Child Welfare* 48 (October 1969):496–499. **H.**

981. Miller, W. "Lower-Class Culture as a Generating Millieu of Gang Delinquency." In S. Eisenstadt, ed. *Comparative Social Problems.* New York: The Free Press, 1965. **F.**

982. Milowe, I. "Patterns of Parental Behavior Leading to Physical Abuse of Children." Paper presented at Workshop Sponsored by the Children's Bureau in Collaboration with the University of Colorado, Colorado Springs, March 21, 22, 1966. **A, D.**

983. Milowe, I., and R. Lourie. "The Battered Child Syndrome: Some Unanswered Questions and Some Variations on the Theme." Paper presented at American Orthopsychiatric Association Meeting, Chicago, 1964. **A.**

984. Milowe, I., and R. Lourie. "The Child's Role in the Battered Child Syndrome" (Abstract). *Journal of Pediatrics* 65 (1964):1079–1081. **A.**

985. Milowe, I., et al. "Some Provocative and Controversial Mental Health Problems Posed by the Battered Child Syndrome." In *Proceedings of the*

Third Annual Conference: Mental Health Career Development Program,
May 26-28, 1964. Washington, D.C. National Institute of Mental Health,
Publication No. 1245, 1964. **H.**

986. Military Medicine. "Child Abuse and Injury." *Military Medicine* "Child
Abuse and Injury." *Military Medicine* 130 (1965):747-762. **A.**

987. Mindlin, R. "Child Abuse and Neglect—Role of Pediatrician and
Academy." *Pediatrics* 54 (1974):393-395. **D.**

988. Minnesota Medicine. "Battered Child Syndrome" Neuro-Pediatrics Conference. *Minnesota Medicine* 49 (1966):1429-1436. **A.**

989. ——. "Physicians Required to Report Child Beatings." *Minnesota Medicine* 46 (September 1963):876. **B.**

990. Mintz, A. "Battered Child Syndrome." *Texas Journal of Medicine* 60
(February 1964):107-108. **A.**

991. Minuchin, S., B. Montalvo, B. Guerney, B. Rosman, and F. Schumer.
Families of the Slums: An Exploration of Their Structure and Treatment.
New York: Basic Books, 1967. **C, F.**

992. Mitchell, B. "Working With Abusive Parents. A Caseworker's View."
American Journal of Nursing 73 (1973):480-483. **E, H.**

993. Mitchell, R. "The Incidence and Nature of Child Abuse." *Developmental
Medicine and Child Neurology* 17 (October 1975):641-644. **A.**

994. Mohr, J., and C. McKnight. "Violence as a Function of Age and Relationship, With Special Reference to Matricide." *Canadian Psychiatric Association Journal* 16 (1971):29-53. **A.**

995. Mondale, W. "Burdened Family." *Trial* (May 1974):12-13 ff. **C.**

996. ——. "Child Abuse—Issues and Answers." *Public Welfare* 32 (1974):9-11.
A.

997. ——. "The Child Abuse Prevention Act." *Congressional Record* 119 (39):
S4444-S4457, 1973. **B.**

998. ——. "We're Tossing Our Children on Scrap Heap." *Miami Herald,* December 10, 1970. **A.**

999. Mnookin, R. "Foster Care: In Whose Best Interest?" *Harvard Educational
Review* 43 (November 1973):599-638. **C.**

1000. Mooney, J. "Needed Modification of Legislation for Management of the
Problem." Paper Read at Southeastern Psychological Association, April
29, 1971. **B.**

1001. Moore, J. "Yo-Yo Children: Victims of Matrimonial Violence." *Child
Welfare* 54 (September 1975):557-566. **C.**

1002. ——. "Reporting of Child Abuse." *Journal of Medical Association
Georgia* 55 (1966):328-329. **B.**

1003. Moorehead, C. "7-Man Team Helps Parents of Battered Babies." *(London)
Times Educational Supplement* 1897 (1970):12. **E.**

1004. Moran, J., N. Ebeling, and D. Hill. "Child Abuse—Intervention and Treatment." *Child Study Journal* 6 (1976):49-51. **D, E.**

1005. Morris, M., and R. Gould. "Role Reversal: A Concept in Dealing With Neglected Battered Child Syndrome." In *The Neglected-Battered Child Syndrome.* New York: Child Welfare League of America, 1963. **E.**

1006. ———. "Role Reversal: A Necessary Concept in Dealing with the 'Battered Child Syndrome'." *American Journal of Orthopsychiatry* 33 (1963): 298–299. **E.**

1007. Morris, M., et al. "Toward Prevention of Child Abuse." *Children* 11 (2): 55–60, April 1964. **H.**

1008. Morris, T., et al. "A Battered Baby with Pharyngeal Atresia." *Journal of Laryngology and Otology* 85 (1971):729–731. **A.**

1009. Morse, C., et al. "A Three-Year Follow-Up Study of Abused and Neglected Children." *American Journal of Diseases of Children* 120 (1970):439–446. **A.**

1010. Morse, H. "Aggression Syndrome." *Georgia State Bar Journal* 9 (1973): 451. **A.**

1011. Moss, S. "Authority—An Enabling Factor in Casework with Neglectful Parents." *Child Welfare* (October 1963):385. **B.**

1012. ———. "How Children Feel About Being Placed Away From Home." *Children* 13 (November 4, 1966):153–157. **A, D.**

1013. Mother's Magazine, L.H.S. Reviewer. "On Seeing an Infant Prepared for the Grave." *Mother's Magazine*, April 1833. **A.**

1014. Mother's Magazine, W.A. Reviewer. "On the Death of Infants." *Mother's Magazine,* May 1834. **A.**

1015. Moyles, P. "Subdural Effusions in Infants." *Canadian Medical Association Journal* 100 (1969):231–234. **A.**

1016. Mulford, R. "Development of Child Protective Services in the United States." In *Interest of Children—A Century of Progress.* Denver, Colorado: Children's Division, American Humane Association, 1966. **A.**

1017. Mulford, R. *Emotional Neglect of Children.* Denver, Colorado: Children's Division, American Humane Association.

1018. ———. "Emotional Neglect of Children: A Challenge to Protective Services." *Child Welfare* (October 1958):19. **A, F.**

1019. ———. "The Caseworker in Court." In *Caseworker and Judge in Neglect Cases.* New York: Child Welfare League of America, 1956, (1970). **B, F.**

1020. Mulford, R., and M. Cohen. *Neglecting Parents—A Study of Psychosocial Characteristics.* Denver, Colorado: Children's Division, American Humane Association, 1968. **B, F.**

1021. Mulford, R., M. Cohen, and E. Philbrick. *Psychosocial Characteristics of Neglecting Parents: Implications for Treatment.* Denver, Colorado: American Humane Association, (pamphlet), 1967. **A, B, E, F.**

1022. Mulford, R., N. Ebeling, and D. Hill. "Child Abuse—Intervention and Treatment." *Child Welfare* 55 (1976):226. **A, C, D.**

1023. Mulford, R., and H. Hoel. *Protective-Preventive Services; Are They*

Synonymous? Denver, Colorado: Children's Division, American Humane Association, 1972. **D, H.**

1024. Mulford, R., et al. *Caseworker and Judge in Neglect Cases.* Denver, Colorado: Children's Division, American Humane Association, 1956. **A, B, F.**

1025. Murdock, G. "The Abused Child and the School System." *American Journal Public Health* 60 (1970):105-109. **G.**

1026. Muse, D. "Black Children's Literature Rebirth of a Neglected Genre." *Black Scholar* 7 (1975):11-14. **F.**

1027. Mushin, A. "Ocular Damage in the Battered-Baby Syndrome." *British Medical Journal* 3 (1971):402-404. **A.**

1028. Mushin, A., et al. "Ocular Injury in the Battered Baby Syndrome. Report of Two Cases." *British Journal of Opthalmology* 55 (1971):343-347. **A.**

1029. Myren, R., and L. Swanson. *Police Work with Children.* Children's Bureau, United States Department of Health, Education, and Welfare, Washington, D.C., Government Printing Office, 1962. **B.**

1030. Nagi, S. "Child Abuse and Neglect Programs: A National Overview." *Today* 4 (May-June 1975):18-21. **A.**

1031. Nation. "Children in Peril." *Nation* March 6, 1972. **A.**

1032. ——. "More of the Same." *Nation* April 6, 1964. **A.**

1033. National Academy of Sciences. "Reduce the Flow of Unwanted Babies." In H. Miller, *Poverty—American Style,* 1966. **H.**

1034. National Conference on Social Welfare. *History of Child Saving in the United States.* Montclair, New Jersey: Patterson, Smith, 1971. **A.**

1035. ——. "Legally Reported Child Abuse: A Nationwide Survey." In *Social Work Practice.* New York: Columbia University Press, 1968. **B.**

1036. National Parent Planning Association Journal. "Neglect: A Symposium. Legal Nature of Neglect." *National Parent Planning Association Journal* 6 (1960):1. **A, B.**

1037. National Study Service. *Planning for the Protection and Care of Neglected Children in California.* Sacramento, California: National Study Service, 1964. **A, D, H.**

1038. Nazzaro, J. "Child Abuse and Neglect." *Exceptional Children* 40 (1974): 351-354. **A.**

1039. Neimann, N. "Child Abuse." *Semaine des Hoptaux de Paris* 44 (May 8, 1968):1523-1525. **A, F.**

1040. Nelson G., and F. Paletta. "Burns in Children." *Surgery, Gynecology, Obstetrics* 128 (1969):518-522. **A.**

1041. New England Journal of Medicine. "More on the Battered Child" (Editorial). *New England Journal of Medicine* 269 (1964):1437. **A.**

1042. ——. "More on the Battered Child." *New England Journal of Medicine* 271 (August 23, 1964):210. **D.**

1043. New England Medical Journal. "Slaughter of the Innocents" (Editorial). *New England Medical Journal* (June 6, 1962). **A.**

1044. New York Medicine. "M.D. Responsibility for the Protection of the Battered Child." *New York Medicine* 26 (1970):59. **B, H.**

1045. New York State Dental Journal. "Dentists Required to Report Cases of Abused and Maltreated Children." *New York State Dental Journal* 39 (1973):629. **A, B, D.**

1046. New York University Intermural Law Review. " 'Discipline' as the Public School Teacher's Defense in Actions for Battery." *New York University Intermural Law Review* 16 (1960):43. **B, G.**

1047. New Yorker. "Shelter: Children's Center Deluged With Child Abuse Cases." *New Yorker,* July 5, 1969. **D.**

1048. New Zealand Medical Journal. "Taking It Out on the Baby." *New Zealand Medical Journal* 66 (1967):394. **A.**

1049. Newbauer, P. "On the Neglect of the Young Child." *American Journal of Orthopsychiatry* 33 (1963):777–778. **A.**

1050. Newberger, E. Book Review, *Violence Against Children* by David Gil. *Pediatrics* 48 (1971):688–690. **A.**

1051. ——. "The Myth of the Battered Child Syndrome." *Current Medical Dialogue* (April 1973):327. **A.**

1052. Newberger, E., and J. Hyde, Jr. *Child Abuse: Principles and Implications of Current Pediatric Practice,* United States Department of Health, Education, and Welfare, Office of Child Development, Washington, D.C., June 1974. **D.**

1053. Newberger, E., et al. "Child Abuse in Massachusetts." *Massachusetts Physician* 32 (1973):31. **F.**

1054. ——. "Reducing the Literal and Human Cost of Child Abuse: Impact of a New Hospital Management System." *Pediatrics* 51 (1973):840–848. **A, D, H.**

1055. Newman, C. "Police and Families: Factors Affecting Police Intervention," *Police Chief* 39 (1972):25–26, 28, 30. **B.**

1056. Newsweek. "The Battered Child." *Newsweek,* June 3, 1968. **A.**

1057. ——. "Hard Case: Alleged Abuse at Artisia Hall, Houston, Texas." *Newsweek,* July 16, 1973. **A.**

1058. ——. "Help For Child Beaters." *Newsweek,* July 24, 1972. **E.**

1059. ——. "Their Prison Was Home." *Newsweek,* August 8, 1960. **A.**

1060. ——. "When They're Angry." *Newsweek,* April 16, 1962. **A.**

1061. Newton, N. "The Relationship Between Infant Feeding Experience and Later Behavior." *Journal of Pediatrics* 38 (1951):28–40. **A, C.**

1062. Ney, P. "Uses and Abuses of Operant Conditioning—Subjective Review." *Canadian Psychiatric Association Journal* 20 (1975):119–132. **E.**

1063. Nichamin, S. "Battered Child Syndrome and Brain Dysfunction." *Journal American Medical Association* 223 (March 19, 1973):1390. **D.**

1064. Nichols, E. *A. Voluntary Agency Adds Child Protective Services,* Denver, Colorado: Children's Division, American Humane Association, 1973. **H.**

1065. Nixon, H., and S. Court. "Non-accidental Injury in Children." *British Medical Journal* 4 (1973):656-600. **A, C.**

1066. Nomura, F. "The Battered Child 'Syndrome'" (Review). *Hawaii Medical Journal* 25 (1966):387-394. **A.**

1067. Nordstrom, J. "Child Abuse: A School District's Response to Its Responsibility." *Child Welfare* 53 (April 1974):257-260. **G.**

1068. Nurse, S. "Familial Patterns of Parents Who Abuse Their Children." In *Smith College Studies in Social Work* 11 (October 1964). **A, C.**

1069. ———. "Parents Who Abuse Their Children." *Smith College Studies in Social Work* 35 (October 1974):11-25. **C.**

1070. Nurses Forum. "Child Abuse." *Nurses Forum* 3 (1964):7-9. **A, D.**

1071. Nyden, V. "Preventing Maltreatment of Children: The Use of Authority." *Public Welfare* 24 (1966):239-245. **B, H.**

1072. Oakland, L., and R. Kane. "The Working Mother and Child Neglect on the Navajo Reservation." *Pediatrics* 51 (1973):849-853. **F.**

1073. O'Brien, J. "Violence in Divorce Prone Families." *Journal of Marriage and Family* 33 (November 1971):692-698. **C.**

1074. O'Doherty, N. "Subdural Hematoma in Battered Babies." *Developmental Medicine and Child Neurology* 6 (1964):192-193. **A.**

1075. Odlum, D. "Neglected Children." *Royal Society of Health Journal* 79 (1959):737. **A.**

1076. Oettinger, K. "Abused Child." *Childhood Education* 41 (January 1965): 135-137. **A.**

1077. Oettinger, K., A. Morton, and R. Mulford. *In the Interest of Children—A Century of Progress.* Denver, Colorado: Children's Division, American Humane Association, 1976. **A, C, H.**

1078. Oettinger, K. "Protecting Children From Abuse." *Parents* 39(11):12, November 1964. **H.**

1079. ———. "The Facts Behind Battered-Child Laws." *Medical Economics* 41 (1964):71-75. **A.**

1080. Ogburn, W. "The Wolf Boy of Agra." *American Journal of Sociology* 64 (March 1959):449-454. **A, G.**

1081. Ohio School Counselors Association. *Guidance For the NOW Student.* Report of the 18th Annual All Ohio Guidance Conference, Ohio School Counselors Association: Division of Guidance and Testing, Ohio State Department of Education, Columbus, Ohio, October 1970. **G.**

1082. Okell, C., and C. Butcher. "Battered Child Syndrome." *The Law Society's Gazette* 66 (1969):587. **A.**

1083. Oliman, J., and S. Friedman. "Parental Deprivation in Psychiatric Conditions. In Personality Disorders and Other Conditions." *Diseases of the Nervous System* 28 (1967):298-303. **C.**

1084. Oliver, J., et al. "A Family Kindren With Ill-Used Children: A Burden to the Community." *British Journal of Psychiatry* 123 (1973):81-90. **C, D, E, H.**

1085. ——. "Five Generations of Ill-Treated Children in One Family Pedigree."
    British Journal of Psychiatry 119 (1971):473-480. **C.**

1086. ——. "Six Generations of Ill-Used Children in a Huntington's Pedigree."
    Postgraduate Medical Journal 45 (1969):757-760. **C.**

1087. Oliver, J. "Parents of Battered Children." *British Journal of Psychiatry*
    128 (May 1976):509. **C, E.**

1088. Oliver, K., and A. Barclay. "Stanford-Binet and Goodenough-Harris Test
    Performances of Head Start Children." *Psychological Reports* 20 (1967):
    175-179. **H.**

1089. Olsen, I. "Some Effects of Increased Aid in Money and Social Services to
    Families Getting AFDC Grants." *Child Welfare* 49 (1970):94-100. **E.**

1090. Olsen, R. "Index of Suspicion: Screening for Child Abusers." *American
    Journal of Nursing* 75 (January 1976):108-110. **A, C.**

1091. O'Neill, J., Jr. "Deliberate Childhood Trauma: Surgical Perspectives."
    Journal of Trauma 13 (1973):361-362. **A.**

1092. O'Neill, J., Jr., et al. "Patterns of Injury in the Battered Child Syndrome."
    Journal of Trauma 13 (1973):332-339. **A.**

1093. O'Neil, M. "A Mother Beats Her Child." *The Social Worker* 37 (1969):
    166-170. **C.**

1094. Oregon Law Review. "Parent and Child—Child Beating—Recent Legisla-
    tion Requiring Reporting of Physical Abuse." *Oregon Law Review* 15
    (1966):453. **B.**

1095. O'Toole, T. "The Speech Clinician and Child Abuse." *Language, Speech,
    and Hearings Services in Schools* 5 (April 1974):103-106. **D, G.**

1096. Ott, J. "Neglect of Physically Abused Children: A Review." *Journal of
    South Carolina Medical Association* 60 (October 1974):309-315. **A.**

1097. Overton, A., and K. Tinker. *Casework Notebook,* St. Paul: Family Centered
    Project, 1957. **D.**

1098. Oviatt, B. "After Child Abuse Reporting Legislation—What?" In C. Kempe
    and R. Helfer, eds., *Helping the Battered Child And His Family.* Phila-
    delphia: J.B. Lippincott, 1972. **B, C.**

1099. Owena, D., and M. Straus. "The Social Structure of Violence in Childhood
    and Approval of Violence as an Adult." *Aggressive Behaviour* (1975). **F.**

1100. Paget, N. "Emergency Parent—A Protective Service to Children in Crisis."
    Child Welfare (July 1967). **D.**

1101. ——. "Involving Protective Service Clients." In *Family Life Education and
    Protective Services.* A Report prepared by the American Humane
    Association, Children's Division, Denver, Colorado, 1966. **H.**

1102. Paget, N., and G. Penner. *Family Life Education and Protection Ser-
    vices.* Denver, Colorado: Children's Division, American Humane Associa-
    tion, 1966. **C, H.**

1103. Parker, F. "Representing the Parent in a 'Care and Protection' Custody
    Hearing." *Massachusetts Law Quarterly* 57 (1972):387. **B.**

1104. Parker, G. "The Battered Child Syndrome." (The Problem in the United States). *Medical Science Law* 5 (1965):160-163. **A.**

1105. Parry, W., et al. "Child Abuse Syndrome." *British Medical Journal* 3 (1972):113-114. **A.**

1106. Parsell, N. *Growing Up in Idaho: The Needs of Young Children.* Boise, Idaho: Idaho State Office of Child Development, 1973. **A.**

1107. Parsons, T., and R. Bales. *Family Socialization and Interaction Process.* New York: Free Press, 1955. **C.**

1108. Pasamanick, B. "A Child is Being Beaten." *American Journal of Orthopsychiatry* 41 (1971):540-556. **A.**

1109. Pashayan, H., et al. "Maltreatment Syndrome of Children." *Nova Scotia Medical Bulletin* 44 (1965):139-142. **A.**

1110. Patterson, P., et al. "Child Abuse in Hawaii." *Hawaii Medical Journal* 25 (1966):395-397. **A.**

1111. Patti, R. "Child Protection in California, 1850-1966. An Analysis of Public Policy." Ph.D. dissertation, University of Southern California, Los Angeles, June 1967. **F, H.**

1112. Patton, R., and L. Gardner. *Growth Failure in Maternal Deprivation.* Springfield, Illinois: Charles C. Thomas, 1963. **C.**

1113. ———. "Influence of Family Environment in Growth: The Syndrome of 'Maternal Deprivation'." *Pediatrics* 30 (December 1962):957-962. **C.**

1114. Paul S. "Recognition of the Entity 'The Battered Child Syndrome' in India." *Indian Journal of Pediatrics* 38 (1972):58-62. **A.**

1115. Paull, D., R. Laurena, and B. Schimel. "A New Approach to Reporting Child Abuse." *Hospitals* 41 (1967):62-64. **A, B.**

1116. Paulsen, M. "Child Abuse Reporting Laws: The Shape of the Legislation." *Columbia Law Review* 67 (1967):1-49. **B.**

1117. ———. "Legal Framework for Child Protection." *Columbia Law Review* 66 (1966):679-717. **B.**

1118. ———. "Legal Protections Against Child Abuse." *Children* 13 (1966):42-48. **B.**

1119. ———. "The Delinquency, Neglect and Dependency Jurisdiction of the Juvenile Court." In *Justice for the Child,* M. Rosenheim, ed. New York: Free Press, 1962. **A, B.**

1120. ———. "The Law and Abused Children." In C. Kempe and R. Helfer, eds., *The Battered Child.* Chicago: University of Chicago Press, 1968. **B.**

1121. ———. "The Legal Rights of Children." *Childhood Education* 50 (1974): 327-330. **B.**

1122. Paulsen, M., G. Parker, and L. Adelman. "Child Abuse Reporting Laws: Some Legislative History." *George Washington Law Review* 34 (1966): 482-506. **B.**

1123. Paulsen, M., et al. "Child Abuse Reporting Laws—Some Legislative History." *George Washington Law Review* 34 (March 1966):482. **B.**

1124. ——. "Legal Protection Against Child Abuse." *Children* 43 (March–April 1966). **B.**

1125. Paulson, M. "Child Trauma Intervention: A Community Response to Family Violence." *Journal of Clinical Psychology* 4 (1975):26–29. **D, E.**

1126. Paulson, M., A. Afifi, A. Chaleff, V. Liu, and M. Thomason. "MMPI Scale for Identifying At-Risk Abusive Parents." *Journal of Clinical Psychology* 4 (1975):22–24. **C, E.**

1127. Paulson, M., and P. Blake. "The Abused, Battered and Maltreated Child: A Review." *Trauma* 9 (1967):3. **A.**

1128. ——. "The Physically Abused Child: A Focus on Prevention." *Child Welfare* 48 (1969):86–95. **H.**

1129. Paulson, M., and A. Chaleff. "Parent Surrogate Roles: A Dynamic Concept in Understanding and Treating Abusive Parents." *Journal of Clinical Child Psychology* 2 (Fall 1973):38–40. **E.**

1130. Paulson, M., et al. "Group Psychotherapy: A Multidisciplinary Approach to the Treatment of Abusive Parents. In R. Helfer and C. Kempe, eds., *The Battered Child.* Chicago: University of Chicago Press, 1972. **E, H.**

1131. Pavenstedt, E., ed. *The Drifters: Children of Disorganized Lower-Class Families.* Boston: Little, Brown, 1967. **A, F.**

1132. ——. "The Meanings of Motherhood in a Deprived Environment." In E. Pavenstadt and V. Bernard, eds. *Crises of Family Disorganization: Programs to Soften Their Impact on Children.* New York: Behavioral Publications, 1971. **C.**

1133. Pavenstedt, E., and V. Bernard, eds. *Cries of Family Disorganization: Programs to Soften Their Impact on Children.* New York: Behavioral Publications, 1971. **D, E, H.**

1134. Pediatric Currents. "Failure to Thrive." *Pediatric Currents* 18 (September 1969):57. **A.**

1135. Pediatrics. "American Academy of Pediatrics Committee on Infant and Pre-School Children. Maltreatment of Children. The Battered Child Syndrome." *Pediatrics* 50 (1972):160–162. **A.**

1136. ——. "Committee on Infant and Pre-School Child. Maltreatment of Children: The Physically Abused Child." *Pediatrics* 37 (February 1966): 377–387. **A.**

1137. Pemberton, D., et al. "Consciously Rejected Children." *British Journal of Psychiatry* 123 (1973):575–578. **A.**

1138. Pena, S., et al. "Child Abuse and Traumatic Pseudocyst of the Pancreas." *Journal of Pediatrics* 83 (1973):1026–1028. **A.**

1139. Penner, G., and H. Welch. *The Protective Services Centre.* Denver, Colorado: American Human Association, 1975. **C, H.**

1140. Pennsylvania Medicine. "M.D. Has Role in Child Abuse Cases." *Pennsylvania Medicine* 73 (1970):102. **D.**

1141. Perira, F. "Application of Psychology of Learning to Rehabilitation of

Abandoned Children." *Revista Latinoamericana De Psicologia* 7 (1975): 391–399. **D.**

1142. Peterson, K. "Contributions to An Abused Childs Unlovability—Failure In Developmental Tasks and In Mastery of Trauma." *Smith College Studies in Social Work* 44 (1973):24–25. **A.**

1143. Peterson, K. "There's a Link Between Animal Abuse and Child Abuse." *PTA Magazine* 68 (June 1974):14–16. **A.**

1144. Pfundt, T. "The Problem of the Battered Child." *Postgraduate Medicine* 35 (1962):426–431. **A.**

1145. Philbrick, E. *Treating Parental Pathology—Through Child Protective Services.* Denver, Colorado: Children's Division, American Humane Association. **C, D, E, H.**

1146. Pickel, S., et al. "Thirsting and Hypernatremic Dehydration. . . A Form of Child Abuse." *Pediatrics* 45 (1970):54–59. **A.**

1147. Pickett, L. "Role of the Surgeon in the Detection of Child Abuse." *Connecticut Medicine* 36 (1972):513–514. **A, B, D.**

1148. Pitcher, R., Jr. "The Police." In C. Kempe and R. Helfer, eds., *Helping the Battered Child and His Family.* Philadelphia: J.B. Lippincott, 1972. **B, E.**

1149. Piven, F., and R. Cloward. *Regulating the Poor: The Functions of Public Welfare.* New York: Pantheon Books, 1971. **F.**

1150. Plaine, L. "Evidentiary Problems in Criminal Child Abuse Prosecutions." *Georgetown Law Journal* 63 (1974):257–273. **B.**

1151. Platou, R., et al. "Battering." *Bulletin Tulane Medical Faculty* 23 (1964): 157–165. **A.**

1152. Podell, L. "Family Planning by Mothers on Welfare." *Bulletin of the New York Academy of Medicine* 49 (1973):931–937. **C, H.**

1153. Polokow, R., and D. Peabody. "Behavioral Treatment of Child Abuse." *International Journal of Offender Therapy* 19 (1975):100–103. **E.**

1154. Polansky, N. "Child Neglect in a Rural Community." *Social Casework* 49 (1968):467–474. **B, F.**

1155. ——. *The Apathy-Futility Syndrome in Child Neglect.* Annual Workshop on Children's Institutions, School of Social Work, University of North Carolina, 1966. **A.**

1156. Polansky, N., R. Borgman, and C. DeSaix. *Roots of Futility.* New York: Jossey-Bass, 1972. **A.**

1157. Polansky, N., R. Borgman, C. Desaix, and B. Smith. "Two Modes of Maternal Immaturity and Their Consequences." *Child Welfare* 49 (1970): 312–323. **C.**

1158. Polansky, N., C. DeSaix, and S. Sharlin. "Child Neglect in Appalachia." In *Social Work Practice.* New York: Columbia University Press, 1971. **F.**

1159. Polansky, N., and N. Polansky. "The Current Status on Child Abuse and Child Neglect in This Country." In *Report to the Joint Commission on Mental Health for Children,* Washington, D.C., February 1968. **A.**

1160. Polansky, N., and L. Pollane. "Measuring Child Adequacy of Child Caring: Further Developments." *Child Welfare* 54 (May 1975):354–359. **C.**

1161. Polansky, N., et al. "Child Neglect in a Rural Community." *Social Casework* 49 (1968):467–474. **A, F.**

1162. ———. *Child Neglect: Understanding and Reaching the Parent.* San Francisco: Jossey-Bass, 1972. **A.**

1163. ———. *Profile of Neglect. A Survey of Knowledge of Child Neglect.* United States Department of Health, Education, and Welfare, Social and Rehabilitative Service, Community Services Administration, Washington, D.C., 1975. **A.**

1164. ———. "Verbal Accessibility in the Treatment of Child Neglect." *Child Welfare* (June 1971):349. **A.**

1165. Polier, J. "Professional Abuse of Children—Responsibility for Delivery of Services." *American Journal of Orthopsychiatry* 45 (1975):357–362. **D.**

1166. Polier, J., and K. McDonald. "The Family Court in an Urban Setting." In C. Kempe and R. Helfer, eds., *Helping the Battered Child and His Family.* Philadelphia: J.B. Lippincott, 1972. **B, C.**

1167. Pollack, J. "What You Can Do to Help Stop Violence, An Interview with Cr. John P. Spiegel, Director, Lemberg Centre for the Study of Violence." *Family Circle,* October 1968. **A, H.**

1168. Pollitt, E., et al. "Psychosocial Development and Behavior of Mothers of Failure-to-Thrive Children." *American Journal of Orthopsychiatry* 45 (July 1975):525–537. **C.**

1169. Pollock, C. "Early Case Finding as a Means of Prevention of Child Abuse." In R. Helfer and C. Kempe, eds., *The Battered Child.* Chicago: University of Chicago Press, 1968. **H.**

1170. Pollock, C., and B. Steele. "A Therapeutic Approach to the Parents." In C. Kempe and R. Helfer, eds., *Helping the Battered Child and His Family.* Philadelphia: J.B. Lippincott, 1972. **C, E, H.**

1171. Polomeque, F., et al. "Battered Child Syndrome: Unusual Dermatological Manifestation." *Archives Dermatology (Chicago)* 90 (1964):326–327. **A.**

1172. Postgraduate Medicine. "Child Abuse and the Physician's Responsibility." *Postgraduate Medicine* 35 (April 1964):446. **D.**

1173. Potter, C. "Infanticides." In M. Leach, eds. *Dictionary of Folklore, Mythology, and Legend,* Vol. 1. New York: Funk and Wagnalls, 1949. **A.**

1174. Potts, W., and O. Forbis. "Willful Injury in Childhood. A Distinct Syndrome." *Journal of the Arkansas Medical Society* 59 (1962):266–270. **A.**

1175. Powell, G., J. Brasel, and R. Blizzard. "Emotional Deprivation and Growth Retardation Simulating Idiopathic Hypopituitarism: I. Clinical Evaluation of the Syndrome." *New England Journal of Medicine* 276 (1967):1217–1278. **D.**

1176. Provence, S., and R. Lipton. *Infants in Institutions.* New York: International University Press, 1962. **C.**

1177. Prugh, D., and R. Harlow. "Masked Deprivation in Infants and Young Children." In *Deprivation of Maternal Care: A Reassessment of Its Effects.* Public Health Papers No. 14, Geneva, Switzerland: W.H.O., 1962. **A, C.**

1178. Psychiatische Praxis. "Social Aspects of Child Abuse." *Psychiatische Praxis* 2 (1975):129–130. **F.**

1179. Psychiatry Annual. "Treatment of Abused and Neglected Preschool-Children in A City Hospital." *Psychiatry Annals* 6 (1976):36. **D.**

1180. Public Health. "Violence at Home." *Public Health* 84 (1970):53–56. **A, C.**

1181. Public Welfare, District of Columbia Department of. *Toward Social and Economic Independence: The First Three Years of the District of Columbia Training Center,* Department of Public Welfare, District of Columbia, 1965. **A, E, F.**

1182. Pugh, R. "Battered Babies." *Lancet* 2 (1970):466–467. **A.**

1183. Raab, E., and G. Selznick. *Major Social Problems.* Illinois: Row, Person, 1959. **A.**

1184. Rabellino, C. "Child Abuse and the Hospital Social Worker." *Canadian Association of Medical Students and Interns Journal* 24 (1965):39. **A, D, H.**

1185. Racine, A. "Introductory Discussion of Child Abuse." *Les Enfants Victims de Mauvais Traitements (Bruxelles)* 28 (1971):5–16. **A, F.**

1186. Radbill, S. "A History of Child Abuse and Infanticide." In R. Helfer and C. Kempe, eds., *The Battered Child.* Chicago: University of Chicago Press, 1968. **A.**

1187. Rafalli, H. "The Battered Child. An Overview of a Medical, Legal and Social Problem." *Crime and Delinquency* 16 (1970):139–150. **B, D.**

1188. Rainwater, L. *Social Stratification in the United States.* Englewood Cliffs, New Jersey: Prentice-Hall, 1969. **F.**

1189. Rall, M. "The Casework Process in Work with the Child and the Family in the Child's Own Home." National Conference of Social Work, *1954 Casework Papers.* New York: Columbia University Press, 1954. **C, D, E, H.**

1190. Rappaport, M., et al. "The Neglected Child: Collaborative Approaches to Recognition and Management." *Clinical Pediatrics (Philadelphia)* 2 (1963): 521–524. **A, D.**

1191. Rathbun, D., L. Di Virgilio, and S. Waldfogel. "The Restitutive Process in Children Following Radical Separation from Family and Culture." *American Journal of Orthopsychiatry* 28 (1958):408–415. **C, H.**

1192. Rathsam, B. *"Sadistische Kindesmisshandlung"* (Sadistic Abuse of Children). *Krim Mh.* 11 (1937):244–248. **A.**

1193. Rauchfle, U. "Social Emotional Problems in Self-Appraisal of Neglected Child." *Praxis der Kinderpsychologie und Kinderpsychiatrie* 21 (1972): 246–254. **A, D.**

1194. Rayford, L., et al. "The Social and Legal Aspects of the Battered Child in the District of Columbia: Panel Discussion." *Clinical Proceedings of the Childrens Hospital, D.C.* 24 (1968):375–393. **B, F.**

1195. Reed, J. "Working With Abusive Parents: A Parent's View" (Interview With Jolly K.). *Children Today* 4 (May 1975):6–9. **C.**

1196. Reed, K., M. Melli, M. Wald, and R. Wesenberg. "A Conference on Child Abuse." *Wisconsin Medical Journal* 71 (1972):226–229. **A.**

1197. Rein, M. *Child Protective Services in Massachusetts.* Waltham, Massachusetts: Florence Heller Graduate School for Advanced Studies in Social Welfare, Brandeis University, November 1963. **D, H.**

1198. Reiner, B., and I. Kaufman. *Character Disorders in Parents of Delinquents.* Family Service Association of America, 1959. **C.**

1199. Reinhart, J., et al. "Love of Children—A Myth?" *Clinical Pediatrics (Philadelphia)* 7 (1968):703–705. **A.**

1200. ——. "The Abused Child. Mandatory Reporting Legislation." *Journal of the American Medical Association* 188 (1964):358–362. **B.**

1201. Reinitz, F. "Special Registration Project of the Abused Child." *Child Welfare* 44 (February 1965):103–105. **H.**

1202. Renvoize, J. *Children in Danger.* New York: Routledge and Kegen, 1975. **A.**

1203. ——. "Have You Stopped Beating Your Baby?" *(London) Times Educational Supplement,* June 14, 1974. **A.**

1204. Reskow, J. "Child Abuse: What the Educator Should Know." *New Jersey Education Association Review* 47 (November 1973):14–15. **G, H.**

1205. Resnick, P. "Child Murder by Parents: A Psychiatric Review of Filicide." *American Journal of Psychiatry* 126 (1969):325–334. **A, C.**

1206. Reul, M. *Territorial Boundaires of Rural Poverty: Profiles of Exploitation.* Lansing, Michigan: Center for Rural Manpower and Public Affairs, 1974. **F.**

1207. Rhode Island Medical Journal. "Mandatory Reporting of Injuries Inflicted by Other than Accidental Means Upon Children Under the Age of Eighteen Years." *Rhode Island Medical Journal* 47 (August 1964):397–399. **B.**

1208. ——. "The Abused Child, Parents and the Law." *Rhode Island Medical Journal* 47 (February 1964):89–90. **A, B, C.**

1209. Riccards, M. *Child Study Journal* 1 (1971):227–232. **A.**

1210. Richette, L. "Cheated Out of Childhood." In L. Richette, *The Throwaway Children.* Philadelphia: J.B. Lippincott, 1969. **A.**

1211. Richette, L. "Who Catches the Throwaway Child?" *Transaction of the Student College Physicians Philadelphia* 40 (1973):219–225. **H.**

1212. Riese, H. *Heal the Hurt Child.* Chicago: University of Chicago Press, 1962. **A.**

1213. Riley, H. "The Battered Child Syndrome: General and Medical Aspects." *Southern Medical Journal* 58 (1970):9–13. **A, D.**

1214. Riley, N. "The Abused Child." *Rocky Mountain Medical Journal* 68 (1971):33–36. **A.**

1215. Riscalla, L. "Professionals Role and Perspectives on Child Abuse." *Journal of Clincal Child Psychology* 5 (1976):24–26. **A, D.**

1216. Roach, J., and O. Gursslin. *Social Stratification in the United States.* Englewood Cliffs, New Jersey: Prentice-Hall, 1969. **F.**

1217. Robbins, J. *The Legal Status of Child Abuse and Neglect in Mississippi.* Sponsoring Agency: Governor's Office of Education and Training, Jackson, Mississippi, April 1974. **B.**

1218. Roberts, A. "Childhood Deprivation." Springfield, Illinois: Charles C. Thomas, 1974. **A.**

1219. ——. "Studies of Children Deprived of Human Contact, Interaction and Affection." In A. Roberts, ed., *Childhood Deprivation.* Springfield, Illinois: Charles C. Thomas, 1974. **C, D, E.**

1220. Roberts, A., and B. Roberts. "Divorce and the Child: A Pyrrhic Victory?" In A. Roberts, ed., *Childhood Deprivation.* Springfield, Illinois: Charles C. Thomas, 1974. **C.**

1221. Roberts, J. "Characteristics of the Abused Child and His Family: An Agency Study." Unpublished thesis submitted for course in Social Work, Carleton University School for Social Work, 1968. **A.**

1222. Roberts, R. "A Comparative Study of Social Caseworkers' Judgments of Child Abuse Cases." *Dissertation Abstracts International,* Ann Arbor, Michigan: University Micro-Films, No. 71-6247. **H.**

1223. Robertson, A. "Children, Teachers and Society: The Over Pressure Controversy, 1880–1886." *British Journal of Educational Studies* 20 (October 1972):315–323. **G, H.**

1224. Robertson, J. "Mothering as an Influence on Early Development." *Psychoanalytic Study of the Child* 17 (1962):245–264. **A, C.**

1225. Rochester, D., et al. "What Can The Schools Do About Child Abuse?" *Todays Education* 57 (September 1968):59–60. **G, H.**

1226. Rodenburg, M. "Child Murder by a Depressed Mother: A Case Report." *Canadian Psychiatric Association Journal* 16 (1971):49–53. **A, B.**

1227. ——. "Child Murder by Depressed Patients." *Canadian Psychiatric Association Journal (Ottawa)* (February 1971):41–48. **A.**

1228. Rodham, H. "Children Under the Law." *Harvard Educational Review* 43 (1973):487–514. **A, B.**

1229. Rogers, D., J. Tripp, A. Bentovim, A. Robinson, D. Berry, and D. Goulding. "Non-Accidental Poisoning—Extended Syndrome of Child Abuse." *British Medical Journal* 1 (1976):793–796. **D.**

1230. Rolston, R. "The Effect of Prior Physical Abuse on the Expression of Overt and Fantasy Aggressive Behavior in Children." *Dissertation Abstracts International* 32 (1971):3016. **A.**

1231. Rosen, S., S. Hirschenfang, and J. Benton. "Aftermath of Severe Multiple Deprivation in a Young Child: Clinical Implications." *Perceptual and Motor Skills* 24 (1967):219–226. **D.**

1232. Rosenblatt, S., D. Schaeffer, and J. Rosenthal. "Effects of Diphenylhydantoin on Child Abusing Parents—Preliminary Report." *Current Therapy* 19 (1976):332–336. **E.**

1233. Rosengard, B. *Research. Demonstration and Evaluation Studies: Fiscal Year 1973.* United States Department of Health, Education, and Welfare, Children's Bureau, Washington, D.C., Division of Research and Evaluation, 1974. **H.**

1234. Rosenheim, M. "The Child and His Day in Court." *Child Welfare* 45 (1966):17–21. **B.**

1235. ——. "The Child and the Law." In B. Caldwell and H. Ricintti, eds., *Review of Child Development,* Vol. 3. Chicago: University of Chicago Press, 1973. **B.**

1236. Roskies, E., P. Bedard, H. Gauvreaugilbault, and D. Lafortune. "Emergency Hospitalization of Young Children—Some Neglected Psychological Considerations." *Medical Care* 13 (1975):570–581. **D.**

1237. Rosten, P. "Spare the Rod and Save the Parent." *McCalls,* August 1973. **E.**

1238. Roth, F. "Practice Regimen for Diagnosis and Treatment of Child Abuse." *Child Welfare* 54 (April 1975):268–273. **D.**

1239. Rowe, D. "Rights of Parents and Children." *New England Journal of Medicine* 283. (1970):156–157. **B.**

1240. Rowe, D., et al. "A Hospital Program for the Detection and Registration of Abused and Neglected Children." *New England Journal of Medicine* 282 (1970):950–952. **B, D, H.**

1241. Rowe, N. "Fractures of the Facial Skeleton in Children." *Journal of Oral Surgery* 26 (1968):505–515. **A.**

1242. Royal Society for Health Journal. "Battered Babies." *Royal Society for Health Journal* 90 (1970):282–283. **A.**

1243. Rubin, J. "Preventing Maltreatment of Children: The Need for Intervention." *Public Welfare* 24 (1966):231. **H.**

1244. ——. "The Battered Child." *Wellesley Alumnae Magazine* 50 (March 1966):8–9. **A.**

1245. Rubin, S. "Children as Victims of Institutionalization." *Child Welfare* 51 (1972):6–18. **A, F.**

1246. Rudeen, S., et al. *The Prenatal, Perinatal, and Postnatal Status of Children in Idaho,* Vol. 1. Idaho State Office of Child Development. Boise, Idaho, 1973. **B.**

1247. Russell, D. "Law Medicine, and Minors—IV." *New England Journal of Medicine* 279 (1968):31–32. **A, B.**

1248. Russell, P. "Subdural Hematomas in Infancy." *British Medical Journal* 2 (1965):446–448. **A.**

1249. Ryan, J. *Social Services and the Family.* Learning Institution of North Carolina, Durham, Department of Health, Education, and Welfare, Office of Child Development, Washington, D.C., 1975. **E.**

1250. Ryan, W. *Infanticide: Its Law, Prevalence, Prevention and History.*
London: J. Churchill, 1862. **A, B, H.**

1251. Salk, L. "On the Prevention of Schizophrenia." *Diseases of the Nervous System* 29 (1968):11-15. **D.**

1252. Salmon, J. "Subdural Hematoma in Infancy. Suggestions for Diagnosis and Management." *Clinical Pediatrics* (October 1971):597-599. **D.**

1253. Saltin, D., and J. Miller. "The Ecology of Child Abuse Within a Military Community." *American Journal of Orthopsychiatry* 41 (1971):675-678. **F.**

1254. Sampson, P. "Medical Progress Has Little Effect on an Ancient Childhood Syndrome." *Journal of American Medical Association* 222 (1972): 1605-1612. **A, E.**

1255. San Diego Law Review. "Battered Child: Logic in Search of Law." *San Diego Law Review* 8 (1971):364. **B.**

1256. Sanders, L., et al. "Child Abuse: Detection and Prevention." *Young Child* 30 (July 1975):332-338. **A.**

1257. Sanders, R. "Resistance to Dealing with Parents of Battered Children." *Pediatrics* 50 (1972):853-857. **E, H.**

1258. Sandler, S. "If You Don't Stop Hitting Your Sister, I'm Going to Beat Your Brains In." *Clinical Child Psychology* 5 (Spring 1976):27 ff. **A.**

1259. Sandusky, A. "Protective Services." *Encyclopedia of Social Work.* New York: National Association of Social Workers, 1965. **A, H.**

1260. ———. "Services to Neglected Children." *Children* 7 (January-February 1960):23-28. **H.**

1261. Sandgrun, A., R. Gaines, and A. Green. "Child Abuse and Mental Retardation—Problem of Cause and Effect." *American Journal of Mental Deficiency* 79 (1974):327-330. **A.**

1262. Sandford, D., and R. Tustin. "Behavioral Treatment of Parental Assault on Children." *New Zealand Psychology* 2 (October 1973):76-82. **E.**

1263. Santhanakrisnan, B., et al. "PITS Syndrome." *Indian Pediatrics* 10 (1972): 97-100. **A.**

1264. Sargent, D. "The Lethal Situation: Transmission of Urge to Kill From Parent to Child." In J. Fawcett ed. *Dynamics of Violence.* Chicago: American Medical Association, 1971. **A, C.**

1265. Sarsfield, J. "Battering: Danger of a Backlash." *British Medical Journal* (1974):57-58. **A, C.**

1266. Sarsfield, J., and A. Dowell. "Parents of Battered Babies." *British Medical Journal* (1974):637. **B, C.**

1267. Satchell, M. "A Series of Three Articles on Battered Children: Innocent Victims of Recession's Stresses." Reprint from *Washington Star News,* April 14, 15, 16, 1975, United States Department of Health, Education, and Welfare. **A.**

1268. Sattin, D., and J. Miller. "The Ecology of Child Abuse Within a Military Community." *American Journal of Orthopsychiatry* 41 (July 1971): 675-678. **F.**

1269. Sauer, L. "Problems of Teen-Age Parents." *PTA Magazine* 59 (October 1964):27-28. **C.**

1270. Savino, B., et al. "Working with Abusive Parents. Group Therapy and Home Visits." *American Journal of Nursing* 73 (1973): 482-484. **E, H.**

1271. Sayre, J., et al. "Community Committee on Child Abuse. A Step Toward a Better Understanding and Co-Operation." *New York State Journal of Medicine* 73 (1973):2071-2075. **C, D, E, H.**

1272. Scarr-Salapatek, S. "Race, Social Class and IQ." *Science* 174 (1971): 1285-1295. **F.**

1273. Schachter, M. "Contribution to the Clinical and Psychological Study of Mistreated Children: Physical and Moral Cruelty." *Psychiatric Neuropathology* 80 (1952):311. **A.**

1274. Schafer, E., and R. Bell. "Development of Parental Attitude Research Instrument." *Child Development* 29 (September 1958):339-361. **C, H.**

1275. Scherl, D., and L. Macht. "An Examination of the Relevance for Mental Health of Selected Anti-Poverty Programs for Children and Youth." *Community Mental Health Journal* 8 (1972):8-16. **D.**

1276. Schlaegel, E., and K. Fordyce. "Schools—Corporal Punishment Without Civil or Criminal Liability." *West Virginia Law Review* 72 (1970): 399-407. **G.**

1277. Schlesinger, B. "Battered Children and Damaged Parents." *Canadian Health and Welfare* 19 (1964):3. **A, C.**

1278. Schleyer, F., and W. Pioch. "Fatal Outcome by Crush Syndrome after Continuous Beatings of a Child." *Mschr. Kinderheilk* 105 (1957):392. **A.**

1279. Scholesser, P. "The Abused Child." *Bulletin from the Menninger Clinic* 28 (1964):260-268. **A.**

1280. Schmitt, B. "What Teachers Need to Know About Child Abuse and Neglect." *Education Digest* 41 (March 1976):19-21. **G, H.**

1281. Schneider, C., et al. "Interviewing the Parents." In C. Kempe and R. Helfer, eds., *Helping the Battered Child and His Family*. Philadelphia: J.B. Lippincott, 1972. **C, E, H.**

1282. Schneider, C., R. Helfer, and C. Polleck. "The Predictive Questionnaire: Preliminary Report." In C. Kempe and R. Helfer, eds., *Helping the Battered Child and His Family*. Philadelphia: J.B. Lippincott, 1972. **H.**

1283. Schoepfer, A. "Legal Implications in Connection With Physical Abuse of Children." In *Protecting the Battered Child*. Denver, Colorado: Children's Division, American Humane Association, 1962. **B.**

1284. Schorr, A. *Children and Decent People*, New York: Basic Books, 1974. **A.**

1285. ——. *Poverty in America*. Ann Arbor: University of Michigan Press, 1968. **F.**

1286. Scrimshaw, N. "Early Malnutrition and Central Nervous System Function." *Merill-Palmer Quarterly* 15 (1969):375-387. **D.**

1287. Schrotel, S. "Responsibilities of Physicians in Suspected Cases of Brutality." *Cincinnati Journal of Medicine* 42 (October 1961):406-407. **D.**

1288. Schulman, I. "On The Management of the Irate Parent." *Journal of Pediatrics* 77 (1970):338-340. **E, H.**

1289. Schultz, L. "The Child Sex Victim: Social, Psychological and Legal Perspectives." *Child Welfare* 52 (1973):147-157. **A, B.**

1290. Schwartz, E. "Child Murder Today" (Playwrights and Psychologists View Filicide in Life, Drama). *The Human Context* 4 (1972):360-361. **A.**

1291. ——. "Facts, Fancies and Reflections." *Human Context (London)* 2 (1970):346-348. **A.**

1292. Schwartz, L. "Psychiatric Case Report of Nutritional Battering with Implications for Community Agencies." *Community Mental Health Journal* 3 (1967):163-169. **A, C, D, E, F.**

1293. Science Digest. "Dealing with Child Abusers." *Science Digest* 76 (October 1974):70-71. **E.**

1294. Scott, P. "Fatal Battered Baby Cases." *Medicine, Science and the Law* 13 (1973):197-206. **A, B.**

1295. ——. "Parents Who Kill Their Children." *Medicine, Science and the Law* 13 (April 1973):120-126. **A, C.**

1296. ——. "Tragedy of Maria Colwell." *British Journal of Criminology* 15 (January 1975):88-90. **A.**

1297. Scranton, W. "State Legislation of 1963 of Interest to Physicians." *Pennsylvania Medical Journal* 66 (October 1963):22-26. **B.**

1298. Segal, J. *Mental Health Program Reports—No. 5.* United States Department of Health, Education, and Welfare, Health Services and Mental Health Administration, Bethesda, Maryland, December 1971. **H.**

1299. Segal, R. "A Comparison of Some Characteristics of Abusing and Neglecting, Nonabusing Parents. Ph.D. dissertation, Columbia University. Ann Arbor, Michigan: University Microfilms, No. 72-1386, 1971. **B, F.**

1300. Seltzer, R. "The Disadvantaged Child and Cognitive Development in the Early Years." *Merill-Palmer Quarterly* 19 (1973):241-252. **A.**

1301. Semaine des Hopitaux de Paris. "Professional Secrecy and Abused Children." *Semaine des Hopitaux de Paris* 47 (Supplement) 14:263-267, November 26, 1971. **D.**

1302. Sgroi, S. "Sexual Molestation of Children." *Children Today* 4 (May–June 1975):18-21. **A.**

1303. Shade, D. "Limits to Service in Child Abuse." *American Journal of Nursing* 69 (1969):1710-1712. **D.**

1304. Shaffer, H. "Child Abuse: Search for Remedies." *Editorial Research Reports* 1 (May 12, 1965):343-359. **H.**

1305. Shanas, R. "Child Abuse: A Killer Teachers Can Help Control." *Phi Delta Kappan* 56 (March 1975):479-482. **G.**

1306. Sharlin, S., and N. Polansky. *American Journal of Orthopsychiatry* 42 (1972):92-102. **D, E.**

1307. Shaw, A. "The Surgeon and the Battered Child." *Surgery, Gynecology, Obstetrics* 119 (1964):355. **A, B, D.**

1308. Shengold, L. "The Effects of Overstimulation: Rat People." *International Journal of Psychoanalysis* 48 (1967):403-415. **A.**

1309. Shenken, L. "A Child is Being Beaten." *Australian and New Zealand Journal of Psychiatry* 7 (December 1973):243-248. **A.**

1310. Shepherd, R., Jr. "The Abused Child and the Law." *Virginia Medical Monthly* 93 (January 1966):3-6. **B.**

1311. ———. "The Battered Child and the Law." *Washington and Lee Law Review* 22 (Fall 1965):180-195. **B.**

1312. Sheridan, M. "The Intelligence of 100 Neglectful Mothers." *British Medical Journal* (January-March 1956):91-93. **A, C.**

1313. ———. *Lancet* 1 (2):722-725, April-June 1959. **A.**

1314. Sheriff, H. "The Abused Child." *Journal of the South Carolina Medical Association* 60 (1964):191-193. **A.**

1315. Sherman, E., et al. *Service to Children in Their Own Homes: Its Nature and Outcome,* New York: Child Welfare League of America, 1973, Sponsoring Agency: United States Department of Health, Education, and Welfare, Community Services Administration. **D.**

1316. Sherman, E., R. Neuman, and A. Shyne. *Children Adrift in Foster Care.* New York: Child Welfare League of America, 1973. **C.**

1317. Sherman, G. "The Abused Child—New York State." *New York Dentist Journal* 36 (1970):109. **A.**

1318. Shopfner, F. "Periosteal Bone Growth in Normal Infants." *American Journal of Roentgen* 97 (1966):154-163. **D.**

1319. Siegel, E., F. Decourcy, and J. Decourcy. "Silent Tragedy—Child Abuse in Community." *American Journal of Public Health* 65(1975): 1349. **A.**

1320. Sierra, S. "Rx to Check Child Molesting." *Illinois Medical Journal* 135 (1969):731-732. **D.**

1321. Silber, D., et al. "The Neurologist and the Physically Abused Child." *Neurology (Minneapolis)* 21 (1971):991-999. **A.**

1322. Silbert, J., and A. Sussman. "Rights of Juveniles Confined in Training Schools." *Crime and Delinquency* 20 (1974):373-388. **B, C, D.**

1323. Silver, H., and C. Kempe. "The Problem of Parental Criminal Neglect and Severe Physical Abuse of Children." *American Journal of Diseases of Children* 98 (1959):528. **C, E.**

1324. Silver, H., et al. "The Problem of Parental Criminal Neglect and Severe Physical Abuse of Children." *American Journal of Diseases of Children* 98 (October 1959):528. **A, C.**

1325. Silver, H., and M. Finkelstein. "Deprivation Dwarfism." *Journal of Pediatrics* 70 (March 1967):317-324. **A, D.**

1326. Silver, L., et al. "Agency Action and Interaction in Cases of Child Abuse." *Social Casework* 52 (1971):164-171. **D, E, H.**

1327. ———. "Child Abuse Laws—Are They Enough?" *Journal of the American Medical Association* 199 (1967):65-68. **B.**

1328. ———. "Child Abuse Syndrome: The 'Gray Areas' In Establishing a Diagnosis. *Pediatrics* 44 (1969):594-600. **I.**

1329. Silver, L. "Child Abuse Syndrome: A Review." *Medical Times* 96 (1968): 303-320. **A.**

1330. ———. "The Psychological Aspects of the Battered Child and His Parents." *Clinical Proceedings of the Childrens Hospital D.C.* 24 (1968):355-364. **A, C.**

1331. Silver, L., C. Dublin, and R. Lourie. "Community Agencies: Actions, Non-Actions and Interactions in Cases of Child Abuse." *Social Casework*, 1976. **H.**

1332. Silver, L., et al. "Does Violence Breed Violence? Contributions From a Study of the Child Abuse Syndrome." *American Journal of Psychiatry* 126 (1969):404-407. **A.**

1333. ———. "Mandatory Reporting of Physical Abuse of Children in the District of Columbia: Community Procedures and New Legislation." *Medical Annual, D.C.* 36 (1967):127-130. **B.**

1334. Silverman, F. "Radiological Aspects of the Battered Child Syndrome." In R. Helfer and C. Kempe eds., *The Battered Child.* Chicago: University of Chicago Press, 1968. **D.**

1335. ———. "The Battered Child." *Manitoba Medical Review* 45 (October 1965): 473-477. **A.**

1336. ———. "The Roentgen Manifestations of Unrecognized Skeletal Trauma in Infants." *American Journal of Roentgen* 69 (1953):413-427. **D.**

1337. ———. "Unrecognized Trauma in Infants. The Battered Child Syndrome and the Syndrome of Ambroise Tardieu." *Radiology* 104 (1972):337-353. **D.**

1338. Silverman, M., and E. Wolfson. "Early Intervention and Social Class: Diagnosis and Treatment of Preschool Children in a Day Care Center." *Journal of the American Academy of Child Psychiatry* 10 (1971):603-618. **D, F.**

1339. Simons, B., et al. *Child Abuse: A Perspective on Legislation in Five Middle-Atlantic States, and a Survey of Reported Cases in New York City.* New York: Columbia University School of Public Health and Administrative Medicine, February 1966. **B.**

1340. ———. "Child Abuse: Epidemiologic Study of Medically Reported Cases." *New York Journal of Medicine* 66 (1966):2783-2788. **A.**

1341. ———. "Medical Reporting of Child Abuse." *New York State Journal of Medicine* 68 (1968):2324-2330. **A, B, D.**

1342. Simpson, J. "Self-Mutilation by a 13-Year-Old Girl." *Pediatrics* 45 (1970): 1008. **A.**

1343. Simpson, K. "The Battered Baby Problem." *Royal Society of Health Journal* 87 (1967):168–170. **A.**

1344. ———. "The Battered Baby Problem." *South African Medical Journal* 42 (1968):661–663. **A.**

1345. Sims, B., et al. "Bite Marks in the 'Battered Baby Syndrome.' " *Medicine Science and the Law,* 13 (1973):197–206. **A.**

1346. Singh, J., and R. Zingg. *Wolf Children and Feral Man.* New York: Harper and Row, 1942. **A.**

1347. Skeels, H., and H. Dye. *Proceedings of American Association on Mental Deficiency,* 44 (1939):114–136. **A.**

1348. Skinner, A., and R. Castle. "Seventy-eight Battered Children: A Retrospective Study." *National Society for the Prevention of Cruelty to Children* London, 1969. **A.**

1349. Slater, P. *The Pursuit of Loneliness: American Culture at the Breaking Point.* Boston: Beacon Press, 1970. **F.**

1350. Smith, A., G. Flick, G. Feriss, A. Selim, and H. Adolph. "Predication of Developmental Outcome at Seven Years From Prental, Perinatal, and Postnatal Events." *Child Development* 43 (1972):495–507. **A.**

1351. Smith, A. "The Beaten Child." *Hygeia* 22 (1944):386. **A.**

1352. Smith, C. "The Battered Child." *New England Journal of Medicine* 289 (1973):322–323. **A.**

1353. Smith, H. "The Legal Aspects of Child Abuse." *Southern Medical Bulletin* 58 (1970):19–21. **B.**

1354. Smith, M. "Subdural Hematoma with Multiple Fractures." *American Journal of Roentgenology* 63 (1950):342. **B.**

1355. Smith, R. "New Ways to Help Battering Parents." *Today's Health* 51 (January 1973):57–64. **A.**

1356. Smith, S. "Child Injury Intensive Monitoring System." *British Medical Journal* 3 (1973):593–594. **E, H.**

1357. ———. "Battered Child Syndrome—Some Research Findings." *Royal Society of Health Journal* 95 (1975):148–153. **H.**

1358. ———. "Failure to Thrive and Anexoria Nervosa." *Postgraduate Medical Journal* 48 (1972):382–384. **A, C.**

1359. Smith, S., and R. Hanson. "Interpersonal Relationships and Child-Rearing Practices in 214 Parents of Battered Children." *British Journal of Psychiatry* 127 (December 1975):513–525. **A.**

1360. ———. *Postgraduate Medical Journal* 48 (1972):382–384. **G, H.**

1361. Smith, S., and S. Noble. "Battered Children and Their Parents." *New Society* 26 (1973):393–395. **A, C.**

1362. Smith, S., et al. "EEG and Personality Factors in Baby Batterers." *British Medical Journal* 3 (1973):20–22. **C.**

1363. ——. "Parents of Battered Babies: A Controlled Study." *British Medical Journal* 4 (1973):388-391. **C.**

1364. Snedecor, S., and H. Wilson. "Some Obstetrical Injuries to Long Bones." *Journal of Bone and Joint Surgery* 31 (1949):378. **A.**

1365. Snedecor, S., R. Knapp, and H. Wilson. "Traumatic Ossifying Periostitis of Newborn." *Surgery, Gynecology and Obstetrics* 61 (1935):385. **A.**

1366. Snedeker, L. "Notes on Childhood Trauma." *New England Journal of Medicine* 275 (1966):1061-1062. **A, B.**

1367. ——. "Traumatization of Children." *New England Journal of Medicine* 267 (September 13, 1962):572. **D.**

1368. Social Welfare Court Digest. "First Degree Murder Indictment of Parents: State vs. House p. 485 2d33 (Oregon), Court of Appeals of Oregon." *Social Welfare Court Digest* 16 (1971):1. **B.**

1369. ——. "Physically Abused Child Held 'Deprived'." In re J.Z. 190 N.W. 2027 (North Dakota), Supreme Court of North Dakota, September 7, 1971. *Social Welfare Court Digest* 17 (1972):3. **B.**

1370. Soeffing, M. "Abused Children are Exceptional Children." *Exceptional Children* 42 (November 1975):126-133. **D.**

1371. Soloom, M. "The spectrum of Abuse in the Battered-Child Syndrome." *Injury* 2 (1971):211-217. **A.**

1372. Solomon, T. "History and Demography of Child Abuse." *Pediatrics* 51 (1973):773-776. **A.**

1373. Solomon, T., et al. *The Mayor's Task Force on Child Abuse and Neglect.* New York: Center for Community Research, 1970. **H.**

1374. Soman, S. *Let's Stop Destroying Our Children: Society's Most Pressing Problem.* New York: Hawthorn Books, 1974. **A.**

1375. Southwest Educational Development Lab., Austin, Texas. *Parenting in 1975: A Listing from PMIC.* U.S. Department of Health, Education, and Welfare, National Institute of Education, Washington, D.C., June 1975. **C.**

1376. Spargo, J. *The Bitter Cry of Children.* New York: Grosset and Dunlop, 1908. **A.**

1377. Spinetta, J., and D. Rigler. "The Child Abusing Parent: A Psychological Review." *Psychological Bulletin* 77 (1972):296-304. **A.**

1378. Spitz, R., and A. Wolf. "Hospitalism: An Inquiry in the Psychiatric Conditions in Early Childhood." *Psychoanalytic Studies of Children* 1 (1946): 53-74. **D.**

1379. Spitz, R. *Hospitalism. In the Psychoanalytic Study of the Child.* New York, International University Press, 1945. **D.**

1380. ——. *Hospitalism: A Follow-Up Report. In the Psychoanalytic Study of the Child.* New York: International University Press, 1946. **D.**

1381. ——. *The Role of the Ecological Factors in Emotional Development in Infancy.* New York: International University Press, 1949. **A.**

1382. Stallones, R., and L. Corsa. "Childhood Accidents in Two California Counties." *Public Health Reports* (January 1961). **D.**

1383. ——. "Epidemiology of Childhood Accidents in Two California Counties."
      Public Health Reports 76 (January 1961):25–36. **F.**

1384. Stanford Law Review. "Observations on the Establishment of a Child-
      Protective-Services System in California." *Stanford Law Review* 21 (1969):
      1129. **D, E, H.**

1385. Stark, J. "Battered Child—Does Britain Need a Reporting Law?" *Public
      Law* (1969). **B.**

1386. Starr, R. "Introduction to 1973 Infant Conference Papers." *Merrill-
      Palmer Quarterly of Behavior and Development* 20 (1974):227–229. **A.**

1387. Starr, R., C. Zook, and P. Hauser. "Children's Rights: Countering the
      Opposition." *Clinical Child Psychology* 5 (Spring 1976):21 ff. **A, B.**

1388. Steele, B. "Parental Abuse of Infants and Small Children." In E. Anthony
      and T. Benedik, eds. *Parenthood: Its Psychology and Psychopathology.*
      Boston: Little, Brown, 1970. **A, C.**

1389. ——. Proceedings of Conference on Patterns of Parental Behavior Leading
      to Physical Abuse of Children." Unpublished. University of Colorado,
      School of Medicine, 1966. **A.**

1390. ——. "Violence in Our Society." *The Pharos of Alpha Omega Alpha* 33
      (April 1970):42–48. **F.**

1391. ——. "Working with Abusive Parents." *Children Today* 4 (May–June
      1975):3–5. **E.**

1392. Steele, B., and C. Pollock. "A Psychiatric Study of Parents Who Abuse
      Infants and Small Children." In R. Helfer and C. Kempe, eds., *The
      Battered Child.* Chicago: University of Chicago Press, 1968. **C, E.**

1393. Steele, B., C. Pollock, and E. Davoren. "Observations on the Treatment of
      Parents Who Attack Their Children." Project on the Battered Child
      Syndrome, Conducted Jointly by the Department of Psychiatry and
      Department of Pediatrics, University of Colorado Medical Center, Unpub-
      lished, 1966. **C.**

1394. Steinmetz, S. "Occupation and Physical Punishment: A Response to
      Straus." *Journal of Marriage and the Family* 33 (November 1971):664–
      666. **A.**

1395. Steinmetz, S., and M. Straus. "Some Myths About Violence in the
      Family." Paper read at the Meetings of the American Sociological Asso-
      ciation, 1971. **A, C.**

1396. ——. "The Family as Cradle of Violence." (Formerly *Transaction*) 10
      (September–October 1973):50–56. **C.**

1397. ——. *Violence in the Family.* New York: Dodd, Mead, 1974. **C.**

1298. Stephens, P., and N. Lo. "When Shall We Tell Kevin—Battered Child
      Revisited." *Child Welfare* 53 (1974):576–581. **D.**

1399. Stern, E. "The Medea Complex: The Mother's Homicidal Wishes to Her
      Child." *Journal of Mental Science (British Journal of Psychiatry)* 94
      (1948):329. **A.**

1400. Stern, L. "Prematurity as a Factor in Child Abuse." *Hospital Practice* 8 (May 1973):117-123. **A.**

1401. Stevenson, W. "Battered Baby Syndrome." *The Medical Journal of Australia* 2 (1973):1073. **A.**

1402. Stolk, M. *The Battered Child in Canada.* Montreal, Canada: McClelland and Stewart, 1972. **A.**

1403. ———. "Who Owns the Child?" *Childhood Education* 50 (March 1974): 158-165. **A.**

1404. Stone, F. "Psychological Aspects of Early Mother-Infant Relationships." *British Medical Journal* (October 23, 1971):224-226. **A, C.**

1405. Stone, J. "Acute Epiphyseal and Peristeal Infections in Infants and Children." *Boston Medical and Surgical Journal* 156 (1907):842. **A.**

1406. Stone, N., et al. "Child Abuse by Burning." *Surgical Clinic of North America* 50 (1970):1419-1424. **A.**

1407. Storey, B. "The Battered Child." *Medical Journal Aust.* 2 (1964):789-791. **A.**

1408. Straus, M. "A General Systems Theory Approach to Theory of Violence Between Family Members." *Social Science Information* 12 (June 1973): 105-125. **A, C.**

1409. ———. "Cultural and Social Organizational Influences on Violence Between Family Members." In R. Prince and D. Barried, eds., *Configurations: Biological and Cultural Factors in Sexuality and Family Life.* Lexington, Mass.: D.C. Heath, Lexington Books, 1974. **C, F.**

1410. ———. "Leveling, Civility, and Violence in the Family." *Journal of Marriage and the Family* 36 (February 1974):13-29. **C.**

1411. ———. "Some Social Antecedents of Physical Punishment: A Linkage Theory Interpretation." *Journal of Marriage and the Family* 33 (November 1971):658-663. **A.**

1412. Strauss, P. "Child Abusers—Psychological Approach." *Archives of French Pediatrics* 28:249. **A.**

1413. Strauss, P., and A. Wolf. "A Topical Subject: The Battered Child." *Psychiatrie de L'Enfant (Paris)* 12:577-628. **A, F.**

1414. Strauss, P. "The Relationship Between Promise and Performance in State Intervention in Family Life." *Columbia Journal of Law and Social Problems* 9 (1972):28-62. **B, G. H.**

1415. Streshinsky, S. "Help Me Before I Hurt My Child!" *Recbook*, June 1974. **E.**

1416. Stringer, E. "Homemaker Service in Neglect and Abuse. II. A Tool for Case Evaluation." *Children* 12 (1965):26-29. **C, E, H.**

1417. Suarez, M., and M. Ricketson. "Facilitating Casework with Protective Service Clients Through Use of Volunteers." *Child Welfare* 53 (May 1974): 313-322. **E.**

1418. Suffolk University Law Review. "Neglected Child: His and His Family's

Treatment under Massachusetts Law and Practice and Their Rights under the Due Process Clause." *Suffolk University Law Review* 4 (1970):631. **B**.

1419. Sulby, A., and A. Diodati. "Family Day Care—No Longer Day Cares Neglected Child." *Young Children* 30 (1975):239-247. **H**.

1420. Sullivan, E,, et al. "Symposium: Battered Child Syndrome." *Clinical Proceedings Children's Hospital (Washington)* 20 (1964):229-239. **A**.

1421. Sullivan, M. "Child Neglect: The Environmental Aspects." *Ohio State Law Journal* 29 (1963):85. **B, F**.

1422. Sullivan, M., M. Spasser, and M. Taber. *The Bowen Center Project.* Chicago, Illinois: Juvenile Protective Association, 1974. **D**.

1423. Sussman, A. "Reporting Child Abuse—Review of Literature." *Family Law Quarterly* 8 (1974):245-313. **A, D**.

1424. Sussman, A., and S. Cohen. *Reporting Child Abuse and Neglect: Guidelines for Legislation.* New York: Ballinger, 1975. **B**.

1425. Sussman, S. "Skin Manifestations of the Battered-Child Syndrome." *Journal of Pediatrics* 72 (1968):99. **A**.

1426. ——. "The Battered Child Syndrome." *California Medicine* 108 (1968): 437-439. **A**.

1427. Swanson, L. "Role of the Police in the Protection of Children from Neglect and Abuse." *Federal Probation* 25 (1961):43-48. **B**.

1428. Swift, J. "A Modest Proposal for Preventing the Children of Ireland from Being a Burden to Their Parents of Country." In W. Eddy, ed., *Satires and Personal Writings.* London: Oxford University Press, 1965. **F, H**.

1429. Swischuk, L. "Spine and Spinal Cord Trauma in the Battered Child Syndrome." *Radiology* 92 (1969):733-738. **D**.

1430. ——. "The Battered Child Syndrome: Radiologic Aspects." *Southern Medical Bulletin* 58 (1970):24-26. **D**.

1431. ——. "The Beaked, Notched or Hooked Vertebra." *Radiology* 5 (1970): 661-664. **C, D**.

1432. Syre, J., F. Foley, L. Zingarella, and H. Kristal. "Community Committee on Child Abuse." *New York State Journal of Medicine* 73 (1973):2071-2075. **A, B, G**.

1433. Taipale, V., et al. "Experiences of an Abused Child." *Acta Paedopsychiatr (Basal)* 39 (1972):53-58. **A**.

1434. Talbert, J., et al. "Identification and Treatment of Thoracoabdominal Injuries in 'Battered Children'," *Southern Medial Bulletin* 58 (1970):37-43. **D**.

1435. Tamilia, P. "Neglect Proceedings and the Conflict Between Law and Social Work." *Duquesne Law Review* 9 (1971):579. **B**.

1436. Tank, E., et al. "Blunt Adbominal Trauma in Infancy and Childhood." *Journal of Trauma* 8 (1968):439-448. **A**.

1437. Tapp, J., V. Ryken, and C. Kaltwasser. "Counseling the Abusing Parent by Telephone." *Crisis Intervention* 5 (1974):27-37. **E**.

1438. Tardieu, A., and F. Silverman. "Unrecognized Trauma in Infants. The Battered Child Syndrome and the Syndrome of Abrise Tardieu." Rigler Lecture. *Radiology* 104 (August 1972):337–353. **D.**

1439. Tascari, A. "The Abused Child." *Journal of Iowa Medical Society* 62 (1972):229–232. **A.**

1440. Tate, R. "Facial Injuries Associated with the Battered Child Syndrome." *British Journal of Oral Surgery* 9 (1971):41–45. **A.**

1441. Taylor, A. "Deprived Infants: Potential for Affective Development." *American Journal Orthopsychiatry* 38 (October 1968):835–845. **A.**

1442. Taylor, R. *Sweatshops in the Sun: Child Labor on the Farm.* Boston: Beacon Press, 1973. **A.**

1443. Teaque, R. "Kentucky Legislature Concerning Reporting of Abused Children." *Journal of Kentucky Medical Association* 64 (1966):584. **B.**

1444. Ten Bensel, R., et al. "The Battered Child Syndrome." *Minnesota Medicine* 46 (October 1963):977–982. **A.**

1445. Ten Broeck, E. "The Extended Family Center—'A Home Away from Home' for Abused Children and their Parents." *Children Today* 3 (1974): 2–6. **A, B, E.**

1446. Ten Have, R. "A Preventive Approach to Problems of Child Abuse and Neglect." *Michigan Medicine* 64 (1965):645–649. **H.**

1447. Teng, C., et al. "Inflicted Skeletal Injuries in Young Children." *Pediatric Digest* (September 1964):53–66. **D.**

1448. ——. "Skeletal Injuries of the Battered Child." *American Journal Orthopsychiatry* 6 (1964):202–207. **D.**

1449. Terr, L. "A Family Study of Child Abuse." *American Journal Psychiatry* 127 (1970):665–671. **C.**

1450. Terr, L., et al. "The Battered Child Rebrutalized: Ten Cases of Medical-Legal Confusion." *American Journal Psychiatry* 124 (1968):1432–1439. **A.**

1451. Texas Medicine. "Battered Child Law Reporting Procedure Places Moral Obligation on Physician." *Texas Medicine* 63 (1967):120. **A, B, D.**

1452. Thomas, D. "The Battered Child Syndrome." *The Child's Guardian* 5 (March 1968). **A.**

1453. Thomas, E. "Child Neglect Proceedings—New Focus." *Indiana Law Journal* 50 (1974):60–81. **B.**

1454. Thomas, M. Jr., "Child Abuse and Neglect: Historical Overview, Legal Matrix, and Social Perspectives." *North Carolina Law Review* 50 (1972): 293. **A, B.**

1455. ——. "Child Abuse Cases—A Complex Problem." *State Government* (October 1965). **B.**

1456. Thomas, W., and F. Znaniecki. *Sociological Theory: A Book of Readings.* New York: Macmillan, 1964. **A.**

1457. Thomson, E., et al. *Child Abuse: A Community Challenge.* New York: Children's Aid Society for the Prevention of Cruelty to Children, 1971. **A, H.**

1458. Thomson, E. "Child Abuse Is No Myth: Interview." *Instructor* 83 (January 1974):84–85. **A.**

1459. Till, K. "Subdural Haematoma and Effusion in Infancy." *British Medical Journal* 3 (1968):804. **A.**

1460. Time. "Battered-Child Syndrome: Child Beating." *Time,* July 20, 1962. **A.**

1461. ——. "Battering Parent; Battered Child Syndrome." *Time,* November 7, 1969. **A, C.**

1462. ——. "Hard Times for Kids Too: Child Abuse as a Consequence of Economic Strain." *Time,* March 17, 1975. **A.**

1463. ——. "Saving Battered Children." *Time,* January 8, 1965. **D.**

1464. Tobias, J. "Deprivation in the Affluent Suburbs." In A. Roberts, *Childhood Deprivation.* Springfield, Illinois: Charles C. Thomas, 1974. **F.**

1465. Today's Child. "Abusing Parents Organize to Help Each Other." *Today's Child* 22 (1974):6. **B.**

1466. Today's Education. "The Abused Child." *Today's Education* 63 (1974): 40–43. **A, H.**

1467. Today's Health. "10,000 Children Battered and Starved." *Today's Health* 43 (September 1965):24. **A, D.**

1468. Togut, M., et al. "A Psychological Exploration of the Non-organic Failure-to-Thrive Syndrome." *Developmental Medicine and Child Neurology* 11 (October 1969):601–607. **D.**

1469. Toland, M. "Abuse of Children—Whose Responsibility?" *Connecticut Medicine* 28 (June 1964):438–442. **A.**

1470. Tormes, Y. *Child Victim of Incest.* Denver, Colorado: Children's Division, American Humane Association, 1968. **D.**

1471. Touloukian, R. "Abdominal Visceral Injuries in Battered Children." *Pediatrics* 42 (1968):642–646. **A.**

1472. ——. "Battered Children with Abdominal Trauma." *General Pathology and Pathological Anatomy* 40 (1969):106–109. **A.**

1473. ——. "Visceral Injury Caused by Trauma." *Modern Medicine* (November 1969). **A.**

1474. Tracy, J., et al. "Child Abuse Project-Follow-Up." *Social Work* 20 (1975): 398–399. **D.**

1475. Tracy, J., and E. Clark. "Treatment for Child Abusers." *Social Work* 19 (1974):338–342. **E.**

1476. Trattner, W. "Care of Destitute, Neglected and Delinquent Children." *Child Welfare* 51 (6):361–368, 1972. **D.**

1477. Tripp, N. "Acting 'in Loco Parentis' as a Defense to Assault and Battery." *Cleveland-Marshall Law Review* 16 (1967):39–49. **A, B.**

1478. Trouern-Trend, J., et al. "Prevention of Child Abuse: Current Progress in Connecticut. I. The Problem." *Connecticut Medicine* 36 (1972):135–137. **A, H.**

1479. Tulkin, S., and J. Kagan. "Mother-Child Interaction in the First Year of Life." *Child Development* 43 (1972):31–41. **C.**

1480. Turner, E. "Battered Baby Syndrome." *British Medical Journal* 5379 (1964):308. **A.**

1481. U.S. Department of Health, Education, and Welfare. *Child Abuse: A Very Real Problem,* (Reprint), U.S. Department of Health, Education, and Welfare, Washington, D.C., February 12, 19, 26, 1975. **A.**

1482. U.S. Department of Health, Education, and Welfare, Office of Child Development. *Child Abuse and Neglect Activities,* U.S. Department of Health, Education, and Welfare, Washington, D.C., December, 1974. **H.**

1483. ——. *Child Abuse and Neglect: The Problem and Its Management. Volume I, An Overview of the Problem.* U.S. Department of Health, Education, and Welfare, Office of Child Development, National Center on Child Abuse and Neglect, Washington, D.C., 1975. **H.**

1484. ——. *Child Abuse . . . Volume II, The Role and Responsibilities of Professionals,* U.S. Department of Health, Education, and Welfare, Office of Child Development, National Center on Child Abuse and Neglect, Washington, D.C., 1975. **H.**

1485. ——. *Child Abuse . . . Volume III, The Community Team: An Approach to Case Management and Prevention.* U.S. Department of Health, Education, and Welfare, Office of Child Development, National Center on Child Abuse and Neglect, Washington, D.C., 1975. **H.**

1486. ——. *Child Welfare Statistics–1967.* Statistical Series No. 92, U.S. Department of Health, Education, and Welfare, Office of Child Development, National Center on Child Abuse and Neglect, Washington, D.C., 1967. **H.**

1487. ——. *Office of Child Development.* U.S. Department of Health, Education, and Welfare, Office of Child Development, National Center on Child Abuse and Neglect, Washington, D.C., 1975. **A.**

1488. ——. *Perspectives on Human Deprivation: Biological, Psychological, and Sociological.* U.S. Department of Health, Education, and Welfare, Office of Child Development, Washington, D.C., 1968. **H.**

1489. ——. *Research, Demonstration and Evaluation Studies on Child Abuse and Neglect.* U.S. Department of Health, Education, and Welfare, Office of Child Development, Washington, D.C., 1975. **H.**

1490. ——. *The Abused Child: Principles and Suggested Language for Legislation on Reporting of the Physically Abused Child.* U.S. Department of Health, Education, and Welfare, Office of Child Development, Washington, D.C., 1963. **B.**

1491. ——. *The Child Advocate. 1970 White House Conference on Children.* Report of Forum 24 (working copy). U.S. Department of Health, Education, and Welfare, Washington, D.C., 1970. **A.**

1492. ——. Children's Bureau, Social and Rehabilitation Service, U.S. Department of Health, Education, and Welfare., *The Child Abuse Reporting Laws: A Tabular View.* U.S. Department of Health, Education, and Welfare, Washington, D.C., 1966 (Revised 1968). **B.**

1493. ——. *National Conference on Child Abuse: A Summary Report.* U.S.

Department of Health, Education, and Welfare, Office of Child Development, National Institute of Mental Health, Rockville, Maryland, 1974. **A.**

1494. U.S. News. "Authorities Face Up To the Child-Abuse Problem." *U.S. News* 80 (May 3, 1976):83-84. **B.**

1495. U.S. Medicine. "High Risk Abuse Should be Identified in Clinical Setting." *U.S. Medicine* (December 15, 1973):6-7. **D.**

1496. University of Detroit Law Review. "Exception to Use of the Physician-Patient Privilege in Child Abuse Cases." *University of Detroit Law Review* 42 (1964):88. **A, B, D.**

1497. University of Florida Law Review. "Battered Child: Florida's Mandatory Reporting Statute." *University of Florida Law Review* 18 (1965):503. **B.**

1498. University of Missouri Law Review. "Parent-Child Tort Immunity: A Rule in Need of Change." *University of Missouri Law Review* 27 (1972):191-207. **B.**

1499. Updating School Board Policies. "How Do Your Employees Handle Child Abusers?" *Updating School Board Policies* 6 (October 1975):10. **G.**

1500. Van Stolk, M. "The Abused Child and the Law." In *Reports of Family Law.* Agincourt, Ontario: The Carswell Company, 1974. **B.**

1501. ———. *The Battered Child in Canada.* Toronto: McClelland and Stewart, 1972. **A, F.**

1502. ———. "Who Owns the Child?" *Childhood Education* 50(5):259-265, March 1974. **A.**

1503. Varon, E. "The Client of a Protective Agency in the Context of the Community: A Field Study of the Massachusetts Society for the Prevention of Cruelty to Children." Ph.D. dissertation, Brandeis University; Ann Arbor, Michigan: University Microfilms, No. 62-1215, 1961. **B, F.**

1504. ———. "Communications: Client, Community and Agency." *Social Work* 9 (1964):51-57. **E.**

1505. Vaughan, M. "Hungry Children Scavenge in Portsmouth Dustbins." *(London) Times Education Supplement,* March 5, 1971. **F.**

1506. Vesin, C., et al. "Mistreatment of Young Children." *Medicine Légale et Dommage Corporal (Paris)* 4 (1971):95-107. **A.**

1507. Vesterdal, J. *The Battered Child Syndrome. Lindau, Nestle Scientific Services, 1972 (Annales Nestle. English Edition No. 27).* **H.**

1508. Villanova Law Review. "Legislation as Protection for the Battered Child." *Villanova Law Review* 12 (1965):313-325. **B.**

1509. Vore, D. "Prenatal Nutrition and Postnatal Intellectual Development." *Merrill-Palmer Quarterly* 19 (1973):253-260. **A, C.**

1510. Wadlington, W. "A New Look at the Courts and Children's Rights." *Children* 16 (1969):138-142. **B.**

1511. ———. *Protective Services and Emotional Neglect.* Denver, Colorado: Children's Division, American Humane Association, 1973. **D, H.**

1512. Waldeck, K. *The Significance in Forensic Medicine of Abuse of Children.* Würzburg: Trilitsch, 1938. **A.**

1513. Walker, C. "Separation and Object Loss: The Plight of the Foster Child." In A.R. Roberts, ed., *Childhood Deprivation*. Springfield, Illinois: Charles C. Thomas, 1974. **C.**

1514. Wall, C. "Child Abuse–Societal Problem with Educational Implications." *Peabody Journal of Education* 52 (1975):222-225. **A, F, H.**

1515. Walters, D. *Physical And Sexual Abuse of Children: Causes and Treatment.* Indiana University Press, 1975. **D.**

1516. Walton, C. "The Battered Baby Syndrome." *New Statesman* 72 (1966): 343. **A.**

1517. Ward, D., and L. Fiegelson. *The Cleveland Story–Community Planning Spotlights Child Protection.* Denver, Colorado: Children's Division, American Humane Association. **H.**

1518. Wardle, M. "The Lordsville Project: Experimental Group Work in a Deprived Area." *Case Western Reserve Conference* 16 (1970):441-446. **E.**

1519. Warren, E. "Battered Child Syndrome." *Journal of Arkansas Medicine Society* 62 (1966):413. **A.**

1520. Washington Law Review. "Legislative Efforts to Control Child Abuse in Washington." *Washington Law Review* 40 (1965):916. **B.**

1521. Wasserman, H. "Early Careers of Professional Social Workers in a Public Welfare Agency." *Social Work* 15 (1970):93-101. **E.**

1522. Wasserman, S. "The Abused Parent of the Abused Child." *Children* 14 (1967):175-176. **C, E.**

1523. ——. "Ego Psychology." In F.J. Turner, ed., *Social Work Treatment.* New York: Free Press, 1974. **E.**

1524. Waterman, J. "Role Reversal: A Necessary Concept in Dealing with a 'Battered Child Syndrome'." *American Journal of Ortho-Psychiatry* 33 (1963):298-300. **D.**

1525. Wedge, P., and H. Prosser. *Born to Fail.* Newton Upper Falls, Mass.: Arrow Books, for the National Childrens Bureau, 1973. **A.**

1526. Weinbach, R. "Case Management of Child Abuse." *Social Work* 20 (1975): 396-397. **D.**

1527. Weinberger, P., and P. Smith. "The Disposition of Child Neglect Cases Referred by Case-Workers to a Juvenile Court." *Child Welfare* 45 (1966): 457-463. **A, B.**

1528. Weininger, O. "Effects of Parental Deprivation: An Overview of Literature and Report on Some Current Research." *Psychological Reports* 30 (1972):591-612. **A, C.**

1529. Weisfeld, D. "Child Abuse Reviews: A Family Phenomenon." *International Journal of Child Psychotherapy.* **C.**

1530. Weisfeld, D., and E. Lord. "The Abused Child." In A.R. Roberts, ed., *Childhood Deprivation.* Springfield, Illinois: Charles C. Thomas, 1974. **A.**

1531. Welsh, R. "Severe Parental Punishment and Delinquency: A Developmental Theory." *Clinical Child Psychology* 5 (Spring 1976):17 ff. **C.**

1532. Wetham, F. "Battered Children and Baffled Parents." *Bulletin of the New York Academy of Medicine* 48 (1972):887–898. **A, C.**

1533. West, S. "Acute Peristeal Swelling in Several Young Infants of the Same Family." *British Medical Journal* 1 (1888):856. **D.**

1534. Western Reserve Law Review. "Ohio's Mandatory Reporting Statute for Cases of Child Abuse." *Western Reserve Law Review* 18 (1967): 1405. **B.**

1535. Weston, J. "Summery of Neglect and Traumatic Cases." In R. Helfer and C. Kempe, eds., *The Battered Child.* Chicago: University of Chicago Press, 1968. **A.**

1536. ——. "The Pathology of Child Abuse." In R. Helfer and C. Kempe, eds., *The Battered Child.* Chicago: University of Chicago Press, 1968. **A.**

1537. Weston, W. "Metaphyseal Fractures in Infancy." *Journal of Bone and Joint Surgery (Britain)* 39B (1957):694. **A.**

1538. What's New. "Willful Injuries to Children." *What's New* 228 (Summer 1962):3. **A.**

1539. White, D. "Protecting the Abused Child in Georgia: Identifying and Reporting." *Journal of Medical Association Georgia* 60 (1971):86–88. **A, B, H.**

1540. White House Conference on Youth. "Children in Trouble: Delinquency, Abuse and Neglect." In *White House Conference on Youth,* 1970, Washington, D.C., Superintendent of Documents, U.S. Government Printing Office, 1971. **A, B.**

1541. Whitehorn, C., and A. Whitehorn. "Cruelty to Children." *Spectator* 206 (May 26, 1961):775–776. **A.**

1542. Whitten, C., M. Pettit, and J. Fischhoff. "Evidence that Growth Failure from Maternal Deprivation is Secondary to Undereating." *Journal of the American Medical Association* 209 (September 15, 1969):1675–1682. **A, C.**

1543. Wickes, I., et al. "Battered or Pigmented?" *British Medical Journal* 2 (1972):404. **A.**

1544. Wigglesworth, R. "Ecology of Child Abuse." *Royal Society of Health Journal* 95 (1975):144–148. **A.**

1545. Wight, B. "The Control of Child-Environment Interaction: A Conceptual Approach to Accident Occurrence." *Pediatrics* 44 (1969):799–805. **D, H.**

1546. Wilkerson, A. *The Rights of Children: Emergent Concepts in Law and Society.* Philadelphia: Temple University Press, 1973. **B.**

1547. William and Mary Law Review. "Legal Response to Child Abuse." *William and Mary Law Review* 11 (1970):960. **B.**

1548. Willamette Law Journal. "Oregon's Child Abuse Legislation: Some Additional Proposals." *Willamette Law Review* 5 (1968):131. **B.**

1549. ——. "Unfit Parents—ORS 419. 523(2)(a)." *Willamette Law Journal* 5 (1968):177. **B.**

1550. Wills, W. "Place Like Home." *British Journal of Psychiatry* 119:220. **C.**

1551. Wilson, J., Jr. "The Battered Child Act—A Summary and Analysis." *Res. Gestae,* 9(6):9-10, June 1965. **B.**

1552. ——. "Fractures and Dislocations in Childhood." *Pediatric Clinic of North America* 14 (1967):659-682. **D.**

1553. Wilson, R. "Legal Action and The Battered Child." *Pediatrics* 33 (1964): 1000. **B.**

1554. Wilson, T. *Ventura Ventures into Child Protective Services.* Denver, Colorado: Children's Division, American Humane Association. **H.**

1555. Winick, M. "Malnutrition and Brain Development." *Journal of Pediatrics* 74 (1969):667-679. **A.**

1556. Winnicot, D. "The Depressive Position in Normal Emotional Development." *British Journal of Medical Psychology* 28 (1955):89-100. **D.**

1557. Winter, A. "Serious Consequences of Minor Head Injuries." *Trauma* 3 (October 1963):3-39. **D.**

1558. Wisconsin Medical Journal. "The Abused Child Law." *Wisconsin Medical Journal* 68 (1969):31-32. **B.**

1559. ——. "The Abused Child Law." *Wisconsin Medical Journal* 69 (1970): 25-26. **B.**

1560. ——. "The Abused Child Law: How It Affects You." *Wisconsin Medical Journal* 66 (1967):23-24. **B.**

1561. Wolkenstein, A. "Evolution of a Program for the Management of Child Abuse." *Social Casework* 57 (May 1976):309 ff. **H.**

1562. Wolff, H. "Are Doctors Too Soft on Child Beaters?" *Medical Economics* (October 3, 1966):84-87. **D.**

1563. Wolman, J., et al. "Clinical Pediatrics Handbook: The Abused or Sexually Molested Child: Clinical Management." *Clinical Pediatrics* 8(5):16B, May 1969. **A.**

1564. Wooley, P. "The Pediatrician and the Young Child Subjected to Repeated Physical Abuse." *Journal of Pediatrics* 62 (1963):628-630. **A, B, D.**

1565. Wooley, P., et al. "Significance of Skeletal Lesions in Infants Resembling Those of Traumatic Origin." *Journal of the American Medical Association* 158 (1955):539-554. **D.**

1566. Wooster, K. "California Legislative Approach to Problems of Willful Child Abuse." *California Law Review* 54 (1966):1805-1831. **B.**

1567. Worling, R. "Maternal Deprivation—A Re-Examination." *Canada's Mental Health* 14 (1966):3-11. **A, C, D.**

1568. Wright, B. "The Control of Child-Environment Interaction: A Conceptual Approach to Accident Occurrence." *Pediatrics* 44 (1969):799-805. **D.**

1569. Wright, L. "Psychologic Aspects of the Battered Child Syndrome." *Southern Medical Bulletin* 58 (1970):14-18. **A.**

1570. Wurfel, L., et al. "Radiographic Features of the Battered Child Syndrome." *Journal of Colloid Radiol. Aust.* 9 (1965):220-223. **D.**

1571. Wylegala, V. "Court Procedures in Neglect Cases. Caseworker and Judge in Neglect Cases." *Child Welfare League of America* 1956 (1970):9-19. **B.**

1572. Yannaconne, V. "Children or Chattels?" *Trial Lawyer's Quarterly* 8 (1972):10. **B.**
1573. Yarber, W. "Tenth Grade Health Students Conduct a Community Program Against Child Molesting." *Journal of School Health* 41(8):425-426, October 1971. **G, H.**
1574. Yarden, P., and I Suranyi. *Diseases of the Nervous System* 29 (1968): 380-384. **E, G.**
1575. Yarrow, M., J. Campbell, and R. Burton. *Child Rearing: An Inquiry into Research and Methods.* San Francisco: Jossey-Bass, 1968. **C.**
1576. Yelaja, S. "The Abused Child . . . A Reminder of Despair." *Canadian Welfare* 49 (1973):8-11. **A.**
1577. ——. "The Concept of Authority and Its Use in Child Protective Service." *Child Welfare* 44 (1966):514-522. **D, H.**
1578. Young, D., Jr. "Problem of Neglect—The Legal Aspects." *Journal of Family Law* 4 (1964):29. **B.**
1579. Young, L. "An Interim Report on An Experimental Program of Protective Services." *Child Welfare* 45 (July 1966):376. **D, H.**
1580. ——. *Wednesday's Children—A Study of Child Neglect and Abuse.* New York: McGraw-Hill, 1964. **A.**
1581. Zadik, D. "Social and Medical Aspects of the Battered Child with Vision Impairment." *New Outlook for the Blind* 67 (June 1973):241-250. **D.**
1582. Zalba, S. "The Abused Child." *Social Work,* Part I. "A Survey of the Problem." (October 1966):30. **A.**
1583. ——. "A Typology for Classification and Treatment." *Social Work* (January 1967):70. **A.**
1584. ——. "Battered Child." *Science Digest* 70 (December 1971):8-13 ff. **A.**
1585. ——. "Battered Children." *Transaction* 8 (1971):58-61. **A.**
1586. Zauner, P. "Mothers Anonymous: The Last Resort." *McCalls,* January 1972. **E.**
1587. Ziering, W., et al. "The Battered Baby Syndrome." *Journal Pediatrics* 65 (1964):321-322. **A.**
1588. Zilboorg, G. "Depressive Reactions Related to Parenthood." *American Journal of Psychiatry* 10 (1931):937. **C.**
1589. Zollinger, R., P. Creedon, and J. Sanguily. "Trauma in Children in General Hospital." *American Journal of Surgeons* 104 (1962):855. **D.**
1590. Zuckerman, K., et al. "Child Neglect and Abuse. A Study of Cases Evaluated at Columbus Children's Hospital in 1968-1969." *Ohio State Medical Journal* 68 (1972):629-632. **A.**

Author Index

403

About the Authors

Joseph J. Costa has been, since 1968, head librarian at the Schuylkill Campus—Pennsylvania State University. He received the B.S. degree from Bloomsburg State, Bloomsburg, Penna., the M.S.L.S. from Villanova University, and the M.Ed. (Reading Specialist) from Kutztown State College, Kutztown, Penna. He has had practical experience in elementary, junior high, and high schools as a teacher and librarian. He is involved in library development in Pennsylvania through the state's Governor's Advisory Council, appointed by Milton S. Shapp, Governor of Pennsylvania.

Gordon K. Nelson, a developmental psychologist, is assistant professor of human development at the Pennsylvania State University. Professor Nelson received the B.A. degree from the University of California at Berkeley and the M.S. and Ph.D. degrees from the University of Wisconsin at Madison. Professor Nelson has written numerous professional articles on child behavior and development and is involved in the planning and assessment of intervention programs for child abuse in eastern Pennsylvania.